SECOND TO NONE

SECOND
TO NONE

A Documentary History
of American Women

Volume I

From the Sixteenth Century to 1865

Edited

by Ruth Barnes Moynihan

Cynthia Russett

and Laurie Crumpacker

University of Nebraska Press

Lincoln & London

Library of Congress Cataloging
in Publication Data
Second to none: a documentary
history of American women / edited
by Ruth Barnes Moynihan, Cynthia
Russett, and Laurie Crumpacker.
p.   cm.
Includes bibliographical references.
Contents: v.1.
From the sixteenth century to 1865 –
ISBN 0-8032-3165-2 (cloth: v.1: alk.
paper).
– ISBN 0-8032-8199-4 (pbk.: v.1: alk.
paper) – ISBN 0-8032-3167-9 (cloth:set). –
ISBN 0-8032-8205-2 (pbk.:set)
1. Women – United States – History –
Sources. I. Moynihan, Ruth
Barnes. II. Russett, Cynthia Eagle.
III. Crumpacker, Laurie, 1941–
HQ1410.S43 1993
305.4′0973 – dc20 93-14347
CIP

THIRD PRINTING: 2000

Our common memory sustains and binds us together as a community. It lifts us up when our courage fails for it calls the roll of women and men who have persevered. It judges us when our lives are false and it does not hesitate to summon us before the bar of truth. Our common memory embraces us in our achievements and it tells out the names of those who made our successes possible. Common memory upholds our common past, directs our common present, and creates our common future.

M. SHAWN COPELAND, O.P.

Contents

Illustrations

Part Two: The Eighteenth Century

Part Three: The Nineteenth Century

Preface

THIS BOOK has been more than twelve years in gestation. First conceived by Ruth, who soon asked Cynthia to share in the process, it was again revised and expanded when we both asked Laurie to join the team. All three of us are indebted to our many fellow scholars of women's history, as well as to all the determined women of previous generations who recorded their history and kept alive the stories of their foremothers.

We editors grieve only that we had to leave out so much material and so many other women's stories. The sources, once one starts looking, exist in great variety and are extensive and rich in detail; the narrative possibilities are almost endless. We hope that in giving birth to these two volumes, we have started a process of exploration and discovery for new readers and enriched the process for those already on the journey.

In some of our earliest documents, spelling and punctuation have been modernized for comprehension and clarity. We have done this only where the original document seemed unusually difficult for a modern reader, and we generally tried to retain as much of the original spelling as is readily comprehensible. We have consistently rendered *y* (as in *ye*) with a *th*, which is the sound that the printed symbol was intended to indicate. Missing or illegible words are indicated by a blank space within brackets, and obvious typographical errors in the originals have been corrected. Occasionally we have added words or sentences in brackets to summarize a longer omission or to provide a definition for an obscure word. Spaced ellipses indicate omissions: a full line of ellipses indicates a substantial omission and change of subject in the original. In a few cases, the original documents contained ellipses; these have been set without spaces to distinguish them from our own.

All permission and publication acknowledgments are to be found in the source notes that accompany each document and illustration. We also wish to give thanks for the indispensable work of numerous librarians, archivists, and colleagues—past and present—without whom this collection would not be possible. Laurie especially wishes to acknowledge the help of her colleague Susan

Porter and of Nichole Cosentino, secretary of the history department at Simmons College. Cynthia thanks the first women undergraduates at Yale who asked, "Why is there no course on women?" For this reason she began teaching her women's history course, one of the first in the country, in 1971. In 1974, Ruth asked the same question as a Yale graduate student. She thanks Jonathan Spence (then director of graduate studies) for suggesting an independent reading course with Cynthia, and Howard Lamar for directing her work on Abigail Scott Duniway. Ruth also thanks the Danforth Foundation for enabling her, and many other women with "interrupted educations," to study for a Ph.D. after eighteen years of "alternative education" in housewifery, community service, and child rearing.

To our mothers, sisters, daughters, students, women friends of many times and places, and also to our fathers, husbands, sons, and men friends, we give thanks for helping us to learn and grow as scholars, as women, and as human beings. The University of Connecticut Research Foundation provided a typing grant, and Yale's A. Whitney Griswold Faculty Research Fund helped with other costs. Ruth thanks Trudy Anderson for her commendable skills in creating order and cleanliness out of creative chaos in the Moynihan household. Cynthia thanks Helen Nielsen for the same service among the Russetts. Our copy editor, Teddy Diggs, has been very helpful. And we owe a huge debt of gratitude to our wonderfully competent typist, Catherine Belanger, who worked on many evenings and weekends in addition to her regular job. Her enthusiastic interest is well matched by her skilled hands and eagle eye for errors. The book could not have been completed without her.

General Introduction

THE PURPOSE of this book is to present a history of American women through a wide-ranging collection of documents. Because we want to let women speak for themselves, because we want to include a diverse selection of individuals and many types of evidence, and because history itself is complex and multifaceted, we have sought as much as possible to allow the documents themselves to tell the story. Recognizing that women's differences (age, race, class, sexual orientation, geographical or ethnic origins, abilities or disabilities) are as significant as their commonalities, we have concentrated on documents that represent the experiences of many different women. We have also tried to show that the daily lives of ordinary women have historical significance, ranging from the ways that women provide for the survival of their communities to their emergence into the public spheres of political, social, and economic life.

The selections are generally brief, and the material is organized to draw the reader through the book, stimulate awareness and curiosity about women's experience, and enhance the reader's knowledge of all of American history. Introductions to each division discuss themes, historical context, and relationships among the selections. Headnotes provide specific information about each document and what it illustrates. Editorial material has been kept to a minimum to allow readers to concentrate on the documents and find meanings for themselves in the words of our historical forebears.

*

American women have been an integral part of all aspects of U.S. history. This is no longer a controversial idea, but whereas there is a vast array of available material to document men's lives, there is still a need for documentary evidence about women's lives. The documents in this volume are meant to show women in the context of traditional American history, intimately connected with everyday survival and with every American event and movement including the establishment and maintenance of the earliest indigenous communities, later pioneer settlement, entrepreneurial development, revolutionary and reform activity, and intellectual trends.

Although we see women as very much a part of the mainstream, we also want to document the problems and circumstances unique to women, circumstances that sometimes limited or changed the nature of individual contributions. For example, among European colonists, preindustrial and early industrial production was a function of the household rather than of individuals. For this reason, it was carried on and recorded in the name of the husband and father no matter how much his wife and daughters were involved. The resulting limitations in the records have led to distortions in perception and ideology about the "traditional" work of women and their economic contributions. Another problem has been the deliberate and widespread exclusion of women from professions such as law, medicine, and entrepreneurial finance as these professions were being developed and consolidated during the nineteenth and early twentieth centuries. This discrimination against women profoundly affected relationships between the sexes and also the particular nature of women's accomplishments. It is necessary to discuss why most men and some women promoted such divisions and how other women either developed alternative professions or circumvented the exclusion.

Another unique characteristic of women's lives is the fact that women alone give birth to children, a biological difference that has affected women's lives one way or another in all generations. Sexual mores, birth and mortality rates, marriage age and sex ratios, birth-control methodology, and child-rearing customs can all make a difference in economic or political behavior as well as in personal lives. Traditional history, which has not recognized the impact of these factors, excludes significant issues in its delineation of reality. This book's documentation should help to redress that imbalance.

By demonstrating, as we do, that gender is a significant category of historical analysis, we hope to aid readers to alter the way they look at history. The nineteenth-century African-American abolitionist, teacher, and novelist Anna Julia Cooper explained, "Tis women's strongest vindication for speaking that the world needs to hear her voice." Without the words of the female half of humanity, Cooper noted, each of us is like a person with one eye bandaged. When the eye is uncovered, "the whole body fills with light."[1] Opening this new lens of gender analysis causes other forms of difference (race, class, age, ability, sexual orientation) to become more visible and thereby shows us a world beyond the narrow limitations of traditional history. The historian Joan Kelly was one of the first to explain the urgency of including gender as a historical

1. Anna Julia Cooper, *A Voice from the South by a Black Woman of the South* (Xenia, Ohio: Aldine Printing House, 1892), p. 144.

category, and more recently the historian Joan Scott, the philosopher Elizabeth Minnich, and others have described the ways that gender analysis can change how we understand our past.[2] For example, knowing that during the era of colonization, Native American women leaders like the *cacica* of Cutifachiqui or Awashonks of the Sakonnets creatively worked to try to keep peace between their societies and the Europeans alters our perception of the interactions between these cultures. Another example is the contribution to the abolitionist movement by black and white women; they pressed for an immediate end to slavery, arguing that it devastated both the morality of southern whites and the families of African Americans. In other words, emphasizing gender as an analytical category can bring women and other formerly marginal groups to the center of our thinking, add incalculably to our knowledge, and ultimately transform our understanding of historical truth.

᭄ As authors, we have been asked how and why we decided on the documents we chose. Our answer goes to the heart of what this book is trying to accomplish. We have relied on our own extensive reading and teaching of women's history to choose materials that we believe enhance our understanding of our collective past, selections that represent voices rarely heard, and documents that make interesting and lively reading. As women's history has done from its inception, we have recognized that there is not one representative "woman's voice" but rather a multiplicity of voices. Understanding this, we have tried to value our many differences and touch on the varied experiences of women from distinct regional, class, ethnic, religious, and racial backgrounds as well as women representing varied ages and sexual orientations.

᭄ We have chosen a social history focus. That is, we have concentrated on the daily existence of ordinary women. This does not mean that we have ignored prescriptive advice to women, nor have we neglected women noted for their historical contributions. We have indeed a number of examples of well-known women and advice givers—from Anne Hutchinson and Elizabeth Cady Stanton in Volume 1 to Dorothy Day and Rosa Parks in Volume 2. The section "Revolutionary Days" includes letters between Abigail and John Adams and their friend Mercy Otis Warren. In the twentieth century, we refer to Sigmund Freud and his popularizers and present documents of women like Margaret Sanger and Brenda Ueland, whose writings reflect changing sexual mores.

In general, we have insisted on letting women tell their own stories and have minimized male documentation. This is less true, however, in the colo-

3

2. Joan Kelly, *Women, History, and Theory: The Essays of Joan Kelly* (Chicago: University of Chicago Press, 1984); Joan Scott, "Gender: A Useful Category of Historical Analysis," *American Historical Review* 91 (1986): 1053–75; Elizabeth Kamarck Minnich, *Transforming Knowledge* (Philadelphia: Temple University Press, 1990).

nial period, when Native American, African-American, and colonial European women left few written records. Wherever possible, we have looked for source material transmitted through the rich oral traditions of Native Americans and African Americans. In other cases, however, we have included a number of descriptive and prescriptive writings by men. Reading these documents carefully is an exercise in separating fact from interpretation, with these writings sometimes revealing as much about the writer's bias as about his subject. This is particularly true of white males' misunderstanding of the lives of Native American women or of enslaved women, though Thomas Jefferson, Edward Clarke, and Adlai Stevenson show similar misunderstanding about all American women. In the later centuries, we have decreased our reliance on male voices as growing literacy and education allowed many women to leave their own written histories.

A particularly exciting aspect of our focus on social history is the way that documents about women's daily lives bring to life our foremothers' important contributions to history even if they did not make the historical "headlines." We bring you women as workers: from Native American women dressing deerskin for clothing and shelter to the early-nineteenth-century button business of Mrs. Williston; from the plantation management of Eliza Lucas Pinckney in the eighteenth century to the cannery workers of the twentieth; from the eighteenth-century childbearing and childbed support of Elizabeth Drinker for her daughter Sally to the twentieth-century political career of Shirley Chisholm.

We have focused on the kinds of work that most women do in households: producing the goods needed for family survival, nurturing and educating children, feeding and clothing their families and nursing the sick, passing on crucial cultural and religious traditions, carrying out the visiting and hostessing duties demanded of even the poorest housewife, and often providing these domestic services in the homes of more prosperous families or slave owners. Beyond household work, the variety of occupations pursued by ordinary women ranges from colonial tavern keeping and journalism to eighteenth- and nineteenth-century entrepreneurial endeavors, from colonial daughters' incessant spinning, cooking, and sewing in their own and their neighbors' homes to nineteenth- and twentieth-century sweatshop laborers, garage mechanics, doctors, politicians, and scientists.

Women emerge as community builders in every age and locale. Keeping this focus allows us to observe not only women's oppression but especially their evolving sense of themselves as empowered human beings. We can trace an emerging sense of pride from Anne Hutchinson's and Mary Dyer's religious self-assertion in the seventeenth century to Annis Boudinot Stockton's satiric rejection of male insults in the 1750s, from Caroline Kirkland's disdain for narrow definitions of the women's sphere in the 1840s to the more overt feminism of women's rights leaders from Elizabeth Cady Stanton to Betty Friedan or Patricia Schroeder.

10 These documents also demonstrate the ways in which economic and social conditions interrelate with ideological definitions of womanhood. Notions about women's proper responsibilities or inherent natures are not immutable; they change from generation to generation in a complex process reflecting the needs and aspirations of all members of society. The difference between ideology and reality is often profound. Thomas Jefferson asserted that American women were unconcerned about women's rights or politics. But Esther DeBerdt Reed organized fund-raising for the Revolutionary Army, and Abigail Adams and others enthusiastically described very effective economic boycotts by American women. While Jefferson was making these statements, Judith Sargent Murray and Mercy Otis Warren were asserting women's need for education and their right to be respected as citizens of the new Republic. There are other examples of male prescriptions presented in the book, among them Cotton Mather's admonitions about proper attitudes for pious mothers-to-be, John Adams's comments on women as "another Tribe" that had "grown discontented," Theodore Roosevelt's fears of "race suicide," and Adlai Stevenson's charge to Smith College graduates in 1955 to use their education to be better wives and mothers. That each piece of advice spawned strong reactions among female hearers underlines our belief that the interaction between prescription and real behavior is one of the dynamics that make the study of our history exciting.

11 Looking closely at the social and economic circumstances of daily life also produces an awareness of both our strengths and our problems. Out of this consciousness is born a belief in the necessity for social change and a recognition of the importance of the benevolent, reform, women's rights, and other political movements that have succeeded in bringing about such changes. Viewing history in this way—from the inside out—supports the validity of the twentieth-century feminist contention that the personal is indeed political.

12 The intent of this book is to move readers gradually through what scholars recognize to be five stages of historical awareness. According to Mary Kay Tetreault, Peggy McIntosh, and other scholars,[3] students usually begin their education with "womanless history"—traditional history that excludes most women and other members of racial, ethnic, and cultural minority groups. The next step for well-meaning teachers and writers is often to include in books and

3. Mary Kay Thompson Tetreault, "Integrating Women's History: The Case of United States High School Textbooks," *History Teacher* 19, no. 2 (February 1986); Peggy McIntosh, "Interactive Phases of Curricular Re-Vision: A Feminist Perspective," Working Paper no. 124 (Wellesley College Center for Research on Women, Wellesley, Mass., 1983).

classes some "notable" women like Jane Addams or Eleanor Roosevelt—members of traditionally excluded groups who have made major contributions to public life. Many books and classes never move beyond this level. It takes courage to move to stage three, where we must recognize the exclusion and indeed victimization of many women and others in our history and permit their stories to be told. But only such painful recognitions allow us to progress beyond notables and victims to a further level, where we celebrate the contributions and triumphs of ordinary women and other excluded groups who have participated in shaping their own realities.

6

This book obviously rejects womanless history and moves its readers through stages two, three, and four, bringing women back into history. In this process, we open the door for an as yet only dimly visualized fifth level—a stage at which women in all their diversity, along with other members of previously excluded groups, move from the margins to the mainstream of our consciousness, transforming our understanding of our country's past and moving us toward the ultimate goal of a truly inclusive human history.

✳

To ensure coverage of essential topics in this book, we have tried to draw our material from many areas of women's lives. The physical environment where women spent their lives, along with their racial, cultural, and class backgrounds, has informed our choices and our analysis of documents. We have also emphasized personal aspects of women's existence, such as health, sexuality, and some of the emotional and spiritual dimensions of their lives. Another focus of these documents is women's work and creativity and the sisterhood and political and social activism that were often parts of their experience. Finally, as noted before, we have included but not emphasized some of the behavioral advice and prescriptions to which all women have been subjected.

The documents in this book are organized chronologically. This is partly because most of these documents resist simple classification into topical categories. Instead, they spill over boundaries, subtly blending into more than one category or illustrating several things at once. Examining the manner in which women's documents resist topical classifications has helped us realize the unsatisfactory nature of arbitrary categories for any analysis of human life, male or female. For example, one may be tempted to consider sexuality as part of the personal dimension of people's lives. Yet it is far more than just personal for women; for example, women's sexuality has often been both controlled by external forces (consider the arrest and imprisonment of prostitutes but not their customers) and exploited by all forms of media (consider sexist advertising and pornography). As historians, we also cannot easily separate women's roles in reproduction from other types of productivity, especially in premodern circumstances.

Childbearing and child rearing are *work,* not merely an aspect of women's personal and biological lives. Raising children represents a contribution not simply to the family but to the entire economy. A particular society's fertility statistics have a profound effect on its political and economic behavior; and certainly any society without children would become extinct within one generation. To closet the bearing and rearing of children in a compartment labeled "personal" distorts reality for both women and men.

7

These considerations apply also to the familiar distinction between public and private spheres of activity. Some men may have managed such separations in their lives; most women never could. For many white women, a private persona, in the days when it was most likely to be that of wife, homemaker, and mother, was also a public persona, lived out in a domestic setting. Her work was service to a particular family, but it had value and significance within the whole economy and polity. Any woman undertaking activity outside the family—whether or not she was a wife or a mother—still found herself linked to the private world of household and child-care responsibilities in a way that men were not. So powerful has been the cultural model of woman as wife and mother that even single women and lesbians have been profoundly affected by its norms—accorded less than a full share of work opportunities and compensation, assumed to maintain (or at least yearn for) some aspects of domesticity, and refused the dignity of a public image or title not defined by gender and marital status.

The chronological organization of this book will be familiar to historians, but the book should also be easy to follow for students or readers new to historical chronology or unclear about events in American history. We have tried to be sensitive to the calls of Gerda Lerner and other women's historians to avoid traditional periodization, which is often based on events of significance to men (i.e., wars and presidencies). When we have considered wars to be especially important in women's lives, they have been given that kind of recognition, for example, in our sections including the American Revolution, the Civil War, and World War II. But we have also given primacy to events of particular significance to women, focusing, for example, on boycotts and resolutions before the Revolution and on the first women's rights convention in 1848.

Within our basic chronological organization, we have made divisions that reflect the variety of women's experiences and events of importance to them in each time period. For example, we begin our book with the section "First Americans" to remind our readers that Native American women were the first American settlers. We then focus on the experiences of emigrating European women in the segment entitled "Building Colonies North and South." Because religion was so important in the colonial era, both the seventeenth- and eighteenth-century units devote considerable space to women's religious experiences; in later centuries, religious concerns are less pervasive, reflecting the secularization of American life. The kinds of documents relating to work and family also change with time, although the topic continues to be appropriate in every century. Gradually, especially in the nineteenth and twentieth centuries, we add more material on paid employment, as areas of women's work move outside the home and as women begin to experience the "double day"—trying to balance external work and domestic responsibilities. These examples demonstrate the value of a flexible approach that concentrates on different women's experiences but also reminds us of continuities over time.

8

We are strongly committed to the belief that women can be most truthfully portrayed as both shaped by and shapers of their society. Some of the liveliest controversies in the field of American women's history today center on the question of the progress (or lack thereof) in women's condition over time. For example, historians have asked whether the colonial period was a kind of "golden age" for women from which their status and prestige declined in the early part of the nineteenth century. Some scholars are redefining power and asking whether or not women have gained power in both public and private spheres. Other historians have questioned to whom we refer when we use the inclusive term *women*. Such questions are immensely complex, as the writings of historians like Sara Evans, Paula Giddings, Mary Beth Norton, Kathryn Sklar, and Thomas Dublin have shown.[4] It may be that no one summary statement can accurately depict the fortunes even of white women of the middle class, let alone of racial minorities or poor women. If progress is defined as greater autonomy and a more equal status with men, then in this country, women have progressed since the seventeenth century, at least in gaining expanded educational, political, and legal rights and increased control over their fertility. But have we gained greater economic or psychological well-being? Violence against women abounds, and the proportion of women and children living in poverty has been increasing rather than decreasing in recent decades. In this book, we have not attempted to offer definitive answers to questions about progress; but we have tried to provide materials that will stimulate the reader to reflection, to further reading and analysis, and even, we hope, to action.

4. Sara M. Evans, *Born for Liberty: A History of Women in America* (New York: Free Press, 1989); Paula Giddings, *When and Where I Enter: The Impact of Black Women on Race and Sex in America* (New York: William Morrow, 1984); Mary Beth Norton, "The Myth of the Golden Age," in Carole Berkin and Mary Beth Norton, eds., *Women of America* (Boston: Houghton Mifflin, 1979); Kathryn Kish Sklar and Thomas Dublin, *Women and Power in American History: A Reader* (Englewood Cliffs, N.J.: Prentice-Hall, 1991).

PART ONE

Cultures Collide,

1540–1700

First Americans

A N INDIAN WOMAN was the first person to welcome a ragged company of English explorers from the Virginia Company to her comfortable village on Roanoke Island, in what we now call North Carolina, in 1584. She provided hospitality, advice, and protection, but the expedition's historian, Richard Hakluyt, recorded only the name of her husband, Granganimo. Her Native American village was destroyed three years later when the first British colonists in North America chose Roanoke as the site of their own settlement.

Forty-four years earlier, other Native American women faced the treachery and savagery of Spanish conquistadores, including the rapacious Hernando de Soto. Even the biased Spanish narratives of that expedition cannot hide the evidence of cruelty and terror, which became known throughout the Indian nations of the South and West. They also reveal both the heroism and the heartbreak of Indian women.

These incidents remind us that the earliest known "native" American women were the people Christopher Columbus mistakenly called "Indians." Their ancestors, the discoverers and settlers of the Americas, had migrated across the land bridge from Asia to Alaska during the last Ice Age, between thirty thousand and ten thousand years ago, and settled throughout the Western Hemisphere. Numerous and various Native American cultures, some of them urban and highly sophisticated, were long established before Europeans knew of the existence of the American continent. According to some estimates, five hundred thousand Native Americans lived along the east coast of North America at the beginning of the seventeenth century. There were probably ten to twelve million north of the Rio Grande.

Myths of creation and corn production, represented here by a Navajo creation myth, are the only narrative "histories" we have of prehistoric American women. But they remind us of women's participation in the crucial events of all American history.

Around 1200 B.C., the Anasazi people and other ancestors of the modern Hopi, Zuni, and Pueblo peoples of Arizona, New Mexico, and Colorado developed a complex agricultural economy based on the domestication of corn, a complicated botanical achievement that would eventually change the diet of the world. They built the settled villages shown in the picture of the Anasazi ruins at Mesa Verde and used terraced fields and irrigation systems to grow their corn, squash, and beans. They made pottery and were skilled basket and cloth weavers.

12   The Mississippian, Hopewell, and Adena peoples of the Ohio and Mississippi River valleys and surrounding areas also lived in large permanent towns, developing tools and skills in agriculture and trade after about A.D. 300. They are called "mound builders" both because of their ruined mound cities and because of their large, mound-type burial dwellings, which (much like Egyptian pyramids) they filled with goods needed for the afterlife. The people of the Pacific Northwest had prosperous villages of fishers and traders. The Woodland peoples of the East and South were somewhat more nomadic but were well adapted to their land and climate—experts at fishing and hunting as well as at growing all the food they needed.

When Europeans arrived in the sixteenth and seventeenth centuries (primarily the English in the East and the Spanish in the South and West), they found well-organized, highly developed Native American societies in which women played a major role in the production of needed goods. As Roger Williams's description of the Narragansetts tells us, corn was the dietary staple of most Native American tribes east of the Rockies and in the old Southwest, and women were responsible for nearly all agricultural work. Among the northeastern woodlands and river tribes, women also helped with hunting and fishing, which provided additional food and other necessities. They smoked, preserved, and prepared food, processed hides for clothing and shelters, and made other products from animals, shellfish, and plants.

Along with agriculture and production, Native American women were in charge of the children in their homes and villages. The English traveler John Lawson observed that they also played crucial roles in commercial transactions. Men frequently left on extended hunting and trading expeditions and on diplomatic and fighting missions. Remaining in the villages, Native American women were the mainstays of economic and community life; men thus treated them with respect and accorded them significant behavioral autonomy. Both tribal respect and women's independence can be seen in the courtship patterns described by French commandant Lamothe Cadillac around the Great Lakes and by John Lawson in the southern territories. Leadership like that of the *cacica* (woman chief) of Cutifachiqui, of Granganimo's wife, and of Awashonks, *sachem* (chief) of the Sakonnets was based on matrilineal family structures and on women's economic importance.

Native American women and men were not prepared for the massive material and cultural invasions that accompanied the Spanish gold hunters of the

sixteenth century and the land-hungry colonizers of the seventeenth and eighteenth centuries. The stories of the *cacica* of Cutifachiqui and of Pocahontas's
relations with the English settlers in Jamestown are among several similar tales
that indicate the diplomatic efforts by Native American women and the be-
trayal or exploitation that often resulted. Kidnapping, conflict, and conquest;
epidemics of lethal diseases; destruction of cornfields, fishing weirs, clam beds,
and hunting territories; and an ever increasing fur trade that disrupted living
patterns and economic relationships—all of these affected both individuals and
the course of history.

Even before the first settlements, European explorers and traders had brought
to North America fatal epidemics of smallpox, measles, chickenpox, and viral
plagues to which Native Americans had no immunity and for which they had
no cures. For example, Indians told de Soto and his men that "two years before,
there had been a pest in the land" that had left whole villages desolate. Some historians think that Native Americans' fears of further epidemics were one cause
of their initial kindness toward colonists; at other times, Native Americans expressed their bitterness about this devastation by lashing out at the settlers. Epidemics did not stop with the colonial period but continued into the nineteenth
century as Europeans spread westward. One unique description of the effects of
such an epidemic is given later in this book in Isaac Knight's captivity narrative.

European colonists also brought unexpected cultural conflict and war. Native
Americans did not at first expect war; they thought that there was ample land
available and, further, that no one individual could "own" land, which had
been given to all living beings to share. Thus, they did not anticipate the con-
flicts that would soon occur over property rights. In addition, Native Americans were shocked by the European custom of killing large numbers of fighters
during battles and of not sparing women, children, and other noncombatants.
Another cultural difference was the treatment of wartime captives. Whereas
Native Americans often adopted captives to replace warriors killed in battle
or women and children lost to disease, Europeans sold most of their captives
into West Indian slavery or forced them into servitude. In 1637, New England
colonists destroyed the southeastern Connecticut Pequots to forestall organized
Native American alliances and to secure European control of trading posts on
the Connecticut River. In 1675, King Philip's War, so called by the English because of their name for the Wampanoag leader Metacom, was a last attempt by
New England's Native Americans to stop the encroachment of the English into
their lands and lives. This book's Awashonks, of the Sakonnets, succeeded in
keeping her people out of this conflict, which brought bloodshed to all of New
England, both Native American and white. In 1676, Bacon's Rebellion in Virginia caused the slaughter of hundreds of Indians as the English battled among
themselves over who would control the Native Americans and their land.

In the Southwest, there was considerable resistance to the Spanish during this same period, beginning with the battle at the Acoma Pueblo, in what is now New Mexico, in 1598. The Spanish response was to massacre and torture the rebellious Pueblo people. Another rebellion beginning at the Taos Pueblo in 1680 drove the Spanish south of the Rio Grande for over a decade, but by 1695 the reconquest was complete. Most resisting Pueblos had been destroyed, and the survivors had been enslaved and divided among the colonists. The Pueblo population of forty thousand in 1600 was reduced by the Spanish conquest to ten thousand in 1800.

Historians estimate that wars, disease, and the often devastating effects of colonization during the seventeenth century decreased the Native American population of this country to one-tenth of its precolonization size. Agricultural abundance declined, along with morale and general living conditions. The European introduction of guns and the commercial demand for furs also upset the carefully controlled economic and ecological balance that had existed before colonization. Like male chiefs, women leaders exhibited both resistance and creative adaptation to colonization. During King Philip's War, Weetamoo, "squaw-sachem" of the Pocassets, tried to negotiate a separate peace, but when that failed, she entered the conflict as an ally of Metacom (King Philip), chief of the Wampanoags. Awashonks, of the Sakonnets, described here by Thomas Church, sought protection for her people through negotiation and cooperation. Pocahontas functioned as an ambassador between her people and the English when her father married her to John Rolfe.

Native American women and the families for which they were responsible suffered profoundly from the disruptions of the colonial period. As Indians were uprooted, defeated, and demoralized, women's roles were transformed. Overworked "squaws" became a symbol to the English of uncivilized degradation. Nevertheless, many Indian women adapted to hard times and used their skills in trading, translating, or scouting to improve their condition or to protect their people. The beadwork and crafts pictured in this book demonstrate the usefulness and beauty of these women's products. Baskets, clothing, jewelry, and other goods were essential to village life and were also remunerative items of trade with the Europeans. Indian women taught English settlers how to grow and cook Native American foods.

Most of our knowledge of Native American women during the colonial era must be pieced together from the not always sympathetic accounts of white male observers, from material evidence, and from anthropological investigations. The writings included here by Richard Hakluyt, Roger Williams, John Lawson, and Lamothe Cadillac give a good idea of courtship, marriage, and childbearing customs and also of the esteem in which Native American women were held among their own people. Often, however, like William Wood, Europeans demonstrated their white cultural bias by ignoring women in their accounts or using them primarily to substantiate the writer's and his audience's expectation that Native American women were either exotic and tempting or savage and repulsive. Sometimes these reporters deplored, instead of admired, the hard but important work of Native American women; rarely did they recognize women's significant leadership functions.

A number of Europeans found Native American life attractive because of its more relaxed sexual and behavioral codes, its spirit of community, and its egalitarian treatment of women and children. In fact, of the six hundred white people captured by the French and Indians from 1689 to 1713, nearly 50 percent chose to stay with their captors. During the same period, very few Native American captives chose to remain in European society. As you read the documents gathered below, you should be aware not only of the impact of European colonization on Indian culture but also of the importance of Native American models to the colonists of this period.

The Changing Woman (Navajo Origin Myth)

Early Native American peoples, like peoples in all preliterate cultures, did not use the written word to tell their stories. Instead, they relied on storytelling and on painted, sculpted, or woven symbols and images. But these stories, passed down from generation to generation (often by grandmothers to their grandchildren), convey the history, lessons, and values of Native American cultures.

Most societies have a creation myth that explains how the first human beings emerged from their mother, the earth. In this Navajo story, First Man and First Woman adopted a creative daughter (Changing Woman), who gave us the changing seasons, sons to destroy threatening monsters, and a way of using corn to repopulate the earth and ensure human survival.

From Dexter Fisher, ed., *The Third Woman: Minority Women Writers of the United States* (Boston: Houghton Mifflin, 1980), p. 44.

❖

In the great desert of multicolored sand stood the Mountain-Around-Which-Moving-Was-Done, and at the foot of this great mountain was found a baby girl.

First Man and First Woman found the child when the earth was still unformed and incomplete. They took her home with them and raised her carefully, and the gods smiled on her and loved her. As she grew into womanhood, the world itself reached maturity as the mountains and valleys were all put into the proper places.

At last she was grown and the world was complete, and to celebrate her becoming a woman, the gods gave her a Blessing Way, Walking-into-Beauty. Songs and chants were sung to her, and her body was shaped with a sacred stick so that it would grow strong and beautiful. Each morning of the ceremony, she ran to greet the sun as it arose. The sacred ceremony was preserved and it is now given to all Navajo girls when they reach adulthood.

But the young girl did not stay the same. Each winter she became withered and white-haired, just as the earth became bare and snow-covered. But each spring as the colors of life grew back on the land, the colors of youth and beauty appeared in her cheeks and in her hair. So she is calling Changing Woman, or "A Woman She Becomes Time and Again."

The sun fell in love with Changing Woman, but she did not know what to do with him. So she went to First Woman for advice. On the advice of First Woman, she met the sun and he made love to her. Nine months later, twin sons were born to her and she raised them with love and care. For monsters had now appeared in the world, and the people were being destroyed. Changing Woman hoped her sons could save the world from the monsters.

When the twin boys were grown, Changing Woman sent them to the sun, their father, to get power from him so that they could fight the monsters. After undergoing severe tests by their father, the boys returned and destroyed all the monsters.

Now the world was complete and the monsters were dead. It was a perfect place for people, but there were very few left. Changing Woman pondered over this problem, and at last she took two baskets of corn. One was of white corn and one was of yellow corn. From the white cornmeal she shaped a man and from the yellow cornmeal she shaped a woman.

And so the earth was populated again, a changing world and a beautiful world—the world of Changing Woman.

A Hopi Wedding

The continuity between legend and historical reality is suggested by the following narrative. Helen Sekaquaptewa described wedding customs, in which she participated in the early twentieth century, as an example of Hopi Indian traditions that had been maintained for hundreds of years. Notice that it was the man's role to card, spin, and weave in this society, while women spent many hours grinding corn.

From Helen Sekaquaptewa *Me and Mine: The Life Story of Helen Sekaquap-*

tewa as Told to Louise Udall (Tucson: University of Arizona Press, 1969), pp. 154–64. © 1969 by the Arizona Board of Regents.

❖

After we decided to get married, I spent every minute that I could grinding in preparation for feeding the wedding guests. Women and girls of my relatives who wanted to help started grinding too. When my sister Verlie walked with me to Bacabi to Susie's house, I carried a big pan full of fine white cornmeal. I never left Susie's house for the entire period (about a month) and was under her watchful care, even slept with her the first three nights.

As a bride I was considered sacred the first few days, being in a room with the shades on the windows, talking to no one. All this time I was steadily grinding corn which was brought in by Emory's kinswomen. Each brought, say, a quart of corn in a basket or on a plaque to be passed in to me to be ground, each lot separately. After the first grinding I handed the corn out and waited while it was roasted and passed back to me to be ground real fine. As each lot was finished, I put it back into its own container, lining it up along the wall with others. When the aunts came back in the evening to get their corn there was food on the table and they ate. White corn was the grist the first day, blue corn on the second and third days. At the end of each day Susie gave me a relaxing rubdown.

Early each morning of the first three days, Cousin Susie went with me to the east edge of the mesa, and there, facing the rising sun, we bowed our heads and each offered a silent prayer for a happy married life. Our days began with the rising of the sun and ended with its setting, because there was no artificial light for night working.

The fourth day is the actual wedding day. Everyone of the relatives is up when the cock crows, to participate in the marriage ritual, the hair washing. Suds are made from the tuber of the yucca root, pounded into a pulp, put into two basins of water, and worked with the hands until the pan is filled with foamy suds.

Two pans were placed side by side on the floor, where Susie and my sister Verlie prepared the suds. Usually the mothers of the bride and groom do this. Susie and Verlie acted for our mothers. While Susie washed my hair, Verlie washed Emory's. Then each took a strand of hair and twisted them together hard and tight as a symbol of acceptance of the new in-law into the clan (family) and also to bind the marriage contract, as they said, "Now you are united, never to go apart."

Next Emory was taken outside and stripped to the waist by the women of my family. Each had brought her small container of water which she poured over his shoulders as he knelt over a tub. They splashed the water over him with their hands. It was still dark, so they could not see him; they put a blanket around him, and he came back into the house to get warm from that icy bath.

Now, with our hair still wet and hanging loose, Emory and I walked together to the eastern edge of the village and once more faced the rising sun, and with bowed heads we prayed in silence for a long time; for a good life together, for children, and to be together all of our lives and never stray from each other. . . .

The making of the robes begins on the morning of the nuptial hair washing. The father or uncle of the groom (in our case Susie's father) took a bag of cotton and, passing through the village, stopped at each house. He was expected, and each housewife opened her door and extended a plaque to receive some cotton (everyone was required to wash his hands before touching the cotton). Immediately all hands went to work cleaning the cotton of seeds, burrs, and little sticks. It was all cleaned that same day.

In the evening the uncles, godfather, and men who wished to help, gathered at the groom's house to card the cotton. The cards were a pair of flat, wire-toothed brushes, four by twelve inches, with wooden handles at a slight angle, on the long side. . . . A small handful of cotton was spread over all the teeth of one card; with the second card, the cotton was combed back and forth until all the lumps were out and it became fluffy. Another motion made it into a strip as long as the card, which strip was put aside and another one started. The men worked late carding big piles of white cotton. Coal-oil lamps lighted their work. During this time the men told stories, with the bride sitting nearby, along with the kinswomen. From time to time the bride thanked the workers for their service. Everyone enjoyed the stories, and before they realized it, it was midnight and quitting time. The men were served refreshments and everyone went home to bed. It took several nights to do the carding.

All the men in the village worked to spin this cotton into thread in one day. Food was obtained and prepared to feed the whole village. Ten or fifteen sheep were required. . . . After his breakfast, each man went to his kiva, taking his spindle (every adult male owns one). Emory's uncle came around early to deliver to each kiva the carded cotton to be spun. In Bacabi there were three kivas. Soon all spindles were humming away. . . .

The weaving took about two weeks, and it began a few days after the spinning was finished. One sheep was butchered this time, and the other foods were made ready for the first day of the weaving. At dawn and before breakfast the three special looms used in wedding weaving were brought out from their storage place to the kiva (one kiva) where they were untied and spread out on the floor. Two or three men at a time worked at the long and tedious job of stringing each loom, rolling the warp back and forth to each other, over the notches close together on the two end poles. . . . The threaded looms were hung from loops in the ceiling beams and fastened to loops on the floor and stretched tight, and the weaving began, the best weavers taking turns during the day. The belt is braided rather than woven.

18

At noon, food was brought to the kiva by relatives. After dinner a man took his place at each loom and worked until evening. . . . The men sat down to eat of piki and beans and leftover food from dinner and somviki, which is tamales made from finely ground blue corn, sweetened and wrapped in corn husks, and tied with yucca strips and then boiled, and made by the bride every evening. . . . Each morning the weaving continued. Only one man could work on each loom at a time, but the best weavers came and took turns during the day. Other men came, bringing their spinning or knitting, or just sat and visited and listened as the older men retold the traditional stories. Sometimes they all sang together. . . .

The activity died down after the first few days anyway, the weavers carrying on until everything was done. I helped with the grinding and cooking until the outfit was completed.

When the weaving was finished the men took the robes from the looms and brought them into the house to be tried on. A border of sixteen running stitches in red was embroidered in the two corners, suggesting a limit of sixteen children, the most a person should have, and four stitches in each of the other two corners in orange, suggesting a minimum number of children. The white moccasins with leggings in one piece were finished just in time to be put on with the rest of the outfit. It was by then evening; food was placed before the guests and everyone ate again. (Hopis do not invite you to eat. They set the food before you, and the food invites.)

The *Cacica* of Cutifachiqui

The ruthless conquistador Hernando de Soto, who had been designated Spanish governor of Florida, the name for the entire southeastern and Gulf area of North America, landed in western Florida to begin his search for gold on May 30, 1539. Spanish expeditions had visited the area in previous years, and some Spaniards had remained to live among the Native Americans. Fatal epidemics as well as waves of conquest had affected Indian tribes for hundreds of miles. Word of de Soto's cruelty and year-long rapacious journey with six hundred armed men on horseback, along with hundreds of Indian *tanemes* (slaves) taken in every village along the way, was passed from tribe to tribe throughout the country. De Soto traveled up into western North Carolina and westward as far as the Arkansas River before dying in 1542 near the future site of Memphis. Deserted villages, as described in the following narrative, were one reason the *cacica* chose to try to pacify her visitor. But her power and diplomacy were no match for the savagery and treachery of the Spanish captain. The narrator of the following excerpt was one of the soldiers accompanying de Soto's expedition. Several others also left narratives of the journey, and each gave a similar version of this story. They blamed de Soto's cruelty and greed for the ultimate failure of the expedition.

From Edward Gaylord Bourne, ed., *Narratives of the Career of Hernando De Soto in the Conquest of Florida* . . . , vol. 1 (New York: A.S. Barnes, 1904), pp. 45–46, 63–68, 69–72.

❖

On the twenty-third day of September the Governor left Napetaca, and went to rest at a river, where two Indians brought him a deer from the Cacique of Uzachil; and the next day, having passed a large town called Hapaluya, he slept at Uzachil. He found no person there; for the inhabitants, informed of the deaths at Napetaca, dared not remain. In the town was found their food, much maize, beans, and pumpkins, on which the Christians lived. The maize is like coarse millet; the pumpkins are better and more savoury than those of Spain.

Two captains having been sent in opposite directions, in quest of Indians, a hundred men and women were taken, one or two of whom were chosen out for the Governor, as was always customary for officers to do after successful inroads, dividing the others among themselves and companions. They were led off in chains, with collars about the neck, to carry luggage and grind corn, doing the labour proper to servants. Sometimes it happened that, going with them for wood or maize, they would kill the Christian, and flee, with the chain on, which others would file at night with a splinter of stone, in the place of iron, at which work, when caught, they were punished, as a warning to others, and that they might not do the like. The women and youths, when removed a hundred leagues from their country, no longer cared, and were taken along loose, doing the work, and in a very little time learning the Spanish language. . . .

A barbacoa [storage place] was found full of parched meal and some maize, which were distributed by allowance. Four Indians were taken, not one of whom would say any thing else than that he knew of no other town. The Governor ordered one of them to be burned; and thereupon another said, that two days' journey from there was a province called Cutifachiqui. . . .

[H]e set out for Cutifachiqui, capturing three Indians in the road, who stated that the mistress of that country had already information of the Christians, and was waiting for them in a town. He sent to her by one of them, offering his friendship and announcing his approach. Directly as the Governor arrived, four canoes came towards him, in one of which was a kinswoman of the Cacica, who, coming near, addressed him in these words:

Excellent Lord:

My sister sends me to salute you, and to say, that she has thought to serve you better by remaining to give orders on the other shore; and that, in a short time, her canoes will all be here, in readiness to conduct you thither, where you may take your repose and be obeyed.

The Governor thanked her, and she returned to cross the river. After a little time the Cacica came out of the town, seated in a chair, which some principal men having borne to the bank, she entered a canoe. Over the stern was spread an awning, and in the bottom lay extended a mat where were two cushions, one above the other, upon which she sate; and she was accompanied by her chief men, in other canoes, with Indians. She approached the spot where the Governor was, and, being arrived, thus addressed him:

Excellent Lord:
Be this coming to these your shores most happy. My ability can in no way equal my wishes, nor my services become the merits of so great a prince; nevertheless, good wishes are to be valued more than all the treasures of the earth without them. With sincerest and purest good-will I tender you my person, my lands, my people, and make you these small gifts.

The Cacica presented much clothing of the country, from the shawls and skins that came in the other boats; and drawing from over her head a large string of pearls, she threw them about his neck, exchanging with him many gracious words of friendship and courtesy. She directed that canoes should come to the spot, whence the Governor and his people passed to the opposite side of the river. So soon as he was lodged in the town, a great many turkeys were sent to him. The country was delightful and fertile, having good interval lands upon the streams; the forest was open, with abundance of walnut and mulberry trees. The sea was stated to be two days' travel. About the place, from half a league to a league off, were large vacant towns, grown up in grass, that appeared as if no people had lived in them for a long time. The Indians said that, two years before, there had been a pest in the land, and the inhabitants had moved away to other towns. In the barbacoas were large quantities of clothing, shawls of thread, made from the bark of trees, and others of feathers, white, gray, vermilion, and yellow, rich and proper for winter. There were also many well-dressed deer-skins, of colours drawn over with designs, of which had been made shoes, stockings, and hose. The Cacica, observing that the Christians valued pearls, told the Governor that, if he should order some sepulchres that were in the town to be searched, he would find many; and if he chose to send to those that were in the uninhabited towns, he might load all his horses with them. They examined those in the town, and found three hundred and fifty pounds' weight of pearls, and figures of babies and birds made of them. [Other narratives of the same expedition say that de Soto raided the sepulchres without permission.] The inhabitants are brown of skin, well formed and proportioned. They are more civilized than any people seen in all the territories of Florida, wearing clothes and shoes. This country, according to what the Indians stated, had been very populous. . . .

In the town were found a dirk and beads that had belonged to Christians, who, the Indians said, had many years before been in the port, distant two days' journey. He that had been there was the Governor-licentiate Ayllon, who came to conquer the land, and, on arriving at the port, died. . . . Without knowing any thing of the country, they went back to Spain.

22   To all it appeared well to make a settlement there, the point being a favourable one, to which could come all the ships from New Spain, Peru, Sancta Marta, and Tierra-Firme, going to Spain; because it is in the way thither, is a good country, and one fit in which to raise supplies; but Soto, as it was his object to find another treasure like that of Atabalipa, lord of Peru, would not be content with good lands nor pearls, even though many of them were worth their weight in gold. . . .

On the third day of May the Governor set out from Cutifachiqui; and, it being discovered that the wish of the Cacica was to leave the Christians, if she could, giving them neither guides nor tanemes, because of the outrages committed upon the inhabitants, there never failed to be men of low degree among the many, who will put the lives of themselves and others in jeopardy for some mean interest, the Governor ordered that she should be placed under guard and took her with him. This treatment, which was not a proper return for the hospitable welcome he had received, makes true the adage, For well doing . . . ; and thus she was carried away on foot with her female slaves.

This brought us service in all the places that were passed, she ordering the Indians to come and take the loads from town to town. We travelled through her territories a hundred leagues, in which, according to what we saw, she was greatly obeyed, whatsoever she ordered being performed with diligence and efficacy. . . .

In seven days the Governor arrived at the Province of Chelaque, the country poorest off for maize of any that was seen in Florida, where the inhabitants subsisted on the roots of plants that they dig in the wilds, and on the animals they destroy with their arrows. They are very domestic people, are slight of form, and go naked. . . .

From Ocute to Cutifachiqui are one hundred and thirty leagues, of which eighty are desert; from Cutifa to Xualla are two hundred and fifty of mountainous country; thence to Guaxule, the way is over very rough and lofty ridges.

One day while on this journey, the Cacica of Cutifachiqui, whom the Governor brought with him, as has been stated, to the end of taking her to Guaxule, the farthest limit of her territories, conducted by her slaves, she left the road, with an excuse of going into a thicket, where, deceiving them, she so concealed herself that for all their search she could not be found. She took with her a cane box, like a trunk, called petaca, full of unlabored pearls, of which, those who had the most knowledge of their value said they were very precious. They were carried for her by one of the women; and the Governor, not to give offence, permitted it so, thinking that in Guaxule he would beg them of her when he should give her leave to depart; but she took them with her, going to Xualla, with three slaves who had fled from the camp.

Granganimo's Wife

The "wife of Granganimo" in this 1584 description was clearly a woman of authority and wealth. But the failure of English explorers to mention her name typifies a common problem in our search for knowledge about the first American women. Europeans assumed that power must be derived from masculine status, and so they often failed to recognize the significance of what they reported. Yet these men could see that Granganimo's wife was "well-favoured." They also admired her coral and pearl jewelry and the fine copper earrings of her many servants—indications of high social status and trade connections with distant places. This account is by one of the two ship captains on the 1584 expedition to Virginia. They sent their reports to Sir Walter Raleigh, who sponsored the voyage. Richard Hakluyt, who first published the reports in 1600, was one of the major publicists of New World exploration—a "best seller" in his time. This narrative reveals women who ran their own lives, made major decisions, and managed a bounteous agricultural society. Granganimo's wife even provided a guard of thirty women to protect the frightened English explorers. Her village on the Carolina coast was burned and destroyed by the first English colonists at Roanoke a few years later.

From Richard Hakluyt, *The Principal Navigations, Voyages, Traffiques, and Discoveries of the English Nation,* vol. 6 (1598–1600; reprint, New York: E.P. Dutton and Co.; London: J.M. Dent and Sons, 1927), pp. 125–29.

❖

The Kings brothers wife, when she came to us (as she did many times) was followed with forty or fifty women alwayes: and when she came into the shippe, she left them all on land, saving her two daughters, her nurse and one or two more.

. . . Wee came to an Island, which they call Roanoak, distant from the harbour by which we entred, seven leagues: and at the North end thereof was a village of nine houses, built of Cedar, and fortified round about with sharpe trees, to keepe out their enemies, and the entrance into it made like a turne pike very artificially; when wee came towardes it, standing neere unto the waters side, the wife of Granganimo the kings brother came running out to meete us very cheerefully and friendly, her husband was not then in the village; some of her people shee commanded to drawe our boate on shore for the beating of the billoe [waves]: others she appointed to cary us on their backes to the dry ground, and others to bring our oares into the house for feare of stealing. When we were come into the utter [outer] roome, having five roomes in her house, she caused us to sit downe by a great fire, and after tooke off our clothes and washed them, and dryed them againe: some of the women plucked off our stockings and washed them, some washed our feete in warme water, and shee her selfe tooke great paines to see all things ordered in the best maner shee could, making great haste to dresse some meate for us to eate.

After we had thus dryed our selves, she brought us into the inner roome, where shee set on the boord standing along the house, some wheate like furmentic, sodden [stewed] Venison, and roasted, fish sodden, boyled, and roasted, Melons rawe, and sodden, rootes of divers kindes, and divers fruites: their drinke is commonly water, but while the grape lasteth they drinke wine, and for want of caskes to keepe it, all the yere after they drink water, but it is sodden with Ginger in it, and blacke Sinamon, and sometimes Sassaphras, and divers other wholesome, and medicinable hearbes and trees. We were entertained with all love and kindnesse, and with as much bountie (after their maner) as they could possibly devise. . . . While we were at meate, there came in at the gates two or three men with their bowes and arrowes from hunting, whom when wee espied, we beganne to looke one towards another, and offered to reach our weapons: but as soone as shee espied our mistrust, shee was very much mooved, and caused some of her men to runne out, and take away their bowes and arrowes and breake them, and withall beate the poore fellowes out of the gate againe. When we departed in the evening and would not tary all night, she was very sory, and gave us into our boate our supper halfe dressed, pottes and all, and brought us to our boate side, in which wee lay all night, remooving the same a prettie distance from the shoare: shee perceiving our jelousie, was much greived, and sent divers men and thirtie women, to sit all night on the banke side by us, and sent us into our boates five mattes to cover us from the raine, using very many wordes to intreate us to rest in their houses: but because wee were fewe men, and if wee had miscaried, the voyage had bene in very great danger, wee durst not adventure any thing, though there was no cause of doubt: for a more kinde and loving people there can not be found in the worlde, as farre as we have hitherto had triall.

The Women Bring in All the Increase

Roger Williams, who founded Rhode Island after his banishment from Massachusetts for religious insubordination, was the most vocal European advocate of Native American rights in early New England, a fluent speaker of the Algonquian language, and a careful, sympathetic observer. He wrote a treatise in 1643, still one of the best early sources, to share with European readers his knowledge of Narragansett work, culture, and language. He recognized that the Narragansett women of southeastern New England, like women in most North American societies, were gatherers, producers, and preservers of the community's main food supply. (Many of these foods, such as squash, corn, pumpkin, lobster, clams, and various berries, were new to the settlers and are now common in the American diet.) He also described Native American marriages, housekeeping customs, and frequent house moves. His book was printed in the form of lists of words or phrases followed by definitions and "observations." The most recent edition of this book was edited by John J. Teunissen and Evelyn J. Hinz and published by Wayne State University Press, Detroit, in 1973.

From Roger Williams, *A Key into the Language of America* (London: Gregory Dexter, 1643), chaps. 6, 16, 19, 23.

❖

NICKQUÉNUM. *I am going home:* Which is a solemne word amongst them; and no man wil offer any hinderance to him, who after some absence is going to visit his Family, and useth this word *Nicquénum* (confessing the sweetnesse even of these short temporall homes.) . . .

WETUOMÉMESE. *A little house;* which their women and maids live apart in, four, five, or six dayes, in the time of their monethly sicknesse, which custome in all parts of the Countrey they strictly observe, and no *Male* may come into that house. . . .

WUTTAPUÍSSUCK. *The long poles,* which commonly men get and fix, and then the women cover the house with mats, and line them with embroydered mats which the women make, and call them *Munnotaúbana,* or *Hangings,* which amongst them make as faire a show as Hangings with us. . . .

WUCHICKAPÊUCK. *Burching barke,* and *Chesnut barke* which they dresse finely, and make a Summer-covering for their houses. . . .

Two Families will live comfortably and lovingly in a little round house of some fourteen or sixteen foot over, and so more and more families in proportion. . . . Instead of shelves, they have severall baskets, wherin they put all their houshold-stuffe: they have some great bags or sacks made of *Hempe,* which will hold five or six bushells. . . . Their women constantly beat all their corne with hand: they plant it, dresse it, gather it, barne it, beat it, and take as much paines as any people in the world, which labour is questionlesse one cause of their extraordinary ease of childbirth. . . . It is almost incredible what burthens the poore women carry of *Corne,* of *Fish,* of *Beanes,* of *Mats,* and a childe besides. . . . They nurse all their children themselves; yet, if she be an high or rich woman, she maintaines a Nurse to tend the childe. . . .

NQUSSÚTAM. *I remove house:* which they doe upon these occasions: From thick warme vallies, where they winter, they remove a little neerer to their Summer fields; when 'tis warme Spring, then they remove to their fields where they plant Corne.

In middle of Summer, because of the abundance of Fleas, which the dust of the house breeds, they will flie and remove on a sudden from one part of their field to a fresh place: And sometimes having fields a mile or two, or many miles asunder, when the worke of one field is over, they remove house to the other: If death fall in amongst them, they presently remove to a fresh place: If an enemie approach, they remove into a Thicket, or Swampe, unlesse they have some Fort to remove unto.

Sometimes they remove to a hunting house in the end of the yeere, and forsake it not untill Snow lie thick, and then will travel home, men, women and children, thorow the snow, thirtie, yea, fiftie or sixtie miles; but their great remove is from their Summer fields to warme and thicke woodie bottomes where they winter: They are quicke; in halfe a day, yea, sometimes at few houres warning to be gone and the house up elsewhere; especially, if they have stakes readie pitcht for their *Mats.* . . . The men make the poles or stakes, but the women make and set up, take downe, order, and carry the *Mats* and householdstuffe. . . .

. . . The *Indians* have an Art of drying their Chesnuts, and so to preserve them in their barnes for a daintie all the yeare. . . . These Akornes also they drie, and in case of want of Corne, by much boyling they make a good dish of them: yea some times in plentie of Corne doe they eate these Acornes for a Novelty. . . . Of these Wallnuts they make an excellent Oyle good for many uses, but especially for their annoynting of their heads. And of the chips of the Walnut-Tree (the barke taken off) some *English* in the Countrey make excellent Beere. . . .

WUTTÁHIMNEASH. *Strawberries.*

Obs. This Berry is the wonder of all the Fruits growing naturally in those parts: It is of it selfe Excellent: so that one of the chiefest Doctors of *England* was wont to say, that God could have made, but God never did make a better Berry: In some parts where the *Natives* have planted, I have many times seen as many as would fill a good ship within few miles compasse: the *Indians* bruise them in a Morter, and mixe them with meale and make Strawberry bread. . . .

Sasèmineash [cranberry] another sharp cooling Fruit growing in fresh Waters all the Winter, Excellent in conserve against Feavers. . . .

ATTITAASH. *Hurtle-berries.* Of which there are divers sorts sweete like Currants, some opening, some of a binding nature.

Saútaash are these Currants dried by the *Natives,* and so preserved all the yeare, which they beat to powder, and mingle it with their parcht meale, and make a delicate dish which they cal *Sautautthig;* which is as sweet to them as plum or spice cake to the *English.*

They also make great use of their Strawberries having such abundance of them, making Strawberry bread, and having no other Food for many dayes, but the *English* have exceeded, and make good Wine both of their Grapes and Strawberries also in some places, as I have often tasted. . . .

Obs. The Women set or plant, weede, and hill, and gather and barne all the corne, and Fruites of the field: Yet sometimes the man himselfe, (either out of love to his Wife, or care for his Children, or being an old man) will help the Woman which (by the custome of the Countrey) they are not bound to.

When a field is to be broken up, they have a very loving sociable speedy way to dispatch it: All the neighbours men and Women forty, fifty, a hundred &c, joyne, and come in to help freely. . . . The *Indian* Women to this day . . . doe use their naturall Howes [hoes] of shells and Wood. . . .

PAUSINNÚMMIN. *To dry the corne.* Which they doe carefully upon heapes and Mats many dayes, before they barne it up, covering it up with Mats at night, and opening when the Sun is hot. . . . The woman of the family will commonly raise two or three heaps of twelve, fifteene, or twentie bushells a heap, which they drie in round broad heaps; and if she have helpe of her children or friends, much more. . . .

SICKÌSSUOG. *Clams.*

Obs. This is a sweet kind of shelfish, which all *Indians* generally over the Countrey, Winter and Summer delight in; and at low water the women dig for them: this fish, and the naturall liquor of it, they boile, and it makes their broth and their *Nasaúmpt* (which is a kind of thickned broth) and their bread seasonable and savory, in stead of Salt: and for that the *English* Swine dig and root these Clams wheresoever they come, and watch the low water (as the *Indian* women do) therefore of all the *English* Cattell, the Swine (as also because of their filthy disposition) are most hatefull to all Natives, and they call them filthy cut throats, &c. . . .

WUSSENETÛOCK, AWETAWÁTUOCK. *They make a match.* Single fornication they count no sin, but after Mariage (which they solemnize by consent of Parents and publique approbation publiquely) then they count it hainous for either of them to be false. . . . In this case the wronged party may put away or keepe the party offending: commonly, if the Woman be false, the offended Husband will be solemnly revenged upon the offender, before many witnesses, by many blowes and wounds, and if it be to Death, yet the guilty resists not, nor is his Death revenged. . . .

Their Number [of wives] is not stinted, yet the chief Nation in the Country, the Narrigansets generally have but one Wife.

Two causes they generally alledge for their many Wives.

First desire of Riches, because the Women bring in all the increase of the Field, &c. the Husband onely fisheth, hunteth, &c.

Secondly, their long sequestring themselves from their wives after conception, untill the child be weaned, which with some is long after a yeare old, generally they keep their children long at the breast. . . .

Obs. Generally the Husband gives . . . payments for a Dowrie, . . . to the Father or Mother, or guardian of the Maide. To this purpose if the man be poore, his Friends and neighbours doe . . . contribute Money toward the Dowrie. . . .

Obs. They commonly abound with Children, and increase mightily; except the plauge fall amongst them, or other lesser sicknesses, and then having no means of recovery, they perish wonderfully [i.e., amazingly]. . . .

Obs. It hath pleased God in wonderfull manner to moderate that curse of the sorrowes of Child-bearing to these poore Indian Women: So that ordinarily they have a wonderfull more speedy and easie Travell, and delivery then the Women of *Europe:* not that I thinke God is more gracious to them above other Women, but that it followes, First from the hardnesse of their constitution, in which respect they beare their sorrowes the easier.

Secondly from their extraordinary great labour (even above the labour of men) as in the Field, they sustaine the labour of it, in carrying of mighty Burthens, in digging clammes and getting other Shelfish from the Sea, in beating all their corne in Morters: &c. Most of them count it a shame for a Woman in Travell to make complaint, and many of them are scarcely heard to groane. I have often knowne in one Quarter of an houre a Woman merry in the House, and delivered and merry again: and within two dayes abroad, and after foure or five dayes at worke, &c. . . .

They put away [i.e., divorce] (as in Israell) frequently for other occasions beside Adultery, yet I know many Couples that have lived twenty, thirty, forty yeares together.

28

Of the Naturall Inhabitants of Virginia

John Smith, of Jamestown, who wrote the first history of English settlement in North America, here describes the Native Americans he encountered in Virginia (the "naturall inhabitants"), the aid given the settlers by Pocahontas, the daughter of Chief Powhatan, and the subsequent kidnapping of Pocahontas by the English. The "princess" became legendary for saving Smith's life when he was captured by her people in 1608; this common custom gave Indian women the right to choose between death and tribal adoption for prisoners taken in battle. Pocahontas later married another prominent Jamestown resident, Captain John Rolfe, who explained to English friends that his passionate "misalliance" with such a "dusky savage" was a means of converting her to Christianity. After the birth of her first baby, he took her to England, where, Smith tells us, she was well received and was presented to Queen Anne. However, the climate was cold and the culture strange. Pocahontas died within a year, at age twenty-one, just before she was to return to America.

From Captain John Smith, *A True Relation, 1608,* and *John Smith's Historie of Virginia, 1624, Book IV,* both reprinted in Lyon Gardiner Tyler, ed., *Narratives of Early Virginia: 1606–1625* (New York: Charles Scribner's Sons, 1907), pp. 99–101, 306–11, 325–30. ❖

The land is not populous, for the men be fewe; their far greater number is of women and children. Within 60 miles of James Towne there are about some 5000 people, but of able men fit for their warres scarse 1500.

. . . The people differ very much in stature, especially in language, as before is expressed. Some being very great as the Sesquesahamocks, others very little as the Wighcocomocoes: but generally tall and straight, of a comely proportion, and of a colour browne, when they are of any age, but they are borne white. Their haire is generally black; but few have any beards. The men weare halfe their heads shaven, the other halfe long. For Barbers they use their women, who with 2 shels will grate away the haire, of any fashion they please. The women are cut in many fashions agreeable to their yeares, but ever some part remaineth long. They are very strong, of an able body and full of agilitie, able to endure to lie in the woods under a tree by the fire, in the worst of winter, or in the weedes and grasse, in Ambuscado in the Sommer. They are inconstant in everie thing, but what feare constraineth them to keepe. Craftie, timerous, quicke of apprehension and very ingenuous. Some are of disposition fearefull, some bold, most cautelous, all Savage. Generally covetous of copper, beads, and such like trash. They are soone moved to anger, and so malitious, that they seldome forget an injury: they seldome steale one from another, least their conjurors should reveale it, and so they be pursued and punished. That they are thus feared is certaine, but that any can reveale their offences by conjuration I am doubtfull. Their women are carefull not to bee suspected of dishonesty without the leave of their husbands. Each houshold knoweth their owne lands and gardens, and most live of their owne labours. For their apparell, they are some time covered with the skinnes of wilde beasts, which in winter are dressed with the haire, but in sommer without. The better sort use large mantels of deare skins not much differing in fashion from the Irish mantels. Some imbroidered with white beads, some with copper, other painted after their manner. But the common sort have scarce to cover their nakednesse but with grasse, the leaves of trees, or such like. We have seen some use mantels made of Turky feathers, so prettily wrought and woven with threeds that nothing could bee discerned but the feathers, that was exceeding warme and very handsome. But the women are alwaies covered about their midles with a skin and very shamefast to be seene bare. They adorne themselves most with copper beads and paintings. Their women some have their legs, hands, brests and face cunningly imbrodered with diverse workes, as beasts, serpentes, artificially wrought into their flesh with blacke spots. In each eare commonly they have 3 great holes, whereat they hange chaines, bracelets, or copper. . . .

Men women and children have their severall names according to the severall humor of their Parents. Their women (they say) are easilie delivered of children, yet doe they love children verie dearly. To make them hardy, in the coldest mornings they wash them in the rivers, and by painting and ointments so tanne their skins, that after year or two, no weather will hurt them.

The men bestowe their times in fishing, hunting, wars, and such manlike exercises, scorning to be seene in any woman-like exercise, which is the cause that the women be verie painefull and the men often idle. The women and children do the rest of the worke. They make mats, baskets, pots, morters, pound their corne, make their bread, prepare their victuals, plant their corne, gather their corne, beare all kind of burdens, and such like.

. . . But to conclude our peace, thus it happened. Captaine Argall, having entred into a great acquaintance with Japazaws, an old friend of Captaine Smiths, and so to all our Nation, ever since hee discovered the Countrie, heard by him there was Pocahontas, whom Captaine Smiths Relations intituleth the Numparell [nonpareil] of Virginia, and though she had beene many times a preserver of him and the whole Colonie, yet till this accident shee was never seene at James towne since his departure. Being at Patawomeke, as it seemes, thinking her selfe unknowne, was easily by her friend Japazaws perswaded to goe abroad with him and his wife to see the ship: for Captaine Argall had promised him a Copper Kettle to bring her but to him, promising no way to hurt her, but keepe her till they could conclude a peace with her father; the Salvage for this Copper Kettle would have done any thing, it seemed by the Relation. For though she had seene and beene in many ships, yet hee caused his wife to faine how desirous she was to see one, that hee offered to beat her for her importunitie, till she wept. But at last he told her, if Pocahontas would goe with her, hee was content: and thus they betraied the poore innocent Pocahontas aboord, where they were all kindly feasted in the Cabbin. . . . [The Captain] told her before her friends, she must goe with him, and compound peace betwixt her Countrie and us, before she ever should see Powhatan. . . .

A messenger forthwith was sent to her father, that his daughter Pocahontas he loved so dearely, he must ransome with our men, swords, peeces, tooles, &c. hee trecherously had stolne.

This unwelcome newes much troubled Powhatan, because hee loved both his daughter and our commodities well, yet it was three moniths after ere hee returned us any answer: then by the perswasion of the Councell, he returned seven of our men, with each of them an unserviceable Musket, and sent us word, that when wee would deliver his daughter, hee would make us satisfaction for all injuries done us, and give us five hundred bushels of Corne, and for ever be friends with us. That he sent, we received in part of payment, and returned him this answer: That his daughter should be well used; but we could not beleeve the rest of our armes were either lost or stolne from him, and therefore till hee sent them.

This answer, it seemed, much displeased him, for we heard no more from him for a longtime after: when with Captaine Argals ship, and some other vessels belonging to the Colonie; Sir Thomas Dale, with a hundred and fiftie men well appointed, went up into his owne River, to his chiefe habitation, with his daughter. With many scornfull bravado's they affronted us, proudly demanding Why wee came thither; our reply was, Wee had brought his daughter, and to receive the ransome for her that was promised, or to have it perforce. They nothing dismayed thereat, told us, We were welcome if wee came to fight, for they were provided for us: but advised us, if wee loved our lives to retire; else they would use us as they had done Captaine Ratcliffe: We told them, Wee would presently have a better answer; but we were no sooner within shot of the shore than they let flie their Arrowes among us in the ship.

Being thus justly provoked, wee presently manned our Boats, went on shore, burned all their houses, and spoiled all they had we could finde; and so the next day proceeded higher up the River, where they demanded Why wee burnt their houses, and wee, Why they shot at us: They replyed, it was some stragling Salvage, with many other excuses, they intended no hurt, but were our friends: We told them, Wee came not to hurt them, but visit them as friends also. Upon this we concluded a peace. . . .

Long before this, Master John Rolfe, an honest Gentleman, and of good behaviour, had beene in love with Pocahontas, and she with him: . . . the bru[i]te [rumor] of this mariage came soone to the knowledge of Powhatan, a thing acceptable to him, as appeared by his sudden consent. . . . And ever since wee have had friendly trade and commerce, as well with Powhatan himselfe, as all his subjects. . . .

32   During this time, the Lady Rebecca, *alias* Pocahontas, daughter to Powhatan, by the diligent care of Master John Rolfe her husband and his friends, was taught to speake such English as might well bee understood, well instructed in Christianitie, and was become very formall and civill after our English manner; shee had also by him a childe which she loved most dearely, and the Treasurer and Company tooke order both for the maintenance of her and it, besides there were divers persons of great ranke and qualitie had beene very kinde to her; and before she arrived at London, Captaine Smith to deserve her former courtesies, made her qualities knowne to the Queenes most excellent Majestie and her Court, and writ a little booke to this effect to the Queene: *To the most high and vertuous Princesse, Queene Anne of Great Brittanie.* . . .

That some ten yeeres agoe being in Virginia, and taken prisoner by the power of Powhatan their chiefe King, I received from this great Salvage exceeding great courtesie, especially from his sonne Nantaquaus, the most manliest, comeliest, boldest spirit, I ever saw in a Salvage, and his sister Pocahontas, the Kings most deare and wel-beloved daughter, being but a childe of twelve or thirteene yeers of age, whose compassionate pitifull heart, of my desperate estate, gave me much cause to respect her: I being the first Christian this proud King and his grim attendants ever saw: and thus enthralled in their barbarous power, I cannot say I felt the least occasion of want that was in the power of those my mortall foes to prevent, notwithstanding al their threats. After some six weeks fatting amongst those Salvage Courtiers, at the minute of my execution, she hazarded the beating out of her owne braines to save mine; and not onely that, but so prevailed with her father, that I was safely conducted to James towne: where I found about eight and thirtie miserable poore and sicke creatures, to keepe possession of all those large territories of Virginia; such was the weaknesse of this poore Commonwealth, as had the Salvages not fed us, we directly had starved.

And this reliefe, most gracious Queene, was commonly brought us by this Lady Pocahontas.

. . . When her father with the utmost of the policie and power, sought to surprize mee, having but eighteene with mee, the darke night could not affright her from comming through the irkesome woods, and with watered eies gave me intelligence, with her best advice to escape his furie; which had hee knowne, hee had surely slaine her. James towne with her wild traine she as freely frequented, as her fathers habitation; and during the time of two or three yeeres, she next under God, was still the instrument to preserve this Colonie from death, famine and utter confusion; . . . if she should not be well received, seeing this King-dome may rightly have a Kingdome by her meanes; her present love to us and Christianitie might turne to such scorne and furie, as to divert all this good to the worst of evill. . . .

Being about this time preparing to set saile for New-England, I could not stay to doe her that service I desired, and she well deserved; but hearing shee was at Branford with divers of my friends, I went to see her. After a modest salutation, without any word, she turned about, obscured her face, as not seem-ing well contented; and in that humour her husband, with divers others, we all left her two or three houres, repenting my selfe to have writ she could speake English. But not long after, she began to talke, and remembered mee well what courtesies shee had done: saying, You did promise Powhatan what was yours should bee his, and he the like to you; you called him father being in his land a stranger, and by the same reason so must I doe you: which though I would have excused, I durst not allow of that title. . . .

. . . It pleased God at Gravesend to take this young Lady to his mercie, where shee made not more sorrow for her unexpected death, than joy to the beholders to heare and see her make so religious and godly an end. Her little childe Thomas Rolfe therefore was left at Plimoth with Sir Lewis Stukly that desired the keeping of it.

Quite Seemly and Respectful

Lamothe Cadillac, the commandant of a French fort on the upper Great Lakes in the 1690s, was amazed by the common practice of sexual abstinence among Native Americans to protect the health of women and children and to maintain mutual respect in the premarital custom of "running the light." Many Indian peoples traced inheritance and family relationships through the mother rather than the father. Thus women retained control over their children and had sig-nificant personal and sexual autonomy. Cadillac wrote his memoirs in 1718, but they were not published until 1877. Edith Moodie translated them into English early in the twentieth century.

From Milo Milton Quaife, ed., *Memoir of Lamothe Cadillac* (Chicago: Lake-side Press, R.R. Donnelly and Sons, 1947), pp. 38–42, 45–46.

❖

It rarely happens that a husband dismisses his wife, or a wife leaves her hus-band, if they have children. But if it does happen, all the offspring, both boys and girls, belong to the mother, and the husband is not allowed to retain any of them against her will; for the mother's title rests on the law of nature, since no one can dispute that she is the mother of the children whom she has brought into the world. . . .

For this reason the Indians trace their genealogy through the women, when they wish to prove their claims to nobility. Among them the number of children is never a burden to the mother. On the contrary, she is more highly respected for them, more honored, more esteemed, and richer. Accordingly she finds it an easier and quicker matter to get married again, for the man who marries her, in becoming her husband becomes also the father and head of the whole family, and is therefore a person of more importance; for if the children are grown-up they support the cabin either by their deeds as warriors or by hunting, or by the alliances they make by taking wives of their own; and if they are still young, the step-father hopes and expects that if he receives any personal wrong or injury he will be avenged when his stepsons, who regard him as their own father, are old enough. . . .

But if a man becomes a widower and his wife leaves him children, then the relatives pick out a wife for him suitable to his circumstances. They make the proposal to her and take her to his cabin. If he refuses her, and in course of time takes another more to his liking, the woman who has received this insult is allowed to abuse him and heap all sorts of insults upon him. Then she smashes up everything in the cabin or plunders and carries off all the finest and best things it contains and takes them to her own home, and neither the man nor his wife, who is considered as a concubine, can stop her or say a word to her, but only hang their heads. . . .

When a woman is confined, she sleeps apart and remains separated from her husband for forty days; on the forty-first day she comes into her cabin, where she makes a new fire with a flint and steel, and then she is purified. When the women or girls have their monthly periods they leave their cabins and each one lodges by herself. The others bring them food in a dish, which they leave at their door, but will not enter nor go near them. As soon as they get over this indisposition they go back to their cabins.

When the women are with child, or nursing, their husbands refrain from sleeping with them, for they maintain that sexual intercourse ruins the nourishment which the child receives from its mother, weakens it, and may cause an abortion. As for nursing mothers, the Indians say that such intercourse spoils their milk and that if they become pregnant they could not nourish the child, having no other food to give it. But the husbands are often duped, for their wives are not satisfied with such arguments and go and gratify themselves secretly elsewhere, paying but little attention to this regimen. However, it is true that there are many who do observe this custom, out of affection for their offspring. . . .

This is the way they conduct their lovemaking. The young men have strips of bark rolled up in the form of a torch. At night they light one end and go through all the cabins they care to visit. The girls are lying down at the side of the passage-way, and when their beloved passes they stop him by seizing a corner of his garment. When the gallant perceives this signal he stoops down, and then his mistress takes his torch and puts it out and makes the young man lie down beside her, and he tells her his love. Despite this privacy and complete freedom, it is not often that anything takes place but what is quite seemly and respectful, so true it is that people think less of what is permitted than of what is forbidden. For it is evident that on these occasions there is nothing to prevent the lovers from indulging their passion; yet generally they do not, especially if they intend to marry. At length, when the girl is tired and wants to go to sleep she tells her lover, who retires as soon as she bids him. This custom is called by them "running the light."

Their Carriage It Is Very Civill

William Wood's pamphlet *New England's Prospect,* published in 1634, was a popular advertisement for the New World. In it, he clearly overstates the biased European view that Native American men were lazy and the women seriously exploited. This was done in part to portray life for European women in New England as pleasant by comparison. The truth was that European women, far from being pampered, worked terribly hard and found it very difficult to adjust their clothing, food preparation, and households to the "wilderness" in which their Native American counterparts existed relatively comfortably. Despite his prejudice, Wood details an impressive list of the productive skills of Native American women in southern New England.

From William Wood, *New England's Prospect,* vol. 1 (Boston: Prince Society, 1865), pp. 105–10. ❖

To satisfy the curious eye of women-readers, who otherwise might thinke their sex forgotten, or not worthy a record, let them peruse these few lines, wherein they may see their owne happinesse, if weighed in the womans balance of these ruder *Indians,* who scorne the tuterings of their wives, or to admit them as their equals, though their qualities and industrious deservings may justly claime the preeminence, and command better usage and more conjugall esteeme, their persons and features being every way correspondent, their qualifications more excellent, being more loving, pittifull, and modest, milde, provident, and laborious than their lazie husbands. Their employments be many: First their building of houses, whose frames are formed like our garden-arbours, something more round, very strong and handsome, covered with closewrought mats of their owne weaving, which deny entrance to any drop of raine, though it come both fierce and long, neither can the piercing North winde finde a crannie, through which he can conveigh his cooling breath, they be warmer than our *English* houses; at the top is a square hole for the smoakes evacuation, which in rainy weather is covered with a pluver [rain flap]; these bee such smoakie dwellings, that when there is good fires, they are not able to stand upright, but lie all along under the smoake, never using any stooles or chaires, it being as rare to see an *Indian* sit on a stoole at home, as it is strange to see an *English* man sit on his heeles abroad. Their houses are smaller in the Summer, when their families be dispersed, by reason of heate and occasions. In Winter they make some fiftie or threescore foote long, fortie or fiftie men being inmates under one roofe; and as is their husbands occasion these poor tectonists [architects or builders] are often troubled like snailes, to carrie their houses on their backs sometime to fishing-places, other times to hunting-places, after that to a planting place, where it abides the longest: an other work is their planting of corne, wherein they exceede our *English* husband-men, keeping it so cleare with their Clamme shell-hooes, as if it were a garden rather than a corne-field, not suffering a choaking weede to advance his audacious head above their infant corne, or an undermining worme to spoile his spurnes [roots]. Their corne being ripe, they gather it, and drying it hard in the Sunne, conveigh it to their barnes, which be great holes digged in the ground in forme of a brass pot, seeled with rinds [bark] of trees, wherein they put their corne, covering it from the inquisitive search of their gurmandizing husbands, who would eate up both their allowed portion, and reserved feede, if they knew where to finde it. But our hogges having found a way to unhindge their barne doors, and robbe their garners, they are glad to implore their husbands helpe to roule the bodies of trees over their holes, to prevent those pioners, whose theeverie they as much hate as their flesh. An other of their employments is their Summer processions to get Lobsters for their husbands, wherewith they baite their hookes when they goe a fishing for Basse or Codfish. This is an every dayes walke, be the weather cold or hot, the waters rough or calme, they must dive sometimes over head and eares for a Lobster, which often shakes them by their hands with a churlish nippe, and bids them adiew. The tide being spent, they trudge home two or three miles, with a hundred weight of Lobsters at their backs, and if none, a hundred scoules [scolds] meete them at home, and a hungry belly for two days after. Their husbands having caught any fish, they bring it in their boates as farre as they can by water, and there leave it; as it was their care to catch it, so it must be their wives paines to fetch it home, or fast: which done, they must dresse it and cooke it, dish it, and present it, see it eaten over their shoulders; and their loggerships having filled their paunches, their sweete lullabies [wives and children] scramble for their scrappes. In the Summer these *Indian* women when Lobsters be in their plenty and prime, they drie them to keepe for Winter, erecting scaffolds in the hot sun-shine, making fires likewise underneath them, by whose smoake the flies are expelled, till the substance remain hard and drie. In this manner they drie Basse and other fishes without salt, cutting them very thinne to dry suddainely, before the flies spoile them, or the raine moist them, having a speciall care to hang them in their smoakie houses, in the night and dankish weather.

In Summer they gather flagges [long, sword-shaped water grass], of which they make Matts for houses, and Hempe and Rushes, with dying stuffe of which they make curious baskets with intermixed colours and protractures of antique Imagerie: these baskets be of all sizes from a quart to a quarter, in which they carry their luggage. In winter time they are their husbands Caterers, trudging to the Clamm bankes for their belly timber [food], and their Porters to lugge home their Venison which their lazinesse exposes to the Woolves till they impose it upon their wives shoulders. They likewise sew their husbands shooes, and weave coates of Turkie feathers, besides all their ordinary household drudgerie which daily lies upon them, so that a bigge bellie [pregnancy] hinders no business, nor a childebirth takes much time, but the young Infant being greased and sooted, wrapt in a Beaver skin, bound to his good behaviour with his feete up to his bumme, upon a board two foots long and one foot broade, his face exposed to all nipping weather; this little *Pappouse* travells about with his bare footed mother to paddle in the Icie Clammbankes after three or foure dayes of age have sealed his passeboard [navel] and his mothers recoverie. For their carriage it is very civill, smiles being the greatest grace of their mirth; their musick is lullabies to quiet their children, who generally are as quiet as if they had neither spleene or lungs. To heare one of these *Indians* unseene, a good eare might easily mistake their untaught voyce for the warbling of a well tuned instrument. Such command have they of their voices. These womens modesty drives them to weare more cloathes than their men, having always a coate of cloath or skinnes wrapt like a blanket about their loynes, reaching downe to their hammes [thighs] which they never put off in company. If a husband have a minde to sell his wives Beaver petticote, as sometimes he doth, shee will not put it off untill shee have another to put on: commendable is their milde carriage and obedience to their husbands, notwithstanding all this their customarie churlishnesse and salvage inhumanitie, not seeming to delight in frownes or offering to word it with their lords, not presuming to proclaime their female superiority to the usurping of the least title of their husbands charter, but rest themselves content under their helplesse condition, counting it the womans portion: since the *English* arrivall comparison hath made them miserable, for seeing the kind usage of the *English* to their wives, they doe as much condemne their husbands for unkindnesse, and commend the *English* for their love.

38

The Conversation of Their Women

With the coming of white men, Indian women faced both sexual and commercial exploitation. The unexpected lasciviousness of some European men, evident in this excerpt, contrasted with the self-restraint practiced among Native Americans and noted by many observers. This narrative by John Lawson, a traveler in North Carolina in 1700, reveals the disdain of European traders, who took aggressive advantage of Native American hospitality and marriage arrangements. Lawson knew about the practice of abortion and apparently assumed that all unmarried Native American women were prostitutes, although these women clearly thought they were preparing for long-term conjugal relationships. Readers may wonder how he obtained some of his detailed knowledge about Indian women!

Lawson observed that women usually managed tribal trade and acted as interpreters, and he admired their intricately designed baskets and mats. Midwives with professional skill and pharmaceutical knowledge helped women in childbirth, and it appears that the health of both women and babies was better than that of Europeans.

From John Lawson, *History of North Carolina* (1714; reprint, Richmond, Va.: Garrett and Massie, 1937), pp. 194–201.

❖

As for the Indian Women which now happen in my Way, when young, and at Maturity, they are as fine shaped Creatures, (take them generally,) as any in the Universe. They are of a tawny Complexion, their Eyes very brisk and amorous, their Smiles afford the finest Composure a Face can possess, their Hands are of the finest Make, with small, long Fingers, and as soft as their Cheeks, and their whole Bodies of a smooth Nature. . . . As for the Trading Girls, which are those designed to get Money by their Natural Parts, these are discernable by the Cut of their Hair; their tonsure differing from all others of that Nation, who are not of their Profession, which Method is intended to prevent Mistakes; for the Savages of America are desirous (if possible) to keep their Wives to themselves, as well as those in other Parts of the World. When any Addresses are made to one of these Girls, she immediately acquaints her Parents therewith, and they tell the King of it, (provided he that courts her be a Stranger) his Majesty commonly being the principal Bawd [matchmaker] of the Nation he rules over, and there seldom being any of these Winchester-Weddings agreed on without his Royal Consent. He likewise advises her what Bargain to make, and if it happens to be an Indian Trader that wants a Bedfellow and has got Rum to sell, be sure the King must have a large Dram for a Fee to confirm the Match. These Indians that are of the elder sort, when any such Question is put to them, will debate the Matter amongst themselves with all the Sobriety and Seriousness imaginable, every one of the Girl's Relations arguing the Advantage or Detriment that may ensue such a Night's Encounter; all which is done with as much Steadiness and Reality as if it was the greatest Concern in the World, and not so much as one Person shall be seen to smile, so long as the Debate holds, making no Difference betwixt an Agreement of this Nature and a Bargain of any other. . . .

The Indian Traders are those which travel and abide amongst the Indians for a long space of time; sometimes for a Year, two, or three. These Men have commonly their Indian Wives, whereby they soon learn the Indian Tongue, keep a Friendship with the Savages; and besides the Satisfaction of a She-Bed-Fellow, they find these Indian Girls very serviceable to them, on Account of dressing their Victuals, and instructing them in the Affairs and Customs of the Country. Moreover, such a Man gets a great Trade with the Savages; for when a Person that lives amongst them, is reserved from the Conversation of their Women, tis impossible for him ever to accomplish his Designs amongst that People.

But one great Misfortune which often times attends those that converse with these Savage Women, is, that they get Children by them, which are seldom educated any otherwise than in a State of Infidelity. . . . On this Score it ever seems impossible for the Christians to get their Children (which they have by these Indian Women) away from them; whereby they might bring them up in the Knowledge of the Christian Principles. Nevertheless, we often find, that English Men, and other Europeans that have been accustomed to the Conversation of these Savage Women and their Way of Living, have been so allured with that careless sort of Life, as to be constant to their Indian Wife, and her Relations, so long as they lived, without ever desiring to return again amongst the English. . . .

They are never to boast of their Intrigues with the Women. If they do, none of the Girls value them ever after, or admit of their Company in their Beds. This proceeds not on the score of Reputation, for there is no such thing, (on that account) known amongst them; and although we may reckon them the greatest Libertines and most extravagant in their Embraces, yet they retain and possess a Modesty that requires those Passions never to be divulged.

The Trading Girls, after they have led that Course of Life, for several Years, in which time they scarce ever have a Child; (for they have an Art to destroy the Conception, and she that brings a Child in this Station, is accounted a Fool, and her Reputation is lessened thereby) at last they grow weary of so many, and betake themselves to a married State, or to the Company of one Man; neither does their having been common to so many any wise lessen their Fortunes, but rather augment them.

40   The Woman is not punished for Adultery, but tis the Man that makes the injured Person Satisfaction, which is the Law of Nations practised amongst them all; and he that strives to evade such Satisfaction as the Husband demands, lives daily in Danger of his Life; yet when discharged, all Animosity is laid aside, and the Cuckold is very well pleased with his Bargain, whilst the Rival is laughed at by the whole Nation, for carrying on his intrigue with no better Conduct, than to be discovered and pay so dear for his Pleasure.

The Indians say, that the Woman is a weak Creature, and easily drawn away by the Man's Persuasion; for which Reason, they lay no Blame upon her, but the Man (that ought to be Master of his Passion) for persuading her to it.

They are of a very hale Constitution; their Breaths are as Sweet as the Air they breathe in, and the Woman seems to be of that tender Composition, as if they were designed rather for the Bed than Bondage. Yet their Love is never of that Force and Continuance, that any of them ever runs Mad, or makes away with themselves on that score. They never love beyond Retrieving their first Indifferency, and when slighted, are as ready to untie the Knot at one end, as you are at the other.

Yet I knew an European Man that had a Child or two by one of these Indian Women, and afterwards married a Christian, after which he came to pass away a Night with his Indian Mistress; but she made Answer that she then had forgot she ever knew him, and that she never lay with another Woman's Husband, so fell a crying and took up the Child she had by him, and went out of the Cabin (away from him) in great Disorder. . . .

The Indian Women's Work is to cook the Victuals for the whole Family, and to make Mats, Baskets, Girdles, of Possum-Hair, and such like. They never plant the Corn amongst us, as they do amongst the Iroquois, who are always at War and Hunting; therefore, the Plantation Work is left for the Women and Slaves to perform, and look after; whilst they are wandring all over the Continent betwixt the two Bays of Mexico and St Laurence.

The Mats the Indian Women make, are of Rushes, and about five Foot high, and two Fathom long, and sewed double, that is, two together; whereby they become very commodious to lay under our Beds, or to sleep on in the Summer Season in the Day-time, and for our Slaves in the Night.

There are other Mats made of Flags, which the Tuskeruro Indians make, and sell to the Inhabitants.

The Baskets our Neighboring Indians make are all made of a very fine sort of Bulrushes, and sometimes of Silk-grass, which they work with Figures of Beasts, Birds, Fishes, &c.

A great way up in the Country, both Baskets and Mats are made of the split Reeds, which are only the outward shining Part of the Cane. Of these I have seen Mats, Baskets, and Dressing-Boxes, very artificially done.

The Savage Women of America have very easy Travail with their Children; sometimes they bring Twins, and are brought to bed by themselves, when took at a Disadvantage; not but they have Midwives amongst them, as well as Doctors who make it their Profession (for Gain) to assist and deliver Women, and some of these Midwives are very knowing in several Medicines that Carolina affords, which certainly expedite, and make easy Births. Besides, they are unacquainted with those severe Pains which follow the Birth in our European Women. Their Remedies are a great Cause of this Easiness in that State; for the Indian Women will run up and down the Plantation the same day, very briskly, and without any sign of Pain or Sickness; yet they look very meagre and thin. Not but that we must allow a great deal owing to the Climate and the natural Constitution of these Women, whose Course of Nature never visits them in such Quantities, as the European Women have. And though they never want Plenty of Milk, yet I never saw an Indian Woman with very large Breasts; neither does the young-est Wife ever fail of proving so good a Nurse as to bring her Child up free from the Rickets and Disasters that proceed from the Teeth, with many other Dis-tempers which attack our infants in England, and other Parts of Europe. . . .

The Women's Dress is, in severe Weather, a hairy Match-coat in the Nature of a Plad, which keeps out the Cold, and, (as I said before,) defends their Children from the Prejudices of the Weather. At other times they have only a sort of Flap or Apron containing two Yards in Length, and better than half a Yard deep. Sometimes it is a Deer-Skin dressed white, and pointed or slit at the bottom, like Fringe. When this is clean it becomes them very well.

Dressing Deerskin

Preparing the skins of animals for use as clothing was one of the most impor-tant of Native American women's productive activities. The work required time, skill, and strength, followed by careful sewing and decorating for appropriate use. Deerskin made the softest and most flexible leather, so it was also quickly adopted by white pioneers. This description was written by a seventeenth-century observer to present to the Royal Society of London, an organization that included most of the scientists and learned men of the seventeenth century.

From Sir Robert Southwell, "The Method the Indians in Virginia and Carolina Use to Dress Buck and Doe Skins," *Philosophical Transactions*, no. 194 (July–September 1691): 532–33.

❖

The Pelt being taken off is first streined by Lines, or otherwise, most like the Clothiers Racks, but for no other purpose but to dry them.

42   The Brains of the Deer, whether Buck or Doe, is taken out and mesled [*sic*], and dawbed on Moss or dryed Grass, and then dryed in the Sun, or by a Fire to preserve them.

When the Hunting time is over, the Women dress the Skins; first, by putting them in a Pond, or Hole of Water, to soak them well. Then they with an old Knife fixed in a Cleft-Stick, force off the Hair, whilst they remain wet. The Hair being taken or forced off, they put as many Skins as they have made so ready, into a Kettle or Earthen Pot, and a proportion of the Deers Brains, before spoken of, into the Kettle with the Skins; and then put them over a Fire till they are more than Blood-warm; which will make them ladder and scour perfectly clean; which done, they with small sticks wrest and twist each Skin as long as they find any Wet to drop from them, letting them remain so wrested some Hours; and then they untwist each Skin, and put them into a sort of a Rack, like a Clothiers Rack (which they fix at every place they come to, with no more Trouble than two small Poles set upright, and two more put athwart, all fixed with their own Barcks,) and extend them every way by Lines, and as the Skin dries, so they with a dull Hatchet, or a Stick slatted, and brought to a round edge, or a Stone fitted by nature for that purpose, rub them all over to force all the Water and Grease out of them, till they become perfectly dry: which is all they do.

And one Woman will dress eight or ten Skins in a day; that is, begin and end them. I intimate this because the Men never do it.

Awashonks, Queen of the Sakonnets

A "squaw-sachem" (woman chief) was not unusual in Native American societies. Usually a woman came to the position by inheritance, but she held it only by quality of leadership. Awashonks was the leader of the Sakonnets, related to the Wampanoag of southeastern Massachusetts; her people lived on the southern edge of Plymouth Colony, not far from Narragansett Bay, a location that left them vulnerable to being surrounded and destroyed. When King Philip's War broke out in 1675, Awashonks employed shrewd diplomacy to protect her people and to keep from being blamed for other Native Americans' actions. She sought the advice of her influential neighbor, Colonel Benjamin Church, who was himself shrewd enough to recognize the status of Awashonks and her power to protect *him* from attack. After advising her to avoid war, he kept his word about helping to protect her people from English retribution. The narrator of this account is Benjamin Church's descendant Thomas.

From Thomas Church, *The History of Philip's War,* 2d ed. (Exeter, N.H.: J.B. Williams, 1829), pp. 20–29. ❖

[King Philip] sent six men to Awashonks, squaw-sachem of the Sogkonate Indians, to engage her in his interests. Awashonks so far listened unto them as to call her subjects together to make a great dance, which is the custom of that nation when they advise about momentous affairs. But what does Awashonks do but sends away two of her men that well understood the English language . . . to invite Mr. [Benjamin] Church to the dance. Mr. Church, upon the invitation, immediately takes . . . his tenant's son, who well understood the Indian language, and rid down to the place appointed where they found hundreds of Indians gathered together from all parts of her dominion. Awashonks herself in a foaming sweat was leading the dance. But she was no sooner sensible of Mr. Church's arrival but she broke off, sat down, calls her nobles round her, orders Mr. Church to be invited into her presence. Complements being passed, and each one taking seats, she told him King Philip had sent six men . . . to draw her into a confederacy with him in a war with the English. Desiring him to give her his advice in the case, and to tell her the truth whether the Umpame [white] men (as Philip had told her) were gathering a great army to invade Philip's country. He assured her he would tell her the truth and give her his best advice. Then he told her it was but a few days since he came from Plymouth, and the English were then making no preparations for war; that he was in company with the principal gentlemen of the Government, who had no discourse at all about war, and he believed no thoughts about it. He asked her whether she thought he would have brought up his goods to settle in that place if he apprehended an entering into war with so near a neighbor. She seemed to be somewhat convinced by his talk, and said she believed he spoke the truth.

. . . Awashonks proceeded to tell Mr. Church that Philip's message to her was that unless she would forthwith enter into a confederacy with him in a war against the English, he would send his men over privately to kill the English cattle and burn their houses on that side of the river, which would provoke the English to fall upon her, whom they would without doubt suppose the author of the mischief. Mr. Church told her he was sorry to see so threatening an aspect of affairs, and stepping to the Mount-hopes [Philip's emissaries], he felt of their bags and finding them filled with bullets, asked them what those bullets were for. They scoffingly replied, to shoot pigeons with.

Then Mr. Church turned to Awashonks and told her, if Philip were resolved to make war, her best way would be to knock those six Mount-hopes on the head and shelter herself under the protection of the English, upon which the Mount-hopes were for the present dumb. But those two of Awashonks' men who had been at Mount-hope expressed themselves in a furious manner against his advice. And Little Eyes, one of the Queen's Council, joined them and urged Mr. Church to go aside with him among the bushes that he might have some private discourse with him, which other Indians immediately forbid, being sensible of his ill design; but the Indians began to side and grow very warm. Mr. Church with undaunted courage . . . bid the company observe those men that were of such bloody disposition, whether Providence would suffer them to live to see the event of the war, which others more peaceably disposed might do.

Then he told Awashonks he thought it might be most advisable for her to send to the Governor of Plymouth and shelter herself and people under his protection. She liked his advice and desired him to go on her behalf to the Plymouth government, which he consented to. And at parting advised her, whatever she did, not to desert the English interest to join with her neighbors in a rebellion which would certainly prove fatal to her. (He moved none of his goods from his house that there might not be the least umbrage from such an action.) She thanked him for his advice and sent two of her men to guard him to his house, which, when they came there, urged him to take care to secure his goods. . . . But [he] desired the Indians that if what they feared should happen, they would take care of what he left and directed them to a place in the woods where they should dispose them; which they faithfully observed.

44

FIRST AMERICANS

1. Anasazi Ruins—Mesa Verde

The Anasazi people, ancestors of the Pueblo and probably of some of the Zuni and Hopi peoples of today, lived in the southwestern United States in the prehistoric period from ca. 1200 B.C. to A.D. 1250. This picture shows their "apartment buildings," multifamily dwellings centering on a ceremonial kiva and built into the cliffs beside rivers, hunting grounds, and areas where the Indians planted their staple crops of corn and other vegetables. Courtesy of the Western History Department, Denver Public Library, Denver, Colorado.

2. Making Pottery at Santa Clara Pueblo

Women of the Santa Clara Pueblo in New Mexico still live in homes like those of their ancestors, and they preserve their history as they make the same kind of distinctive pottery. Here two women create their wares as a small child watches. Courtesy of the National Anthropological Archives, National Museum of Natural History, Smithsonian Institution, Washington, D.C. Photo no. 4561.

3. A Cheiff Ladye of Pomeiooc

The Indian women depicted by the Roanoke expedition artist John White in the 1580s were robust and active, as yet untouched by the disease and disasters that Europeans would bring in the seventeenth century. The little girl here plays with what looks like a corncob doll while her mother carries "a gourd full of some kind of pleasant [nonalcoholic] liquor." The child wears a type of G-string made of moss, and the mother wears a carefully fringed, soft deerskin skirt. Reprinted by permission of the publishers from Paul Hulton, ed., *America 1585: The Complete Drawings of John White* (Chapel Hill: University of North Carolina Press, 1984), figure 12. Copyright © 1984 by the University of North Carolina Press and by British Museum Publications.

4. Indian Village of Pomeiooc

The Native American societies of the East (Algonquian, Delaware, Iroquois, Huron, Pequot, Narragansett) lived along the coast or in woodlands and river valleys. The women made and decorated their lodges, using materials, such as bark and branches, from the woodland areas. These villages moved with the seasons, from valleys where the Indians could grow corn and other staples in the spring and summer to sheltered woodland areas where ice fishing and hunting small animals provided winter fare. All of the family members in one mother's line generally shared a lodge, although in certain groups, single families might have their own lodges. Reprinted by permission of the publishers from Paul Hulton, ed., *America 1585: The Complete Drawings of John White* (Chapel Hill: University of North Carolina Press, 1984), plate 32. Copyright © 1984 by the University of North Carolina Press and by British Museum Publications.

5. Indians Planting a Crop

Jacques Le Moyne, the official artist for a French expedition to Florida in 1564, depicted the cooperative division of labor between Indian men clearing and breaking the soil and women preparing and planting the rows of seeds. The composition of his painting is stylized in accord with European artistic conventions, but the size of the planting fields and the robust physique of the men and women imply well-organized agricultural abundance among precolonial Indians. Women made the large woven baskets that were essential for grain storage, but these men seem to be using metal grub hoes of European origin, an indication of established trade relationships long before European settlement in North America. From Jacques Le Moyne de Morgues painting, engraved and printed by Theodore de Bry, *Brevis Narratio Eorum Quae in Florida Americae Provicia* . . . (Frankfurt, 1591). Courtesy of the Special Collections, Lehigh University Libraries, Bethlehem, Pennsylvania.

6. Ojibwa Embroidered Pouch

Native American women were accomplished in the decorative arts. They made
many kinds of beadwork on cloth or leather or, as in this southeastern Ojibwa
pouch, produced intricate designs with natural materials. This pouch was embroidered with porcupine quills in a thunderbird design. Courtesy of the Pea-
body Museum of Archaeology and Ethnology, Harvard University, Cambridge,
Massachusetts.

7. Passamaquoddy Birch-Bark Box
This small, beautifully designed box could have had many storage uses, holding salt
or medicinal herbs or perhaps prized personal ornaments. It is another example of
the artistry of Native American women, who surrounded themselves with useful
and aesthetically pleasing objects of their own creation. Courtesy of the National
Museum of the American Indian, Smithsonian Institution.

8. Pocahontas Rebecca Rolfe

This portrait in vivid color shows Pocahontas in the garb of an English lady of her
period, the type of dress she wore when she was presented to Queen Anne. She
may have found these constraining fashions as unpalatable as the English weather,
because shortly afterwards she became ill and died in England at the age of twenty-
one. Oil on canvas by Antonien Zeon Shindler, ca. 1890. Courtesy of the National
Museum of American Art, Smithsonian Institution, Washington, D.C.

Building Colonies North and South

THE FIRST European child born in colonial North America was a girl—Virginia Dare in 1587 at Roanoke Island, Virginia. Historians seldom comment on the oddity of the fact that England's first major exploratory settlement included a pregnant woman. The Roanoke colony and little Virginia Dare had disappeared by 1591, never to be traced, an enduring enigma of early colonial history. But a few women were present and survived with the Jamestown colony, which was established in 1607. And the first Pilgrim to set foot on Plymouth Rock was Mary Chilton. Dorothy Bradford, the wife of William Bradford, the governor of Plymouth Colony, was the first person to die while the Pilgrims were exploring the Massachusetts coast in 1620. Bradford wrote that his wife, "accidentally falling overboard, was drowned in the harbor." It is suspected that the grim surroundings of the New World led her to suicide. Perhaps she was fortunate to escape the fate of the many women and men who died of cold and starvation that first year.

When one considers the harsh realities of survival in Europe's "New World," it seems remarkable that either men or women chose to venture forth in the tiny, crowded, leaking ships that brought them to America. Women particularly, as in all migrations, lamented leaving homes and families in their native lands. And they feared the forested "wilderness" broken only by newly cleared fields and mosquito-infested swamps—so different from the long-tilled land of their English origins. The poet Anne Bradstreet, an early settler of the Massachusetts Bay Colony, tells us that after she arrived, her "heart rose" with unhappiness, and she became ill for a long while. Only after she was convinced that "it was the way of God" did she submit and "join the church at Boston."

Many women, like Anne Bradstreet, dutifully followed their husbands or fathers to America. A few women, like Anne Hutchinson (in the next section), followed their ministers, out of religious conviction. Still other women, like the French Huguenot Judith Manigault, left Europe to escape religious persecution. Finally, a great many fled poverty, family abuse, criminal records, or unwanted sexual advances. This last group, responding to advertisements such as

William Alsop's pamphlet, often came as indentured servants whose contracts allowed no release from their bondage until they reached the age of twenty-one or twenty-five. African women were kidnapped from West Africa, were forced to endure the slave ship horrors of the fifty-day "middle passage," and if they survived, were sold as slaves in the West Indies or the American colonies.

46   Permanent settlements could not survive without cooks, laundresses, and caretakers, whose skills were unknown to most men of that era. Records of the Virginia Company and several other groups show that some white women were "imported" to be wives for the many single men among the southern colonists. Comparing the passenger lists for settlers of Virginia with those for New England reveals regional differences. Family relationships accounted for most women among the New Englanders, whereas among the early southern colonists, women were fewer in number and most often unattached—probably servants.

On landing, most of these early immigrants settled in tiny one-room, thatched-roof houses in the midst of what Governor Bradford described as "a hideous and desolate wilderness." In Boston, some even spent their first winter in caves. Even though living conditions improved, crowding was normal; this could lead to family disputes and sometimes to casual sexual behavior, as in "A Bedroom Story." The huge open fireplaces needed for cooking and heat contributed to frequent fires. Anne Bradstreet's anguished poem "Upon the Burning of Our House" describes the not unusual loss of home and precious possessions in the early colonies.

For women in families, ties to husbands and children usually made the pioneering experience more bearable. Particularly in seventeenth-century New England, Puritan doctrine emphasized that the family was the building block for the entire social structure. Even though family hierarchy always placed wives below husbands and just above children and servants, marriages in the New World were more egalitarian than those in Europe. Women and men were more likely to choose their own mates and to expect personal compatibility in the economic and social partnership that was a colonial marriage. Contrary to modern stereotypical notions, Puritan theologians like Samuel Willard advocated both mutual respect and sexual attraction as essential to marital stability. Anne Bradstreet's poem to her husband is an expression of the deep and passionate bonds encouraged between seventeenth-century husbands and wives.

In southern colonies, a demographic shortage of women led to more marriages at a young age, often in adolescence, and also to earlier deaths due to frequent childbearing. Family life for most other seventeenth-century white women meant marriage in their early twenties and up to eight or nine surviving children, usually at two-year intervals. Childbirth was attended by skilled midwives, and more women died from infectious diseases than from childbirth complications; still, giving birth was a fearful experience for which every woman prepared as if for death. Anne Bradstreet wrote a poem about that fear. And because families broken by deaths and reconstituted by remarriage were the rule rather than the exception in colonial America, Bradstreet's poem cautions her husband about his probable remarriage and about protecting her children from a stepmother's mistreatment.

A majority of seventeenth-century American white women were, for some years, servants whose lives were full of hard work, harsh discipline, and sometimes sexual exploitation. John Winter's letter details some of the work expected of serving maids and the punishment received if they displeased their masters and mistresses. Often the friction between master or mistress and servant led to the serving maid's resistance or, as a last resort, to her running away. Charity Dallen took her complaints about mistreatment to court and won a new master. Elizabeth Greene was not so fortunate. When she gave birth to a baby out of wedlock, she killed it—probably to avoid the severe sanctions on unwed servant mothers. She was caught, however, and hanged for the offense. The unwed mother in the anonymous document chose to protect her lover and suffer the consequences—which usually included additional years of servitude. Life was especially bleak in the Chesapeake colonies, where servants often died at an early age from disease, overwork, and malnutrition. Court records show that rape was not uncommon in both the North and the South; the victims were likely to be blamed, as court testimony shows in "Wilt Thou Not Drinke to Me?"

The legal situation of seventeenth-century enslaved African people was at first quite similar to that of white indentured servants. Slaves might be freed after their period of service, and both white and black servants frequently died of overwork and harsh living conditions. A Dutch ship brought the first slaves to Jamestown in 1619, but only small numbers were imported during the seventeenth century (five thousand by the end of the century), and very few were women. Although during the early years of the century, the legal status of enslaved peoples had much in common with that of white indentured servants, there were significant differences. For example, unlike white female servants, enslaved black women in the South were sent into fields to labor alongside men, and southern slaves were not permitted to marry. The scattered nature of early farms did not allow for much contact between the sexes or for the easy establishment of stable families among either blacks or whites. One result was numerous mulatto children, like Elizabeth Key, whose story demonstrates that there was still flexibility in mid-century laws regarding slave status and racial intermarriage.

Southern whites would soon tighten restrictions. As tobacco became a major southern crop, requiring a large cheap labor force to maintain profits, the demand for enslaved laborers increased. In 1664, Virginia became the first colony to enact restrictive laws that mandated lifetime slavery (which children inherited from their mother no matter who their father was), deprived enslaved blacks of most legal rights, and effectively dissuaded potentially rebellious white laborers from making common cause with black allies. In contrast to enslaved women in the South, those in the North rarely worked in the fields, and less restrictive codes allowed them to marry, attend church, receive some education, and even enjoy a few legal rights. There were, of course, fewer slaves in the North; in the South, by 1700, the institution of black slavery was rapidly becoming a factor in the lives of all women.

The labor of both black and white women was essential for the survival of their communities. "Making Linen" provides one example of the kind of productive and time-consuming work that filled the lives of all seventeenth-century women, whether servants or mistresses. In addition to this work, many white women also managed large households. All women worked in dairies and kitchen gardens, processed and preserved the family's food and medicine, made and maintained cloth and clothing, milked cows, collected eggs, produced cheese and butter, made soap, bartered for necessities, nursed the sick, cooked and served meals for their families and hired help, and taught the skills of house-wifery to their daughters. It is no wonder that a favorite biblical verse of the period maintained that a virtuous woman "eateth not of the bread of idleness" (Prov. 31:27). Where family units were strong, women's contributions were re-spected, and women retained some control over when and how they would work. For example, Plymouth Colony's governor, William Bradford, explained that the colony's experiment in communal labor and ownership failed largely because of the disapproval of its women. In the South, where family units were more rare and commercial farming was more common, white women were likely to live on scattered farms rather than in the closely knit villages common in the North.

But some class division did exist in the colonies, as we can see from the 1674 portrait of Elizabeth Freake and her daughter Mary. From Elizabeth's lovely lace and velvet, we know that the Freake family was wealthy. We also see, how-ever, that although Mrs. Freake had the wealth to command a staff of servants, she still wore a matron's apron (ornamental though it certainly was), indicat-ing that she defined herself as a working person who probably often labored alongside her servants and younger female family members. The baby daughter would be trained in the same family and household responsibilities and also in the Puritan religious tradition of her mother and father.

48

For the Increase of the Plantation

A few women came with the Jamestown settlers in 1607. They were included in the expedition to perform the many subsistence tasks that men did not know how to do. By 1620, the date of the following document, the Virginia Company decided to send large groups of potential wives to Jamestown to deflect the male colonists from pure profit-taking. The company was concerned that colonists might refuse to stay if women did not help establish a permanent community, as the company secretary noted in these excerpts from the company records. By 1622, these women were all married, but unfortunately one-third of the population died in a 1623 massacre. Apparently only about thirty-five of several hundred women survived. Spelling and punctuation of the document have been modernized.

From Susan M. Kingsbury, ed., *Records of the Virginia Company of London*, vol. 1 (Washington, D.C.: Government Printing Office, 1906), pp. 256, 566.

❖

Lastly he [the governor] wished that a fit hundredth might be sent of women, Maids young and uncorrupt to make wives to the Inhabitants and by that means to make the men there more settled & less moveable, who by defect thereof (as is credibly reported) stay there but to get something and then to return for England, which will breed a dissolution, and so an overthrow of the Plantation. These women if they marry to the public farmers, to be transported at the charges of the Company; If otherwise, then those that takes them to wife to pay the said Company their charges of transportation, and it was never fitter time to send them than now. . . .

. . . The Third Roll was for sending of Maids to Virginia to be made Wives, which the Planters there did very much desire, by the want of whom have sprang the greatest hindrances of the increase of the Plantation, in that most of them esteeming Virginia not as a place of Habitation but only of a short sojourning have applied themselves and their labors wholly to the raising of present profit and utterly neglected not only staple Commodities but even the very necessities of man's life. In regard whereof and to prevent so great an inconvenience hereafter, whereby the Planters minds may be the faster tied to Virginia by the bonds of Wyves and Children, care hath been taken to provide them young handsome and honestly educated maids whereof 60 are already sent to Virginia, being such as were specially recommended unto the Company for their good bringing up by their parents or friends of good worth: Which maids are to be disposed in marriage to the most honest and industrious Planters who are to defray and satisfy to the Adventurers the charges of their passages and provisions at such rates as they and the Adventurers' Agents there shall agree.

50

Passengers to Virginia

The following passengers, listed with their age, were transported to Virginia on the *Elizabeth de Lo* in August 1635. They were all single and unrelated, in contrast to the family groups that emigrated to Massachusetts. And they were young, the men mostly between fourteen and thirty and the women between nineteen and twenty-eight except for one unattached mother and her daughter.

From *The New England Historical and Genealogical Register* 15 (1861): 142.

❖

Jo. Benford	20	Wm. Thurrowgood	13
Lodowick Fletcher	20	Samuel Mathew	14
Jo. Bagbie	17	Tho. Frith	17
Robt. Salter	14	Jo. Austin	24
Edward White	18	Paul Fearne	24
Stephen Pierce	30	Thomas Royston	25
Rich. Beanford	18	Jo. Taylor	18
Rich. Chapman	18		
Andrew Parkins	18		
Jo. Baker	16	WOMEN	
Jo. Walker	16		
Jo. Vaughan	17	Katherine Jones	28
Yeoman Gibson	16	Eliz. Sankster	24
Tho. Leed	16	Ellin Shore	20
Geo Trevas	18	Alice Pindon	19
Wm Shelborn	20	Sara Everedge	22
Samuel Growce	38	Margaret Smith	28
Wm. Glasbrooke	21	Elizab. Hodman	20
Edward Dicks	30	Moules Naxton	19
Jo. Bennett	18	Marie Burback	17
Michael Saundby	25	Eliz. Rudston	40
		Eliz. Rudston	5

Passengers to Massachusetts

The following passengers sailed from Weymouth, England, to Massachusetts on March 20, 1635. Most were family members, in contrast to the single young people who went to Virginia. There were women of all ages—wives, daughters, and kinswomen of various tradesmen, husbandmen (farmers), and the minister, who led the group. Even the servants were likely to be relatives.

From *The New England Historical and Genealogical Register* 25 (1871): 13–15.

❖

1. Joseph Hull, of Somerset, a minister, aged 40 years
2. Agnes Hull, his wife, aged 25 years
3. Joan Hull, his daughter, aged 15 years
4. Joseph Hull, his son, aged 13 years
5. Tristram, his son, aged 11 years
6. Elizabeth Hull, his daughter, aged 7 years
7. Temperance, his daughter, aged 9 years
8. Grissell Hull, his daughter, aged 5 years
9. Dorothy Hull, his daughter, aged 3 years
10. Judith French, his servant, aged 20 years
11. John Wood, his servant, aged 20 years
12. Robert Dabyn, his servant, aged 28 years
13. Musachiell Bernard, of Batcombe, clothier in the county of Somerset, 24 years
14. Mary Bernard, his wife, aged 28 years
15. John Bernard, his son, aged 3 years
16. Nathaniel, his son, aged 1 year
17. Rich. Persons, salter and his servant, 30 years
18. Francis Baber, chandler, aged 36 years
19. Jesope, joyner, aged 22 years
20. Walter Jesop, weaver, aged 21 years
21. Timothy Tabor, in Somerset of Batcombe, tailor, aged 35 years
22. Jane Tabor, his wife, aged 35 years
23. Jane Tabor, his daughter, aged 10 years
24. Anne Tabor, his daughter, aged 8 years
25. Sarah Tabor, his daughter, aged 5 years
26. William Fever, his servant, aged 20 years
27. John Whitmarke, aged 39 years

28. Alice Whitmarke, his wife, aged 35 years
29. James Whitmarke, his son, aged 11 years
30. Jane, his daughter, aged 7 years
31. Onseph Whitmarke, his son, aged 5 years
32. Rich. Whitmarke, his son, aged 2 years

52

33. William Read, of Batcombe, taylor in Somerset, aged 28 years
34. [name not entered]
35. Susan Read, his wife, aged 29 years
36. Hannah Read, his daughter, aged 3 years
37. Susan Read, his daughter, aged 1 year
38. Rich. Adams, his servant, 29 years
39. Mary, his wife, aged 26 years
40. Mary Cheame, his daughter, aged 1 year
41. Zachary Bickewell, aged 45 years
42. Agnes Bickewell, his wife, aged 27 years
43. John Bickewell, his son, aged 11 years
44. John Kitchin, his servant, 23 years
[45. omitted from ms.]
46. George Allin, aged 24 years
47. Katherine Allin, his wife, aged 30 years
48. George Allin, his son, aged 16 years
49. William Allin, his son, aged 8 years
50. Matthew Allin, his son, aged 6 years
51. Edward Poole, his servant, aged 26 years
52. Henry Kingman, aged 40 years
53. Joan, his wife, being aged 39
54. Edward Kingman, his son, aged 16 years
55. Joanne, his daughter, aged 11 years
56. Anne, his daughter, aged 9 years
57. Thomas Kingman, his son, aged 7 years
58. John Kingman, his son, aged 2 years
59. John Ford, his servant, aged 30 years
60. William King, aged 40 years
61. Dorothy, his wife, aged 34 years
62. Mary King, his daughter, aged 12 years
63. Katheryn, his daughter, aged 10 years
64. William King, his son, aged 8 years
65. Hannah King, his daughter, aged 6 years
66. Thomas Holbrooke, of Broadway, aged 34 years
67. Jane Holbrooke, his wife, aged 34 years
68. John Holbrooke, his son, aged 11 years

69. Thomas Holbrooke, his son, aged 10 years
70. Anne Holbrooke, his daughter, aged 5 years
71. Elizabeth, his daughter, aged 1 year
72. Thomas Dible, husbandman, aged 22 years
73. Francis Dible, sawyer, aged 24 years
74. Robert Lovell, husbandman, aged 40 years
75. Elizabeth Lovell, his wife, aged 35 years
76. Zacheus Lovell, his son, 15 years
77. Anne Lovell, his daughter, aged 16 years
78. John Lovell, his son, aged 8 years
79. Ellyn, his daughter, aged 1 year
80. James, his son, aged 1 year
81. Joseph Chickin, his servant, 16 years
82. Alice Kinham, aged 22 years
83. Angell Hollard, aged 21 years
84. Katheryn, his wife, 22 years
85. George Land, his servant, 22 years
86. Sarah Land, his kinswoman, 18 years
87. Richard Jones, of Dinder
88. Robert Martin, of Batcombe, husbandman, 44
89. Humphrey Shepard, husbandman, 32
90. John Upham, husbandman, 35
91. Joan Martin, 44
92. Elizabeth Upham, 32
93. John Upham, Junior, 7
94. Sarah Upham, 26
95. William Grane, 12
96. Nathaniel Upham, 5
97. Elizabeth Upham, 3
98. Dorset Richard Wade, of Simstyly, cooper, aged 60
99. Elizabeth Wade, his wife, 6[?]
100. Dinah, his daughter, 22
101. Henry Lush, his servant, aged 17
102. Andrew Hallett, his servant, 28
103. John Hoble, husbandman, 13
104. Robert Huste, husbandman, 40
105. John Woodcooke, 2[?]
106. Rich. Porter, husbandman, 3[?]

A Huguenot Refugee

A woman had to share hard labor with her husband if either was to survive in early frontier settlements. Yet in the South, such labor was already considered working "like a slave," as described in this account. Judith Giton (ca. 1665–1711) was about twenty when she and many other Protestant Huguenots escaped, penniless, from French persecution to settle in South Carolina in 1685. She described the harrowing experience in this letter to her brother. After an early widowhood, she remarried and operated a boardinghouse while her second husband ran a distillery. Judith Manigault died too young to know that her labor had helped establish one of the South's wealthiest families.

From "Letter of Judith Giton Manigault," translated and quoted in Charles W. Baird, *History of the Huguenot Emigration to America,* vol. 2 (New York: Dodd, Mead and Co., 1885), pp. 112–14.

❖

For eight months we had suffered from the contributions and the quartering of the soldiers, on account of religion, enduring many inconveniences. We therefore resolved on quitting France at night, leaving the soldiers in their beds, and abandoning the house with its furniture. [They hid for ten days with another Huguenot, then went on through Lyons and Lorraine to Wesel in the Rhineland, only about ninety miles from her soldier brother's winter quarters.] Our deceased mother and I entreated my eldest brother to consent that we should go that way. . . . It was in the depth of winter. But he would not hear of it, having nothing in his mind but "Carolina," and dreading to miss any chance of coming hither. The thought that we thus lost so good an opportunity to see you at least once more, has been a constant source of grief to me, ever since. After this, we passed into Holland, in order to go to England. We were detained in London for three months, waiting for a vessel ready to sail for Carolina. Once embarked, we were miserably off indeed. The scarlet fever broke out in our ship, and many died, among them our aged mother. . . . Our vessel put in [at Bermuda] for repairs, having been badly injured in a severe storm. Our captain . . . was thrown into prison, and the ship was seized. It was with the greatest difficulty that we secured our passage in another ship, for our money had all been spent. After our arrival in Carolina, we suffered all sorts of evils. Our eldest brother died of a fever, eighteen months after coming here. . . . We ourselves have been exposed, since leaving France, to all kinds of afflictions, in the forms of sickness, pestilence, famine, poverty, and the roughest labor. I have been for six months at a time in this country without tasting bread, laboring meanwhile like a slave in tilling the ground. Indeed, I have spent three or four years without knowing what it was to eat bread whenever I wanted it. God has been very good to us in enabling us to bear up under trials of every kind.

Why Servant Women Should Come to America

The myth of increased opportunities for women under frontier conditions because of the high ratio of men to women has been echoed by many historians, past and present. For those of the lower classes in the seventeenth century, however, self-improvement was very limited. The following bawdy statement encouraged poor women to go to the New World to find husbands and to avoid prostitution in London's Lewknors Lane. But it minimized the hardships of New World servitude and the possibility of injustice and exploitation.

From William Alsop, pamphlet, in Clayton Colman Hall, ed., *Narratives of Early Maryland, 1633–1684* (New York: Charles Scribner's Sons, 1910), pp. 358–59.

❖

The Women that go over into this Province as Servants, have the best luck here as in any place of the world besides; for they are no sooner on shoar, but they are courted into a Copulative Matrimony, which some of them (for aught I know) had they not come to such a Market with their Virginity, might have kept it by them untill it had been mouldy, unless they had let it out by a yearly rent to some of the Inhabitants of Lewknors-Lane, or made a Deed of Gift of it to Mother Coney, having only a poor stipend out of it, untill the Gallows or Hospital called them away. Men have not altogether so good luck as Women in this kind, or natural preferment, without they be good Rhetoricians, and well vers'd in the Art of perswasion, then (probably) they may ryvet themselves in the time of their Servitude into the private and reserved favour of their Mistress, if Age speak their Master deficient.

In short, touching the Servants of this Province, they live well in the time of their Service, and by their restrainment in that time, they are made capable of living much better when they come to be free.

Surviving in the Wilderness

William Bradford, a leader of New England's first colony at Plymouth, Massachusetts, arrived with the Mayflower in 1620. In his lengthy history of the Pilgrim settlement, he described the explorations of the coastline. "Wise Seneca" is the Wampanoag, Squanto, who was kidnapped twice (in 1605 and 1612) from his native village of Pautuxet and taken to England to "advertise" the New World. When the exploring party, with Squanto, reached the site of Pautuxet, they discovered that the people of that village had been wiped out by disease; there the Pilgrims decided to establish their colony of Plymouth. The wilderness that Bradford's party explored must have seemed just as "hideous" to the women of his party remaining on their ship; indeed Dorothy Bradford, his wife, was the group's first casualty, drowning beside the *Mayflower* (an apparent suicide) soon after arrival.

Bradford, who became governor in 1621 after the death of Governor John Carver and nearly half of the other colonists, also described the idealistic colony's early abandonment of community property in favor of family ownership of land and products, making clear that the complaints of overworked women were a major factor in the decision. This action demonstrates that women's opinions could not be ignored when their labor was seen as essential to the survival of the community. Spelling has been modernized.

From William T. Davis, ed., *Bradford's History of Plymouth Plantation, 1606–1646* (New York: Charles Scribner's Sons, 1908), pp. 95–97, 146–47.

❖

Being thus arrived in a good harbor and brought safe to land, they fell upon their knees and blessed the God of heaven, who had brought them over the vast and furious ocean, and delivered them from all the perils and miseries thereof, again to set their feet on the firm and stable earth, their proper element. And no marvel if they were thus joyful, seeing wise Seneca was so affected with sailing a few miles on the coast of his own Italy; as he affirmed, that he had rather remain twenty years on his way by land, than pass by sea to any place in a short time; so tedious and dreadful was the same unto him.

But here I cannot but stay and make a pause, and stand half amazed at this poor peoples present condition; and so I think will the reader too, when he well considers the same. Being thus passed the vast ocean, and a sea of troubles before in their preparation (as may be remembered by that which went before), they had now no friends to welcome them, nor inns to entertain or refresh their

weatherbeaten bodies, no houses or much less towns to repair to, to seek for succor. It is recorded in scripture as a mercy to the apostle and his shipwrecked company, that the barbarians showed them no small kindness in refreshing them, but these savage barbarians when they met with them (as after will appear) were readier to fill their sides full of arrows than otherwise. And for the season it was winter, and they that know the winters of that country know them to   57
be sharp and violent, and subject to cruel and fierce storms, dangerous to travel to known places, much more to search an unknown coast. Besides, what could they see but a hideous and desolate wilderness, full of wild beasts and wild men? and what multitudes there might be of them they knew not. Neither could they, as it were, go to the top of Pisgah, to view from this wilderness a more godly country to feed their hopes; for which way soever they turned their eyes (save upward to the heavens) they could have little solace or content in respect of any outward objects. For summer being done, all things stand upon them with a weatherbeaten face; and the whole country, full of woods and thickets, represented a wild and savage hue. If they looked behind them, there was the mighty ocean which they had passed, and was now as a main bar and gulf to separate them from all the civil parts of the world. If it be said they had a ship to succor them, it is true; but what heard they daily from the mr. and company? . . . Yes it was muttered by some, that if they got not a place in time, they would turn them and their goods ashore and leave them. . . . What could now sustain them but the spirit of God and his grace? . . .

. . . They began to think how they might raise as much corn as they could, and obtain a better crop than they had done, that they might not still thus languish in misery. At length, after much debate of things, the Governor (with the advice of the chiefest amongst them) gave way that they should set corn every man for his own particular, and in that regard trust to themselves. . . . And so assigned to every family a parcel of land, according to the proportion of their number. . . . This had very good success, for it made all hands very industrious, so as much more corn was planted than otherwise would have been by any means. . . . The women now went willingly into the field, and took their little ones with them to set corn; which before would allege weakness and inability; whom to have compelled would have been thought great tyranny and oppression.

The experience that was had in this common course and condition, tried sundry years and that amongst godly and sober men, may well evince the vanity of that conceit of Plato's and other ancients applauded by some of later times; that the taking away of property and bringing in community into a common-wealth would make them happy and flourishing; as if they were wiser than God. . . . For men's wives to be commanded to do service for other men, as dressing their meat, washing their clothes, etc., they deemed it a kind of slavery, neither could many husbands well brook it.

Conjugal Love

Among Puritan theorists, the whole social order was seen to rest on the stability of family life even more than on individual virtue. Samuel Willard (1640–1707), the influential pastor of Boston's prestigious Old South Church for thirty years, described the ideals of Puritan marriage. He was not "puritanical" about sex; Willard's first principle of conjugal love was the necessity of a good sexual relationship. He also stressed mutuality of affection and responsibility and as much domestic equality as possible. But wives were to remain subordinate to husbands and other public authorities because women's misbehavior could destroy "Humane Societies."

From Samuel Willard, *A Compleat Body of Divinity* (1726; New York: Johnson Reprint Corp., 1969), pp. 609–10.

❖

Private Families . . . are the first foundation of Humane Societies . . . out of which all other do arise; and do necessarily require that there be Order in them, without which Mankind would fall into a Rout. . . . The natural Necessity of this Relation [between husband and wife] was founded in the Order and End of Man's Creation. Humane Nature was at first confined to one Man, and one Woman, by whom it was to be Propagated and Multiplyed in its Individuals, which was the reason why God made a distinction of Sex between them: And to prevent Confusion, God from the First appointed Marriage . . . And in this He laid a foundation for distinct Families, to set up each by themselves. . . . So that if this Order be not upheld, either Mankind must cease, or Mankind must degenerate into the State and Order of Brutes, which is altogether disagreeable.

. . . In the further Prosecution of the Duties between these, we are to take Notice, that of all the Orders which are unequals, these do come nearest to an Equality, and in several respects they stand upon even ground. These do make a Pair, which infers so far a *Parity:* They are in the Word of God called *Yoke-Fellows,* and so are to draw together in the Yoke. Nevertheless, God hath also made an imparity between them, in the Order prescribed in his Word, and for that reason there is a Subordination, and they are ranked among unequals. And from this we may observe some Duties that are *mutual* or common between them, and others that are *proper* to each. . . .

1. . . . . That therefore which belongs to Married Persons is *Conjugal Love;* which is therein distinguished from that which is due to any other Relation whatsoever. There is also a *Special Love,* which comprehends the whole Duty of

the Husband to his Wife, in all the parts of it; and is put in contradistinction to the Submission, which expresseth the whole Duty of the Wife. . . . But this Conjugal Love is *Mutual,* and is the proper Cement of this Relation: And it is enforced from that Conjugal Union, by which they become One Flesh: And tho' this Oneness be not *Natural,* but *Voluntary,* yet it is the nearest relative Conjunction in the World, and on that account it requires the intimatest Affection; and if it be rightly made, it follows from a Preference that these have each of the other in their hearts, above all the World, on account of this Relation: For which reason it is compared to Love between Christ & his Church. . . . And the true Comfort which is to be hoped for from this Relation, must derive from this Love, without which it will prove to be, of all the most unhappy.

2. A *Special Care and Tenderness one of another.* And this follows from the Love now mentioned, and is indeed the end and use of it: And in this they ought with an holy emulation, to strive which shall outstrip the other. They are to be Helps one to another, and this Helpfulness is equally incumbent on them. . . . They should, so far as may be without sinning against God, endeavour to give each other *Content,* that they may fortify and preserve Amity and Sweetness in their whole Conversation, remembring that by Marriage they are made inseparable, and cannot without Sin, at least on one side, be put asunder, or depart one from the other. Hence they ought to study each others Tempers, and prudently accommodate themselves thereunto, so as not to irritate the Corruption that is in them; to bear with each others Infirmities, Natural or Sinful, considering themselves as the frail Children of fallen *Adam;* and making the Allowances which they stand in need of having made to them. . . . They should be careful of each others Health: And carry to one another with greatest Tenderness in Time of Sickness, expressing a very peculiar Compassion. They are to be very tender of each others Reputation; not only to bear, but also to cover and not discover any thing, which may render them a reproach to others. . . .

3. A *Mutual endeavour to promote each others Eternal Salvation.* To do all they can to help one another to Heaven; and in nothing can they equally show their best Love. . . .

4. A *joint Interest in governing the rest of their Family.* If God in his Providence hath bestowed on them Children or Servants, they have each of them a share in the government of them; tho' there is an inequality in the degree of this Authority, and the Husband is to be acknowledged to hold a *Superiority,* which the Wife is practically to allow; yet in respect of all others in the Œconomical Society, she is invested with an Authority over them by God; and her Husband is to allow it to her, and the others are to carry it to her as such . . . for tho' the Husband be the Head of the Wife, yet she is an Head of the Family.

The Tenth Muse

America's first published poet was the pious Puritan Anne Bradstreet (1612–72), whose book of poems, *The Tenth Muse Lately Sprung Up in America*, was published in London in 1650. Her lyrics are among the best of the seventeenth century and reveal a great deal about women's lives in the colonies at a time when virtually no other American women, and few men, were writing. In the first of the poems below, Bradstreet describes her passionate love for her husband, Simon, a government official who was often absent from their Ipswich home on business for the Massachusetts Bay Colony. The second poem reveals the thoughts of a seventeenth-century woman preparing for the birth of a child as if for death. Bradstreet had been disappointed to have no children during the first eight years of her marriage, but after her arrival in America, she finally became pregnant and went on to have eight children, all of whom survived. For this she was very thankful, and in this poem she cautions her husband to protect her children from a stepmother's mistreatment should she die and he remarry. In the third poem, Bradstreet laments the burning of her third home in North Andover, Massachusetts, in 1660 and the loss of her precious possessions, which may have included other writings. She struggles, as any good Puritan should, to resign herself to God's will.

From John Harvard Ellis, ed., *The Works of Anne Bradstreet in Prose and Verse* (Charlestown, Mass.: Abram E. Cutter, 1867), pp. 40–42, 393–95.

❖

To My Dear and Loving Husband

If ever two were one, then surely we.
If ever man were lov'd by wife, then thee;
If ever wife was happy in a man,
Compare with me ye women if you can.
I prize thy love more than whole Mines of gold,
Or all the riches that the East doth hold.
My love is such that Rivers cannot quench,
Nor aught but love from thee, give recompense.
Thy love is such I can no way repay,
The heavens reward thee manifold I pray.
Then while we live, in love let's so persever,
That when we live no more, we may live ever.

❖

Before the Birth of One of Her Children

All things within this fading world hath end,
Adversity doth still our joys attend;
No ties so strong, no friends so dear and sweet,
But with deaths parting blow is sure to meet.
The sentence past is most irrevocable,
A common thing, yet oh inevitable;
How soon, my Dear, death may my steps attend,
How soon't may be thy Lot to lose thy friend,
We both are ignorant, yet love bids me
These farewell lines to recommend to thee,
That when that knot's unty'd that made us one,
I may seem thine, who in effect am none.
And if I see not half my days that's due,
What nature would, God grant to yours and you;
The many faults that well you know I have,
Let be interr'd in my oblivion's grave;
If any worth or virtue were in me,
Let that live freshly in thy memory.
And when thou feel'st no grief, as I no harms,
Yet love thy dead, who long lay in thine arms:
Thy loss shall be repaid with gains
Look to my little babes, my dear remains.
And if thou love thy self, or loved'st me
These O protect from step Dames injury.
And if chance to thine eyes shall bring this verse,
With some sad sighs honour my absent Herse;
And kiss this paper for thy loves dear sake,
Who with salt tears this last Farewel did take.

❖

Upon the Burning of Our House, July 10th, 1666

In silent night, when rest I took,
For sorrow near I did not look,
I wakened was with thundering noise
And piteous shrieks of dreadful voice.
That fearful sound of "Fire!" and "Fire!"
Let no man know is my Desire.

I, starting up, the light did spy,
And to my God my heart did cry
To strengthen me in my Distress,
And not to leave me succorless.
Then coming out, beheld apace,
The flame consume my dwelling-place.

And when I could no longer look,
I blest his Name that gave and took,
That laid my goods now in the dust;
Yea, so it was, and so 'twas just—
It was his own; it was not mine.
Far be it that I should repine.

He might of all justly bereft,
But yet sufficient for us left.
When by the ruins oft I passed,
My sorrowing eyes aside did cast,
And here and there the places spy
Where oft I sat, and long did lie.

Here stood that trunk, and there that chest;
There lay that store I counted best;
My pleasant things in ashes lie,
And them behold no more shall I.
Under thy roof no guest shall sit,
Nor at thy table eat a bit.

No pleasant tale shall e'er be told,
Nor things recounted done of old;
No candle e'er shall shine in thee,
Nor bridegroom's voice e'er heard shall be.
In silence ever shalt thou lie,
Adieu, Adieu; all's vanity.

Then straight I 'gan my heart to chide:
And did thy wealth on earth abide?
Didst fix thy hope on mouldering dust,
The arm of flesh didst make thy trust?
Raise up thy thoughts above the sky,
That dunghill mists away may fly.

Thou hast an house on high erect;
Framed by that mighty Architect,

With glory richly furnished,
Stands permanent though this be fled.
It's purchased, and paid for too,
By Him who hath enough to do—

A prize so vast as is unknown,
Yet, by his gift, is made thine own.
There's wealth enough; I need no more;
Farewell, my pelf; farewell, my store.
The world no longer let me love,
My hope and treasure lies above.

Making Linen

Women brought seeds from England and planted flax almost as soon as they arrived in the New World, both north and south. Producing linen required months of work from numerous laborers in the colonial household. It was part of a housewife's job to organize the complicated home-industrial process here described by a nineteenth-century woman historian. Linen was a necessity for baby clothes, sanitary napkins, and men's and women's long-wearing shirts, as well as for fine tablecloths and luxury items. Linen cloths often became prized possessions, tangible wealth to be lovingly preserved for generations and mourned if destroyed, as in the story of a domestic tragedy quoted at the end of this selection.

From Alice Morse Earle, *Margaret Winthrop* (New York: Charles Scribner's Sons, 1895), pp. 71–76, 188–89. ❖

In May the flax and hemp were ripe, were ready to be gathered. The plants were not cut off, but were pulled up by the roots and laid flat a day and a night, spread out on the ground. The stalks were then tied up in bundles, which were called "baits" or "bates,"—universally so called in the seventeenth century, though that use of the word is not found in our modern dictionaries. These baits were stacked upright till the time came to water the flax or hemp. This was done preferably in running water, as the rotting flax was very offensive, and poisoned fish. Stakes were set in the water in the form of a square, and the baits of flax or hemp were filled in solidly between them, each alternate layer laid at right angles with the one beneath it, and at the top a cover of boards, weighted with heavy stones, kept the flax absolutely immovable beneath the water. After about four days and four nights, the baits of flax were taken out of the water, and all the rotted leaves and filth were removed; and they were then set upright in the sun by the side of the house, the fence, or wall, to dry thoroughly. Before watering, "carl" flax usually went through an extra amount of drying, and a process called "rippling," to remove the seed. A "ripple comb" was drawn over the baits to break off the round seed vessels,—"bobs," as they were called.

64   A brake of wood was then applied with violent blows to separate the woody part from the fibres, to take out the "hexe from the rind." This was done twice, once with an "open wide tooth or mixt brake," then with a "close and strait brake." This had to be done in clear sunny weather, for the flax had to be "dry as tinder," else it would not break well. The fibres were then made into large bundles, which were no longer called baits, but "strikes." Chaucer says, "Down it hung like a strike of flax." The flax usually went through the process of breaking twice. These strikes then were swingled and scraped with a wooden swingling-knife, dagger-shaped, to get out thoroughly the hard "bun" in the centre. The refuse was beaten a second time, and from it was gathered what was called "swingle-tree hurds," from which very coarse cloth like bagging could be spun and woven; or, if it were carded through coarse wool-cards, what were termed "harden" sheets could be made of it. If the flax was then to be sold, this single swingling was all the farm household did; but if it were to be spun at home, it went through a second swingling, and the refuse of this process was called "hempen hurding," or "flax hurding."

These carefully swingled strikes were then bunched up in great rolls, with a broach or spit thrust through them, and set in a chimney corner again to dry thoroughly. The flax was then ready to be beetled. The roll was placed in a wooden trough and pounded with a heavy pestle-shaped beetle till soft, then the roll was opened and laboriously beaten again. Then came the heckling or hatcheling,—a dusty, dirty, wearing work. The heckle was a comb-like instrument which cleaned and straightened the fibres. This heckling was done thrice,—first with a coarse wide-toothed comb, then with finer ones. The hurds or refuse of this process was also carefully saved and spun. The flax could now be spun into thread or linen yarn by rock or wheel. By the former, which was the old classic distaff, a finer thread could be made; the latter was swifter. From the spindles or spools the thread was reeled off upon reels two feet long; then made into skeins or lays of eighty threads, and twenty of these lays were called a knot or slipping. It would seem as if the housewife had already spent all the time and labor on her flax that could be endured, but worse was to come. These slippings of thread were laid in warm water for four days, the water being changed each day, and the slippings wrung out carefully and frequently by hand; then finally they were washed in the brook till the water which was passed from them came perfectly clean and pure. Then came the bucking, so called from the bucking-tub in which it was done. A layer of wood ashes was placed in the bottom of this great tub; then a layer of slippings of thread; then more ashes, and so on to the top, where it was covered with a cloth. A peck or two of ashes was placed thereon, and water poured over it. In this lye the slippings lay all night. In the morning came the exhausting process known as "driving a buck of yarn." The linen yarn was for four hours basted with hot lye, and wrung out as hot as possible, put in fresh lye and beaten, and so over and over again. Then it was kneaded by hand "a pretty while." For a week thereafter it lay in water which was constantly changed. Then came a grand seething, beating, rinsing, washing, and drying, when, being deemed thoroughly scoured and whitened, the slippings were wound in round balls and were ready for weaving. There were other and a trifle less tedious processes of bleaching the yarn,—one with bran and warm water, another with osier-sticks,—but they were deemed rather shiftless methods. 65

The linen thread was often woven into linen cloth away from home at a weaver's; but wherever the web was made, it was not even then deemed finished. It seems almost too much to know that it went again through the process of bucking, "possing," and drying. Then loops were sewed on the selvedge edges, stakes were driven in the turf, and the web was spread between them, drawn tightly in the sun for weeks. It had to be kept slightly wet all this time, but not too wet, lest it mildew.

Thus months were occupied in these exhausting processes. Sometimes the linen was "bucked" and "belted" twenty times during its manufacture before it was purely white. It is really with a keen sense of relief that we read that sometimes "swort housewives" bucked the web with lye and green hemlock, which was a much more speedy method; but, alas, this was deemed highly discreditable, being "foul and uncertain."

. . . .

A godly woman of the church of Boston, dwelling sometime in London, brought with her a parcel of very fine linen of great value, which she had set her heart too much upon, and had been at charge to have it all newly washed, and curiously folded and pressed, and so laid to press over night. She had a negro maid went into the room very late, and let fall some snuff of the candle upon the linen, so as by the morning all the linen was burned to tinder, and the boards underneath, and some stools and a part of the wainscot burned, and never perceived by any in the house, though some lodged in the chamber over head and no ceiling between. But it pleased God that the loss of this linen did her much good, both in taking her heart off from worldly comforts, and in preparing her for a far greater affliction in the death of her husband.

She Was Faine to Ly uppon Goates Skins

Priscilla is a "perplexing" servant in this 1639 letter from John Winter in Richmond Island, Maine. She is probably one of the many indentured servants who worked in early colonial households for four or five years to pay off the cost of their passage from England. Other servants in these households were often nieces, cousins, or the children of friends who were "put out" to learn the skills of housewifery. In a Puritan household, servants were to be treated as subordinates but also as members of the family. This meant that they were to receive religious training and sometimes also minimal education in reading. Masters and mistresses were not supposed to behave cruelly toward servants, just as servants were to perform their tasks willingly. But Master Winter feels this servant deserved the beating that she complained about. His protests reveal much about the work and living conditions in early colonial households and the labor shortage that enabled servants in America to act with much greater freedom than their counterparts in England.

From *Trelawny Papers: Collections of Maine Historical Society,* vol. 3, pp. 166–68; quoted in Lucy Maynard Salmon, *Domestic Service* (New York: Macmillan, 1897), pp. 33–34.

❖

You write me of some yll reports is given of my Wyfe for beatinge the maid; yf a faire waye will not do yt, beatinge must, sometimes, uppon such Idlle girrells as she is. Yf you think yt fitte for my wyfe to do all the worke & the maide sitt still, she must forbeare her hands to strike, for then the worke will ly undonn. She hath bin now 2 yeares ½ in the house, & I do not thinke she hath risen 20 times before my Wyfe hath bin up to Call her, & many tymes light the fire before she Comes out of her bed. She hath twize gon a mechinge [mucking?] in the woodes, which we have bin faine to send all our Company to seeke. We Cann hardly keep her within doores after we ar gonn to beed, except we Carry the kay of the doore to beed with us. She never Could melke Cow nor goat since she Came hither. Our men do not desire to have her boyle the kittle for them she is so sluttish. She Cannot be trusted to serve a few piggs, but my wyfe most Commonly must be with her. She hath written home, I heare, that she was faine to ly uppon goates skins. She might take som goates skins to ly in her bedd, but not given to her for her lodginge. For a yeare & quarter or more she lay with my daughter uppon a good feather bed before my daughter being lacke [gone] 3 or 4 daies to Sacco, the maid goes into beed with her Cloth & stockins, & would not take the paines to plucke of[f] her Cloths: her bedd after was a doust bedd &

she had 2 Coverletts to ly on her, but sheets she had none after that tyme she was found to be so sluttish. Her beating that she hath had hath never hurt her body nor limes. She is so fatt & soggy she Cann hardly do any worke. This I write all the Company will Justify. Yf this maid at her lasy tymes, when she hath bin found in her ill accyons [actions] do not deserve 2 or 3 blowes, I pray Judge You who hath most reason to Complaine, my wyfe or the maid. . . . She hath an unthanke-ful office to do this she doth, for I thinke their was never that steward yet amonge such people as we have Could give them all Content. It does not pleas me well being she hath taken so much paines & Care to order things as well as she Could, & ryse in the morning rath, go to bed soe latte, & to have hard speches for yt.

The Case of Charity Dallen

Mistreatment of women servants was much more common in the plantation-oriented southern colonies, though it was not usually so cruel as in the Charity Dallen case. Unlike black slaves, servants had recourse to the courts for enforce-ment of their indenture contracts and for a modicum of physical protection. This court ruled that Charity Dallen's indenture should be sold to a new mas-ter, and it fined her former mistress. Here, in 1649, an English woman servant was laboring in the fields with men as well as doing domestic work.

From *County Order Book,* Lower Norfolk, Virginia, 1646–51, fol. 120. Micro-film copies at Virginia State Library, Richmond.

❖

The deposition of Joseph Mulders Aged 23 years or thereabouts Sworne and ex-amined Sayeth

That Deborah Fernehaugh, the Mistress of this deponent, did beate her mayd Sarvant in the quartering house before the dresser more Liken a dogge than a Christian, and that at a Certaine time, I felt her head, which was beaten as soft as a sponge, in one place, and that as there shee was a weeding, shee com-playned and sayd, her backe bone as shee thought was broken with beating, and that I did see the mayd's arme naked which was full of blacke and blew bruises and pinches, and her necke Likewise and that afterwards, I tould my Mistress of it and said, that two or three blowes, could not make her in such a Case, and after this my speeches shee Chidge [chided] the said mayd, for shewing her body to the men, and very often afterwards she the said mayd would have showen mee, how shee had beene beaten, but I refused to have seene it, saying it concernes me not, I will doe my worke and if my Mistress abuse you; you may complaine, and about 8 dayes since, being about the time shee last went to Complaine, I knew of her goeing, but would not tell my mistress of it, although shee asked mee, and sayd I could not chuse but know of it, and further hee sayeth not

sworne the 31th July 1649
Thomas Bridge Clerk of Court

68

The Marke of Joseph X Mulders

Upon the depositions of Joseph Mulders and Michaell Mikaye of the misusage of Charetie dallen, by her Mistress Deborah Fernehaugh, and by many other often Complaints, by other sufficient testimonies, and although the said Deborah hath had advertisement thereof from the Court yet persisteth in the very Ill usadge of her said sarvant, as appeareth to the board, It is therefore ordered that the said Charetie Dallen shall no longer remaine in the house or service with her said Mistress, but is to bee and Continue at the house of Mr. Thomas Lambard [Lambert], untill such time as the said Deborah Fernehaugh shall sell or otherwise dispose of her said servant, for her best advantage of her the said Deborah.

The Case of Elizabeth Greene

The primitive living conditions and regulations imposed on servant women, especially on southern plantations, could sometimes lead to desperation and even death. Elizabeth Greene, without relatives or women friends, perhaps even ignorant of female functions, apparently committed infanticide. This bare but heartrending account reveals that after migrating from a country village near Norwich, England, Elizabeth lived with other servants, all men, without privacy even during childbirth. A midwife, Grace Parker, was called to examine her and verify her crime. Elizabeth Greene probably knew that the penalty for pregnancy during indenture was additional years of servitude. She took her chances at concealment and claimed she had had a miscarriage in her fourth month, but her subterfuge did not succeed and she was hanged for her offense. Spelling and punctuation have been modernized.

From J. Hall Pleasants, ed., *Archives of Maryland* (Baltimore: Maryland Historical Society, 1883), vol. 49, *Proceedings of the Provincial Court of Maryland, 1663–66*, pp. 232–36. ❖

The Examination of Elizabeth Greene taken this 5th day of July 1664 Before the Governor and Councill—being asked if her name was Elizabeth Greene, answered yes, and what Country Woman she was, said born five miles from Norwich. Asked where she lived, answered she lived last with John Gary. You are accused of having a Bastard Child and that you did murder it. She answered she had One but did not murder it, nor did not see what she had whether it was a Child formed or not. What made you so barbarous to make it away? She answered she was gone but 4 months. Had you a Child born or not? Answered she did not see such a thing but was delivered being put into a fright by some runaways.

William Wheeler and Thomas Taylor as witnesses against Elizabeth Greene examined, William Wheeler first. Do you know Elizabeth Greene? Yes I lived in the house with her. Did you know whether she was with Child? He did not know but she was very big—then the said William Wheeler was demanded whether he heard any thing Cry with a voyce in the likeness of a Child. Yes something he did hear like the voyce of a Child at the time that she was sick.

Thomas Taylor examined saith that he Came into the house when she was lying on the Ground and asked her what she ailed and bid her go to bed, and that she had milk and water in her breasts two months before—

Grace Parker Examined saith That she was a stranger to the wench and did not see her above once all the time she was with Child and that she did search her breast and the wench denied she was with Child but there was milk in her breasts. And it was agoing away being hard and Curdled—And she desiring her to declare after she was delivered what she had done with her Child she said she had buried it in such a place but when they Came to search for it they Could find no such thing. . . .

The Jury for the Right Honorable the Lord Proprietary do present Elizabeth Greene of Garriden in Calvert County, spinster, [who] the sixth day of May in the year of Our Lord God 1664 being big with Child by God's Providence was delivered of a Certain living man Child which said living man Child She then said Elizabeth Greene did throw into the fire, And so that the said Elizabeth Greene the living man Child by throwing into the fire in manner and form aforesaid, then and there feloniously and of malice forethought did Kill and Murder Contrary to the peace of his said Lordship his Rule and Dignity. . . . [The jury declared her guilty.]

Then was it demanded of Elizabeth Greene, what she had to say for herself, Answered that she threw herself on the mercy of the Board, being again demanded if that was all she had to say, she Answered Yes—Then Sentence of Death passed upon her by the Governor and Judge in these words . . . Elizabeth Greene You shall be Carried to the place from whence you Came, from thence to the place of Execution, and there be hanged by the neck till you are dead, and so God have mercy upon your Soul.

On the Morrow being the 8th July 1664 warrant issued to the Sheriff of St. Mary's County for the performance of Execution.

A Bedroom Story

The earliest dwellings of most European settlers in America were small, usually with only one or two rooms centered around a large fireplace, with a loft above. Families had no privacy and neither did their servants. Because these houses were so small, often many people slept together in one room—masters, mistresses, and servants, men, women, and even children, two or three to a bed. The following excerpt from a witness's statement in a court case shows what forbidden activities might result from these living arrangements.

From Middlesex, Massachusetts, County Court Records, folder 62, group 6, Massachusetts Archives, Boston.

❖

Benjamin Chamberlene aged about 21 years doth testifie that on the 30th of September last, Joseph Graves was at the house of Thomas Goble in Concord, in the night time, and tarrying there after the said Thomas Goble was in bed, who lay in the same roome, and also two mayds in another bed, viz: Ester Necholls and Mary Goble. the said Joseph Graves went and set by the bedside and talked with them privately and after that sung some short songs to them. and after a while I saw the said Joseph Graves in bed with them.—the cloathes were over him. The said mayds as he apprehends being in their naked beds.

An Unwed Mother

To deal with the problem of illegitimate births in Massachusetts, a 1672 law required the father to be responsible for the child's costs. The law specified that the father was whomever the mother named during labor. Puritans assumed that no woman would risk eternal damnation by telling a lie on the brink of death. Not all women had such tender consciences, however.

From anonymous letter in Middlesex, Massachusetts, County Court Records, folder 30, group 4, Massachusetts Archives, Boston.

❖

der love i remember my love to you hoping your welfar and i hop[e] to imbras the[e] but now i rit to you to let you nowe that i am a child by you and i wil ether kil it or lay it to an other and you shal have no blame at al for I have had many children and none [of their fathers?] have none of them.

Wilt Thou Not Drinke to Me?

A woman's life on early southern plantations was often far different from the genteel images of later generations. Except for the wealthy minority, most women—both black and white—mixed quite freely at work and in taverns. The result in this 1681 case was, apparently, rape. Several men, including John Aust, testified that Katherine Watkins had brought it on herself; Humphrey Smith was the only man to testify in her behalf. Katherine herself claimed that she had been raped by "Mulatto Jacke" on her way home.

From Henrico, Virginia, County Deed Book, 1677–92, pp. 192–95. Microfilm copies at Virginia State Library, Richmond.

❖

The examination of Katherine Watkins, the wife of Henry Watkins of Henrico County in Virginia, taken this 13 of September 1681 before us William Byrd and John Farrar two of his Majesties Justices of the County aforesaid as followeth (vizt.)

The said Katherine aforesaid on her Oath and examination deposeth, That on fryday being in the Month of August aboute five weeks since, the said Katherine mett with John Long (a Mulatto belonging to Capt. Thomas Cocke) at or neare the pyney slash betweene the aforesaid Cockes and Henry Watkins house, and at the same tyme and place, the said John threw the said Katherine downe (He starting from behinde a tree) and stopped her Mouth with a handerkerchief, and tooke up the said Katherines Coates [i.e., petticoats], and putt his yard into her and ravished her; Upon which she the said Katherine Cryed out (as she deposeth) and afterwards (being rescued by another Negroe of the said Cockes named Jack White) she departed home, and the said John departed to his Masters likewise, or that way; after which abuse she the said Katherine declares that her husband inclinable to the Quakers [who were pacifists], and therefore would not prosecute, and she being sicke and her Children likewise, she therefore did not make her complaint before she went to Lt. Col. Farrars (which was yesterday, Morning) and this day in the Morning she went to William Randolphs' and found him not at home, But at night met with the gentlemen Justices aforesaid at the house of the aforesaid Cocke in Henrico County in Virginia aforesaid before whom she hath made this complaint upon oath. . . .

The deposition of John Aust aged 32 years or thereabouts Deposeth, That on fryday being the twelvth of August or thereabouts he came to the house of Mr. Thomas Cocke, and soe went into his Orchard where his servants were a cutting downe weeds, whoe asked the deponent to stay and drinke, soe the deponent stayed and dranke syder with them, and Jacke a Mulatto of the said Thomas Cocke went in to draw syder, and he stay'd something long whereupon the deponent followed him, and coming to the doore where the syder was, heard Katherine the wife of Henry Watkins say (Lord) Jacke what makes the[e] refraine our house that you come not oftner, for come when thou wilt thou shalt be as well come as any of My owne Children, and soe she tooke him about the necke and Kissed him, and Jacke went out and drawed Syder, and she said Jack wilt thou not drinke to me, who sayd yes if you will goe out where our Cupp is, and a little after she came out, where the said Thomas Cockes Negroes were a drinking and there dranke cupp for cupp with them (as others there did) and as she sett Negroe dirke passing by her she tooke up the taile of his shirt (saying) Dirke thou wilt have a good long thing, and soe did several tymes as he past by her; after this she went into the roome where the syder was and then came out againe, and between the two houses she mett Mulatto Jacke a going to draw more syder and putt her hand on his codpiece, at which he smil'd, and went on his way and drew syder and she came againe into the company but stay'd not long but went out to drinking with two of the said Thomas Cockes Negroes by the garden pale, And a while after she tooke Mingoe one of the said Cocke's Negroes about the Necke and fling on the bedd and Kissed him and putt her hand into his Codpiece, Awhile after Mulatto Jacke went into the Fish roome and she followed him, but what they did there this deponent knoweth not for it being near night this deponent left her and the Negroes together, (He thinking her to be much in drinke) and soe this deponent went home about one houre by sunn.

Humphrey Smith aged 26 years, deposeth, That he heard John Aust say (about September last past) what Matter is it what I swore to and likewise the deponent saw Katherine's Mouth (the wife of Henry Watkins) torne and her lipps swell'd, And the handkerchief that she said the Mulatto Stopt her Mouth with very much bloody And the deponent heard the Mulatto confess that he had beene to aske the said Watkins wife forgiveness three tymes, and likewise the Mulatto sayd that Henry Watkins (the last tyme he went) bidd him keepe of[f] his plantation or else he would shoote him and further saith not.

Concerning the Freedom of Elizabeth Key

Mulatto children born to slave women and white fathers created much uneasiness among early Virginia settlers. Some fathers, in accordance with English common law, which required that a child's legal status be based on that of the father, tried to ensure the freedom of their children born to slave women. Elizabeth Key's was such a case in 1654, and the court reluctantly granted her petition. William Greensted, the lawyer who represented her, then married her. Soon thereafter, however, legislation was passed forbidding racial intermarriage and making all mulattoes slaves for life, no matter who the father. Punctuation has been added.

From County Order Book, Northumberland, Virginia, 1652–65, fols. 40, 46, 49. Microfilm copy at Virginia State Library, Richmond.

❖

It appeareth to us [a committee of the Virginia assembly] that shee is the daughter of Thomas Key by severall Evidences, and by a fine imposed upon the said Thomas for getting her mother with Child of the said Thomas; That she hath bin by verdict of a Jury impannelled 20th January 1655 in the County of Northumberland found to be free by severall oathes which the Jury desired might be Recorded; That by the Comon Law the Child of a Woman slave begott by a freeman ought to bee free; That shee hath bin long since Christened, Col. Higginson being her God father, and that by report shee is able to give a very good account of her fayth; That Thomas Key sould her onely for nine yeares to Co. Higginson with severall conditions to use her more Respectfully then a Comon servant or slave; That in case Col. Higginson had gone for England within nine yeares hee was bound to carry her with him and pay her passage and not to dispose of her to any other; For these Reasons wee conceive the said Elizabeth ought to bee free and that her last Master should give her Corne and Cloathes and give her satisfaction for the time shee hath served longer than Shee ought to have done. . . . 21th July 1656 Jurat in Curia.

These are to Certifie [to] whome it may concerne that William Greensted and Elizabeth Key intends to be joyned in the Holy Estate of Matrimony. If any one can shew any Lawfull cause why they may not be joyned together lett them Speake or ever after hold their tongues. Signum William Greensted, Signum Elizabeth Key. 21th July 1656.

An Act Concerning Negroes and Other Slaves

Black women in the southern colonies were apparently at first indentured under terms similar to those of whites. But in 1664 the colony of Maryland (with Virginia soon following) declared that "all Negroes or other slaves" (probably Indians) could never become free. Black women's children would inherit their mother's slavery. In addition, to enforce the separation of the races, the law stated that the offspring of Englishwomen who married slaves would inherit their *father's* slavery. Thus all women were victimized, whereas no one punished "forgetful" Englishmen who sired slave children. Spelling and punctuation have been modernized.

From William Hand Browne, ed., *Archives of Maryland: Proceedings and Acts of the General Assembly of Maryland,* January 1637-38–September 1664 (Baltimore: Maryland Historical Society, 1883), pp. 533–34.

❖

Be it enacted . . . by the advice and consent . . . of this present General Assembly That all Negroes or other slaves already within the Province And all Negroes and other slaves to be herafter imported into the Province shall serve Durante Vita. And all Children born of any Negro or other slave shall be Slaves as their fathers were for the term of their lives. And forasmuch as divers freeborn English women, forgetful of their free Condition and to the disgrace of our Nation, do intermarry with Negro Slaves, by which also divers [law]suits may arise touching the Issue of such women, and a great damage doth befall the Masters of such Negroes, for prevention whereof for deterring such freeborne women from such shameful Matches Be it further Enacted by the Authority advice and Consent aforesaid That whatsoever free born woman shall intermarry with any slave . . . shall serve the master of such slave during the life of her husband And that all the Issue of such freeborn women so married shall be Slaves as their fathers were. And Be it further Enacted that all the Issues of English or other freeborn women that have already married Negroes shall serve the Masters of their Parents till they be Thirty years of age and no longer.

BUILDING COLONIES NORTH AND SOUTH

9. A Pioneer's House, Salem, Massachusetts

The earliest dwellings of most European settlers on the East Coast were small, dark, and cold, designed as a refuge from the "wilderness" outside. Thatched roofs were typical, as were tiny windows to keep out the cold and defend against feared attacks by Native Americans. Log cabins did not appear in America until Swedish settlers came to the middle colonies in the late seventeenth century. This photo is of a replica built in Pioneer Village, Salem. Courtesy of the Essex Institute, Samuel Chamberlain Collection, Salem, Massachusetts.

10. *Colonial Kitchen*

The kitchen was the central room of a colonial house. This home would probably have had only unheated anterooms for storage and a dairy on the first floor with one or two loft storage rooms or bedrooms above. Both men and women worked in this one room, usually called the hall. It also functioned as a living room and bedroom. Colonial housewives worked extremely hard at a vast variety of tasks, but at least they were not isolated from other women and men as were many twentieth-century women. Courtesy of the National Archives, Washington, D.C.

11. Embroidered Pocket

Every woman needed, among other things, a handmade pocket, separate from
her clothing and fastened by strings around her waist, to hold needles, thread,
yarn, and other everyday necessities. This one was carefully embroidered by an
unknown seamstress. Bruce Alexander, photography. Courtesy of the Strawbery
Banke Museum, Portsmouth, New Hampshire.

12. *Mrs. Elizabeth Freake and Her Daughter Mary*

Born in 1642, the daughter of a merchant, Elizabeth Clarke married the merchant and lawyer John Freake in 1661. By 1674 she had given birth to eight children. Baby Mary was six months old at the time of this portrait. Elizabeth's velvet gown, her lace collar and cap, and her jewelry indicate the prosperity of her family. Her apron is a proud mark of her status as mistress of a large household. Portrait dated 1671 and updated 1674; artist unknown. Courtesy of the Worcester Art Museum, Worcester, Massachusetts.

Enterprising Women

FOR MOST EARLY colonial white settlers, energetic and successful women were simply obeying God's advice as given in their favorite exemplary passage from the Old Testament (Proverbs 31:10–31). There Solomon's mother, Bathsheba, tells her son that the "virtuous" woman's price is "worth more than rubies." This woman buys and sells land, works day and night, and manages a large household (including servants and slaves); by her entrepreneurial success, she earns the respect of her husband and community, and "her works praise her in the gates" of the city. Religious women, therefore, expected to work hard either within or outside their households. "Mothers in Israel," a biblical expression frequently used by Puritan preachers, writers, and women, modeled themselves on strong Old Testament women in this new Puritan Israel; American "Jezebels," named after the infamous biblical Jezebel, were accused of rebelling against religious teachings or social mores. All were enterprising women in their own ways.

White and black men and boys and enslaved black women were usually the laborers in the fields in both the northern and the southern colonies. White women rarely worked in the fields, especially after the earliest settlements were well established, but they did sometimes engage in commercial dealings outside their homes. Although only about 5 percent of colonial white women probably engaged in such trade, their presence suggests that such activity did not meet with disapproval. Rather, most colonial villages encouraged widows and single women without families to provide for themselves instead of relying on town charity, which was usually scarce and grudgingly dispensed. At least one accusation of witchcraft appears to have been grounded in the reaction of New England townspeople to a woman reduced to begging for herself and her children. Sarah Good, accused of witchcraft in 1692 in Salem, resorted to begging after two successive unscrupulous husbands used up her small inheritance. She was an unpleasant beggar who often cursed ("muttered against") those neighbors who refused to give her alms, hence contributing to their guilt and the belief that her curses might have the power of witchcraft and could come true.

Most women tried every other recourse before resorting to begging. Among these documents is a description of Sister Bradish, a popular baker and brewer, in Cambridge, Massachusetts, whose skills were a mainstay of her family and community. Single women and widows could establish businesses of their own. Some married women did too, but unless they had a prenuptial agreement (often called antenuptial marriage settlements), married women were not legally entitled to any dowry they might have brought to their marriages or to any of their earnings during marriage. Single women, on the other hand, could own property and keep their earnings; they commonly engaged in businesses that were an extension of women's work at home, such as millinery shops, the "healing arts," dairies, or dry goods' sales. Women also engaged in midwifery and healing, tavern- and shopkeeping, weaving, sewing, or running "dame" schools for neighborhood children. Often, the most needy women were widows who had to support themselves and their children. Sometimes, widows invested money from their husbands' estates or took over and managed their husbands' businesses. Among them were two seafaring women from seventeenth-century New Amsterdam and Long Island: Martha Turnstall Smith ran a prosperous whaling business, and Margaret Phillipse was the preeminent shipping magnate of her era.

Arriving on these shores with considerable wealth, Margarett Brent was a respected and influential landowner in seventeenth-century Maryland. The governor called on her for advice; and although Maryland legislators denied her voting rights, they did express their admiration for her managerial skills. Like Mistress Brent, a few other women received land grants in early Salem, Massachusetts, on Long Island, and in New Amsterdam. Men treated these wealthy women with respect largely out of admiration for their entrepreneurial abilities and social status.

Whether women labored inside or outside their homes, religion was often at the center of their lives. For most, religion could be a source of both oppression and self-esteem. Articulating the situation of many other women, Anne Bradstreet described for her children her lifelong struggle to practice her faith. Because her piety was energetic and sincere, she was considered an exemplary "Mother in Israel" by the Puritan community. Yet neither she nor other women were permitted to speak publicly on religious matters or to disagree with authorities. Anne Hutchinson, who dared to do both, was brought to trial, excommunicated, and banished from Massachusetts in 1638. (One reason she was perceived as such a threat to the community was that she had so many prominent men as well as women among her followers.) Quaker women and men, who were encouraged by their sect to be preachers and witnesses, received even harsher treatment. They were mutilated, whipped, and executed by the Puritan authorities. To bear witness to her faith, the heroic Mary Dyer (see illustration) deliberately returned to Massachusetts to face death by hanging on Boston Common in 1660.

Ministers' sermons emphasized the prevailing religious message: rather than claiming a direct relationship with God, women were supposed to obey authority, remain silent in adversity, and thank God if they survived tragic circumstances. But in spite of the proscription against their speaking out, many women found meaning in religious commitment and gained from it courage in adversity. Blaming her own sinfulness for her capture by Indians during King Philip's War in 1675 and praising God for her eventual rescue, Mary Rowlandson wrote a captivity narrative that shows both dutiful submission to God's will and also extraordinary resourcefulness in a terrifying situation. Although she had no sympathy or understanding for the equally devastating plight of her captors, Rowlandson's courageous piety and often bloodcurdling rendition of her captivity made her account a seventeenth-century best-seller.

The 1692 Salem Village witch trials provide an appropriate concluding episode for this section; ideas about proper female behavior, attitudes that had plagued Anne Hutchinson and Mary Dyer, resurfaced in Salem. As in many earlier seventeenth-century trials, women were both the accused and the accusers, and excerpts from court records show how women's own dissatisfactions, as well as social and economic issues, contributed to the witchcraft hysteria. These trial records provide a fitting transition to the next century because much of what happened in Salem Village was related to the development of the New England colonies from a rural agricultural economy into a more urban mercantile economy. Also, in New England, land was becoming scarce, and the movement of single young men to the frontier created anxiety among the young women left behind. Where, they wondered, would they find husbands with whom to establish households of their own?

All through the colonies, by the end of the seventeenth century, traditional beliefs about religion and morality were in question; and all of these changes led to the tense and exciting period of transition that followed in the eighteenth century. As Anne Bradstreet's poem suggests, colonial women often saw themselves as "weary pilgrims" indeed. The seventeenth century was hardly a "golden age" for American women.

Martha Turnstall Smith

Martha Smith used her inheritance as the widow of a wealthy landowner to establish a whaling business. The propriety-conscious nineteenth-century historian Benjamin Thompson informs us that she also "was said to have been a remarkably intelligent and well-bred lady, and minutely skilled in domestic economy."

From Benjamin F. Thompson, *The History of Long Island,* 2d ed., vols. 1 and 2 (New York: Gould, Banks and Co., 1843), 1:420, 438, 2:445.

❖

As an evidence of the extent to which boat-whaling was carried, on this part of Long Island, at the beginning of the eighteenth century, we present [writes Benjamin Thompson] the following items from a manuscript in the hand-writing of Madam Martha, widow of Col. Wm. Smith of St. George's Manor:

"Jan. ye 16, 1707, (she says,) my company killed a yearling whale, made 27 barrels. Feb. ye 4, Indian Harry, with his boat, struck a stunt whale and could not kill it—called for my boat to help him. I had but a third, which was 4 barrels. Feb. 22, my two boats, and my son's, and Floyd's boats, killed a yearling whale, of which I had half—made 36, my share 18 barrels. Feb. 24, my company killed a school whale, which made 35 barrels. March 13, my company killed a small yearling, made 30 barrels. March 17, my company killed two yearlings in one day; one made 27, the other 14 barrels."

The following is the receipt for duties:

"New York, this 5th June, 1707, then received of Nathan Simson, the sume of fifteen pounds, fifteen shillings, for acct of Mad[am] Martha Smith, it being the 20th part of her eyle [oil], by virtue of a warrant from my Ld. Cornbury, dated 25th of March, last past, 1707.   Per me, Elias Boudinot."

Margaret Hardenbroeck Phillipse

Like Martha Smith, Margaret Phillipse invested the money from her first husband's estate, selling some of the property to begin a commercial shipping business, which carried on a lucrative trade in furs and other commodities between Britain and the colonies. She married again and retained control of her business through an antenuptial agreement. She left her second husband a very wealthy man when she died in 1690. The assessment of her success in the account printed here comes from an early example of "women's history," a book about women in colonial New Amsterdam written by a nineteenth-century woman, May King Van Rensselaer.

From Mrs. John King Van Rensselaer, *The Goede Vrouw of Mana-ha-ta* (New York: Charles Scribner's Sons, 1848), pp. 32–35.

❖

Perhaps the most enterprising of all the Dutch colonists, male or female, was Margaret Hardenbroeck. She had married early in life Peter Rudolphus de Vries, and followed her husband to America, where he bought a plantation from the West India Company, on Staten Island, and began a settlement there. De Vries left an account of some of his voyages from Europe to America, that shows him to have been an intelligent, thoughtful man; but he had a quick and domineering temper and was always fighting with the Wilden, his neighbors, or the authorities. As he failed to carry out the terms of his agreement with the company and establish a colony at his own expense, his manorial rights reverted to the government, and after his death his widow sold the property and invested the money in ships, in which she traded between the two continents, establishing what was probably the first line of packets that crossed the Atlantic Ocean. . . .

During one of the first voyages that Madame Hardenbroeck made as owner of a vessel she fell in love with one of her passengers, named Frederick Phillipse, a young trader who was carrying a large stock of furs to Europe. They were married in 1662. . . .

. . . [Some Labbadist missionaries] sailed from Holland on Sunday, June 25, 1679, "in a small flute ship" called the Charles, "of which Thomas Singleton was Master, but the superior authority over both ship and cargo was in Margaret Filipse [Phillipse], who was the owner of both, and with whom we agreed for our passage from Amsterdam to New York, in New Netherland, at 75 guelders for each person, payable in Holland." The ship sailed without the owner, who overtook it in "her yacht and came on board," says the missionary, "with her husband and daughter (Eva de Vries) and a Westphalian woman (who was a widow) and a girl, both of whom were in Margaret's service."

The passengers suffered many hardships on the voyage from overcrowding, filth, and improper food, and the missionary charged the owner of the vessel with unblushing avarice.

The wrath of the passengers was aroused when the ship lay in an English port, before starting on the long voyage across the Atlantic, when Madame Phillipse "sold to the captain of an English ship a hogshead of beer, for which her little daughter was honoured with a good lump of gold and Margaret was presented with some good apples." The passengers had nearly finished their own provisions, as they had not foreseen and provided for the detention in the English ports, and they saw before them, with dismay, the prospect of a long voyage with little to eat, and they were indignant that Madame Phillipse should sell any of the provender on board of her ship (although it was her own property), fearing that they would fall short of provisions before they reached America.

80

The thrift of husband and wife enabled them to purchase large tracts of land in the New Netherlands that was subsequently "erected into a manor, with grants of fisheries, mines, hunting, and tenorial rights," under the English rule. This is the well-known Phillipse Manor, where a comfortable house was erected, which now stands in the city of Yonkers. They also owned a house on Mana-ha-ta, near the White Hall, or governor's mansion. . . .

Madame Phillipse died about 1690, and her husband married, within two years, the young and handsome widow of John Duval, the daughter of his opposite neighbor, Oloff Van Cortlandt, and by her had two sons and a daughter, Annekje, who, by her marriage with Philip French, became the ancestress of many prominent colonial women.

Sister Bradish

Thomas Dudley, the president of Harvard College in 1654, commended "Sister Bradish," a Cambridge brewer and baker. Dudley was a founder and overseer of the college. He apparently needed to defend her from charges of leading students astray with her good cooking!

From Archives of the County Court of Middlesex, 1654, quoted in Elisabeth Anthony Dexter, *Colonial Women of Affairs* (Boston: Houghton Mifflin, 1924), p. 49.

❖

Honored Gentlemen, as far as it may stand in the wholesome orders and prudential laws of the country for the publick weal, I can very freely speak with and write in the behalf of sister Bradish, that shee might be encouraged and countenanced in her present calling for baking of bread and brewing and selling of penny bear [beer] without which shee canot continue to bake: In both which callings such is her art, way and skill, that shee doth vend [sell] such comfortable penniworths for the reliefe of all that send unto her as elsewhere they can seldom meet with. Shee was complained of unto me for harbouring students, unseasonably spending their time and parent's estate; but upon examination I found it a misinformation and that she most was desirous that I should limit or absolutely prohibit any; that in case of sickness or want of comfortable bread or bear in the College only they should thither resort and then not to spend above a penny a man nor above two shillings in a quarter of a year, which order she carefully observed in all ordinary cases.

Came Mistress Margarett Brent

A few wealthy seventeenth-century women received grants of land on the same terms as men. Among them were the aristocratic sisters Margarett and Mary Brent, who financed their own way to the colony of Maryland in 1636. Their land, like that of every other woman, would legally belong to a husband if they married. Pressures to do so were such that the Maryland legislative assembly even asked the proprietor, Lord Baltimore, to require any single woman to forfeit her land if she did not marry within seven years. He refused, and the sisters never did marry.

Margarett Brent was so capable a businesswoman that in 1647 the dying governor named her his executor. She then asked the Maryland assembly for a vote (or rather two votes) like that given all other landholders, based on her ownership of land and on her power of attorney for the deceased governor. The assembly refused because she was a woman. But later, when Lord Baltimore found fault with her management of the governor's estate, the assembly unanimously insisted that the estate had been safer "in her hands than in any man's else in the whole Province." The "Heinous Rebellion" referred to below is Ingles Rebellion of 1646–47. Led by Protestants who were trying to displace and outlaw Catholics, it was put down by Lord Baltimore's troops. Because the governor died, Margarett Brent had to find a way to pay the soldiers and forestall mutiny—which she did. Spelling and punctuation have been modernized.

From *Archives of Maryland*, vol. 1, *Assembly Proceedings*, January–March 1647–48 (Baltimore: Maryland Historical Society, 1883), pp. 215, 238–39.

❖

Came Mistress Margarett Brent and requested to have vote in the house for her self, and voice also for that [because] at the last Court 3rd Jan. it was ordered that the said Mistress Brent was to be looked upon and received as his Lordship's Attorney. The Governor denied that the said Mistress Brent should have any vote in the house. And the said Mistress Brent protested against all proceedings in this present Assembly, unless she may be present and vote as aforesaid.

. . . .

[To Lord Baltimore] Great and many have been the miseries, calamities and other Sufferings which your Poor distressed People, Inhabitants of this Province have sustained and undergone here since the beginning of that Heinous Rebellion . . . for two years continued . . . during all which time your Honour cannot be ignorant what pains and travail your Friends underwent in aiding your dear Brother for the subduing of those Rebels and after again in conserving the Province for your Lordship. . . . As for Mistress Brent's undertaking and meddling with your Lordship's Estate here (whether she procured it with her own and others importunity or no) we do Verily Believe and in Conscience report that it was better for the Colony's safety at that time in her hands than in any man's else in the whole Province after your brother's death. [F]or the Soldiers would never have treated any other with that Civility and respect and, though they were even ready at several times to run into mutiny, yet she still pacified them, till at the last things were brought to that strait that she must be admitted and declared your Lordship's Attorney by an order of Court . . . or else all must go to ruin Again, and then the second mischief had been doubtless far greater than the former. . . . We conceive from that time she rather deserved favour and thanks from your Honour for her so much Concurring to the public safety, than to be justly liable to all those bitter invectives you have been pleased to Express against her.

82

A Pilgrim's Legacy

Anne Bradstreet, whose poetry appeared earlier in this book, wrote this testamentary letter to her eight children. For their benefit, she revealed herself as a devout Puritan woman who was also plagued with religious doubts. Her "heart rose" fearfully and rebelliously when, as a new bride, she had to leave her comfortable home in England and come to America. In Massachusetts, she developed chronic rheumatoid arthritis made worse by the cold climate. Like all good Puritans, she attributed her troubles to God's punishment for her sins, but she conquered her doubts and knew "whom [she had] trusted."

The poem that follows was also written near the end of Bradstreet's life. In it, she describes her lifelong pilgrimage as a Christian woman. Her "dangers past and travails done," she bids farewell to "cares and fears" and also to the "wild fruits" of joy and passion. Her pilgrimage, with all of its pains and pleasures, could be said to represent the journeys of many of the other seventeenth-century European women we have read about in this section. It is no wonder that after a life of arduous toil, these women, like Anne Bradstreet, sought a welcome rest. In the concluding lines of the poem, Bradstreet finds comfort in the belief that she will be united with Christ (the "Bridegroom") after death.

From John Harvard Ellis, ed., *The Works of Anne Bradstreet in Prose and Verse* (Charlestown, Mass.: Abram E. Cutter, 1867), pp. 3–10, 42–44.

❖

My Dear Children,

. . . In my young years, about 6 or 7 as I take it, I began to make conscience of my ways, and what I knew was sinful, as lying, disobedience to parents, etc., I avoided it. If at any time I was overtaken with the like evils, it was as a great trouble, and I could not be at rest 'till by prayer I had confessed it unto God. . . . 83 I also found much comfort in reading the Scriptures, especially those places I thought most concerned my condition, and as I grew to have more understanding, so the more solace I took in them. . . .

But as I grew up to be about 14 or 15, I found my heart more carnal, and sitting loose from God, vanity and the follies of youth take hold of me.

About 16, the Lord laid His hand sore upon me and smote me with the smallpox. When I was in my affliction, I besought the Lord and confessed my pride and vanity. . . .

After a short time I changed my condition and was married, and came into this country, where I found a new world and new manners, at which my heart rose. But after I was convinced it was the way of God, I submitted to it and joined to the church at Boston.

After some time I fell into a lingering sickness like a consumption together with a lameness, which correction I saw the Lord sent to humble and try me and do me good, and it was not altogether ineffectual.

It pleased God to keep me a long time without a child, which was a great grief to me and cost me many prayers and tears before I obtained one, and after him gave me many more of whom I now take the care, that as I have brought you into the world, and with great pains, weakness, cares, and fears brought you to this, I now travail in birth again of you till Christ be formed in you.

Among all my experiences of God's gracious dealings with me, I have constantly observed this, that He hath never suffered me long to sit loose from Him, but by one affliction or other hath made me look home, and search what was amiss; so usually thus it hath been with me that I have no sooner felt my heart out of order, but I have expected correction for it, which most commonly hath been upon my own person in sickness, weakness, pains, sometimes on my soul, in doubts and fears of God's displeasure and my sincerity towards Him; sometimes He hath smote a child with a sickness, sometimes chastened by losses in estate. . . . Then have I gone to searching and have said with David, "Lord, search me and try me, see what ways of wickedness are in me, and lead me in the way everlasting," and seldom or never but I have found either some sin I lay under which God would have reformed, or some duty neglected which He would have performed, and by His help I have laid vows and bonds upon my soul to perform His righteous commands. . . .

I have often been perplexed that I have not found that constant joy in my pilgrimage and refreshing which I supposed most of the servants of God have, although He hath not left me altogether without the witness of His holy spirit. . . . I have sometimes tasted of that hidden manna that the world knows not, and . . . have resolved with myself that against such a promise, such tastes of sweetness, the gates of hell shall never prevail; yet have I many times sinkings and droopings, and not enjoyed that felicity that sometimes I have done. But . . . I know whom I have trusted, and whom I have believed, and that He is able to keep that I have committed to His charge. . . .

This was written in much sickness and weakness, and is very weakly and imperfectly done, but if you can pick any benefit out of it, it is the mark which I aimed at.

As Weary Pilgrim

As weary pilgrim, now at rest,
 Hugs with delight his silent nest,
His wasted limbs now lie full soft
 That mirey steps have trodden oft,
Blesses himself to think upon
 His dangers past and travails done.
The burning sun no more shall heat,
 Nor stormy rains on him shall beat.
The briars and thorns no more shall scratch,
 Nor hungry wolves at him shall catch.
He erring paths no more shall tread,
 Nor wild fruits eat instead of bread.
For waters cold he doth not long
 For thirst no more shall parch his tongue
No rugged stones his feet shall gall,
 Nor stumps nor rocks cause him to fall.
All cares and fears he bids farewell
 And means in safety now to dwell.
A pilgrim I, on earth perplexed
 With sins, with cares and sorrows vext,
By age and pains brought to decay,
 And my clay house mold'ring away.
Oh, how I long to be at rest
 And soar on high among the blest.
This body shall in silence sleep,
 Mine eyes no more shall ever weep,
No fainting fits shall me assail,
 Nor grinding pains my body frail,

84

With cares and fears ne'er cumb'red be
    Nor losses know, nor sorrows see.
What though my flesh shall there consume,
    It is the bed Christ did perfume,
And when a few years shall be gone,
    This mortal shall be clothed upon.
A corrupt carcass down it lays,
    A glorious body it shall rise.
In weakness and dishonour sown,
    In power 'tis raised by Christ alone.
Then soul and body shall unite
    And of their Maker have the sight.
Such lasting joys shall there behold
    As eer ne'er heard nor tongue e'er told.
Lord make me ready for that day,
    Then come, dear Bridegroom, come away.

American Jezebel

Anne Marbury Hutchinson (1591–1643) was excommunicated from her church in Boston and banished by the Massachusetts Bay government in 1638 for being a threat to civil and religious authority. The brilliant daughter of an eminent Puritan clergyman, wife of a successful merchant, and mother of fifteen children, Anne Hutchinson was also a capable and popular midwife. Governor John Winthrop, who wrote this account, feared that the religious meetings she held in her large Boston home were encouraging political opposition. Her knowledge of theology and Scripture, and of her civil rights, along with an "unwomanly" lack of humility, infuriated the magistrates who questioned her. Found guilty by the civil court, Hutchinson was then also subjected to a church interrogation, which resulted in her excommunication. The young Mary Dyer was the only member willing to stand by her "at the dore" as she left. Dyer followed Hutchinson to Rhode Island.

From John Winthrop, "A Short Story of the Rise, Reign, and Ruine of the Antinomians . . . of New England . . . ," London, 1644, in Charles Francis Adams, ed., *Antinomianism in the Colony of Massachusetts Bay* (1894; reprint, New York: Burt Franklin, 1967), pp. 157–71, 228.

❖

A woman had been the breeder and nourisher of all these distempers, one Mistris *Hutchinson,* . . . a woman of a haughty and fierce carriage, of a nimble wit and active spirit, and a very voluble tongue, more bold than a man, though in understanding and judgement, inferiour to many women. This woman had learned her skil in *England,* and had discovered [revealed] some of her opinions in the Ship, as shee came over, which had caused some jealousie of her, which gave occasion of some delay of her admission, when shee first desired fellowship with the Church of *Boston,* but shee cunningly dissembled and coloured her opinions, as shee soon got over that block, and was admitted into the Church, then shee began to go to work, and being a woman very helpfull in the times of child-birth, and other occasions of bodily infirmities, and well furnished with means for those purposes, shee easily insinuated her selfe into the affections of many . . . and indeed it was a wonder upon what a sudden the whole Church of *Boston* (some few excepted) were become her new converts, and infected with her opinions, and many also out of the Church, and of other Churches also, . . . then shee kept open house for all commers, and set up two Lecture dayes in the week, when they usually met at her house, threescore or fourescore persons, the pretence was to repeate Sermons, but . . . shee would comment upon the Doctrines, and interpret all passages at her pleasure, and expound dark places of Scripture. . . . Shee had not failed of her ayme, to the utter subversion both of Churches and civill state, if the most wise and mercifull providence of the Lord had not prevented it by keeping so many of the Magistrates, and Elders, free from the infection. . . . But blessed bee the Lord, the snare is broken, and wee are delivered, and this woman who was the root of all these troubles, stands now before the seat of Justice. . . .

Court Mistris Hutchinson, You are called hither as one of those who have had a great share in the causes of our publick disturbances, partly by those erroneous opinions which you have broached and divulged amongst us, . . . partly by casting reproach upon the faithfull Ministers of this Countrey, . . . and partly by maintaining weekly and publick meetings in your house. . . . Have you countenanced, or will you justifie those seditious practices which have been censured here in this Court?

Hutch. Do you ask mee upon point of conscience?

Court No, your conscience you may keep to your self, but if in this cause you shall countenance and incourage those that thus transgresse the Law, you must bee called in question for it. . . .

Hutch. What Law have they transgressed? the Law of God?

Court Yes, the fifth Commandement, which commands us to honour Father and Mother, which includes all in authority, but these seditious practices of theirs, have cast reproach and dishonour upon the Fathers of the Commonwealth.

Hutch. Do I intertaine, or maintaine them in their actions, wherein they stand against any thing that God has appointed?

Court Yes, you have justified Mr. *Wheelwright* his Sermon, for which you know hee was convict of sedition, and you have likewise countenanced and encouraged those that had their hands to the Petition.

Hutch. I deny it, I am to obey you only in the Lord.

Court You cannot deny but you had your hand in the Petition.

Hutch. Put case, I do feare the Lord, and my Parent doe not, may not I entertain one that feares the Lord, because my Father will not let mee? . . .

Court That's nothing to the purpose, but wee cannot stand to dispute causes with you now, what say you to your weekly publick meetings? Can you shew a warrant for them?

Hutch. I will shew you how I took it up, there were such meetings in use before I came, and because I went to none of them, this was the speciall reason of my taking up this course, wee began it but with five or six, and though it grew to more in future time, yet being tolerated at the first, I knew not why it might not continue.

Court There were private meetings indeed, and are still in many places, of some few neighbours, but not so publick and frequent as yours, . . . but answer by what authority, or rule, you uphold them.

Hutch. By Tit. 2 [in the Bible] where the elder women are to teach the younger.

Court So wee allow you to do, as the Apostle there meanes, privately, and upon occasion, but that gives no warrant of such set meetings for that purpose; and besides, you take upon you to teach many that are elder than your selfe, neither do you teach them that which the Apostle commands, *viz.* to keep at home.

Hutch. Will you please to give mee a rule against it, and I will yeeld?

Court You must have a rule for it, or else you cannot do it in faith, yet you have a plaine rule against it: I permit not a woman to teach.

Hutch. That is meant of teaching men.

Court If a man in distresse of conscience or other temptation, &c. should come and ask your counsell in private, might you not teach him?

Hutch. Yes.

Court Then it is cleare, that it is not meant of teaching men, but of teaching in publick.

Hutch. It is said, I will poure my Spirit upon your Daughters, and they shall prophesie, &c. If God give mee a gift of Prophecy, I may use it.

Court First, the Apostle applies that prophecy unto those extraordinary times. . . . Secondly, in teaching your children, you exercise your gift of prophecy, and that within your calling.

87

Hutch. I teach not in a publick congregation: . . . we do no more but read the notes of our teachers Sermons, and then reason of them by searching the Scriptures.

Court . . . You open your teachers points, and declare his meaning, and correct wherein you think he hath failed, &c. and by this meanes you abase the honour and authority of the publick Ministery, and advance your own gifts, as if hee could not deliver his matter so clearly to the hearers capacity as your self.

Hutch. Prove that, that anybody doth that.

Court Yes, you are the woman of most note, and of best abilities, and if some other take upon them the like, it is by your teaching and example. . . .

Hutch. I call them not, but if they come to me, I may instruct them.

[After condemnation at her civil trial, Hutchinson was also excommunicated by her church.]

. . . So the Pastor . . . propounding it to the Church, to know whether they were all agreed, that she should be cast out, and a full consent appearing . . . by their silence, after a convenient pause he proceeded, and pronounced the sentence of excommunication against her, and she was commanded to depart out of the Assembly. In her going forth, one standing at the dore, said, The Lord sanctifie this unto you, to whom she made answer, The Lord judgeth not as man judgeth, better to be cast out of the Church then to deny Christ.

A Cruel Warrant

Many Quaker women, including Mary Dyer, who was hanged on Boston Common in 1660 for her faith, gave witness to the religious activism of that newly developed seventeenth-century sect. Quakers emphasized the individual's relationship with God, through an "Inner Light" rather than through the mediation of preachers. (They called all preachers "priests.") Thus, the Society of Friends encouraged personal equality and unusual leadership responsibilities for women; missionaries like young Mary Fisher even visited the Turkish sultan's court in the 1650s. Women "called as Witnesses" traveled throughout the colonies—and the authority of such callings enabled them to become leaders and shapers within a strong-minded network of fellow believers.

Fully aware of the Puritan laws of the 1650s that required all heretics to be whipped from one town to the next, three Quaker women traveled to southern New Hampshire (still part of Massachusetts) in 1662. A contemporary Quaker historian wrote this account of their preaching and persecution. Afterward, two of the women, Mary Tomkins and Alice Ambrose, continued their ministry, including an extensive trip to frontier Virginia and the Carolinas.

From George Bishop, *New England Judged, by the Spirit of the Lord* (London: T. Sowle, 1703), pp. 361–72. ❖

Towards the Winter, it came into the Hearts of *Alice Ambrose,* and *Mary Tomkins,* and *Ann Coleman,* to go and visit the Seed of God amongst them that had received the Truth in *Piscatagua*-River, where they were not long, but a flood of Persecution arose, by the Instigation of the Priest, who caused them to be apprehended, by Vertue of your Cart-Law; an Order was made to Whip, and pass them away. . . .

A cruel Warrant, through Eleven Townships by name, . . . to Whip three tender Women, and one of them little and crooked, with ten stripes a-piece, at each Place, in the bitter cold Weather, through such a length of Ground, near Eighty Miles, enough to have beaten their Flesh raw, and their Bones bare. . . .

. . . They were brought before *Walden,* who began to tell them of your Law against Quakers; *Mary Tomkins* reply'd, *So there was a Law that* Daniel *should not pray to his God. Yes,* said *Walden, and* Daniel *suffered, and so shall you.* . . .

So, in a very cold Day, your Deputy, *Walden,* caused these Women to be stripp'd naked, from the middle upward, and tyed to a Cart, and after a while cruelly whipp'd them, whilst the Priest stood and looked, and laughed at it, which some of their Friends seeing, testified against, for which *Walden* put two of them in the Stocks: Having dispatch'd them in this Town, and made way to carry them over the Waters, and thro' Woods to another: The Women deny'd to go, unless they had a Copy of their Warrant; so your Executioner sought to set them on Horse-back, but they slid off; then they endeavour'd to tie each to a Man on Horse-back, that would not do neither, nor any course they took, till the Copy was given them; insomuch that the Constable professed, that he was almost wearied with them: But the *Copy* being given them, they *went* with the Executioner to *Hampton.* . . .

At *Hampton, William Fifield,* the Constable, having received the Women, to Whip them there, said, *I profess you must not think to make Fools of Men;* meaning thereby, as if he would not be out-done, upon the Relation of the Constable of *Dover,* what work he had with them. The Women answered, *They should be able to deal with him, as well as the other.* So this Constable, *Fifield,* who professed himself so Stout, the next Morning would have whipp'd them before Day; but they refused, saying, *That they were not ashamed of their Sufferings.* Then he would have whipp'd them on their Cloaths, contrary to the Warrant, when he had them at the Cart. But they said, *Set us free, or do according to the Order;* which was to whip them on their naked Backs. Then he spake to a Woman to take off their Cloaths.

The Woman said, *She would not do it for all the World;* and so did other Women deny to do it. Then he said, *I profess I will do it my self.* So he stripp'd them, and then stood Trembling with the Whip in his Hand, as a Man Condemned, and did the Execution as a Man in that Condition.

90 ... [Later, two other constables] laid Hands on *Alice Ambrose,* as she was in Prayer, and taking her, the one by the one Arm, and the other by the other Arm, they unmercifully dragged her out of Doors, with her Face towards the Snow, which was knee deep, over Stumps and old Trees, near a Mile; ... and so laid her up Prisoner in a very wicked Man's House ... [with] *Mary Tomkins* also, and kept them both all night ... ; and in the Morning, it being exceeding Cold, they got a certain Boat or Canoo, or kind of Trow, hewed out of the Body of a Tree, which the *Indians* use on the Water, and in it they determined to have the three Women down to the Harbour's Mouth, and there put them in, threatning, *That they would now so do with them, that they would be troubled with them no more.* ... They forced them down a very steep place, in deep Snow, and furiously they took *Mary Tomkins* by the Arms, and dragg'd her on her Back, over the Stumps of Trees, down a very steep Hill, to the Water-side, so that she was much bruised, and often was dying away; and *Alice Ambrose* they plucked violently into the Water, and kept Swimming by the Canoo, being in danger of Drowning, or to be frozen to Death ... And *Ann Coleman* they put in great danger of her Life also, ... but on a sudden, a great Tempest arose, and so their cruel and wicked Purpose was hindred; and back they had them to the House again, and kept them Prisoners there till near Midnight, and then they cruelly turn'd them all out of doors in the Frost and Snow, *Alice Ambrose*'s Cloathes being before frozen like Boards ... but the Hand of the Lord, who keeps all those who wait upon him, preserved, and upheld them; to whom be the Glory. *Amen.*

The Captivity of Mrs. Mary Rowlandson

Mary Rowlandson was a minister's wife in the frontier town of Lancaster, Massachusetts, when Indians destroyed the town, killed many of her relatives, and took her captive during King Philip's War in February 1675. Mrs. Rowlandson's social status made her a prized source of ransom, and her strong-willed resourcefulness impressed her desperate captors. The Wampanoag chief Metacom, called King Philip by the English, even offered to share his pipe with her. This excerpt reveals her ability to market sewing skills and barter for food with both men and women among the Indians as they all struggled for survival. It also shows the variety of social status among Native American women including the "proud" Wattimore, one of the wives of Rowlandson's "master" and a Pocasset sachem herself, called Weetamoo by other authors. Some Indian women comforted Rowlandson and even shared with her their meager food supplies as they ran for their lives from the English. Like all good Puritans, Rowlandson believed that her Christian faith and the direct intervention of God had both tested and saved her. Her long captivity narrative became one of America's first best-sellers.

From Charles H. Lincoln, ed., *Narrative of the Indian Wars, 1675–1699* (New York: Charles Scribner's Sons, 1913), pp. 118–61.

❖

But now, the next morning, I must turn my back upon the Town, and travel with them into the vast and desolate Wilderness, I knew not whither. . . . One of the Indians carried my poor wounded Babe upon a horse, it went moaning all along, I shall dy, I shall dy. I went on foot after it, with sorrow that cannot be exprest. At length I took it off the horse, and carried it in my armes till my strength failed, and I fell down with it: Then they set me upon a horse with my wounded Child in my lap, and there being no furniture upon the horse back, as we were going down a steep hill, we both fell over the horses head. . . .

After this it quickly began to snow, and when night came on, they stopt: and now down I must sit in the snow, by a little fire, and a few boughs behind me, with my sick Child in my lap; and calling much for water, being now (through the wound) fallen into a violent Fever. My own wound also growing so stiff, that I could scarce sit down or rise up. . . .

. . . Thus nine dayes I sat upon my knees, with my Babe in my lap, till my flesh was raw again. . . . About two houres in the night, my sweet Babe like a Lambe departed this life . . . It being about six yeares, and five months old. It was nine dayes from the first wounding, in this miserable condition, without any refreshing of one nature or other, except a little cold water. . . . I have thought since of the wonderfull goodness of God to me, in preserving me in the use of my reason and senses, in that distressed time, that I did not use wicked and violent means to end my own miserable life. In the morning, when they understood that my child was dead they sent for me home to my Masters Wigwam. . . .

[A month later] . . . I fell a weeping which was the first time to my remembrance, that I wept before them. Although I had met with so much Affliction, and my heart was many times ready to break, yet could I not shed one tear in their sight: but rather had been all this while in a maze, and like one astonished. . . . Then came one of them and gave me two spoon-fulls of Meal to comfort me, and another gave me half a pint of Pease; which was more worth than many Bushels at another time. Then I went to see King Philip, he bade me come in and sit down, and asked me whether I woold smoke it [his pipe] (a usual Complement nowadayes amongst Saints and Sinners) but this no way suited me. . . . I remember with shame, how formerly, when I had taken two or three pipes, I was presently ready for another, such a bewitching thing it is: But I thank God, he has now given me power over it; surely there are many who may be better imployed than to ly sucking a stinking Tobacco-pipe. . . .

. . . During my abode in this place, Philip spake to me to make a shirt for his boy, which I did, for which he gave me a shilling: I offered the mony to my master, but he bade me keep it: and with it I bought a piece of Horse flesh. Afterwards he asked me to make a Cap for his boy, for which he invited me to Dinner. I went, and he gave me a Pancake, about as big as two fingers; it was made of parched wheat, beaten, and fryed in Bears grease, but I thought I never tasted pleasanter meat in my life. There was a Squaw who spake to me to make a shirt for her *Sannup*, for which she gave me a piece of Bear. Another asked me to knit a pair of Stockins, for which she gave me a quart of Pease: I boyled my Pease and Bear together, and invited my master and mistriss to dinner, but the proud Gossip, because I served them both in one Dish, would eat nothing, except one bit that he gave her upon the point on his knife. . . .

But I was fain to go and look after something to satisfie my hunger, and going among the Wigwams, I went into one, and there found a Squaw who shewed her self very kind to me, and gave me a piece of Bear. . . . In the morning I went to the same Squaw, who had a Kettle of Ground nuts boyling; I asked her to let me boyle my piece of Bear in her Kettle, which she did, and gave me some Ground-nuts to eat with it: and I cannot but think how pleasant it was to me.

. . . Then came an Indian to me with a pair of stockings that were too big for him, and he would have me ravel them out, and knit them fit for him. I shewed my self willing, and bid him ask my mistriss if I might go along with him a little way; she said yes, I might . . . . he gave me some roasted Ground-nuts, which did again revive my feeble stomach. . . .

My master had three Squaws, living sometimes with one, and sometimes with another one, this old Squaw, at whose Wigwam I was, and with whom my Master had been those three weeks. Another was Wattimore, with whom I had lived and served all this while: A severe and proud Dame she was, bestowing every day in dressing her self neat as much time as any of the Gentry of the land: powdering her hair, and painting her face, going with Neck-laces, with Jewels in her ears, and Bracelets upon her hands: When she had dressed her self, her work was to make Girdles of Wampom and Beads. The third Squaw was a younger one, by whom he had two Papooses. . . . [As the time of release drew closer, Wattimore] laid a Mat under me, and a good Rugg over me; the first time I had any such kindness shewed me. I understood that Wattimore thought, that if she should let me go and serve with the old Squaw, she would be in danger to loose, not only my service, but the redemption-pay also. And I was not a little glad to hear this; being by it raised in my hopes, that in Gods due time there would be an end of this sorrowfull hour. Then came an Indian, and asked me to knit him three pair of Stockins, for which I had a Hat, and a silk Handkerchief. Then another asked me to make her a shift, for which she gave me an Apron. . . .

When the Letter [from the council] was come, the Saggamores met to consult about the Captives, and called me to them to enquire how much my husband would give to redeem me. . . . Now knowing that all we had was destroyed by the Indians, I was in a great strait: I thought if I should speak of but a little, it would be slighted, and hinder the matter; if of a great sum, I knew not where it would be procured: Yet at a venture, I said Twenty pounds, yet desired them to take less; but they would not hear of that, but sent that message to Boston, that for Twenty pounds I should be redeemed. . . .

I have seen the extreme vanity of this world. One hour I have been in health and wealth, wanting nothing; but the next hour in sickness and wounds and death, having nothing but sorrow and affliction. . . . And that scripture would come to my mind, *Heb.*, 12:6: *For whom the Lord loveth He chasteneth, and scourgeth every son whom He receiveth.* But now I see the Lord had His time to scourge and chasten me. The portion of some is to have their afflictions by drops, now one drop and then another; but the dregs of the cup, the wine of astonishment, like a sweeping rain that leaveth no food, did the Lord prepare to be my portion. . . .

Yet I see [that] when God calls a person to anything, and through never so many difficulties, yet He is fully able to carry them through and make them see, and say they have been gainers thereby. . . . I have learned to look beyond the present and smaller troubles, and to be quieted under them, as Moses said, *Exod.*, 14:13: *Stand still and see the salvation of the Lord.*

Examination of Sarah Good and Martha Corey

About three hundred New England women were accused of witchcraft during the seventeenth century, far fewer in proportion to the population than the many thousands who had been executed as witches from the fifteenth through the seventeenth centuries in Europe but clear evidence of a continued belief in supernatural evil as the source of social trouble. The last and most famous episode in America occurred in Salem, Massachusetts, in 1692. More than one hundred people were accused, including a few men, and twenty were put to death before the trials were halted. Community tensions over religion, a changing economy, and the declining availability of land, wealth, and opportunity for youth of both sexes seem to have been causes for the sudden vivid accusations against mostly older women by a number of hysterical young girls.

One of the first "witches" to be arrested was Sarah Good, a poverty-stricken, unpleasant woman whose husband disliked her and who appeared suspicious even when she was reciting a psalm. Another, Martha Corey, had been heard to say that the magistrates needed their eyes opened and should not believe the "distracted children" who made accusations. At her trial, she even laughed at the magistrates' questions until she began to realize her danger. The following excerpts from the court records reveal the developing drama.

94

From Charles W. Upham, *Salem Witchcraft*, vol. 2 (Boston: Wiggin and Lunt, 1867), pp. 13–15, 43–50. ❖

"Sarah Good, what evil spirit have you familiarity with?—None.

"Have you made no contracts with the Devil?—No.

"Why do you hurt these children?—I do not hurt them. I scorn it.

"Who do you employ then to do it?—I employ nobody.

"What creature do you employ then?—No creature: but I am falsely accused.

"Why did you go away muttering from Mr. Parris his house?—I did not mutter, but I thanked him for what he gave my child. . . .

"What is it you say when you go muttering away from persons' houses?—If I must tell, I will tell.

"Do tell us then.—If I must tell, I will tell: it is the Commandments. I may say my Commandments, I hope.

"What Commandment is it?—If I must tell you, I will tell: it is a psalm.

"What psalm?

"(After a long time she muttered over some part of a psalm.)

"Who do you serve?—I serve God.

"What God do you serve?—The God that made heaven and earth (though she was not willing to mention the word 'God'). Her answers were in a very wicked, spiteful manner, rejecting and retorting against the authority with base and abusive words; and many lies she was taken in. It was here said that her husband had said that he was afraid that she either was a witch or would be one very quickly. The worshipful Mr. Hathorne, asked him his reason why he said so of her, whether he had ever seen any thing by her. He answered 'No, not in this nature; but it was her bad carriage to him: and indeed,' said he, 'I may say with tears, that she is an enemy to all good.'"

. . . .

"Mr. Hathorne: [to Martha Corey] You are now in the hands of authority. Tell me, now, why you hurt these persons.—I do not.

"Who doth?—Pray, give me leave to go to prayer.

"(This request was made sundry times.)

"We do not send for you to go to prayer; but tell me why you hurt these.—

I am an innocent person. I never had to do with witchcraft since I was born. I am a gospel woman.

"Do not you see these complain of you?—The Lord open the eyes of the magistrates and ministers: the Lord show his power to discover the guilty.

"Tell us who hurts these children.—I do not know.

"If you be guilty of this fact, do you think you can hide it?—The Lord knows.   95

"Well, tell us what you know of this matter.—Why, I am a gospel woman; and do you think I can have to do with witchcraft too? . . .

"(Children: There is a man whispering in her ear.)

"Hathorne continued: What did he say to you?—We must not believe all that these distracted children say.

"Cannot you tell what that man whispered?—I saw nobody.

"But did not you hear?—No.

"(Here was extreme agony of all the afflicted.)

"If you expect mercy of God, you must look for it in God's way, by confession. Do you think to find mercy by aggravating your sins?—A true thing.

"Look for it, then, in God's way.—So I do.

"Give glory to God and confess, then.—But I cannot confess.

"Do not you see how these afflicted do charge you?—We must not believe distracted persons.

"Who do you improve to hurt them?—I improved none.

"Did not you say our eyes were blinded, you would open them?—Yes to accuse the innocent . . . .

"Here are more than two that accuse you for witchcraft. What do you say?—I am innocent.

"(Then Mr. Hathorne read further of Crosby's evidence.)

"What did you mean by that,—the Devil could not stand before you?

"(She denied it. Three of four sober witnesses confirmed it.)

"What can I do? Many rise up against me.

"Why, confess.—So I would, if I were guilty.

"Here are sober persons. What do you say to them? You are a gospel woman; will you lie?

"(Abigail cried out, 'Next sabbath is sacrament-day; but she shall not come there.')

"I do not care.

"You charge these children with distraction: it is a note of distraction when persons vary in a minute; but these fix upon you. This is not the manner of distraction.—When all are against me, what can I help it?

"Now tell me the truth, will you? Why did you say that the magistrates' and ministers' eyes were blinded, you would open them?

"(She laughed, and denied it.)

"Now tell us how we shall know who doth hurt these, if you do not?—Can an innocent person be guilty?

"Do you deny these words?—Yes.

"Tell us who hurts these. We came to be a terror to evil-doers. You say you would open our eyes, we are blind.—If you say I am a witch.

"You said you would show us.

"(She denied it.)

"Why do you not show us?—I cannot tell: I do not know.

"What did you strike the maid at Mr. Tho. Putnam's with?—I never struck her in my life.

"There are two that saw you strike her with an iron rod.—I had no hand in it.

"Who had? Do you believe these children are bewitched?—They may, for aught I know: I have no hand in it.

"You say you are no witch. Maybe you mean you never convenanted with the Devil. Did you never deal with any familiar?—No, never.

"What bird was that the children spoke of?

"(Then witnesses spoke: What bird was it?)

"I know no bird.

"It may be you have engaged you will not confess; but God knows.—So he doth.

"Do you believe you shall go unpunished?—I have nothing to do with witch-craft.

"Why was you not willing your husband should come to the former session here?—But he came, for all.

"Did not you take the saddle off?—I did not know what it was for.

"Did you not know what it was for?—I did not know that it would be to any benefit.

"(Somebody said that she would not have them help to find out witches.)

"Did you not say you would open our eyes? Why do you not?—I never thought of a witch.

"Is it a laughing matter to see these afflicted persons?

"(She denied it. Several prove it.)

"Ye are all against me, and I cannot help it.

"Do not you believe there are witches in the country?—I do not know that there is any.

"Do not you know that Tituba confessed it?—I did not hear her speak.

"I find you will own nothing without several witnesses, and yet you will deny for all.

"(It was noted, when she bit her lip, several of the afflicted were bitten. When she was urged upon it that she bit her lip, saith she, What harm is there in it?)

"(Mr. Noyes: I believe it is apparent she practiseth witchcraft in the congregation: there is no need of images.)

"What do you say to all these things that are apparent?—If you will all go hang me, how can I help it?

"Were you to serve the Devil ten years? Tell how many.

"(She laughed. The children cried there was a yellow bird with her. When Mr. Hathorne asked her about it, she laughed. When her hands were at liberty, the afflicted persons were pinched.)

"Why do not you tell how the Devil comes in your shape, and hurts these? You said you would.—How can I know how?

"Why did you say you would show us?

"(She laughed again.) . . .

"Do not you see these children and women are rational and sober as their neighbors, when your hands are fastened?

"(Immediately they were seized with fits: and the standers-by said she was squeezing her fingers, her hands being eased by them that held them on purpose for trial.

"Quickly after, the marshal said, 'She hath bit her lip;' and immediately the afflicted were in an uproar.)

"[Tell] why you hurt these, or who doth?

"(She denieth any hand in it.)

"Why did you say, if you were a witch, you should have a pardon?—Because I am a [pause] woman."

ENTERPRISING WOMEN

13. Anne Bradstreet, Stained-Glass Window

Although she was the daughter and then wife of prominent leaders of Massachusetts Bay Colony and was America's first published poet, there are no known pictures or physical descriptions of Anne Dudley Bradstreet. This stained-glass render-
ing of Bradstreet appears in a church in the English town from which she emigrated
to America in 1630. It shows a Puritan matron carrying a nest with eight birds, as
she referred to her children in one poem. Detail from a window in St. Botolph's
Church, designed by Harry Grylls, ca. 1946, Boston, Lincolnshire. Reproduced
by kind permission of the vicar and church wardens. Photo courtesy of Elizabeth
Wade White.

14. Mary Dyer

This sculpture of Mary Dyer is one of only two images of women near Boston Common. The sculptures of Dyer and Anne Hutchinson, whom Dyer followed into exile in 1638, both stand in front of Boston's State House. As a Quaker, Mary Dyer had a missionary zeal that caused her to violate Massachusetts laws against Quaker preaching—three times in the late 1650s. On her third trip, after a gallows reprieve the second time, she was hanged on the Common in 1660. On her way to the hanging she said, "Yea, and willingly I go." Sculpture by Sylvia Shaw Judson, date of installation, 1959, Boston, Massachusetts. Photo by Laurie Crumpacker.

PART TWO

The Eighteenth Century

My Time Is Not My Own

I N THE BRITISH colonies during the first half of the eighteenth century, English colonists were being transformed into Americans. Their maturing self-sufficiency included changing ideas about religion, morals, and politics. Women were, of course, an active part of the change, both responding to cultural currents and establishing new patterns of behavior for themselves. In the South, black and white women who participated in the rapidly expanding commercial agriculture system were usually isolated on rural farms or plantations; in the North, where a mercantile trading system was emerging, women were more likely to live in established towns and villages. The backcountry South, northern and western New England, New Jersey, and Pennsylvania were areas of new immigration and frontier settlements. Throughout the colonies, society was still predominantly rural, though the seaport cities of Newport, Charleston, Boston, New York, and Philadelphia provided the commercial and social advantages of an expanding urban economy. During this period, regional differences, as well as contrasts between urban and rural life-styles, were beginning to intensify.

In the early years of the eighteenth century, the sex ratio in long-settled areas of the colonies became more balanced; no longer were there many fewer women than men. This meant that an eighteenth-century widow, unlike her seventeenth-century counterpart, was quite likely to remain unmarried. The widow Rebekah Badger's petition for a liquor license reveals a frequent problem: she and other single women might become destitute in an inflationary economy and an increasingly stratified society. In the South and on the frontiers especially, women married earlier and produced more children than previous generations. Like the English aristocracy, old southern families consolidated their holdings by arranging advantageous marriages for their daughters; but other white American women were more likely than their European counterparts to have a relatively free choice of marriage partners.

Eighteenth-century white American families were large, and far more children lived to maturity than in Europe. Infant care differed regionally, since southern white women were more likely than northern mothers to use the services of a wet nurse (often an enslaved black woman) to feed their babies. Throughout the colonies, a woman's life expectancy averaged ten years less than a man's (the opposite of today) mainly because of the hazards of too-frequent pregnancies and births and the exhaustion of caring for small children. (Statistics show that if a woman lived beyond fifty, her life expectancy might equal any man's.) One-quarter of all children died before the age of twenty-one; thus every woman had to be prepared for her own or her children's deaths. The graveyard inscription from the tomb of Margaret Edwards explains that she died giving birth to her tenth child when she was only thirty-four; the death from infection of the slave Betty Oliver may have occurred because of her weakened condition after childbirth.

For most Americans, the first half of the eighteenth century was still predominantly a time of preindustrial household production, along with barter relationships and commodity exchanges in which women participated as readily as did men. Although their work was valued during the colonial period, women who worked for wages, no matter what their race or class, were always paid less than free men or hired-out slave men. As cash commercial exchanges became more common, women began to lose control of many household transactions that had been their province in earlier periods. Their produce was usually recorded under their husbands' or fathers' names, and their ability to trade was limited by their lack of access to cash.

The northern economy gradually made the shift from a domestic to a market economy, causing changes in both the content of women's work and the cultural meanings imposed on it. Time-consuming production increasingly took place in commercial enterprises in other homes or in small manufactories and shops. Among more prosperous families, production was relegated to servants or slaves. The portrait of the wealthy Royall family, painted in 1745, shows women dressed differently from Mrs. Freake in 1674. In prosperous families like the Royalls, women no longer performed manual labor, as their seventeenth-century grandmothers had; they doffed their aprons, caps, and serviceable clothing and substituted the silks, laces, and velvets that demonstrated their husbands' prosperity and their social class. They still *worked*, however: managing households and servants, supervising garden and dairy production, ordering and shopping for goods that their grandmothers and less prosperous contemporaries produced at home, sewing and doing fine needlework, "governing" (training) their children, and completing the social obligations deemed essential for women of their class.

There was seldom any leisure at all for rural women, women on the frontier, impoverished women, servants, or enslaved women. Frontier pioneers in newly established Georgia and along the valleys of the Appalachian Mountains were less concerned with women's proper roles and more concerned that everyone's hard work was necessary for family survival. Many of these settlers came from English prisons, like the "Irish convict" couple described in the ad for a runaway servant or like "Bedlam Bess." Often they had been convicted of debt or petty crimes and redeemed from prison by their willingness to accept indentured servitude in the New World. Others were among the waves of immigrant families from northern Ireland, Scotland, and Germany. For the most part, the work of these women remained the same backbreaking labor as it had been in the seventeenth century. In frontier conditions, or among immigrant servants and slaves, women's work roles were not rigidly separated from men's. John Lawson, for example, describes the field work, canoeing, and hunting of "the most industrious sex" on the Carolina frontier. A comparison of the illustrations of a frontier cabin with the plans for a New England farmhouse or (in a later section of the book) the prosperous Sargent-Murray home in Massachusetts helps to clarify the large distinctions among eighteenth-century social classes.

Emphasizing social and legal distinctions between indentured white servants and enslaved Africans, as Robert Beverley did in his *History of Virginia,* was one way of maintaining political stability in the eighteenth-century South, where blacks soon outnumbered whites in two colonies. A booming English-American slave trade after 1690 expanded and consolidated the slave labor system in the American South. More black women were imported, which began to rectify the unbalanced sex ratio among African Americans. This increase enabled close-knit African-American kinship networks to develop in the Chesapeake and Carolina tidewater areas, providing family stability and continuity for some despite the rigors and separations that slavery brought to others. Since the 1660s, slave codes had been growing more rigid, gradually removing all legal rights, making a slave's status inherited and permanent, and forbidding marriage, education, and the retention of individual earnings.

Slave code laws increasingly separated blacks from whites. At the same time, opportunities were increasing for skilled and mobile white immigrants and servants. When a white servant like the runaway tinker Hannah escaped her indenture, she was likely to find employment because all households needed someone who could repair pots and pans. A runaway slave was in a more desperate situation, as was another Hannah, an enslaved black woman who escaped from her abusive master. Lash marks on her back testified to his cruelty and her helpless resistance. Unlike the white Hannah or John Winthrop III's servant, as a slave this Hannah had no recourse to legal remedies for abuse and little likelihood of escaping successfully.

At the same time that white women were being urged to greater "refinement" and delicacy, enslaved black women were being subjected both to the most difficult domestic tasks and to field labor. The *Maryland Gazette* and *Georgia Gazette* advertisements for wet nurses demonstrate the relegation to black women of tasks now deemed undesirable by some whites. Betty Oliver's story is perhaps the saddest of the documents in this section because it presents the dying days of an enslaved woman whose death was probably related to poor medical and obstetrical practice. Her master's care for her is attributable to her value as a worker and mother and not to any particular compassion on his part.

Kezia Murphey's inheritance of two slaves illustrates the way that the slave system entwined generations of white and black women in its exploitative patterns.

Numerous white women were able, and indeed needed, to establish their own businesses during the eighteenth century. A capable housewife frequently augmented a family's scarce cash resources by selling her extra produce or by participating in her husband's trade. Women sold everything from garden seeds and herbs to dry goods and other necessities. Many women kept taverns and lodging houses, as is evident from Rebekah Badger's petition. Women managed plantations for absent male relatives or cooperated in family businesses. The widow Elizabeth Timothy, like several others, continued a successful independent printing business after her husband's death. For most of her eighty-seven years, "Mrs. Whitmore," of Vermont, was one of the many successful midwives in the colonies. And a 1733 petition for governmental consideration, presented by a group of New York widowed "she-merchants" and landowners, was probably at least partly serious. In spite of these examples, however, before the American Revolution, independent businesswomen were exceptional and located mostly in urban areas. Indeed, the average housewife knew very little about business and provided the family's cash income only when forced to by the absence or death of a male provider.

One reason that most women knew little about their family's finances was that few received any education beyond that necessary to be housewives. Only half as many women as men could read and write by mid-century, and those, like Elizabeth Foote, who learned to "read and cypher" received further education only if it was available from indulgent fathers or from listening to brothers' tutors. A few privileged young women attended the female academies that were springing up in New England and the middle colonies. These schools specialized in needlework but also taught rudimentary reading, writing, arithmetic, music, dancing, and sometimes a smattering of French, geography, and botany. The young girls who attended these schools testified that they learned to respect themselves as skilled craftswomen and that they established friendships that lasted throughout their lifetimes. Women's needlework, like the embroidered bedcovers illustrated here, was creative as well as practical and provided a valued form of self-expression.

Comfortably Housed

This contemporary description of Chesapeake-area houses remarks on the similarity of house styles in the early stages of settlement of this area. But only people of "some means" could add white plaster to the inside walls, making the difference between light and dark for isolated housewives. White southerners built kitchens separate from their living space because of their reliance on slaves and also to keep cool in summer. The form was maintained even by those without servants, thus effectively separating female workspace from other household activities.

From Gilbert Chinard, ed., *A Huguenot Exile in Virginia; or, Voyages of a Frenchman Exiled for His Religion, with a Description of Virginia and Maryland* (1687; reprint, New York: N.p., 1934), pp. 119–20.

❖

Some people in this country are comfortably housed; the farmers' houses are built entirely of wood, the roofs being made of small boards of chestnut, as are also the walls. Those who have some means, cover them inside with a coating of mortar in which they use oyster-shells for lime; it is as white as snow, so that although they look ugly from the outside, where only the wood can be seen, they are very pleasant inside, with convenient windows and openings. They have started making bricks in quantities, and I have seen several houses where the walls were entirely made of them. Whatever their rank, and I know not why, they build only two rooms with some closets on the ground floor, and two rooms in the attic above; but they build several like this, according to their means. They build a separate kitchen, a separate house for the Christian slaves, one for the negro slaves, and several to dry the tobacco, so that when you come to the home of a person of some means, you think you are entering a fairly large village.

The Most Industrious Sex

Second- and third-generation white women in the southern colonies, no longer plagued by the high death rates and indenture restrictions of their seventeenth-century predecessors, tended to marry during adolescence rather than in their early twenties. These added years of childbearing resulted in larger families. This was especially true along the newly settled Appalachian frontier, like the western

Carolinas, which John Lawson described in 1700. Most of these women were not servants; they were self-sufficient producers of their own cloth and food and dairy products. Many women even learned survival skills such as canoeing and shooting. They also joined their menfolk in field work when necessary.

From John Lawson, *History of North Carolina* (1714; reprint, Richmond, Va.: Garrett and Massie, 1937), pp. 85–86.

❖

The Women are the most industrious Sex in that Place, and, by their good Housewifery, make a great deal of Cloath of their own Cotton, Wool and Flax; Some of them keeping their Families, (though large,) very decently appareled, both with Linnens and Woollens, so that they have no occasion to run into the Merchants Debt, or lay their money out on Stores for Cloathing. . . .

. . . They marry very young; some at Thirteen or Fourteen; and She that stays till Twenty is reckoned a stale Maid, which is a very indifferent Character in that warm Country. The Women are very fruitful, most Houses being full of Little Ones. . . . Many of the women are very handy in Canoes and will manage them with great Dexterity and Skill, which they become accustomed to in this watery Country. They are ready to help their Husbands in any servile Work, as Planting, when the Season or the Weather requires Expedition; Pride seldom banishing good Housewifery. The Girls are not bred up to the Wheel and Sewing only, but the Dairy, and affairs of the House they are very well acquainted withal; so that you shall see them, whilst very young, manage their Business with a great deal of Conduct and Alacrity.

Gravestone of Mrs. Margaret Edwards

Death in the eighteenth-century colonies was ever present—particularly from the many infectious diseases and, for women, from frequent childbirths. This graveyard inscription reveals the not uncommon fertility and early death of a woman from a prosperous family. She married young and bore children almost yearly, always behaving like an obedient wife and "humble Christian" woman.

From Mabel L. Webber, "Inscriptions from the Independent or Congregational (Circular) Church Yard, Charleston, S.C.," *South Carolina Historical and Genealogical Magazine* 29 (July 1928): 238.

❖

Underneath / lies what was mortal of / Mrs. Margaret Edwards / Wife of Mr. John Edwards, Merchant of this place / Daughter of Mr Alexander Peronneau, Gent / She Died / in Travail with her tenth Child / Aged 34 years and about 4 months / A sincere, modest and humble Christian / A Member of this Church / who adorned her holy Profession / Triumphed over the last Enemy / Exulting in the Riches of free Grace / She committed her Soul to Him whom she ardently loved / and died without fear or a groan / Augt 27th, 1772.

> "My flesh shall slumber in the Ground
> Till the last Trumpet shall sound
> Then burst the chains with sweet surprise
> And in my Saviour's Image rise"

A Bedlam Bess

Servant women left few records, since most of them could not read or write and were working too hard to do so even if they could. This poem, by a purported visitor to eighteenth-century Maryland, describes the factors (workers) on a sotweed (tobacco) plantation. Here he tells the maid's story, surmising that she had run away from home or sold herself into indenture because of a premarital love affair ("supping e'er the Priest said Grace"). She claimed to have been kidnapped and fooled as she tried to avoid an unwanted marriage. The word "Bedlam" referred to a notorious prison-asylum in eighteenth-century London.

From Ebenezer Cook, *The Sotweed Factor; or, A Voyage to Maryland* (London: D. Bragg, at the Raven in Pater-Noster-Row, 1708), pp. 6–7.

❖

> I scarce cou'd find my way to Bed;
> Where I was instantly convey'd
> By one who pass'd for Chamber-Maid,
> Tho' by her loose and sluttish Dress,
> She rather seemed a Bedlam-Bess:
> Curious to know from whence she came,
> I prest her to declare her Name.
> She Blushing, seem'd to hide her Eyes,
> And thus in Civil Terms replies;
> In better Times, e'er to this Land,
> I was unhappily Trapann'd;
> Perchance as well I did appear,
> As any Lord or Lady here,
> Not then a Slave for twice two Year.
> My Cloaths were fashionably new,

Nor were my Shifts of Linnen Blue;
But things are changed, now at the Hoe,
I daily work, and Bare-foot go,
In weeding Corn or feeding Swine,
I spend my melancholy Time.
Kidnap'd and Fool'd, I hither fled,
To shun a hated Nuptial Bed,
And to my cost already find,
Worse Plagues than those I left behind.
Whate'er the Wanderer did profess,
Good-faith I cou'd not chuse but guess
The Cause which brought her to this place,
Was supping e'er the Priest said Grace.

Cruell Usage

John Winthrop III, of New London, Connecticut, complained in a letter to his father about the insubordination of a young Irish serving woman. One-third of colonial households employed indentured servants. Winthrop's servant may have been serving a four- or five-year term in exchange for her passage to America. During her servitude, she was expected to do most of the hard manual work in the household; she could not marry and was supposed to remain obedient to both master and mistress. Obviously, this servant had been rebelling— perhaps against the hard work, the restrictions on social life, or just the years of servitude she saw ahead. The threat of being sent to Virginia, where conditions were far worse, was real, but labor shortages in America enabled her to insist on a freedom of behavior she would never have been allowed in England.

From letter of John Winthrop III (1717), quoted in Lucy Maynard Salmon, *Domestic Service* (New York: Macmillan Co., 1897), p. 36.

❖

It is not convenient now to write the trouble & plague we have had with this Irish creature the year past. Lying & unfaithfull; would doe things on purpose in contradiction & vexation to her mistress; lye out of the house anights, and have contrivances with fellows that have been stealing from our estate & gett drink out of the cellar for them; saucy & impudent, as when we have taken her to task for her wickedness she has gon away to complain of cruell usage. I can truly say we have used this base creature with a great deal of kindness & lenity. She would frequently take her mistresses capps & stockins, hanckerchers &c.,

and dress herself, and away without leave among her companions. I may have said some time or other when she has been in fault, that she was fitt to live nowhere butt in Virginia, and if she would not mend her ways I should send her thither; tho I am sure no body would give her passage thither to have her service for 20 yeares, she is such a high spirited pernicious jade. Robin has been run away near ten days, as you will see by the inclosed, and this creature knew of his going and of his carrying out 4 dozen bottles of cyder, metheglin [fermented honey beverage], & palme wine out of the cellar amongst the servants of the towne, and meat and I know not what.

Of the Servants and Slaves of Virginia

Hard as things were for servant women, conditions were worse for enslaved women brought to America from Africa. Robert Beverley, a prominent Virginian, intended to clarify this distinction when he wrote his *History of Virginia* in 1705. Wanting to encourage white servants to emigrate, he emphasized their status and opportunities, especially the fact that servant women never worked in the fields, as slave women did.

From Robert Beverley, *The History of Virginia, in Four Parts,* 2d rev. ed. (1722; reprint, Richmond, Va.: J. W. Randolph, 1855), pp. 219–22.

❖

Their servants they distinguish by the names of slaves for life, and servants for a time.

Slaves are the negroes and their posterity, following the condition of the mother, according to the maxim, *partus frequitur ventrem.* They are called slaves, in respect of the time of their servitude, because it is for life.

Servants, are those which serve only for a few years, according to the time of their indenture, or the custom of the country. The custom of the country takes place upon such as have no indentures. The law in this case is, that if such servants be under nineteen years of age, they must be brought into court to have their age adjudged; and from the age they are judged to be of, they must serve until they reach four and twenty; but if they be adjudged upwards of nineteen, they are then only to be servants for the term of five years.

The male servants, and slaves of both sexes, are employed together in tilling and manuring the ground, in sowing and planting tobacco, corn, &c. Some distinction indeed is made between them in their clothes, and food; but the work of both is no other than what the overseers, the freemen, and the planters themselves do.

Sufficient distinction is also made between the female servants, and slaves; for a white woman is rarely or never put to work in the ground, if she be good for anything else; and to discourage all planters from using any women so, their law makes female servants working in the ground tithables, while it suffers all other white women to be absolutely exempted; whereas, on the other hand, it is a common thing to work a woman slave out of doors, nor does the law make any distinction in her taxes, whether her work be abroad or at home.

A Runaway Servant and a Runaway Slave

The first ad, for an Irish couple, contrasts sharply with the second one, for the slave Hannah. Thousands of poor English and Irish people convicted of petty crimes or debt were sold into servitude in America as an alternative to prison. White servants had often learned valuable skills and could escape much more easily than could slaves. The Irish couple had an extensive wardrobe, money, tools, a knowledge of English, the help of one another, and no scars from whipping.

The ad for the slave girl Hannah, on the other hand, mentions so many scars that one wonders how she stayed alive long enough to escape. She was a "yellow Negro wench"—light enough to try to "pass for a free woman"—so she obviously had a white father or grandfather who had not cared about his daughter or granddaughter being enslaved. Her owner even disparaged her Christian faith, which would probably have been considered an asset for a white woman.

From *Virginia Gazette* (Williamsburg), March 26, 1767.

❖

Run away from the subscriber, in Northumberland county, two Irish convict servants named William and Hannah Daylies, tinkers by trade, of which the woman is extremely good; they had a note of leave to go out and work in Richmond county and Hobb's Hole . . . ; soon after I heard they were run away. The man wore a light coloured coarse cloth frock coat, a blue striped satin jacket, and plaid one, a pair of leather breeches, a pair of Russia drill white stockings, a little brown bog wig, and his hat cocked up very sharp. . . . The woman had on an old stuff gown and a light coloured petticoat, and under petticoat of cotton with a blue selvedge at the bottom, a blue striped satin gown, the same with his jacket, two check aprons, and a pair of pale blue calimanco shoes. They both wore white shirts, with very short ruffles, and white thread stockings. They had a complete set of tinkers tools. They were seen to have two English guineas and a good deal of silver. . . . Whoever will apprehend both or either of said servants, and brings them to me, shall have five pounds reward for each, and reasonable travelling charges allowed by William Taite.

. . . .

Run away about the 15th of December last, a small yellow Negro wench named Hannah, about 35 years of age; had on when she went away a green plains petticoat, and sundry other clothes, but what sort I do not know, as she stole many from the other Negroes. She has remarkable long hair, or wool, is much scarified under the throat from one ear to the other, and has many scars on her back, occasioned by whipping. She pretends much to the religion the Negroes of late have practised, and may probably endeavour to pass for a free woman, as I understand she intended when she went away, by the Negroes in the neighbourhood. She is supposed to have made for Carolina. Whoever takes up the said slave, and secures her so that I get her again, shall be rewarded according to their trouble, by Stephen Dence.

Kezia Murphey's Legacy

This excerpt from a Virginia farmer's will illustrates the interconnection of white and black women's lives in the slave-plantation economy. When Benjamin Terry died in 1769, his large holdings of land were divided among his sons; the main legacy to his wife and several daughters was in the form of slaves. A married woman could not legally free, sell, or will any of her property, including her slaves, so Terry also provided for future distributions to his grandchildren. Some plantation mistresses enjoyed few material goods; Mistress Terry inherited only one frying pan, two pots, a featherbed, and some furniture in addition to the farm animals and equipment. But the four slaves were a valuable legacy: they would provide domestic help and future capital "increase" in the form of their children. Even women who disapproved of slavery could not lightly give up the only "wealth" they had. Punctuation and spelling have been modernized.

From Benjamin Terry, "Last Will and Testament," December 28, 1769, probated 1771 in Halifax County, Virginia, copy in James Scott Papers, David Duniway Collection, University of Oregon, Eugene.

❖

In the Name of god Amen. I Benjamin Terry, Senior, of Pittsylvania County and Parish of Camden . . . for the settling of my Temporal estate . . . Send to my beloved wife Elizabeth Terry four negroes, namely Abraham, Melinder and her Child[ren] Babe and Siner, Six Cows and Calves with all my hogs, one feather bed and furniture, one frying pan, Two Iron pots & hooks with all the plantation Working Tools, one black mare known by the name of Hazerd and her Colt SoberJohn and the sorrel Clowmare, all During her natural Life and at her decease to be Disposed of as in this my will. [He specifies tracts of land and two slaves for each of his five sons and their "heirs forever."] To my Daughter Kezia Murphey two negroes, namely Harris & Fillis, During her natural life, and after her Decease to be equally Divided between all her Children . . . by her former husband James Scott and all her other Children that she has or should have by her present husband Richard Murphey; but if the said Richard Murphey should not pay his wife's first Children she had by James Scott their Legacy that is or will be Due them out of their Father James Scott's Estate which I am security for, that it shall be paid them out of the two said negroes Harry [*sic*] & Fillis. I send to my Daughter Leviney King two negroes, namely Abbey & Jerry, During her natural Life & then to be equally Divided, they and their increase, between her Daughter Grace Terry and all her Children that she has got or may have. [Daughters Sarah Terry, Elizabeth Buckingham, and Mary Terry each received two slaves—including Old Jenney, Melinder and Butler, Cyner and Cythinia, and their "future increase," to be theirs and their heirs forever.]

Ads for a Wet Nurse

"Genteel" white women in the South usually followed the upper-class European custom of hiring wet nurses to breast-feed their babies. Enslaved African-American nurses usually had to give up feeding their own babies to nurse their employers' children. The practice accentuated the contrast between free women and slaves while it also contributed to increased fertility among plantation mistresses. Travelers often remarked that slave women nursed children of the most distinguished families and that each child would imitate the gestures and accent of its "Mammy." Children also grieved to see their nurses whipped, a sad irony of the inhuman system. If no slave women were currently producing milk, it was sometimes necessary to advertise.

From *Maryland Gazette,* April 4, 1750; *Georgia Gazette,* October 1, 1766.

❖

WANTED,

A NURSE with a good Breast of Milk, of a healthy Constitution, and good Character, that is willing to go into a Gentleman's Family. Such a one may hear a very good Encouragement, by enquiring of the Printer hereof.

❖

Wanted by the Month

A HEALTHY CAREFUL NEGROE WENCH for a WET NURSE. One without a child will be most agreeable, or with a child not above six months old.

Betty Oliver's Illness

Illness stalked the lives of colonial men and women, and often the medical treatment was as bad as the illness. The diary of one of Virginia's most notable landholders graphically details both illness and treatment. In this case, the slave Betty Oliver, early in her pregnancy, apparently contracted malarial fever, a common disease in the southern American colonies. It often led to kidney and liver trouble or early death and was particularly dangerous for pregnant women of every class. Betty also gave birth during a smallpox epidemic and developed an infection from bad obstetrical care. The bleeding and laxatives and other medicines she endured before she died were standard treatments. Whereas Carter's own daughter refused them as worse than no treatment at all, an enslaved woman had to do as she was told.

From Jack P. Greene, ed., *The Diary of Colonel Landon Carter of Sabine Hall, 1752–1778*, vol. 1 (Charlottesville: Virginia Historical Society and University Press of Virginia, 1965), pp. 144–46, 154–56. Reprinted by permission of the University Press of Virginia.

❖

[Feb. 23, 1757] Betty Oliver very ill. This is a fine wench but now much affected. She had first a fever in the summer of the raging bilious kind from which she was releived as others were by evacuants, but her pregnancy preventing a repitition of them she relapsed with the Season into an inflamatory disorder for which she was twice blooded and recovered so as to imploy herself about light works. A week before her lying in she was attacked with a numbness in her right side from her hips and into her side but she describing it only by a pain and her being loaded she was again bled and mended till she lay in, at which time the infant was imprudently or unskillfully taken away from her in a wrong position and this Numbness returned with a swelling in her groin. Her Lochial evacuations were very great, and as she was attended with hysterical Symptoms I ordered her some Nervins which releived her, and I always heard she was better and even yesterday 'twas said she was much mended and walkt about clear of a fever, but at night she was again taken very ill and this morning I visited her [and] found a prodigious rattling Cold on her, a very feverish pulse and her Nerves greatly affected. She protested she never went out to expose herself. Note: as she was purged since her lying in by Dr. Flood's directions, I never attempted to do anything of that kind but just to procure a motion or two per day with rhubarb given in small quantitys with castor etc. which had every good affect, but it is to be fear[ed] there is a Collection of matter internally in the swelling in her groin, for she says it keeps to its state, feels soft and as if it was hollow. I sent for Dr. Flood. . . .

[February 24, 1757] Betty Oliver mended much yesterday after taking the Sal Ammoniae but in the night the Hysteric Symptoms returned and with them a fever. She says she was near Choaked by the usual lumps rising. She expectorated a great deal of viscid matter and is this morning quite easy and cheer full. I was in hopes the Ammoniae would have assisted her nerves from their peculiar quality assigned to them in Spasmodick Symptoms, and it is noted likely, but they were prevented, although she is pretty full in Complaining, being of the kind of Moaning weak hearted Constitution. Note: she says the swelling in her groin has not been uneasy to her these 2 days. . . .

[March 8, 1757] Betty Oliver, who was thought to be on the Recovery a little, has relapsed this weak and continues to return into all her old Symptoms which are severely Hysterical. She took a week vomit last night by Dr. Flood's orders, it brought off such Yellow bile, and drank wine whey with Cammonile Flowers infused in it to work it and after it was done some wine and water to strengthen her. She said it gave her great ease in her stomach and fell a Sleep. . . .

[March 9, 1757] Betty Oliver mended all day yesterday and was distracted for an Opiate last night. I deceived her with wine and brown sugar water. She slept well till midnight and then was Siezed with an ague and fever, a new Symptom not before discoverable in her disorder from beginning to ending. If this should not have been a rigor I shall hope the disorder is terminating into an intermittant but then the ague is to me a demonstration of obstructions in the Hepatic [liver] duct and I suppose we shall see some discharge upwards or downwards of green bile. She goes on with Flood's hysteria medicine.

[March 10, 1757] Betty Oliver disappoints all our hopes, a Cold Rigor siezed her again, and is thought to be a dying.

I Shall Continue the Paper as Usual

Women in a variety of professions and businesses were not uncommon in any of the colonies. Often they worked as partners in a family enterprise, carrying on alone whenever they had to. America's first woman journalist was Elizabeth Timothy, who took over the responsibility for her husband's newspaper after his death. Her son succeeded her in a few years, when he came of age; *his* widow, Ann Timothy, later succeeded him and eventually became South Carolina's state printer.

From Elizabeth Timothy, notice in *South Carolina Gazette,* January 11, 1739.

❖

Whereas the late Printer of this Gazette hath been deprived of his life by an unhappy Accident, I take this opportunity of informing the Publick, that I shall continue the said Paper as usual, and hope by the assistance of my Friends to make it as entertaining and correct as may be reasonably expected. Wherefore I flatter myself, that all those Persons, who, by Subscriptions or otherwise, assisted my late Husband, in the Prosecution of the said undertaking, will be kindly pleased to continue their Favours and good Offices to his poor afflicted Widow with six small children and another hourly expected.

Garden Seeds and Flour of Mustard

In the increasingly commercial economy of the eighteenth century, women were encouraged to engage in almost every kind of business or trade. Shops for selling groceries, china, or dry goods (cloth and sewing supplies) were among the most common, but some women managed blacksmith or harness shops. Lydia Dyar specialized in seeds, a necessity for urban housewives' gardens as well as for country dwellers. Mary Crathorne's wholesale and retail business sold a large variety of foods and imported spices and even bought raw materials for processing.

From *Boston Evening Post,* March 11, 1751; *Pennsylvania Gazette* (Philadelphia), February 11, 1768.

❖

To be sold by Lydia Dyar
at the North End, near the Salutation,

The very best of Garden Seeds, early Cabbage, early Lettuce Seeds, early Dutch, early Sugarloaf, early Yorkshire, green Savoy, yellow ditto, large winter Cabbage, Colliflower, early Dutch Turnip, round red Turnip, yellow ditto, large Winter Turnip, three sorts of Carrots, early Charlton Pease, early Hotspur Pease, Marrow fat Pease, Dwarf Pease, all sorts of other Seeds, Windsor Beans, Hotspur Beans, with a variety of fine Flower Seeds, imported in the very last Ship from London.

❖

MARY CRATHORNE,

Begs leave to inform the public (and particularly those that were her late husband's customers) that she has removed from the house she lately occupied in Laetitis Court, to the house lately occupied by Mrs. Aris, at the corner of the said court, in Market-street, where she continues to sell by wholesale and retail,

The genuine FLOUR of MUSTARD, of different degrees of fineness; chocolate, well manufactured, and genuine raw and ground coffee, tea, race and ground ginger, whole and ground pepper, alspice, London fig blue, oat groats, oatmeal, barley, rice, corks; a fresh assortment of spices, domestic pickles, London loaf sugar, by the loaf or hundred weight, Muscovado sugars, choice raisins by the keg or less quantity, best thin shell almonds, olives and capers, with sundry other articles in the grocery way; likewise Madeira, Lisbon and Fyall wines in half pipes and quarter casks, and claret in bottles.

As the articles of mustard and chocolate are manufactured by her, at those incomparable mustard and chocolate works at the Globe mill, on Germantown road, which her late husband went to a considerable expence in the erecting, and purchasing out Benjamin Jackson's part; and as she has a large quantity of choice clean mustard seed by her, and the singular advantage of being constantly supplied with that article, she flatters herself, that upon timely notice, she can supply any person with large quantities of the said articles of mustard and chocolate, either for exportation, or for retailing again, when a good allowance will be made, and the same put up in any kind of package as may best suit the buyer.

N.B. All the mustard put up in bottles, has the above stamp pasted on the bottles, and also the paper round each pound of chocolate has the said stamp thereon; and least any person may be discouraged from bringing small quantities of mustard seed to her, from the singular advantages already mentioned, she therefore informs those persons that may either have great or small quantities to dispose of, that she will always be ready to purchase of them, and give the highest price.

She Never Lost a Patient

Midwives were the doctors of choice for almost all colonial women in child-birth. Men were neither trained nor allowed to treat women's illnesses except in emergencies. The changeover to male practitioners began slowly in the middle of the century and then only among well-off urban dwellers or for special cases that seemed to require forceps or other invasive procedures. In newly settled villages, competent midwives were indispensable and highly respected.

From Zadock Thompson, *History of Vermont, Part III* (Burlington, Vt.: Chauncy Goodrich, 1842), p. 110.

❖

The settlement [of Marlborough, in southeastern Vermont] was commenced as early as the spring of 1763. . . . [Thomas] Whitmore . . . settled in the south part of the town, and [Abel] Stockwell . . . settled in the eastern border. These families spent nearly a year in town, and endured many hardships, without any knowledge of each other, each considering his own the only family in town. Whitmore brought his provisions from Deerfield, Mass., on his back, distance from 20 to 30 miles. Mrs. Whitmore spent most of the winter of 1765 alone, her husband being absent in the pursuit of his calling, as a tinker. Mrs. Whitmore was very useful to the settlers, both as a nurse and a midwife. She possessed a vigorous constitution, and frequently travelled through the woods on snow shoes, from one part of the town to another, both by night and day, to relieve the distressed. She lived to the advanced age of 87 years, officiated as midwife at more than 2,000 births and never lost a patient.

Rebekah Badger's Petition

The petition of Rebekah Badger is typical of the attempts of many needy widows in the eighteenth century to earn a living for themselves and their children. As land became more scarce and economic troubles increased among the poor, town officials were glad to grant tavern licenses and encourage women to sup-port themselves. Besides, keeping taverns and boardinghouses appeared to be a natural extension of women's normal housework and hospitality. The grammar of this petition indicates that someone wrote the document for Rebekah Badger.

From Miscellaneous Bound Collection, Petition of July 20, 1768. Reprinted by permission of the Massachusetts Historical Society, Boston.

❖

That it is now about eleven Years since you (I) Was Left a Widow by the death of her late Husband Benjamin Badger, and having struggled with many difficulties in the support of her Family till this time, she now finds her self So enfeebled by Sickness, that She cannot hope to maintain them any longer without keeping a Shop, which her Friends advise her immediately to open at her House in Prince Street leading to Charlestown Ferry, provided she can obtain the privilege of selling strong Drink to the Country People who come into Town by said Ferry—Your Petitioner begs leave to observe that she has had a Daughter at home confined by Sickness since January last, who before lived with Mr. William Greenleaff, but is now in the Opinion of Dr. Perkins in so weak a state as will forbid her ever working again for a livin, & must consequently become a Town Charge unless supported in the way proposed—She therefore humbly prays your Honnors to take her Case into your compassionate Consideration, when she hopes as well as prays that she may obtain the indulgence of a License to Retaile Rum & other Spirits at her said House, which indulgence has been frequently granted to the Widows of such Persons as have paid much less Taxes than had been paid by her late Husband for many Years together.

Procrastination Is Surely the Thief of Time

The sisters Abigail and Elizabeth Foote were the daughters of a farmer living in Colchester, Connecticut, during the time of the American Revolution. Like most of their contemporaries, the Foote sisters needed to perform manual labor constantly, both in their own households and by exchanging work with other families. They were skilled spinners, bakers, quilters, and seamstresses at an early age, often called on to perform these tasks for pay. Elizabeth, born on May 19, 1750, was almost twenty-five years old at the time she wrote this diary. Yet she was still learning "to read and cypher." Her diary is more concerned with local gossip and household events than with education or the exciting events surrounding the colonies' war for independence. Still, Elizabeth mentions making "biscuit" for local minutemen going off in April to fight the British "regulars" immediately after the Battles of Lexington and Concord. She adds that she is feeling "Nationly" when she contributes to boycotts of British goods by spinning her own yarn. Even though the sisters' work schedules were extremely demanding, Elizabeth had time for visiting, both to watch at a sickbed and to socialize with peers. Trying to count up the number of her hours devoted to housework dispels the notion that, for women at least, the period before industrialization could ever be called "the good old days."

From "Elizabeth Foote's Journal," 1775–76. Reprinted by permission of the Connecticut Historical Society, Hartford.

❖

January 1775

Sunday   1 – I stayed at home and learnt to read and cypher

M   2 – I went to school in the forenoon and stay'd at home with Molly and Nabby in the a'ternoon and at night Ellen and I wrote letters

T   3   I went to school & writ

W   4   I wash'd & went to school and cypher'd in Compound Multiplication.

T   5   I went to school and began Reduction

(Feb.)

S   18   I went to Mr. Otis's in the forenoon after some green Worsted to mend Mother's Ridinghood and Ellen's Pulleys and Shafts which I forgot yesterday and came home sick with Ague in my face

Sunday   19   I stayed at home my face sweld up and Dr Scot and Dr. Caples came to see me could not draw my teeth my face was so swell'd

M   20   I was sick with ague in my head

T   21   I got so well as to write this page of my journal but it makes me sweat like rain and so I believe I'll lie down

(Mar.)

M   6   I did housework and knit in the forenoon & finished my worsted stockings and in the afternoon went to see Elizabeth Wells

T   21   I spun lining [linen] and received a verry elegant piece of Writing from Mr Caples & at night Mrs Miriam Shailor paid us a short viset & Mr Foster, Israel Newton, Asa Bigelow, Enos Wells and David Wilds & Israel Foot was here & hannah & I worked on a Cheese Basket which we began last night but I forgot to write that

(Apr.)

T   13   I made a gown for Mrs Wells & about noon went to Mr Torers from thence to Mr otis's & hannah came home with me to work and we fixed our wheels to spin linnen & Mr Wells's ow'd me 2s 6d for my work being 1 s[hilling] per day

M   17   I fix'd our folks of[f] to Marlborough & after that clean'd up the house and made 2 X Gowns for Lieut Levy Wells's wife & at night hannah & I went over to Mr amos Wells's to see Liza & Rhoda

T 18   I rose before the sun & made apple pies & Dumplins for breakfast & Susa Toner & Sally Otis came back with us last night we meeting of them & so stay'd to breakfast but they said they would not if it had not raind. I did housework & spun a little and went to Mr Martin Kellog's & in the evening he came here Rhoda Wells being here.

T 20   I did House Work and made Gowns for Lieut Wells's wife at Night it rained and they stay'd all night   in the morning they pay'd me the money & so went home

F 21   in the morning we heard they had began to fight at Boston about noon there came an Indian and his wife (he said it was) here and I bought a snuff bottle of 'em with bread & cheese & cider   I did housework and Quill'd for Ellen as I have done all this week.

S 22   I just got the work done up and the Quills filld when Jonah came and telld me that I must go to making biscuit for to carry to fight the regulars which I did [illegible] and bak'd a pudding & you may guess at the rest & at night David came to take his farewell of Ellen, & hannah & nat & sarah Otis's all came over here a little while for hannah went home in the forenoon to help fix of[f] nat

T 27   I spun Linnen and went to Rhoda Chamberlains Funeral & made Margaret a short visit & went to Mr Breads after a Needle to knit my apron & to Mr demings after some Needles & to mr Pomroy's after some Goose Quills & to naby foots where I got a peony root & from thence to Mr Azariah Wrights & then home

Sunday 30   I went to town to Meeting & Mr Lovet Preached at noon I went to Esquire Foots & we had Pork & Beans for dinner & yesterday we heard Foster was in Hartford Jail & I'm of the opinion 'twould be as well for the publick if somebody else was with him, at Night I went to Mr Otis's to work & they ow'd me 2 Run of Linnen towards changing works. . . .

M 1   May   I spun linnen and did 50 knots and at night hannah & I went to Elias's to see Edmund & his wife & C

T 2   I spun above 2 runs of linnen Last night Sal had a spark [boyfriend] but she hid him

W 3   I spun linnen at Mr Otis's and at night came home & hannah with me & I went to Mr Martin Kellog's to get a horse to ride to town.

T	4	I did house work and went to get a horse to go to Town but was disappointed &c
F	5	the Girls all went to mr Wells's to Quilting but Ellen & I, I did house work and iron'd
T	11	they call it Election I carded Tow all day Nabby & Prude & Mercy spun & went to see Bethiah Kellogg....

(Oct.)

S	9	I began the border of my apron
W	18	I came home in the morning from Mr Otis's & at night Alice Welch came here to work & spun half a run of wool fillen & I carded
T	19	I carded & Alice spun 2 run
F	20	I carded & Alice spun 2 run
S	21	I carded & Alice spun 30 knots
Sunday	22	I went afoot to Meeting to Town & Israel caried Molly at night Alice had the stomach ach
M	23	I carded 2 pound of whole wool & went to Mr Otis's after the cards Alice went home & at night came & spun to take of 10 knots & felt Nationly into the bargain
T	24	I lay a bed till sun an hour high got up and carded a little while & then writ Journal for 5 [?] weeks back & Alice went home sick after she had spun 4 knots. Procrastination is surely the Thief of Time

121

We Pay Our Taxes

"She-merchants," as they called themselves, were found in all colonial towns, but those in New York seem to have been the first to complain publicly of neglect by the government. Pointing out that they were taxpayers, like everyone else who did business or owned any property, in 1733 the women wrote a letter to New York's feisty newspaper editor John Peter Zenger, demanding some government recognition of their services.

From *New York Journal,* January 21, 1733.

❖

Mr. Zenger,

We, the widdows of this city, have had a Meeting, and as our case is something Deplorable, we beg you will give it Place in your *Weekly Journal,* that we may be Relieved, it is as follows.

We are House keepers, Pay our Taxes, carry on Trade, and most of us are she Merchants, and as we in some measure contribute to the Support of Government, we ought to be Intituled to some of the Sweets of it; but we find ourselves entirely neglected, while the Husbands that live in our Neighborhood are daily invited to Dine at Court; we have the Vanity to think we can be full as Entertaining, and make as brave a Defence in Case of an Invasion and perhaps not turn Taile so soon as some of them.

MY TIME IS NOT MY OWN

15. A Frontier House

This frontier cabin in Virginia suggests sharp contrasts between the lives of frontier women and those of upper-class "genteel" women of more settled areas. On the frontier, families lived in small one- or two-room cabins, made with logs or planks and chinked with clay or flimsy mortar. A large fireplace at one end served all cooking and heating needs. Cleanliness and order were rudimentary; both privacy and "frivolous" possessions were usually unobtainable. Courtesy of Colonial Williamsburg Foundation, Williamsburg, Virginia. Photo by Thomas L. Williams.

16. The Adams Family Homestead

In contrast to the isolation of women in most southern homesteads, New Englanders were likely to live in small villages within walking distance of one another. An
early-nineteenth-century descendent drew the family home of Abigail and John
Adams in Braintree (now Quincy), Massachusetts. It shows the proximity of the
homes of family members to each other. From this farm, Abigail Adams wrote influential letters to her husband in Philadelphia during the early days of the American Revolution. Drawing by Eliza S. Quincy, 1822. Courtesy of the Massachusetts
Historical Society, Boston.

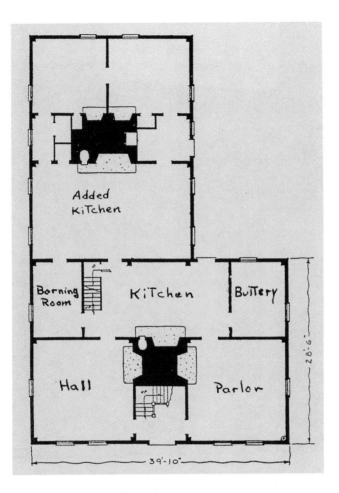

17. Floor Plan of a New England Farmhouse

The kitchen of a New England homestead was central to its design. A woman's domestic work was connected to all the ongoing activities of house and farm. Eggs, cheese, butter, and milk were produced or stored in her buttery. A bedroom next to the kitchen was her "borning room," and family and friends frequently gathered in the hall, or "keeping room." The hall served as a kitchen in smaller or earlier homes, but expanding families built one-story lean-tos across the back or full-sized ell-shaped wings for married children. Passageways and added barns, for convenience in cold northern winters, also joined male and female workspaces. Drawing by Richard Moynihan. Based on Russell Barnes house, Wallingford, Connecticut, built by Benjamin Lewis, ca. 1700. The house has been rebuilt in Stamford, Connecticut.

18. *Embroidered Bed Rug*

Women of all races and classes designed and made bed coverings that were original, beautiful, and useful. The rug pictured here was made by Grace Billings Noyes
in 1741 for Phebe and Ebenezer Billings. Note that the couple's initials and the
date appear near the center of the rug. The colors are tan and gold embroidered
on a deep-blue wool background; the design is entirely the artist's own. Bequest
of Henry B. Moseley, © Addison Gallery of American Art, Philips Academy,
Andover, Massachusetts. All rights reserved.

19. Crewelwork Bed Hangings

Mary Bulman, of York, Maine, embroidered this entire set of bed hangings around 1745. It is the only complete set of American origin to survive from that century. Crewelwork is a type of embroidery named for the worsted yarn (crewel) used to make the design. The valences are stitched with the verses of "Meditation in a Grove," by the English religious poet and hymnist Isaac Watts. Mary Bulman is thought to have designed and embroidered this set while her husband was serving as a surgeon in the army. Courtesy of Old York Historical Society, York, Maine.

20. *Isaac Royall and His Family*

Class divisions were widening in eighteenth-century American society. Isaac Royall was an extremely wealthy Medford, Massachusetts, merchant whose prosperity arose from the Orient trade suggested by the rug used as a table covering in this portrait. Isaac is shown as the dominant figure in a family that included his wife, sister, sister-in-law, and daughter. Family wealth made manual labor unnecessary for these women; the lavish fabrics of their garments were costly and certainly inappropriate for any such work. These women were not idle, however. They managed a large household staff (which included a few slaves), made or supervised all purchases, took charge of the education of children and servants, and worked with servants on the spinning and sewing. They also did all of the visiting and other social obligations essential to maintaining their status in society. Painting by Robert Feke, 1745. Courtesy of Harvard Law Art Collection, Cambridge, Massachusetts.

Changing Identities

WORK ROLES and educational opportunities changed dramatically for only a small proportion of women during the eighteenth century, but social and cultural expectations were in transition for all women during this time. Prescriptive documents—which offered advice, were written by men, and were popular reading among literate women—indicate differing male expectations for women of this period. Sermons and treatises by ministers like Cotton Mather extolled a model of uncomplaining piety for women, but Mather also admired strong-willed pious women and believed that because of their greater suffering in childbirth, women had more opportunities than men to gain salvation. George Savile, the marquis of Halifax, wrote a widely read though more secular manual entitled "Advice to a Daughter." Unlike Mather, he showed little respect for women and instead told his large female audience that they should accept dependent status and use their feminine wiles to make the best of their unenviable options.

Women, however, rarely accepted such advice without question. For example, in her journal, Esther Burr wrote of her "Smart Combat" with a young minister when he tried to dictate appropriate female conversation. Burr usually preferred trusting her own and her friends' opinions on weighty matters of morals rather than relying on male experts. Eliza Lucas Pinckney, who at eighteen was already managing her absent father's plantation, described a typical week of work in the eighteenth-century South, with no hint of subservience. She exercised her right of refusal when her father suggested suitors whom she could not "esteem." A healthy woman given to idleness was considered irreligious as well as lazy. It was an insult to be only "ladies of leisure." In one of her letters, Eliza Pinckney interpreted the writings of the philosopher John Locke and used his psychology to explain her own feelings; and the writer Annis Boudinot Stockton used poetic satire to refute male criticism of female minds.

In the middle of the eighteenth century, a series of religious revivals known as the Great Awakening shook the colonies and had a major impact on many women's lives. These evangelical revivals placed new emphasis on the emotional content of true piety. Since women had always been identified primarily with the "heart," many of them experienced these teachings as a validation of their special capacities. Indeed, female religious converts outnumbered males by about two to one. Some women took the Awakening as an opportunity to establish spiritual sisterhoods—groups of friends who gathered first for prayer and often later for charitable work and sometimes for political activities during the revolutionary era. The mother and the sisters of Jonathan Edwards, one of the most notable of the Awakening's preachers and of all American theologians, had been holding such religious gatherings since his childhood. Edwards claimed to have been profoundly influenced by their ideas and those of his wife.

Although certain theologians deplored the "excesses" of the Awakening, many women found in these revivals an opportunity to speak out and become leaders. For example, Sarah Osborn claimed a religious mandate to pray with others and became a well-known teacher of both young girls and slaves in Newport, Rhode Island. The Quaker preacher Sophia Hume felt called by God to preach a gospel of simplicity, modesty, and self-respect, directed especially at the frivolous life-styles of the decadent British and of some upper-class women in her home state of North Carolina. During the Great Awakening, pious women like Burr, Osborn, and Hume found both comfort and self-esteem through their religious beliefs. For them and countless other women and men, white and black, evangelical religion was also a challenge to established authority and customs. By becoming enthusiastic converts to the Baptist, Methodist, Quaker, or other Protestant denominations, many American women found a rationale for creative action as well as peace and hope in their hard lives.

Out of the religious sisterhoods of the Awakening came some of the earliest consciousness of female inequality. Esther Burr, among others, gained the confidence to speak her mind from female friends and from her pride in women's piety. So did her friend Annis Boudinot Stockton, who spoke out in print (at the urging of women friends) when she felt that her sex had been insulted. Though occasionally women like Sophia Hume became preachers themselves, women's protests were likely to be infrequent, private, and often couched in satire or uneasy humor. Instead of engaging in public protest, early-eighteenth-century women developed individual self-confidence and sisterly networks based on their piety and their productive capacities. Their shared awareness of female identity and women's disadvantages would continue to grow during the period of the American Revolution.

Poor Daughters of Eve

In the premodern era, a woman's life expectancy was precarious. People believed that women's "Peculiar Weaknesses" and the pains of childbirth were the legacy of Eve's original sin. It was God's punishment that women should suffer in childbirth, and it was laws of nature that required them to bear children. Cotton Mather (1663–1728), an influential Massachusetts clergyman who was also fascinated by science and medicine, wrote many treatises on disease. Here he notes that doctors usually had twice as many women patients because of the "Special Maladies" related to childbirth and the reproductive system. Mather completed this manuscript in 1724, but it was not published until the twentieth century.

Mather was an admirer of strong women, including those in his own family, so it is not surprising that he was genuinely concerned about female health. Some of his medicines—like "Preparations of Steel" for "Green Sickness," which we know today as iron-deficiency anemia—may have been helpful. He championed the new, unpopular practice of smallpox inoculation in a 1720 epidemic, even though religious opponents thought it contrary to natural law and God's will. But he considered it "unnatural" for women to complain about the duties of frequent childbearing. He stated that their suffering should make them more humble and pious. Most of his recipes for household medicines and his accompanying spiritual admonitions make one wonder how women survived at all.

From Cotton Mather, *The Angel of Bethesda*, ed. Gordon W. Jones (Barre, Mass.: American Antiquarian Society and Barre Publishers, 1972), pp. 233–48.

❖

THE Sex that is called, *The Weaker Vessel,* has not only a share with us, in the most of our Distempers, but also is liable to many that may be called, Its *Peculiar Weaknesses.* Many others besides *Varandaeus,* have written Large Treatises *of Womens Diseases.* I have read (in *Graunts* Observations,) That Physicians have *Two Women-Patients* to *One Man:* And it is only likely to be True. But inasmuch as both Sexes Dy in a more Equal Proportion, This is very much for the Honour of the Physicians, who cure them, or for the Dishonour of us *Men,* who Dy as much by our *Extravagancies* as *Women* do by their *Infirmities.*

Poor Daughters of *Eve,* Languishing under your *Special Maladies, Look back* on your *Mother,* the *Woman,* who *being Deceived,* was first *in the Transgression,* that has brought in upon us, *all our Maladies.* Beholding your *Affliction* and your *Misery,* in the midst of your *Lamentations* under it, *Remember that Wormwood and Gall* of the Forbidden Fruit; Lett your *Soul have them still in Remembrance, and be humbled in you.* Under all your Ails, think, *The Sin of my Mother, which is also my Sin, has brought all this upon me!*

But then, *Look up* to your SAVIOUR, who will one Day sett you free from all these *Maladies:* And in the mean time will make *all things work together for good unto you. . . .*

I. There is a Malady which is called, *The White Jaundice,* as well as, The *Green Sickness. . . .* It will be well, that they who are under the pernicious Obstructions, which their Viscid Blood suffers in this Distemper; feeling all their Powers Un-active, and Languishing; their Appetite impaired, and perhaps very Depraved and Vitious; their Breathing Difficult; especially upon any Motion; and their Bowels rumbling with Wind filling of them: would consider their Distemper as a Lively Picture, of *A Mind listless to all that is good.* Even such is the *Carnal Mind,* which is a continual Matter of Complaint, with such as *know themselves.*

Yea, *Hearken, O Daughter, and Consider!* And *beholding thy Natural Face in a glass;* beholding how pale, how wan, how like a ghost it looks; consider, the worse, and more ghastly Aspect of thy Soul in thy Sins.

But then, Lett the Terror of thy Condition drive thee to thy SAVIOUR, and make thee Cry out unto Him, *O Lord, Say unto my Soul, I am thy Salvation!*

The most famous and potent Remedies, in this Distemper, are Prepara-tions of *Steel.* Consult a Skilful and Faithful Physician, about the best Way of giving them.

Take a convenient Quantity of *Sheeps-Dung;* Make an Infusion of it in White Wine, or Cyder; Standing a Night in the Embers. Drink a Glassful of this, Twice a Day.

Elixir Proprietatis, taken in agreeable *Wine,* every morning, has been found a considerable Remedy.

For three mornings together, about the Time of Expectation, give a Dram, of the Galls and Livers of *Eels* dried and powdered.

The Tops of white *Hore-hound* infused in *White-Wine,* drunk for a few Days, has been found a Remarkable Remedy:—and a mighty Strengthener of the *Stomach,* and what will recover out of an *Ill Habit* of Body.

II. But then, there is a Distemper very Contrary unto this: Exemplified in the *Eighth* of *Luke* and the *Forty-third* [a continuous flow of blood].

In this Case, the first Thing to be done, is what was done by the Good Woman, who could have no Help from the *Physicians:* and who took a Course, to commemorate which, there has been in a Tradition of Antiquity, a *Statue* Erected for her. *Touch the Fringe of thy* SAVIOURS *Garment; Begging and Hoping for Healing Vertue to proceed from the* SON *of God cloathed in our Flesh.*

Now, try a Decoction, (or a *Tea*) of the Inner Rind of a White *Oak Bark.*

Two Ounces of an Infusion of *Hogs-dung* mixt with one Spoonful of *Nettle-Juice,* and given Morning and Evening, is a famous Remedy. Some add, wearing a Shift, which has been wett with a Strong Decoction of *Hogs-dung*.

A yett pleasanter Medicine, rarely fails. A Mixture of *Claret* Wine, and Old Conserve of *Roses;* and Old Marmalade of *Quinces*.

. . . Some Advice is now to be offered, unto a *Daughter* of *Eve,* . . . who Expects anon the Arrival of a Time, when her *Loins* will be *filled with Pain, Pangs will take hold on her, the Pangs of a Woman which travaileth.* Tis *Now.* Sure, if ever, a Time wherein it may be Expected, that she will hearken to the Counsils of God: *This,* if any, is the Time, wherein the Methods and Motions of Divine Grace, will *find her.* Certainly, she will be concerned that a *Sudden Destruction,* and a fearful and endless One, may not *come as Travail upon a Woman with Child,* when the *Time of Travail* shall come upon her. The Truth is, That tho' the Hazards and Hardships undergone by Travailing Women, be a considerable Article of the *Curse,* which the *Transgression* whereinto our *Mother* was *Deceived* has brought upon a Miserable World, yett our Great REDEEMER has procured this *Grace* from God unto the *Daughters of Zion,* that the *Curse* is turned into a *Blessing.* The Approach of their *Travails,* putts them upon those Exercises of PIETY, which render them truly *Blessed* ones; *Blessed* because their *Transgression is forgiven; Blessed* because they are *Turned from their Iniquities.* And hence in Part it may come to pass, that tho' thro' the Evident Providence of God, watching over Humane Affairs, there is pretty near an Equal Number of *Males* and *Females* that are Born into the World, the Number of the *Males* who are apparently *Pious,* and partakers of a *New Birth,* is not so great as that of the *Females.* Be sure, twil argue a wonderful Stupidity of Soul, and Obstinacy in Sin, if the View of an *Approaching Travail,* do not make the poor Women Serious, and Cause them seriously to Consider their Condition, and bring them into a Considerate, Sollicitous, Effectual Preparation for Eternity.

Ye Daughters of Marah; it is to be proposed unto you in the *first* place: That you do not indulge any indecent *Impatience* or *Discontent,* at the State, which you find ordered for you. Finding yourselves in a State of *Pregnancy,* Froward Pangs of *Dissatisfaction,* harboured and humoured in you, because you see that *in Sorrow you bring forth Children,* may displease Heaven, and bring yett more *Sorrow* upon you. How *Unnatural* will it look in you, to complain of a State, whereinto the *Laws of Nature* Established by God, have brought you! The *Will* of the Great God has been declared in those terms; *I will that the younger Women Marry, and bear Children.* When you find that a Conception has brought you into *Child-bearing* Circumstances, Lett your Submission to the *Will* of God cause you with all possible Resignation to say, *Great God, I am Thine; And I am willing to be all that thou wilt have me to be!* One principal End of *Marriage,* is thus far in an *Honourable Way* of being answered with you. Tis what was acknowledged a *Mercy* in *the old Time,* among the *Women who trusted in God,* and who counted themselves *mercifully visited of God,* when they had Conceived.

128

Advice to a Daughter

Patriarchal notions of decorum were important to wealthy southerners with aristocratic aspirations and close relations to British culture. One frequently reprinted advice book found in many eighteenth-century ladies' libraries was written by an English nobleman for his own daughter. It dictated female subservience by emphasizing the "Œconomy of the World" rather than the biblical order stressed by northern Puritans. The author's disapproval of wifely insubordination corresponded to his fear of "Unlimited Liberty" in politics. Emphasizing obedience and the legal impossibility of divorce, the marquis considered masculine deception inevitable and feminine guile a woman's only proper antidote. His definitions of sex roles remained part of American culture for generations.

From George Savile, Marquis of Halifax, *Miscellanies* (London: Printed for W. Rogers, Benj. Tooke, and D. Midwinter and T. Leigh, 1704), pp. 12–15, 16–17, 21–22, 31.

❖

That which challengeth the place in your Thoughts, is how to live with a *Husband* . . . the part of your *Life* upon which your *Happiness* most dependeth.

It is one of the *Disadvantages* belonging to your *Sex,* that young Women are seldom permitted to make their own *Choice;* their Friends' Care and Experience are thought safer Guides to them, than their own *Fancies;* and their *Modesty* often forbiddeth them to refuse when their Parents recommend, though their *inward Consent* may not entirely go along with it. In this case there remaineth nothing for them to do but to endeavour to make that easie which falleth to their *Lot,* and by a wise use of every thing they may dislike in a *Husband,* turn that by degrees to be very supportable, which, if neglected, might in time beget an *Aversion.*

You must first lay it down for a Foundation in general, That there is *Inequality* in the *Sexes,* and that for better Œconomy of the World, the *Men,* who were to be the Law givers, had the larger share of *Reason* bestow'd upon them; by which means your Sex is the better prepar'd for the *Compliance* that is necessary for the better performance of those *Duties* which seem to be most properly assign'd to it. This looks a little uncouthly at the first appearance; but upon Examination it will be found, that *Nature* is so far from being unjust to you, that she is partial on your side. She hath made you such large *Amends* by other Advantages, for the seeming *Injustice* of the first Distribution, that the Right of

Complaining is come over to our Sex. You have it in your power not only to free your selves, but to Subdue your Masters, and without violence throw both their *Natural* and *Legal Authority* at your Feet. We are made of differing *Tempers*, that our *Defects* may the better be mutually supplied: Your *Sex* wanteth our *Reason* for your *Conduct*, and our *Strength* for your *Protection: Ours* wanteth your *Gentleness* to soften, and to entertain us. The first part of our Life is a good deal   129
subjected to you in the *Nursery*, where you Reign without Competition, and by that means have the advantage of giving the first *Impressions*. Afterwards you have stronger influences, which, well manag'd, have more force in your behalf, than all our *Privileges* and *Jurisdictions* can pretend to have against you. You have more strength in your *Looks*, than we have in our *Laws*, and more power by your *Tears*, than we have by our *Arguments*.

It is true, that the *Laws* of *Marriage* run in a harsher stile towards your *Sex*. *Obey* is an ungenteel word, and less easie to be digested. . . .

But the Answer to it, in short is, That the *Institution* of *Marriage* is too sacred to admit a *Liberty* of *objecting* to it; That the supposition of yours being the weaker *Sex*, having without all doubt a good Foundation, maketh it reasonable to subject it to the *Masculine Dominion*; . . . it is safer some *Injustice* should be *conniv'd* at in a very few instances, than to break into an Establishment, upon which the Order of Humane Society doth so much depend.

You are therefore to make your best of what is *settled* by *Law* and *Custom*, and not vainly imagine, that it will be *changed* for your sake. But that you may not be discouraged, as if you lay under the weight of an *incurable Grievance*, you are to know, that by a *wise* and *dexterous* Conduct, it will be in your power to *relieve* your self from any thing that looketh like a disadvantage in it. For your better direction, I will give a hint of the most ordinary *Causes* of *Dissatisfaction* between Man and Wife, that you may be able by such a *Warning* to live so upon your *Guard*, that when you shall be married, you may know how to *cure* your Husband's *Mistakes*, and to *prevent* your own.

First then, you are to consider, you live in a time which hath rendred some kind of Frailties so habitual, that they lay claim to large *Grains* of *Allowance*. The World in this is somewhat unequal, and our Sex seemeth to play the *Tyrant*, in distinguishing *partially* for our selves, by making that in the utmost degree *Criminal* in the *Woman*, which in a *Man* passeth under a much *gentler Censure*. The Root and Excuse of this Injustice is the *Preservation* of Families from any Mixture that may bring a Blemish to them: And whilst the *Point of Honour* continues to be so plac'd, it seems unavoidable to give your *Sex* the greater share of the Penalty. But if in this it lieth under any *Disadvantage*, you are more than recompens'd; by having the *Honour* of *Families* in your keeping. . . . This Power the World hath lodg'd in you can hardly fail to restrain the Severity of an *ill* Husband, and to improve the Kindness and Esteem of a *good* one. This being so, remember, That next to the danger of *committing* the Fault your self, the greatest is that of *seeing* it in your *Husband*. Do not seem to look or hear that way. . . . Modesty no less than Prudence ought to restrain her; since such an undecent Complaint makes a *Wife* much more Ridiculous, than the Injury that provoketh her to it. But it is yet worse, and more unskilful, to *blaze* it in the World, expecting it should rise up in Arms to take her part: Whereas she will find, it can have no other Effect, than that she will be served up in all Companies, as the *reigning Jest* at that time. . . . Be assur'd, that in these Cases your *Discretion* and *Silence* will be the most *prevailing Reproof*. . . . Besides, it will naturally make him more *yielding* in other things: And whether it be to *cover* or *redeem* his *Offense* you may have the good Effect of it whilst it lasteth, . . . such a Behavior at last will intirely convert him. There is nothing so glorious to a *Wife*, as a Victory so gain'd: A Man so reclaim'd, is for ever after subjected to her *Vertue;* and her *bearing* for a time, is more than rewarded by a Triumph that will continue as long as her Life. . . . [Other examples follow of male brutality, infidelity, drunkenness, stupidity, and appropriate wifely endurance.]

I am tempted to say . . . That a *Wife* is to thank God her *Husband* hath *Faults*. . . . The *Faults* and *Passions* of *Husbands* bring them down to you, and make them content to live upon less unequal Terms, than Faultless Men would be willing to stoop to; so haughty is Mankind till humbled by common Weaknesses and Defects, which in our corrupted State contribute more towards the reconciling us one to another, than all the *Precepts* of the *Philosophers* and *Divines*. So that where the *Errors* of our *Nature* make amends for the *Disadvantages* of yours, it is more your part to make use of the *Benefit*, than to quarrel at the *Fault*. . . .

The last supposition I will make is, That your *Husband* should be *weak* and *incompetent* to make use of the Privileges that belong to him; . . . such a one leaveth room for a great many Objections; but God Almighty seldom sendeth a *Grievance* without a *Remedy*, or at least such a Mitigation as taketh away a great part of the sting, and the smart of it. . . . That a *Wife* very often maketh the better Figure, for her *Husbands* making no great one. . . . If you will be more ashamed in some Cases, of such a *Husband*, you will be less afraid than you would perhaps be of a wise one; his *Unseasonable Weakness*, may no doubt sometimes grieve you, but then set against this, that it giveth you the *Dominion*, if you will make the right use of it; it is next to his being dead, in which case the Wife hath right to Administer; therefore be sure, if you have such an Ideot, that none, except your self, may have the benefit of the forfeiture: Such a Fool is a dangerous Beast, if others have the keeping of him; and you must be very dextrous, if when your *Husband* shall resolve to be an *Ass,* you do not take care he may be *your Ass*. . . . In short, the surest and the most approved method will be to do like a wise *Minister* to an easy *Prince;* first give him the Orders you afterwards receive from him. . . .

With all this, that which you are to pray for, is a *Wise Husband*, one that by knowing how to be a *Master,* for that very reason will not let you feel the weight of it; one whose Authority is so soften'd by his Kindness, that it giveth you ease without abridging your *Liberty;* one that will return so much tenderness for your *Just Esteem* of him, that you will never want *power,* though you will seldom care to use it. Such a *Husband* is as much above all the other Kinds of them, as a *rational Subjection* to a Prince, great in himself, is to be preferr'd before the disquiet and uneasiness of *Unlimited Liberty.*

131

How I Triffle Away My Time

The Englishwoman Eliza Lucas Pinckney (1722–93) was only seventeen when her father sent his family to South Carolina while he remained as lieutenant governor of Antigua in the West Indies. Because her mother was seriously ill, Eliza was designated the manager of three large plantations, regularly reporting to her father about her exports, imports, and agricultural experiments. The New World environment also gave her the freedom to insist on her own choice of husband, as she did with much diplomacy in the following letter to her father. Some years later she married the widower Charles Pinckney, had four children in five years, was widowed at thirty-six, and then took over her husband's business. It is probably no accident that in the period of the American Revolution, two of the South's foremost statesmen were her sons.

For Eliza's sickly mother, the plantation may have been a kind of exile, but for her daughter, it represented opportunity. Well-educated and independent, Eliza wrote the following letters to her English friends Madam Boddicott and Miss Bartlett; she said that she missed the amenities of England but that her "fertile brain at schemeing" thrived on new responsibilities, extensive reading, and the companionship of Charleston friends. For example, Eliza Lucas's experiments in growing indigo established one of South Carolina's major export industries. At the same time, she was reading the contemporary philosopher John Locke to develop her intellect. In accord with ladylike expectations, however, she insisted that she did not wish to "appear learned" and that she "reckoned . . . expence and the prophets [profits]" only as an "innocent and useful amusement."

From Elise Pinckney and Marvin R. Zahniser, eds., *The Letterbook of Eliza Lucas Pinckney, 1739–1762* (Chapel Hill: University of North Carolina Press, 1972), pp. 5–8, 19, 34–35. Copyright © 1972 by the University of North Carolina Press. Used by permission of the publisher.

❖

Hond. Sir. [her father]   1740

Your letter . . . was an additional proof of that paternal tenderness which I have always Experienced from the most Indulgent of Parents . . . , and the subject of it is of the utmost importance to my peace and happiness.

As you propose Mr. L. to me I am sorry I can't have Sentiments favourable enough of him to take time to think on the Subject, . . . so much Generosity on your part claims all my Obedience, but as I know 'tis my happiness you consult, must beg the favour of you to pay my thanks to the old Gentleman for his Generosity and favourable sentiments of me and let him know my thoughts on the affair in such civil terms as you know much better than any I can dictate; and beg leave to say to you that the riches of Peru and Chili if he had them put together could not purchase a sufficient Esteem for him to make him my husband.

As to the other gentleman you mention . . . , I have so slight a knowledge of him I can form no judgment of him, and a Case of such consiquence requires the Nicest distinction of humours and Sentiments. But give me leave to assure you, my dear Sir, that a single life is my only Choice and if it were not, as I am yet but Eighteen, hope you will [put] aside the thoughts of my marrying yet these 2 or 3 years at least.

. . . I hope heaven will always direct me that I may never disapoint you; and . . . I am well aware you would not . . . make me a Sacrifice to Wealth, and I am as certain I would indulge no passion that had not your aprobation, as I truly am Dr. Sir, Your most dutiful & affecte. Daughter.

Dear Madam [Boddicott]   May the 2nd [1740]

I flatter myself it will be a satisfaction to you to hear I like this part of the world, as my lott has fallen here—which I really do. I prefer England to it, 'tis true, but think Carolina preferable to the West Indias, and was my Papa here I should be very happy.

We have a very good acquaintance from whom we have received much friendship and Civility. Charles Town, the principal one in this province, is a polite, agreeable place. The people live very Gentile and very much in the English taste. The Country is in General fertile and abounds with Venison and wild fowl; the Venison is much higher flavoured than in England but 'tis seldom fatt.

My Papa and Mama's great indulgence to me leaves it to me to choose our place of residence either in town or Country, but I think it more prudent as well as most agreeable to my Mama and self to be in the Country during my Father's absence. We are 17 mile by land and 6 by water from Charles Town—where we have about 6 agreeable families around us with whom we live in great harmony.

I have the business of 3 plantations to transact, which requires much writing and more business and fatigue of other sorts than you can imagine. But least you should imagine it too burthensom to a girl at my early time of life, give me leave to answer you: I assure you I think myself happy that I can be useful to so good a father, and by rising very early I find I can go through much business. But least you should think I shall be quite moaped with this way of life I am to inform you there is two worthy Ladies in Charles Town, Mrs. Pinckney and Mrs. Cleland, who are partial enough to me to be always pleased to have me with them, and insist upon my making their houses my home when in town and press me to relax a little much oftener than 'tis in my honor to accept of their obliging intreaties. But I some times am with one or the other for 3 weeks or a month at a time, and then enjoy all the pleasures Charles Town affords, but nothing gives me more than subscribing my self

> Dear Madam,
> Yr. most affectionet and
> most obliged humble Servt.
> Eliza. Lucas

Dear Madam [Pinckney]   [1741]

At my return hither everything appeared gloomy and lonesome. I began to consider what alteration there was in this place that used so agreeably to sooth my (for some time past) pensive humour, and made me indiferent to every thing the gay world could boast; but found the change not in the place but in my self, and it doubtless proceeded from that giddy gayety and want of reflection which I contracted when in town; and I was forced to consult Mr. Lock over and over to see wherein personal Identity consisted and if I was the very same self. I don't affect to appear learned by quoting Mr. Lock, but would let you see what regard I pay to Mr. Pinckney's recommendation of Authors—and, in truth, I understand enough of him to be quite charmed. I recon it will take me five months reading before I have done with him.

I am now returned to my former Gravity and love of solitude and hope you won't conclude me out of my Witts because I am not always gay. I, you know, am not a proper judge in my own Case. I flatter my self you will be favourable in your oppinion of me—tho' 'tis become so much the fashion to say every body that is grave is religiously mad. But be it as it will, those unhappy people have some times intervals, and you may be assured I am in my right Sences. . . .

[ca. April 1742]

Why, my dear Miss B[artlett], will you so often repeat your desire to know how I triffle away my time in our retirement in my fathers absence. Could it afford you advantage or pleasure I should not have hesitated, but as you can expect neither from it I would have been excused; however, to show you my readiness in obeying your commands, here it is.

In general then I rise at five o'Clock in the morning, read till Seven, then take a walk in the garden or field, see that the Servants are at their respective business, then to breakfast. The first hour after breakfast is spent at my musick, the next is constantly employed in recolecting something I have learned least for want of practise it should be quite lost, such as French and short hand. After that I devote the rest of the time till I dress for dinner to our little Polly and two black girls who I teach to read, and if I have my papa's approbation (my Mamas I have got) I intend [them] for school mistres's for the rest of the Negroe children—another scheme you see. But to proceed, the first hour after dinner as the first after breakfast at musick, the rest of the afternoon in Needle work till candle light, and from that time to bed time read or write. 'Tis the fashion here to carry our work abroad with us so that having company, without they are great strangers, is no interruption to that affair; but I have particular matters for particular days, which is an interruption to mine. Mondays my musick Master is here. Tuesdays my friend Mrs. Chardon (about 3 mile distant) and I are constantly engaged to each other, she at our house one Tuesday—I at hers the next and this is one of the happiest days I spend at Woppoe. Thursday the whole day except what the necessary affairs of the family take up is spent in writing, either on the business of the plantations, or letters to my friends. Every other Fryday, if no company, we go a vizeting so that I go abroad once a week and no oftener.

Now you may form some judgment what time I can have to work my lappets [needlework streamers for fashionable eighteenth-century headdresses]. I own I never go to them with a quite easey conscience as I know my father has an aversion to my employing my time in that boreing work, but they are begun and must be finished. I hate to undertake any thing and not go thro' with it; but by way of relaxation from the other I have begun a peice of work of a quicker sort which requires nither Eyes nor genius—at least not very good ones. Would you ever guess it to be a shrimp nett? For so it is.

O! I had like to forgot the last thing I have done a great while. I have planted a large figg orchard with design to dry and export them. I have reckoned my expence and the prophets [profits] to arise from these figgs, but was I to tell you how great an Estate I am to make this way, and how 'tis to be laid out you would think me far gone in romance. Your good Uncle I know has long thought I have a fertile brain at schemeing. I only confirm him in his opinion; but I own I love the vegitable world extremly. I think it an innocent and useful amusement. Pray tell him, if he laughs much at my project, I never intend to have my hand in a silver mine and he will understand as well as you what I mean.

Letters to a Friend

Esther Edwards Burr (1732–58) was the daughter of the great revivalist-theologian Jonathan Edwards and Sarah Pierpoint Edwards. She was the wife of the second president of Princeton University, Aaron Burr, and the mother of Aaron Burr, America's third vice-president. These selections are part of a three-year letter-journal that she wrote to her close friend Sarah Prince, in Boston.

Like other literate eighteenth-century women, Esther Burr was fond of reading pious and moral literature. Because Samuel Richardson's novels *Pamela* (1740) and *Clarissa* (1748) were considered edifying tales of middle-class morality, they were allowable reading and quite popular among literate American women. What is interesting about Burr's interpretation of the novel is her independent judgment about whether the serving girl Pamela's virtue was rewarded by marriage to Mr. B, who acted like a "libertine" throughout the book. She accuses "Mr. Fielding" (whom she has momentarily confused with Richardson) of degrading her sex by suggesting that marriage to this upper-class profligate was a satisfactory solution to Pamela's problems.

In the second group of letters, starting with the August 23 entry, Esther, who had been married for four years, responds to Sarah's dilemmas about an ongoing courtship. This interchange affirms the right of women to choose their spouses; it also suggests the tremendous importance placed on this decision, which, after all, governed a woman's companionship, her social and economic status, and her geographical location for the rest of her life. The devout Sarah Prince was apparently worried about her suitor's lack of religious commitment, despite her love for him. She was twenty-seven when these letters were written, so her mature age may have been a factor in her extremely independent decision-making about marriage. She did marry, probably this suitor, in 1759.

The final letter recounts Esther Burr's defense of female friendship against criticism by the Princeton tutor John Ewing. Eighteenth-century philosophers claimed that friendship, defined as the highest form of intellectual endeavor, was possible only among men because women were not sufficiently rational. The Great Awakening modified this belief by suggesting that emotion is an appropriate component of any loving Christian relationship. Burr thus defends women's capacity for friendship based in part on their supposedly more emotional nature. This spirited argument and her journal itself were conscious attempts to assert the equality and intelligence of women.

From Carol F. Karlsen and Laurie Crumpacker, ed., *The Journal of Esther*

Edwards Burr, 1754–57 (New Haven: Yale University Press, 1984), pp. 98–99, 102, 105, 107–8, 145, 192–95, 231–33, 257. Copyright © 1984 by Yale University.

❖

[March 10, 1755]
Monday P.M.

136   Phoo, folks always coming. Eve. I have borrowed Pamelia and am reading it now. I fancy I shan't like it so well as I did Clarissa, but prejudice must have its weight. I remember you said that in your opinnion it did not equel her. Your judgment my dear has a very great influence on mine. Nay I would venture to report that such a Book surpast such an one, if you said so, if I had never laid my Eyes on 'em—but forall I intend not to be so complaisant but I will have a judgment of my own. Tis quite late. May guardian angels protect my dear friend this night.

[March 11, 1755]
Teusday P.M.

. . . Eve. Pray my deer how could Pamela forgive Mr. B all his Devilish conduct so as to consent to marry him? Sertainly this does not well agree with so much virtue and piety. Nay I think it a very great defect in the performance, and then is'n't it seting up Riches and honnour as the great essentials of happyness in a married state? Perhaps I am two rash in my judgment for I have not read it half out tho' I have enough to see the Devil in the Man.

[March 12, 1755]
Wednesday P.M.

. . . Eve. I am quite angry with Mr. Fielding. He has degraded our sex most horridly, to go and represent such virtue as Pamela, falling in love with Mr. B in the midst of such foul and abominable actions. I could never pardon him if he had not made it up in Clarissia I guss he found his mistake, so took care to mend the first opportunity. . . .

[March 20, 1755]
Thursday. P.M.

. . . I think there is some excelent observations on the duties of the Married state in *Pamela*. I shant repent my pains I guss.

[April 2, 1755]
Wednsday A.M.

. . . I am highly pleased with some of *Pamela*'s remarks on Married life, as well as her Conduct in it—She was more than Woman—An *Angel imbodied*. . . .

[April 8, 1755]
Teusday.

. . . To day I have [been] reading an account of Mr. B.s going after the *Coun[tess]* of _____ . This appears very strange to me considering the [title] of the Book, which is, *Virtue rewarded*—I could but ju[st] stomach to allow it that title before, for he was a sad fello[w] to be sure, had one Child, *bastard,* and did his indevour to get many more as it seems by *Lady Davers,* and his own confession two—but I dont know—I have a poor judgme[n]t of my own. I wish you would be so good as to let me ha[ve] your thoughts on this affair, and I should be glad if it is not two much trouble on the whole History. I know you have made every usefull remark that could be made—there is certainly many excellent observations and rules laid down [*so*] that I shall never regret my pains—you need not wonder if I write a little upon the scrawl for I have Sally in my Lap— in my humble opinion *Riches,* and *honour,* are set up two much—can Money reward virtue? And besides Mr Bs being a *libertine* he was a *dreadful high-spirited Man, impatient of contradiction* as he says of himself—*Pamela* had a task of it, with all Mr Bs good qual[i]ties. She was as much affraid of him as of a Lyon—if the author had [le]ft it to me to have intitled the Books, I think I should hav[e] chose Virtue tryed, instead of rewarded—in that af[fair] of the Countess he was vastly to blame, and would no dou[bt] have kept with her some part of his time at least, as his [wife?] if he had not been prevented just when he was. . . .

[April 11, 1755]
Fryday [A.]M.

Well—*Pamelas* virtue is *rewarded* at last, Mr B. is become a good Man. I confess I had waited for this *reward* 'till I was quite discouraged, and after that *black* affair of the Countess I wholy dispared of a *reward* in this World—but I was to find a little fault for-all—Might not Mr *Fielding* as well have spared himself the pains of this last tryal? Was not her virtue thoroughly tryed before? . . .

[August 23, 1755]
Saturday Morn.

I shall be obliged to send this paquet before I can say all I want to say in reply to your last—but I'll say as much as I can and be as short as I can not from choice but of nesesity because of Mr Burrs Illness—Mr Burr desires me to add for him that he thinks a sertain person will make a kind and affectionate husband. . . .

You charge me with being two severe on a sertain Gentleman—but pray recollect what you have said your self and you'll find you have been much before me—I thought I might follow an example set me by such a Lady as Miss Prince. To be sure I did not expect a reproof from her for it—but when persons get in Love, they themselves may talk against the object beloved as much as they pleas, but if any body elce says a Naughty word, but only in jest, tis Treason. . . .

These poor fettered folks [married people] you seem to pity so much I look upon as the happest part of the world, and if I was to wish you any ill for your severity on us, it should be that you might never be married, but such a friend as I am cant wish you a very great ill nor any ill—We are not obliged to you for your seeming Pity, for in the first place we dont want it, and in the second place you dont pity us, but Envy us for our happy lot. *Say* dont you?

The Old saying is, you may know who is shot by their fluttering. Now nothing is more common than for persons to run out against the married state, and say they never intend to be married, etc. when they are just upon the point of determining to except of the first offer. Hant you observed·this? . . .

[April 14, 1756]
Wednsday Eve

. . . —If you dont come this spring I shall dispare of ever seeing you in these parts, for if you M-a-r-r-y as I think you will before a nother spring I suppose we shall see no more of you in our world—Well tis a mighty strang piece of conduct of that sertain Gentleman—I wonder what ails him—I surspect he is bashfull. You must e'ne do the business for him—Tackle up your Chair and go a Courting, and bring the matter to an issue, [so] that a body may know what to depend on—Its vastly uncomfortable to be hung up between the Heavens and Earth as it were Gibbeted—if Mr Burr goes to Boston he will do something in the affair you may be sertain, for you know he loves to be poking about matches. . . .

[April 16, 1756]
Fryday Morn

. . . 11.o'Clock received No. 19 by Mrs Potter—I have read the Private papers and hant patience to read any more till I vent a litle by writing—I never was so near being angry at you in my life. If you was her[e] I should sertainly Cuff you—Indeed my dear I think you are a little Proud—I have incouraged you in it two under a notion of *nobleness of mind, and greatness of soul* but to be plain you have carried matter of this sort two far. *You have stood upon points two much, and two long,* and I should have told you so before if I knew as much as I do now. (You must pardon my severity for I am two warm about it but I cant bare to see you *murder your self.* . . .) Why you would not have the Man act like a fool would you? Well why will you oblige him to either become a fool or give up the affair, and without desighn in you two for you dont chuse nither—I am almost two vext to write—I wonder in the name of honesty what business you had to run a way time after time when you knew he was a coming—You may repent it when it is two late—for I dont know of such another match on all accounts not on all our shore.

139

You should consider my dear that he does not, nor cant know the reasons of your conduct—tis most likly that he thinks that you dislike him, or elce that you are a Mortal proud creture, which must sink you in his opinnion, and may lay a foundation for unhapyness all your days after Marriage for my dear no man likes a woman the better for being shy when she means the very thing she pretends to be shy off. . . .

[October 17, 1756]
Sabbath P.M. Oct. 17

. . . I am so distressed for you in your perplexed situation that I cant tarry till the Sabbath is over before I tell you I Pity you from the Bottom of my soul, and have after my poor cold manner many times this day prayed for you, that you may be Directed, that you may be inclined to do what shall be most for the glory of God and your own good and comfort boath for time and Eternity—Once I was the subject of much such perplexities. One case in petecular was very similar to yours. Then I have reason to think God was my director and trust he will be yours—dont sink. All is Wisely Ordered and best—I doubt not but duty will be made plain—When did you ever commit any case to the Lord but he directed your paths. . . .

[October 21, 1756]
Thursday P.M.

3rd Objection in my opinnion has more weight in it than all the rest—that you dont think you can esteem him enough—if you cant, tis sufficient objection—for *Let the Wife see that she Reverence her Husband*—if you cant esteem you cant reverence—so there it must end—but I immagine you are mistaken. You cant help esteeming a person of so many good quallifycations as are under the head of Inducements. . . . Objection 4th—that you cant expect relegious conversation from him—*How knowest thou O Woman but thou mayest gain thy*

Husband. I think there is a good deal of reason to hope it as he has such a desire to have a religious Wife.

I know it to be the opinnion of my Honored Parents that a person aught not to make concience of this matter. They said that some other things were more necessary to happyness in a Married state, (which things you have mentioned of him) but when Relegion meets those other things it Crowns all—tis proporly the Crown, but my dear this alone will not do—look around, you will soon see that tis not every good Man that you could live happily with in that state. . . .

[October 23, 1756]
Saturday

Upon the Whole—The important point must turn here. If upon mature deliberation and serious consideration you find you cant think of spending your days with that Gentleman with Complaciency and delight, *say No*—but if on the contarary, I think you may venture to answer in the affermative—This must turn the point so you only can determine for your self. . . .

[April 12, 1757]
Teusday A. M. 10 O'Clock

I have had a Smart Combat with Mr. Ewing about our Sex—he is a man of good parts & Lerning but has mean thoughts of Women—he began the dispute in this Manner, Speaking of Miss Boudinot I Said She was a Sociable friendly creture, a Gentleman Seting by joined with me, but Mr. Ewing Says—*She and the Stocktons are full of talk about Friendship and society and such stuff—and made up a Mouth as if much disgusted*—I asked what he would have 'em talk about—whether he chose they should talk about fashions & dress—*he said things that they understood. He did not think women knew what Friendship was. They were hardly capable of anything so cool & rational as friendship*—(My Tongue You know hangs prety loose, thoughts Crouded in—so I sputtered away for dear life.) You may Guss what a large field this speach opened for me—I retorted several severe things upon him before he had time to speak again. He Blushed and seemed confused. The Gentleman Seting by said little but when [he] did speak it was to my purpose and we carried on the dispute for an hour—I talked him quite silent. He got up and said your Servant and went off—I dont know that ever I met with one that was so openly and fully in Mr. Pope's sordid scheam—One of the last things that he said was that he never in all his life knew or heard of a woman that had a little more lerning than [common?] but it made her proud to such a degree that she was disgusfull [to] all her acquaintance.

On the Death of a Sister

These two letters illustrate mid-century evangelical women's attitudes about death. Sarah Prince (1728–1771) is responding to the death of her dear friend Esther Burr (whose letters appear above). In her eulogy, she suggests the new definitions of ideal womanhood growing out of the Great Awakening, and she also describes the strong bonds of sisterhood that had united her with her friend. Like Sarah Parsons, whose letter follows, she seeks resignation to God's will.

Sarah Parsons was Esther Burr's real sister, and in her letter to another sister she laments not only Esther's death but also that of their father, Jonathan Edwards, who had died a month before. "Poor Lucy" is yet another sister, and the "Dear Little babes" are Esther's children, four-year-old Sally and two-year-old Aaron. She closes with the wish that she and her sister can learn from their grief ("improve the same") and be better prepared for their own deaths.

From "Journal of Meditations of Sarah Prince" (1743–1764), courtesy of the Trustees of the Boston Public Library; letter of Sarah Edwards Parsons to Mary Edwards Dwight, April 18, 1758, Franklin Trask Library, Andover Newton Theological School, Andover, Massachusetts.

❖

April 21, 1758

"GOD will have no Rival in the heart which he sanctifies for himself."

God in Holy but awfull severity has Again struck at one of My Principle springs of Earthly Comfort. In taking from me the Beloved of my heart, my dearest Friend Mrs Burr—This is the heaviest Affliction next to the Death of My dear Sister *Mercy* I ever met with. My whole Prospects in this World are now Changed. My whole dependance for Comfort in this World gone: she was dear to me as the Apple of my Eye—she knew and felt all my Griefs. She laid out herself for my good and was ever assidously studying it. The God of Nature had furnished her with all that I desir'd in a Friend—her Natural Powers were superior to most Women, her knowledge was extensive of Men and Things, her Accomplishments fine—her Prudence forethought and sagacity wonderfull— her Modesty rare—In Friendly Quallity none Exceeded her—she was made for a Refin'd Friend. How Faithfull? how sincere? how Open hearted? how Tender how carefull how disinterested—And *she was mine!* O the tenderness which tied our hearts!—O the Comfort I have Enjoy'd in her for allmost 7 years[!] O the Pleasant days and nights we have spent in opening our whole souls and pouring them into Each others breasts! O the dear Prudent Advice she gave me under all my difficulties—O the Pleasure of seeing hearing loving Writing Conversing thinking we took in Each other. O the Lovely Pattern she set me—The Grace appearing in her Exalted her above all—a bright Example of Personal and Relative social and Divine Duties—A Dutifull Affectionate Respectfull Obedient Tender Daughter and Wife—The Tender yet discreet and wise Mother and Mistress— The every way loving and lovely Sister and Friend—A Pattern of Meekness Patience and submission under heavy trials—The Mortified Humble self denied lively Christian—Generous Affable Courteous and Kind to all—But—she is gone! Fled this World forever. Tired, she longed for rest—dead to this world, she Prayed and panted and Agonised for a Better and with her went allmost *the All* in which I had sum'd up my Earthly Good! O Painfull seperation! O Desolate World, how Barren art thou *now to me!* A Land of Darkness and a vale of Tears and no (...) lightsome ray is left me—My Earthly joy is gone! Not only so but My God hides his Face! Can't see Love in this dispensation! All seems anger yea Wrath to me! What shall I do. Whither shall I turn, Not to Creatures for there is none to comfort me! And I do not find Comfort from God—O Wretched Me. God Points his Arrows at me and I'm ready to say My Way is hid from the Lord. My judgement is passed over from My God and that he has set me as a Mark for his Arrows! I'm ready to sink and I cant find my wonted Comfort! O how shall I drag thro' Life—If God supports not, I shall inevitably sink. (...) A Great part of my atachment to this World is gone. O! were I ready I wou'd gladly wellcome the kind summons to follow my dear Beloved into the Valley of DEATH. Had I the Evidence I want of a title to Glory, joyfully wou'd quit Earth and all that Earthly minds admire. I want to lay low at the Foot of God and resign to him. I chuse to live at loose from the World, and live only on him and have done with Idols and get prepared for Heaven and get more intimate and [Dare?] Acquaintance with Him, the all *in all.* Lord Grant these Mercies for thy Sons sake. AMEN.

❖

Stockbridge April 18th 1758

Dr Sister

I received your kind Letter by my Husband for which return you my hearty thanks—but what or how to write or speak I know not. Last Saturday we had another Expre[ss] from Princeton which brought us the sorrowful Tidings that Dear Sister Burr was dead and buried yesterday week and no doubt have join'd the Company of our dear dear Friends lately deceased (...) who have all got safe home to their heavenly Fathers House, are *come to the New Jerusalem the City of the living God and to innummerable Company of Angels, and to Jesus the Mediator of the new Covenant and to God the judge of all, and to the spirits of just Men made perfect*—O how loud the call to us that survive (...) of this Family, be ye also ready.

How much does it concern [us] to be as servants with their Loins girt and their Lamps trimmed and burning waiting for the coming of their Lord, now we are so plainly taught not only in Gods word but by his Providence, that we know not what hour our Lord will come—God is now Chastizing us. May he not only Correct but teach us what he would have [us] to do. We are now loudly called upon to search our hearts and try our ways and turn our feet into God['s] tes- timonies—Sister I hope you are in a much better [way] under these tryals than I am. I find I'm far from being in such a tender Humble frame as I ought to be in—It is what has lain with great weight on my Heart and has ever since the Moment I heard of my Fathers death that Gods dealings might be sanctified. Oh! my heart [trem]bles at the thought of disposing [these Chastizings] of the Lord. God grant these Corrections may be in Covenant love and faithfullness.

The residue of the spirit is with God. May we all cry mightily that his gracious Presence and [ ] may not be buried with our Friends, but that he would grant that a double portion of the spirit of Christ that was in them might rest on us but in order to [do] this as you observe we had need to [give] our selves to every duty.

My Brother Timo' set out this Day from here to go to Princeton. I cant but feel much Concerned about him but twas judg[ed] by all his call was clear— poor Lucy, Im grievd for her. May she get much spiritual liquor in this Furnace of affliction—and oh the Dear Little babes, my heart overflows with Pity and Compassion towards them. Timo expects to bring them up with him but is not Certain. Sister Burr made a Will but we dont know the Contents as to that Matter fully—Mr Cummins was to Preach her Funeral Sermon upon her desire— she died of an acute Feavour, by Lucys account was much like the Feavour that Carried my Sister Jerusha out of the World, lived but just a Week after she was taken. Her illness appeared not at all threatening till Tuesday (she was taken on Friday Night). She was then taken with a violent Headake and soon delirious and so remained till she died on Friday the 7 Instant—Oh how fast has she been ripening for that world she is now gone. What amercy that God should take those out of [ ] that were ready to die and is warning us hereby and yet giving further opportunity to prepare. May we have hearts to improve the same.

My Mother and Sisters and Brothers join with me in kind [love] to you and Brother and your Little ones.

From your very affectionate and Sympathizing Sister

Sarah Parsons

She Was Regarded with Respect

Most of women's public activities remained undocumented in the records kept by colonial men, unless women were taken to court for charges of misbehavior, malicious gossip, or suspected witchcraft. But occasional glimpses show a practice that was not uncommon—women meeting regularly to study the Bible and other books. Such meetings enabled women to keep informed about community affairs and mutual needs, as well as about intellectual and religious matters. The widow Esther Stoddard Edwards, grandmother of Esther Burr and mother of the theologian Jonathan Edwards, lived in East Windsor in the mid-eighteenth century and was well remembered by those who attended her meetings.

From Sereno E. Dwight, "Life of President Edwards," in *The Works of President Edwards,* vol. 1 (New York: S. Converse, 1829), p. 18.

❖

Mrs. Edwards was always fond of books, and discovered a very extensive acquaintance with them in her conversation; particularly with the best theological writers. A table always stood in the middle of her parlor, on which lay a large quarto Bible, and treatises on doctrinal and experimental religion. In the afternoon, at a stated hour, such of the ladies of the neighbourhood, as found it convenient, went customarily to her house, accompanied not unfrequently by their children. Her daughter [Mary] regularly read a chapter of the Bible, and then a passage from some religious author, but was often stopped by the comments and remarks of her mother, who always closed the interview with prayer. On these occasions, it was a favorite point with the neighbouring females, even with those who were young, to be present; all of them regularly attending when they were able, and many of them, among whom was my informant, dating their first permanent attention to religion from the impression here made. In this way she was regarded with a respect bordering on veneration, and was often spoken of by Mr. Perry [the local minister] as one of his most efficient auxiliaries.

Despicable in Your Eyes

Women were active promoters of religion among southern Quakers, Baptists, and Methodists in the eighteenth century. Sophia Hume—granddaughter of the intrepid Mary Fisher, one of the first American Quaker missionaries—became a famous Quaker preacher after the death of her husband. Like many other women converted during the Great Awakening around 1740, she was accused of "Delusion" and "religious Madness." But despite the disapproval of her children and former friends, she traveled extensively for more than thirty years, writing and preaching both in England and in the colonies. A frequently reprinted eighty-four-page sermon, from which the following segment is drawn, advocated many kinds of moral reformation. Among other things, Sophia Hume favored simplicity of dress, women breast-feeding their own infants, and a woman's right to follow her conscience. Hume's rhetoric also expresses eighteenth-century class distinctions as they affected women's behavior and is an early example of the anti-British feelings that helped lay a foundation for political revolution.

From Sophia Hume, *An Exhortation to the Inhabitants of the Province of South Carolina* (Philadelphia: B. Franklin and D. Hall, 1774), pp. 3–4, 17, 24, 34, 46, 47–48, 65–66. ❖

After an Absence of near six Years from this Province (my native Country) and my Arrival among you, I have beheld the Faces of many of the Inhabitants whom I have known, and been known to, some Years: But the Novelty of my religious Sentiments, and Meanness of my Appearance, has, I find, render'd me despicable in your Eyes. . . .

But notwithstanding . . . that I suffered your Ridicule and Reproach, . . . I am willing to become more vile in your Eyes. . . . I would not have you imagine that any Consideration, less than [God's] Favour, could have prevailed with me to have appeared thus publickly in Print, or otherwise. . . . I am not insensible, that the Reason I have offered for writing, as well as the Subject itself, may probably be consider'd as the Production of a distemper'd and enthusiastick Brain; as it is possible, on such a novel and uncommon Occasion, as a Woman's appearing on the Behalf of God and Religion, you may . . . be induced to consider such an One under some unaccountable Delusion, or affected with religious Madness; and more especially, as the Things recommended to your Consideration, are offer'd by a simple Female of your own Country: Some, in this Case, I expect, will afford me a Smile of Contempt, while others (acted by a more generous Passion) pity my Folly, and kindly wish me a Return of my Senses. . . .

I would now observe to you who indulge yourselves in the false Pleasures, vain Amusements and Recreations of the Age, which once I had a Fondness for, as well as you now have; that when the Almighty was pleased in his Mercy to open the Eyes of my Understanding, I plainly perceived by that Light (he had placed in my Conscience, which enabled me to discern between Right and Wrong, the Precious and the Vile) that a Life of Pleasure and Diversion was inconsistent with the Life of a Christian. . . .

. . . Where is the least Room for GOD among those People who are ridiculously term'd *People of Fashion,* especially in *Great Britain,* where the Hours of People of this Name are spent in Folly, Impertinence and Wickedness? As Home is burthensome to Persons of this Cast, 'tis now fashionable to go Abroad to Breakfast, and . . . They count it Pleasure to riot in the Day-time; some of these dance a great Part of the Morning away, while others are entertained with Drollery, Mimick'ry and Buffoon-ery. When they are sufficiently tired with the Levity and Wantonness, the next Appearance of the Women at least, is at the Mercer's, Milliner's, or Toy-shop, spending in Folly, Superfluity and Extravagance, while the Husbands of some of them are perplexing their Brains how to support his Wife's Vanity, which is now become his own, as he proudly considers it a Reproach to himself, that his Wife should be less fine and fashionable than his Neighbour's. . . .

And indeed since I have thought at all, I mean to any good Purpose, I have been amazed at my own Stupidity and Folly, when I have consider'd and recollected how anxious I had formerly been 'till I was in Possession of this gay Silk, and the other fine Lace; and I have blushed with an holy Shame, when I reflected how I had sometimes doated on a Ribbon, or any other Toy or Bauble, that had but the Title of *new-fashion'd* annex'd to it! . . . If we will but look around and consider how many Families are reduced to Poverty, Wretchedness and Misery, from this very Source Pride, from whence springs luxury, in all its hideous Forms and Shapes. The Disorder . . . is become *almost epidemical,* as the inferior Class of People endeavour all in their Power to appear as grand and fashionable as their Superiors. And when I have consider'd, how usual it is for the lower Part of Mankind to be sway'd by the Example of the higher, I have thought it greatly behoved People of Rank and Condition to exhibit Patterns of Humility, Temperance, Sobriety and Moderation, with every other Christian Virtue, to their Inferiors. . . .

I shall now mention another particular Evil, . . . which relates only to the Female Part of the World, so justly chargeable on them. . . . The Fault I mean, is Neglect of Duty, and natural Obligation to our helpless Infants, which is so obvious at their first Appearance in Life, when we deny them that Nourishment Nature has provided for them, and by framing some insignificant Excuse, forsake and leave them to others. This inhumane Treatment of our tender little Ones, I can't help thinking has its Foundation in Pride. . . . Even a few Weeks after our tender Babe beholds the Light, lest it should occasion us some extraordinary Trouble and Care, or prevent some little Delicacy in our Shape or Dress, or detain us from making unedifying and impertinent Visits, &c., we consign the poor Innocent into the Hands of a Stranger, to be fostered by Women, oftentimes, of savage Tempers, and vile Affections. . . . And, 'tis the Opinion of some, that the Death of many an Infant . . . may be chargeable on their Parents, on this score. . . . For how can we reasonably expect that a Stranger shou'd take that due and tender Care, and faithfully discharge so troublesome an Office, which a Parent, suppos'd to have a natural Engagement for her Infant, declines and refuses.

I Gain by Spending

Sarah Haggar Wheaten Osborn (1714–96) of Newport, Rhode Island, was a twenty-year-old widow when she began teaching school to support herself and her baby. She was among many who were inspired by the Great Awakening, and she founded one of the first women's religious societies. It became both a means of personal fulfillment and a network for social action.

Though it was then customary for women to teach only "dame schools" for small children, Sarah Osborn took on more and more educational responsibilities, including classes for African Americans, both slave and free—education that many people opposed. Acutely conscious of the prejudice against female preachers, the same prejudice that had punished Anne Hutchinson 130 years earlier, Sarah Osborn defended her work to her minister friend, carefully defining it so that no one could forbid her to continue. She also found it necessary to insist that she was not neglecting her family.

From letter of Sarah Osborn to Rev. Joseph Fish, February 28–March 7, 1767, Osborn Collection, American Antiquarian Society, Worcester, Massachusetts. Reprinted with permission of the Society. Excerpts are from letters transcribed by Mary Beth Norton in her article " 'My Resting Reaping Times': Sarah Osborn's Defense of Her 'Unfeminine' Activities, 1767," *Signs* 2 (1976): 522–29.

❖

Permit me . . . to Give you the Most Satisfactory account of my conduct as to religious affairs I am capable. I will begin with the Great one respecting the poor Blacks on Lords day Evenings, which above all the rest Has been Exercising to my Mind. And first Let me assure you Sir it would be the Joy of my Heart

148

to commit it into Superior Hands did any arrise for their Help. My Revd Pastor and Brethren are my wittnesses that I have earnestly Sought, yea in bitterness of Soul, for their assistance and protection. . . . To avoid Moving beyond my Line, while I was anxiously desirous the poor creatures should be favrd with some suitable one to pray with them, I was Greatly distresst; but as I could not obtain [help] I have Given it up and They Have not Had above one [prayer] Made with them I believe Sir Since you was here. I only read to them talk to them and sing a Psalm or Hymn with them, and then at Eight o clock dismiss them all by Name as upon List. They call it School and I Had rather it should be calld almost any thing that is good than Meeting, I reluct so much at being that Head of any thing that bears that Name. Pray my dear Sir dont Look upon it as a rejecting your council. . . . It is Such a tender point with me while the poor creatures attend with so Much decency and quietness you Might almost Hear as we say the shaking of a Leaf when there is More than an Hundred under the roof at onece (I mean with the young Mens Society in the chamber) for all there was so Many. . . . They cling and beg for the Priviledge and no weathers this winter stops them from Enjoying it, nor Have I been once prevented from attending them.

I know of no one in the town now that is against me. My dear Mrs. Cheseborough and Mrs. Grant have both been to see me and thank'd me for persisting Stedily in the path of duty against their discouragements, ownd they were at first uneasy but now rejoicd and wish'd a blessing. Mr C is quite silent. Every Intimate brother and friend intreats and charges me not to dismiss So Long as things rest as they are, telling me it would be the worst days work that Ever I did if I should, as God him Self Has thus Employd me. If any disturbance or disorder Should arise Either to the breaking of Public or family Peace, that would immediately Make the path of duty Plain for dismissing *at once,* but on the contrary Ministers and Magistrates send their Servants and approve. And other Masters and Misstresses frequently send me presents in token of gratitude, Express their thanks Speaking of the good Effects that thro the blessing of the Lord it Has had upon their Servants. . . .

As to some, the Marks of reformation I am informed are these: from unwillingness to Learn or know any thing good, they are now intent upon Learning to read etc. at Home and abroad; some that were unwilling to serve and saucy are become diligent and condecending; some that were guilty of drinking gaming Swearing Sabath breaking and uncleanness are at present reform'd. . . .

. . . I Have Seldom Less than 16 or 17 Boys. *Still* they will come and on Tusday Evenings upwards of 30 almost all weathers from Eight or nine years old to fifteen or sixteen. . . .

There is usualy 30 odd young garls every Monday Evening Except the weather is excessive bad and indeed it is surprising to see their constancy thro almost all weathers. . . . My companies are all Volunties—our Society on Wensday Evenings is I Hope not on the decline but rather growing Hand[ily]—

The children for catechising on Thursday afternoon Hold on with surprising chierfulness and steadiness. . . . The room is usualy full consisting of all denominations. I Have Hope that God Has awakened some few of the Little Garls to a concern about their precious Souls. . . .

As to friday Evning friends, my dear Sir I by no means Set up for their instructor. They come indeed for Mutual Edification and Sometimes condescend to direct part of conversation to me and so far I bear a part as to answer etc. but no otherway. . . . That these Gatherings at our House Sir I imagine no way tend to Separations rents or diversions but are rather a Sweet Sementing bond of union that Holds us together in this critical day. My dear Mr Osborn thro infirmity is unable to Go often to the Deacons on Thursdays Evenings and is very fond of this friday Nights visit, and they are Sweet refreshing Evenings my resting reaping times and as God Has Gatherd I dare not Scatter. In any wise I trust My reasons for Encouraging rather than dispersing will prevent your thinking me Obstinate in bad sence. . . .

As to Strength Sir it is Evident I gain by Spending . . . for years together. I have Lain by but one this winter and comparatively know nothing about weariness to what I did when I Had so Great a School and ten or more children in family to attend. I always feel stronger when my companies break up then when they come in and blessed by God I Have a Good appetite and sleep well. . . .

As to time consistent with other duties it is Most true dear Sir that I am calld by the Providence of God as well as by His word to be a redeemer of time Precious time. And Ille tell my Worthy friend How I do my wakeing time. . . . Mr Osborn rises while it is yet dark. . . . From which time I am alone as to any inturruption, for driven by infirmity and want to conveniency I was about a doz years ago constrained to Make my bed my closet, curtains drawd Except Just to Let in Light. I do not Lie there but turn upon my knees my stomach soported with bolster and Pillows, and I am thus securd from the inclemency of all Seasons and from all inturruptions from family affairs. There I read and write almost Every thing of a religious Nature. Thus I redeem an Hour or two for retirement without which I must *starve* and this priviledge blessed by God I Have been Enabled to Hold thro all my Sesans [seasons] of business, sickness in family only Excepted. I never go down till breakfast is Near ready—after Breakfast family worship; then Giving Some orders as to family affairs, I apply to my School, to which you know Sir a kind providence Has Limited my Earning time for soport of my family. And if in this time I Educate the children of poor Neighbours who Gladly pay me in washing Ironing Mending and Making, I Imagine it is the Same thing as if I did it with my own Hands. I think my family does not Suffer thro My Neglect tho doubtless if I Had a full purse and Nothing to do but Look after them some things Might be done with more Exactness then now, but Every dear friend is ready to set a stitch or Help me in any wise and all is well Here. . . .

. . . Now sir, if my Evenings were not thus improved I could not spend them to so much advantage that I know of any other way, for indeed I am not so capable after the Exercises of the day of working at my Needle; that overpowers me vastly more than the duties I am Engagd in. . . . These seem then to refresh recruit and enliven my Exhausted spirits. My family Has the advantage of all these seasons.

Forbear Unkind Ungenerous Muse

The poet Annis Boudinot Stockton (1736–1801), a good friend of Esther Burr's, used the press to air her own and her friends' grievances. Boudinot married Richard Stockton, a New Jersey signer of the Declaration of Independence. She became popular as a patriotic poet during the American Revolution. This selection from her journal was written during the French and Indian War (ca. 1759). She begins by copying, from a local newspaper, a poem insulting to women; she then presents her reply, which she said was written at the request of her female friends.

From Annis Boudinot Stockton, "Colonial and Revolutionary Poems," Department of Rare Books and Special Collections, Princeton University Library, by permission of Robert Field Stockton.

❖

"A Satire on the Fashionable Pompoons Worn by the Ladies
in the Year 1759 . . ."

"How dull the age when ladies must express
Each darling wish in emblematic dress
See how the wheels in various colours roll
Speaking the wish to every female soul
Oh let a windmill decorate the hair
A windmill proper emblem of the fair
As every blast of wind impells the vane
So every blast of folly whirls their brain."

. . . .

Forbear unkind ungenerous muse forbear
To brand with folly the whole race of fair

Thousands whose minds each manly grace improve
Soften'd by smiles by elegance and love
Might well in spite of satire's keenest hate
Redeem them from an undistinguished fate—
Sure all the poets laurels now must fade
Or some dread blight must blast the Cyprian shade
Or jaundic'd eye must tinge each verdant scene
That we fall victims to the scribbling vein
But what the fabled lion said is true
And if appl'd may serve for *us* and *you*
Were we but writers we'd reform the age
And make your kews adorn some jingling page
For metaphors a bubble should suffice
Whose consequence the softest breath destroys
Oh men behave like men, offend no more
Cherish our virtues and our faults pass o're
Roused be your talents in your countries cause
Fight for her interests liberty and laws
And let the sex whom nature made your care
Claim you as guards to banish all their fear.

CHANGING IDENTITIES

21. *First, Second, and Last Scene of Mortality*

Prudence Punderson (1758–84) embroidered this unusual framed needlework sometime before her marriage to Dr. Timothy Wells Rossiter in 1783. Prudence's mother and her aunt were also notable for their needlework, of which many examples still exist in the Connecticut Historical Society. They lived in Preston, a small southeastern Connecticut village. Done in crimped silk floss with ink on satin, the picture expresses the basic realities of an eighteenth-century woman's life. Flanked by a cradle (tended by a woman slave) and a coffin (with her own initials, PP, on top), an aproned young woman works on her embroidery. Prudence's awareness of approaching death proved justified when she died in childbirth at age twenty-six, one year after her marriage. Courtesy of the Connecticut Historical Society, Hartford.

Revolutionary Days

FOR ALL Americans, the revolutionary war was an important event. But the changes it brought for women were very different from those it brought for men. This section is crowded with examples of women working at home, on farms, and in aid of the armies while men were away fighting or legislating. Yet, in spite of their contributions to the war effort, women made few gains in terms of status, work, and public roles. The equality and natural rights hailed by the Declaration of Independence and the Constitution did not apply to white women, African Americans, Native Americans, or even white working men without property. But even though expanded legal rights remained elusive, many women experienced considerable growth in their self-esteem, organizational skills, and political sense in the period during and after the war.

The time is long past when Betsy Ross and Martha Washington were the only female names connected with the era of the American Revolution. Many women actively participated in the political upheavals of this period. Large numbers of women organized economic boycotts of imported British teas and fabrics. They substituted coffee and herb brews for tea, and they spun and wove homespun garments to replace imported finery. Women's boycotts not only enraged English manufacturers but also set the stage for the development of an American textile industry. In New England, newspapers printed paeans to the Daughters of Liberty, an organization formed to encourage the boycotts; in Edenton, North Carolina, and in other places, groups of women signed resolutions asserting their support of this economic warfare. From 1772 to 1779, Mercy Otis Warren anonymously published five widely circulated "propaganda" plays satirizing the British. Later she popularized the Revolution internationally with her three-volume history of the conflict.

As the war became a reality, many women found themselves managing farms or businesses for absent spouses. Abigail Adams, married to a prominent member of the Continental Congress, described herself as a "Farmeress" when John was away; for years, her work produced the entire family income while he engaged in politics. In her letters, she shared the trials of frightening dysentery and smallpox epidemics and her decision, in her husband's absence, to inoculate their children. She also sent him a recipe for making gunpowder. Esther DeBerdt Reed, of Philadelphia, cited examples of influential women throughout history to support her own controversial fund-raising projects for the "cause." She also attempted to influence the way her group's donation was spent, but General George Washington let her know that *he* would decide on the disposition of the funds; she and the other women in her group were advised to make shirts for the army if they wanted to be helpful. Other women, particularly wage earners and the wives of soldiers, accompanied the Continental army as "camp-followers," doing most of the cooking and laundry. There were also women spies for each side. And Mary Hooks Slocumb describes nursing the wounded, another common wartime experience that brought some women close to the front lines in battles.

Many Loyalist women were victimized by the Patriots because of their British sympathies. Some, like Philadelphian Grace Growden Galloway, were separated from their families and driven from their homes; others found that their neighbors would no longer patronize their stores or taverns. Like many other Loyalists, Ann Hulton, the sister of Boston's customs officer, left the colonies during the war, going to Canada and then back to England. Some never returned. Comparing Hulton's account of the Battles of Lexington and Concord with that of patriotic Jane Franklin Mecom demonstrates how very different the conflict looked from opposing sides.

Despite its horrors, the war had a liberating effect on some women's lives. For the first time, women organized their own activist political groups, a precedent that would bear fruit in the next generation. The pleasure of shared effort, the responsibility and recognition, and the hope of greater justice and freedom for all gave these women a lasting sense of personal accomplishment. But poor women often lost more than they gained. Years before the war, Jane Franklin Mecom had told her brother Benjamin of her plans to open a small millinery (hat-making) shop if he would help her obtain the necessary raw materials. After her husband's death, she opened the shop and also took in boarders to make ends meet. Wartime depression and inflation ruined small businesses like Jane Mecom's shop.

For most African Americans, the war brought no change in their slave status. Phillis Wheatley, one of a number of individual slaves freed by their northern owners during this period, wrote poetry comparing the bondage of enslaved Africans to the British tyranny over the American colonists. But in spite of the Revolution's rhetoric of liberty and equality for all, the slave system remained intact in the South.

White women also made few gains. For example, Mary Katherine Goddard's prestige could not protect her from her brother's ambition and greater legal rights when he insisted on taking over her printing business in 1784, even though she had been the official printer of the Declaration of Independence. When Abigail Adams asked her husband to "Remember the Ladies" as the Continental Congress planned the new government's legal system, he treated her request like a joke.

How do we assess the gains made by diverse groups of American women during the era of the Revolution? We might ask a question similar to that posed by the historian Joan Kelley about the Renaissance: "Was there a Revolution for American women?" The answer, according to two historians of the period, Mary Beth Norton and Linda Kerber, is yes, some women made limited gains in many areas during this time. Women formed their first political organizations, which acted effectively to aid the revolutionary cause. While men fought or made policy, women contributed by running households and businesses and by nursing and providing other support services. From these activities, women gained skills, self-respect, and often the admiration of powerful men. Male admiration translated not into immediate political or legal gains but into a recognition of women's importance to the economy and, sometimes, an admission that women possessed rational minds needing education for the benefit of the new Republic. These women adopted much of the Enlightenment and revolutionary rhetoric to analyze their own situations; they continued to believe in the efficacy of activist organizations; and they began to gain the education and confidence they would need to struggle for their own rights in the next century.

Spinning Bees

Before the Revolution, the Townshend Acts of 1767 imposed duties on many British imports, including tea. In response, American women organized groups, called Daughters of Liberty, to boycott British goods and substitute home manufactures. In 1767, the *Massachusetts Gazette* advised women to wear homespun garments and not consider any suitors who wore British fashions. In 1769, the *Boston Evening Post* sang the praises of the Newport, Rhode Island, Daughters of Liberty.

From *Massachusetts Gazette*, November 1767; *Boston Evening Post*, May 29, 1769.

❖

Young ladies in town and those that live round
　　Let a friend at this season advise you.
Since money's so scarce and times growing worse,
　　Strange things may soon hap and surprise you.
First then throw aside your high top knots of pride

Wear none but your own country linen.
Of economy boast. Let your pride be the most
    To show cloaths of your own make and spinning.
What if homespun they say is not quite so gay
    As brocades, yet be not in a passion,
For when once it is known this is much wore in town,
    One and all will cry out 'Tis the fashion.
And as one and all agree that you'll not married be
    To such as will wear London factory
But at first sight refuse, till e'en such you do choose
    As encourage our own manufactory.

❖

A Gentleman of New-Port Writes—"As I am a great Lover of Liberty, of Beauty, of Music, of my Country. . . . I was extremely pleased by having admittance into the company of Eleven of the daughters of Liberty . . . each laudably employed in playing on a musical instrument called a Spinning Wheel . . . . I found that, as these daughters of Liberty delight in each others company, they had agreed to make circular visits to each of their houses, and in order to excite emulation in serving their country, promoting temperance and industry, had determined to convert each visit into a spinning match, and to have no entertainment but what is the produce of their own country; and to appear as much as possible clothed with our own manufactures, and that more especially which is the effect of their own labour—The above forsaid ladies spun between 6 o'clock in the morning, and 6 o'clock in the evening, 37 skeins and 15 threads, which upon an average make three skeins, five knots and five threads."

Boycott Resolutions

In 1770, the *Boston Evening Post* reported that three hundred "Mistresses of Families" had agreed not to drink tea (except for medicinal purposes) until the Townshend Acts were repealed. Southern women were as fervently patriotic as their northern sisters, though their language was less assertive and emphasized their supportive role. The resolution prepared and signed by the women of Edenton, North Carolina, was reported even in London newspapers. British cartoonists (see illustration) ridiculed such female efforts and certainly underestimated their influence in revolutionary America. Even if these actions had limited economic impact, they succeeded in mobilizing American public opinion. The boycotts were certainly a contributing cause of the repeal of the duties (except for the one on tea) in March 1770.

From *Boston Evening Post,* February 12, 1770; *Morning Chronicle and London Advertiser,* January 16, 1775, quoted in Samuel A'Court Ashe, *History of North Carolina,* vol. 1 (Greensboro, N.C.: Charles L. Van Neppen, 1908), pp. 428–29.

❖

Boston, January 31, 1770

The following agreement has lately been come into by upwards of 300 Mistresses of Families in this Town; in which Number the Ladies of the highest rank and influence, that could be waited upon in so short a Time, are included.

"At a time when our invaluable Rights and Privileges are attacked in an unconstitutional and most alarming Manner, and as we find we are reproached for not being so ready as could be desired, to lend our Assistance, we think it our Duty perfectly to concur with the true Friends of Liberty in all Measures they have taken to save this abused Country from Ruin and Slavery. And particularly, we join with the very respectable Body of Merchants and other inhabitants of this Town, who met in Faneuil Hall the 23rd of this Instant, in their resolutions, totally to abstain from the Use of Tea; and as the greatest part of the Revenue arising by Virtue of the late Acts, is produced from the Duty paid upon Tea, which Revenue is wholly expended to support the American Board of Commissioners; We, the Subscribers, do strictly engage, that we will totally abstain from the Use of that Article, (Sickness excepted) not only in our respective Families, but that we will absolutely refuse it, if it should be offered to us upon any Occasion whatsoever. This Agreement we cheerfully come into, as we believe the very distressed Situation of our Country requires it, and we do hereby oblige ourselves religiously to observe it, till the late Revenue Acts are repealed."

❖

Edenton, North Carolina, October 25, 1774

The provincial deputies of North Carolina, having resolved not to drink any more tea, nor wear any more British cloth, etc., many ladies of this province have determined to give a memorable proof of their patriotism, and have accordingly entered into the following honorable and spirited association. . . .

"As we cannot be indifferent on any occasion that appears nearly to affect the peace and happiness of our country, and as it has been thought necessary, for the public good, to enter into several particular resolves by a meeting of members deputed from the whole province, it is a duty which we owe, not only to our near and dear connections, who have concurred in them, but to ourselves, who are essentially interested in their welfare, to do everything, as far as lies in our power, to testify our sincere adherence to the same; and we do therefore accordingly subscribe this paper as a witness of our fixed intention and solemn determination to do so: (51 signatures).

158 Poem on Her Own Slavery

One of the many women's voices raised against British "tyranny" in the years before the Revolution was that of a young West African slave woman from Boston. Phillis Wheatley (1753–84) had been bought by Quakers (who opposed slavery) when she was six years old. They educated her "like a daughter" and promoted her writing talent. When her poems were published in 1773, she visited England and was presented to the king. Freed when her mistress died, but without money in revolutionary Boston, she married an abusive husband. He deserted her, impoverished, and a few years later she and her three children died in an epidemic. This excerpt is from a longer poem to the earl of Dartmouth, a supporter of America's cause.

From Phillis Wheatley, "To the Right Honourable William, Earl of Dartmouth . . . ," *Poems on Various Subjects* (London, 1773), reprinted in Julian D. Mason, Jr., ed., *The Poems of Phillis Wheatley* (Chapel Hill: University of North Carolina Press, 1989), p. 83.

❖

No more, America, *in mournful strain*

Of wrongs, and grievance unredress'd complain,
No longer shalt thou dread the iron chain,
Which wanton *Tyranny* with lawless hand
Had made, and with it meant t'enslave the land.
     Should you, my lord, while you peruse my song,
Wonder from whence my love of *Freedom* sprung,
Whence flow these wishes for the common good,
By feeling hearts alone best understood,
I, young in life, by seeming cruel fate
Was snatch'd from *Afric's* fancy'd happy seat:
What pangs excruciating must molest,
What sorrows labour in my parent's breast?
Steel'd was the soul and by no misery mov'd
That from a father seiz'd his babe belov'd:
Such, such my case. And can I then but pray
Others may never feel tyrannic sway?

A Journal Second to None

Mary Katherine Goddard, along with her brother William, learned the printing and newspaper business from her mother, Sarah Updike Goddard, in Rhode Island. Goddard's *Providence Gazette* had been influential in the anti–Stamp Act protests in 1765. With her *Maryland Gazette*, Mary Katherine Goddard was a leading supporter of the American Revolution; the Continental Congress made her the official printer of the Declaration of Independence.

From Elisabeth Anthony Dexter, *Colonial Women of Affairs* (Boston: Houghton Mifflin Company, 1924), pp. 172–73. Copyright 1924 and 1931, renewed in 1952 by Elizabeth Anthony Dexter. Reprinted by permission of Houghton Mifflin Company. All rights reserved.

❖

William Goddard was a restless person, and in February, 1774, he left Annapolis, where he was then editing the "Maryland Gazette," in order to work on the establishment of the postal system. His sister, Mary Katherine Goddard, took over the paper, at first temporarily. As he did not return, in the following year she dropped his name and assumed full responsibility. She conducted it with success throughout the trying years of the war. The paper sometimes had to be reduced in size, but it appeared, approximately on time, "a journal second to none in the colonies in interest." In her issue of November 16, 1779, she announced with truth, that her paper circulated as extensively as any on the continent. . . . In addition to her editorial work, she was for many years the postmistress of Annapolis, at a time when postal revenues were very uncertain; at times she paid the riders "hard money," as she described it, from her own purse. Furthermore, she did good job printing, and kept a bookstore. In 1784, when the war was over, and the paper running well, her brother returned, and she relinquished it to him. The position as postmistress she held until 1789, and after that simply kept the bookstore. She died in 1814, aged about seventy-nine, and left a small property to a colored woman who had been her servant.

Giting a Living and Keeping up Curidg

Jane Franklin Mecom (1712–94) was the sister of eighteenth-century America's famous scientist, entrepreneur, and statesman Benjamin Franklin. A woman of intelligence and spirit, she married at fifteen and had twelve children. When her husband died in 1765, Jane remarked that he had "injoyed Litle & suffered much by Sin & Sorrow." Several of her children were mentally ill, and after the death of a favorite daughter in 1767, she wrote, "Sorrows roll upon me like the waves of the sea." Her life, which was so full of hardship and loss, was made only slightly easier by the kindness of her brother.

For many years Jane Mecom kept a boardinghouse in Boston, not far from the old State House. Legislators roomed there, like the "six good Honist old Souls" in her second letter. They gave her information about public issues, such as the question of compensation for officials whose homes had been pillaged by Boston mobs in the Stamp Act crisis. After her husband died, Jane and her daughter also opened a millinery (hat-making) shop, and she asked Benjamin to send her cloth from England.

In her third letter, Mecom writes of her flight from Boston in the chaos following the Battles of Lexington and Concord on April 19, 1775. Like many other Bostonians, she took refuge away from the city, in Warwick, Rhode Island, with distant relatives. The "Generl" she mentions is the British general William Howe, and "Poor Quensey" is Josiah Quincy, by whom Benjamin Franklin had sent his letter but who had died on the journey. Compare Mecom's account of the battle with the Loyalist Ann Hulton's description below.

From Carl Van Doren, ed., *The Letters of Benjamin Franklin and Jane Mecom* (Princeton, N.J.: Princeton University Press, 1950), pp. 86–88, 93–94, 153–55. Copyright © 1950 by Princeton University Press. Reprinted by permission of Princeton University Press.

❖

Boston, Dec. 30, 1765

Dear Brother . . .

My famely is now in a beter state of Helth than they have been for two years Past old Sarah Lives yet & is got Down stars again. I have son Flagg boards with me & cousen Ingersols two Daughters, Mrs. Bowls is also Returned after a twelve months absence, but I have them all at a Low Rate because I can Do no beter, so that my Income suplys us with vitles fiering candles & Rent but more it cannot with all the Prudence I am mistres of, but thus I must Rub along till Spring when I must strive after some other way. . . . I feel now as if I could carey on some Biusnes if I was in it but at other times I fear my years are two far advancd to do any thing but jog on in the old track but my two Daughters if they have there Helth are capeble & willing to Do there Part towards giting a Living. . . . I have wrote & spelt this very badly but as it is to won who I am shure will make all Reasonable allowances for me and not let any won Els see it I shall venter to send it & subscrib my self yr Ever affectionat Sister

Jane Mecom

Nov. 8, 1766

. . . . You wonce told me my Dear Brother that as our Numbers of Bretheren & Sisters Lessened the Affections of those of us that Remain should Increes to Each other. you & I only are now Left. my Affection for you has all ways been so grate I see no Room for Increec, & you have manifested yrs to mee in such Large measure that I have no Reason to suspect Itts strength & therefore know it will be agreable to you to hear that my self & the childrin I have the care of are in no wors situation than when I Last wrot you. . . . I hope in god you . . . will live Long to make yr Inemies ashamed, yr Ansurs to the Parlement are thought by the best Judges to Exeed all that has been wrot on the subject & being given in the maner they were are a Proof they Proceeded from Prinsiple & suficent to stop the mouths of all gain-sayers, the vile Pretended Leter which no Doubt you have seen gave me some uneaseyness when I heard of it before I could git a sight of it, as considering when a grat Deal of Durt is flung some is apt to stick but when I Read it I see it was filld with such bare faced falshoods as confuted them selves, theyre treetment of you among other things makes the World Apear a miserable world to me not withstanding yr good opinyon of it, for would you think it our General Court has sett allmost a Fortnight cheaffly on the subject of Indemnifieing the sufferers by the Late mobs & cant yet git a Vote for it tho they sitt Late in the Evening & the friends to it strive hard to git it acomplishd. I have six good Honist old Souls who come groneing Home Day by Day at the Stupidety of there Bretheren   I cant help Interesting my self in the case & feel in mere Panicks till they have Brought the matter to a conclusion. . . .

& I have a small Request to ask tho it is too trifeling a thing for you to take care of   Mrs. Steevenson I Dont Doubt will be so good as to do it if you will give her the meterals   it is to Procure me some fine old Lining [linen] or cambrick (as a very old shirt or cambrick hankercheifs) Dyed into bright colors such as red & green a Litle blew but cheafly Red for with all my own art & good old unkle Benjamins memorandoms I cant make them good colors. & my Daughter Jeney with a litle of my asistance has taken to makeing Flowers for the Ladyes Heads & Boosomes with Prity good acceptance. & If I can Procure them coulars

I am In hopes we shall git somthing by it worth our Pains if we live till Spring. it is no mater how old the Lining is   I am afraid you never have any bad a nouf. . . .

Warrick 14 May 1775

162   My Ever Dear & much Hond Brother

God be Praised for bring you saif back to America & soporting you throw such fatuges as I know you have sufered while the minestry have been distresing Poor New England in such a cruil maner. yr last by Poor Quensey Advises me to: keep up my curidg & that faul wither does not last all ways in any country. but I beleve you did not then Imagin the Storm would have Arisen so high as for the Generl to have sent out a party to creep out in the night & Slauter our Dear Brethern for Endevering to defend our own Property, but God Apeard for us & drove them back with much Grater Lose than they are willing to own, there countenances as well as confeshon of many of them shew they were much mistaken in the people they had to Deal with, but the distress it has ocationed is Past my discription. the Horror the Town was in when the Batle Aprochd within Hearing Expecting they would Proceed quite in to town, the comotion the Town was in after the batle ceasd by the Parties coming in bringing in there wounded men causd such an Agetation of minde I beleve none had much sleep, since which we could have no quiet, as we under stood our Bretheren without were determined to Disposes the Town of the Regelors, & the Generol shuting up the town not Leting any Pass out but throw such Grate Dificulties as were allmost insoportable, but throw the Goodnes of God I am at last Got Saif Hear & kindly Recved by Mr Green & His wife (who to my grate comfort when I had got Pact up what I Expected to have liberty to carey out intending to seek my fourtune with hundred others not knowing whither) sent me an Invitation in a leter to Mrs Patridg of which I gladly acepted an the day I arived at Provedence had the unspeakable Pleasure of hearing my Dear Brother was saif arived at His own home, Blessed be God for all His mercys to me an unworthy creature, these People seem formed for Hospetality Apear to be Pleasd with the vast Adition to there famely which consists of old Mr Gough & wife, there sons wife & negro boy, Mr Thomas Leverett's wife 2 children & a made, my self an Grand Daughter who I could not leve if I had it would have been her Death, & they Expect this Day 3 more of Mr Leveretts chilen young Mr Gouge, Suckey & Mrs Pateridg & Daughter. & seem as tho there harts were open to all the world   they sent for old Mrs Downs but dont know if she designs to come as it is so Extremly dificult to git a line to pass to Each other, Mrs Leveritt is trying to git a house to keep house by her self. My Poor litle Delicat nabour Mrs Royall & Famely came out with me not knowing where she should find a Place   I left them at Cambridg in a most shocking Disagreable Place but since hear she is gone to wooster, my own Daughter had been at Board at Roxbury almost a year before but she with the famely were obliged to fly in to the woods & tho they Returnd again they think them selves very unsaif & she was in grate concern what cours to take when the day before I left her she Recd a leter from her husband that He was saif Arived at Bedford in Dartmouth not Dareing to venture in to salem from whence they saild, this also was a grat ease to my mind as she might now soon Expect her husband to take the care of her,

I am Still under grate concern for cousen williams   He was out of Town at the time of the batle & was Advised to keep out & His Poor wife slaved her self almost to Death to Pack up & Secure what She could & sent away her two Daughters Intending to go to Him & behold in comes he in to town the day before I cam out Imagining (as I was told for I did not see him) that was the saifest Place   I can hear nothing of Him since,

you will have seen the Generl leter to conettacut & be able to Judge of the truth of His Insineuations by his fidelity to us Poor bostonians.

I have wrot a grat number of leters to you the winter & Spring Past but cannot Prercive by yr self or cousen Jonathan that you have recved any of them I sent won about a month ago but as you are Returnd it is no mater if you never git it.

Present my love to my cousens Beaches' & the Dear children

& Exept the same from yr Ever

Affectionat Sister

Jane Mecom

Is Jonan come with you if he is remember my love to Him

Dear Brother I am tould you will be joynd to the Congress & that they will Remove to conetecut   will you Premit me to come & see you there Mrs Green says she will go with me

The Barbarism of the Times

Ann Hulton was a British Loyalist, the sister of Henry Hulton, commissioner of customs in Boston from 1767 to 1775. Because her father had been sent to Boston to enforce the unpopular Townshend Acts, Hulton was understandably partial to the British cause and alarmed at the rough treatment of some British officials at the hands of the Patriots. In this letter, she presents the Tory view of the Battles of Lexington and Concord. Compare her description with Jane Mecom's Patriot perspective on the same events. Late in 1775, the Hulton family left Boston for England, where Ann died in 1779.

From *Letters of a Loyalist Lady, Being the Letters of Ann Hulton, Sister of Henry*

Hulton, Commissioner of Customs at Boston, 1767–1776 (Cambridge: Harvard University Press, 1928), pp. 76–80. Reprinted by permission of Harvard University Press. Copyright © 1927 by the President and Fellows of Harvard College.

❖

April (?) 1775

164   I acknowledged the receipt of My Dear Friends kind favor of the 20th Sept. the begin'ing of last Month, tho' did not fully Answer it. . . . At present my mind is too much agitated to attend to any subject but one, and it is that which you will be most desirous to hear particulars of, I doubt not in regard to your friends here, as to our Situation, as well as the Publick events. I will give you the best account I can, which you may rely on for truth.

On the 18th inst[ant] at 11 at Night, about 800 Grenadiers & light Infantry were ferry'd across the Bay to Cambridge, from whence they marchd to Concord, about 20 Miles. The Congress had been lately assembled at that place, & it was imagined that the General had intelligence of a Magazine being formed there & that they were going to destroy it.

The People in the Country (who are all furnished with Arms & have what they call Minute Companys in every Town ready to march on any alarm), had a signal it's supposed by a light from one of the Steeples in Town, Upon the Troops embar[kation]. The alarm spread thro' the Country, so that before daybreak the people in general were in Arms & on their March to Concord. About Daybreak a number of the People appeard before the Troops near Lexington. They were called to, to disperse, when they fired on the Troops & ran off, Upon which the Light Infantry pursued them & brought down about fifteen of them. The Troops went on to Concord & executed the business they were sent on, & on their return found two or three of their people Lying in the Agonies of Death, scalp'd & their Noses & ears cut off & Eyes bored out—Which exasperated the Soldiers exceedingly—a prodigious number of People now occupying the Hills, woods, & Stone Walls along the road. The Light Troops drove some parties from the hills, but all the road being inclosed with Stone Walls Served as a cover to the Rebels, from whence they fired on the Troops still running off whenever they had fired, but still supplied by fresh Numbers who came from many parts of the Country. In this manner were the Troops harrased in thier return for Seven on eight Miles, they were almost exhausted & had expended near the whole of their Ammunition when to their great joy they were releived by a Brigade of Troops under the command of Lord Percy with two pieces of Artillery. The Troops now combated with fresh Ardour, & marched in their return with undaunted countenances, recieving Sheets of fire all the way for many Miles, yet having no visible Enemy to combat with, for they never woud face 'em in an open field, but always skulked & fired from behind Walls, & trees, & out of Windows of Houses, but this cost them dear for the Soldiers enterd those dwellings, & put all the Men to death. Lord Percy has gained great honor by his conduct thro' this day of severe Servise, he was exposed to the hottest of the fire & animinated the Troops with great coolness & spirit. Several officers are wounded & about 100 Soldiers. The killed amount to near 50, as to the Enemy we can have no exact acc[ount] but it is said there was about ten times the Number of them engaged, & that near 1000 of 'em have fallen.

The Troops returned to Charlestown about Sunset after having some of 'em marched near fifty miles, & being engaged from Daybreak in Action, without respite, or refreshment, & about ten in the Evening they were brought back to Boston. The next day the Country pourd down its Thousands, and at this time from the entrance of Boston Neck at Roxbury round by Cambridge to Charlestown is surrounded by at least 20,000 Men, who are raising batteries on three or four different Hills. We are now cut off from all communication with the Country & many people must soon perish with famine in this place. Some families have laid in store of Provissions against a Siege. We are threatned that whilst the Out Lines are attacked with a rising of the Inhabitants within, & fire & sword, a dreadful prospect before us, and you know how many & how dear are the objects of our care. The Lord preserve us all & grant us an happy Issue out of these troubles.

Remember the Ladies

Abigail and John Adams maintained a regular and voluminous correspondence during his many extended absences as a colonial politician. While John was in Philadelphia as a member of the Continental Congress, the two kept each other well-informed about both public and private affairs. Abigail even answered her husband's request about how to make saltpeter, a basic ingredient for producing the colonial army's gunpowder. In Braintree, Massachusetts, Abigail Adams managed the family farm, which provided their living during her husband's long absences. She did not hesitate to advise him on political theory, urging a declaration of American independence two months before the fact *and* the legal rights of women. One letter describes women of Boston taking revolutionary action of their own. In another, John responds to Abigail's serious advice with a joke about "another Tribe" of "discontented" women. Both of them allude to the Marquis of Halifax's *Advice to a Daughter* about a woman's power to subdue her "masters" by means of her sexuality instead of laws.

Close friendships with other women provided mutual support and a potential basis for action "in behalf of our Sex." Abigail Adams and Mercy Otis Warren were both members of activist Patriot families during the period of the

American Revolution. They corresponded for years, discussing the course of the war and the condition of women. In her letter to Mercy Warren, Abigail comments more sarcastically on John's response to her suggestion for women's rights. Modeling themselves on the "worthy matrons" of Roman history, the two women gave each other nicknames: Abigail was "Portia."

166   From Lyman Butterfield, ed., *The Adams Family Correspondence,* 4 vols. (Cambridge: The Bellknapp Press of Harvard University Press, 1950), 1:371, 375, 396–98, 2:295. Copyright © 1963 by the Massachusetts Historical Society. Reprinted by permission of the publishers.

❖

[Abigail Adams to John Adams]   Braintree March 31 1776

I long to hear that you have declared an independancy—and by the way in the new Code of Laws which I suppose it will be necessary for you to make I desire you would Remember the Ladies, and be more generous and favourable to them than your ancestors. Do not put such unlimited power into the hands of the Husbands. Remember all Men would be tyrants if they could. If perticuliar care and attention is not paid to the Laidies we are determined to foment a Rebelion, and will not hold ourselves bound by any laws in which we have no voice, or Representation.

That your Sex are Naturally Tyrannical is a Truth so thoroughly established as to admit of no dispute, but such of you as wish to be happy willingly give up the harsh title of Master for the more tender and endearing one of Friend. Why then, not put it out of the power of the vicious and the Lawless to use us with cruelty and indignity with impunity.

April 5, 1776

I want to hear much oftener from you than I do. March 8 was the last date of any that I have yet had.—You inquire of whether I am making Salt peter. I have not yet attempted it, but after Soap making believe I shall make the experiment. I find as much as I can do to manufacture cloathing for my family which would else be Naked. I know of but one person in this part of the Town who has made any. . . . I have lately seen a small Manuscrip de[s]cribing the proportions for the various sorts of powder, fit for cannon, small arms and pistols. If it would be of any Service your way I will get it transcribed and send it to you. . . .

April 11, 1776

I take my pen and write just as I can get time, my Letters will be a strange Mixture. I really am cumberd about many things and scarcly know which way to turn my-self. I miss my partner, and find myself uneaquil to the cares which fall upon me; I find it necessary to be the directress of our Husbandery and farming. Hands are so scarce, that I have not been able to procure one, and add to this that Isaac has been sick with a fever this fortnight, not able to strick a Stroke and a Multiplicity of farming Business pouring in upon Us.

In this Dilemma I have taken Belcher into pay, and must secure him for the Season, as I know not what better course to stear. I hope in time to have the Reputation of being as good a *Farmeress* as my partner has of being a good Statesmen.

[John Adams to Abigail Adams]   Ap. 14, 1776

. . . As to your extraordinary Code of Laws, I cannot but laugh. We have been told that our Struggle has loosened the bands of Government every where. That Children and Apprentices were disobedient—that schools and Colledges were grown turbulent—that Indians slighted their Guardians and Negroes grew insolent to their Masters. But your Letter was the first Intimation that another Tribe more numerous and powerfull than all the rest were grown discontented —This is rather too coarse a Compliment but you are so saucy, I wont blot it out.

Depend upon it, We know better than to repeal our Masculine systems. Altho they are in full force, you know they are little more than Theory. We dare not exert our Power in its full Latitude. We are obliged to go fair, and softly, and in Practice you know We are the subjects. We have only the Name of Masters, and rather than give up this, which would compleatly subject Us to the Despotism of the Peticoat, I hope General Washington, and all our brave Heroes would fight. . . .

[Abigail Adams to Mercy Otis Warren]   Braintree April 27 1776

I set myself down to comply with my Friends request, who I think seem's rather low spiritted.

I did write last week, but not meeting with an early conveyance I thought the Letter of But little importance and tos'd it away. I acknowledg my Thanks due to my Friend for the entertainment she so kindly afforded me in the Characters drawn in her Last Letter, and if coveting my Neighbours Goods was not prohibited by the Sacred Law, I should be most certainly tempted to envy her the happy talant she possesses above the rest of her Sex, by adorning with her pen even trivial occurances, as well as dignifying the most important. Cannot you communicate some of those Graces to your Friend and suffer her to pass them upon the World for her own that she may feel a little more upon an Eaquality with you?—Tis true I often receive large packages from P[hiladelphi]a. They contain as I said before more News papers than Letters, tho they are not for-gotton. It would be hard indeed if absence had not some alleviations.

I dare say he writes to no one unless to Portia oftner than to your Friend, because I know there is no one besides in whom he has an eaquel confidence. His Letters to me have been generally short, but he pleads in Excuse the criti-cal state of affairs and the Multiplicity of avocations and says further that he has been very Busy, and writ near ten Sheets of paper, about some affairs which he does not chuse to Mention for fear of accident.

He is very sausy to me in return for a List of Female Grievances which I transmitted to him. I think I will get you to join me in a petition to Congress. I thought it was very probable our wise Statesmen would erect a New Gover-ment and form a new code of Laws. I ventured to speak a word in behalf of our Sex, who are rather hardly dealt with by the Laws of England which gives such unlimitted power to the Husband to use his wife Ill.

I requested that our Legislators would consider our case and as all Men of Delicacy and Sentiment are averse to Excercising the power they possess, yet as there is a natural propensity in Humane Nature to domination, I thought the most generous plan was to put it out of the power of the Arbitary and tyranick to injure us with impunity by Establishing some Laws in our favour upon just and Liberal principals.

I believe I even threatned fomenting a Rebellion in case we were not consid-erd, and assured him we would not hold ourselves bound by any Laws in which we had neither a voice, nor representation.

In return he tells me he cannot but Laugh at My Extrodonary Code of Laws. That he had heard their Struggle had loosned the bands of Goverment, that children and apprentices were dissabedient, that Schools and Colledges were grown turbulant, that Indians slighted their Guardians, and Negroes grew in-solent to their Masters. But my Letter was the first intimation that another Tribe more numerous and powerfull than all the rest were grown discontented. This is rather too coarse a compliment, he adds, but that I am so sausy he wont blot it out.

So I have help'd the Sex abundantly, but I will tell him I have only been making trial of the Disintresstedness of his Virtue and when weigh'd in the bal-ance have found it wanting. . . .

Portia

[Abigail Adams to John Adams]   May 7, 1776
A Government of more Stability is much wanted in this colony, and they are ready to receive it from the Hands of the Congress, and since I have begun with

Maxims of State I will add on another viz. that a people may let a king fall, yet still remain a people, but if a king let his people slip from him, he is no longer a king. And as this is most certainly our case, why not proclaim to the World in decisive terms your own importance?

Shall we not be dispiced by foreign powers for hesitateing so long at a word?

I can not say that I think you very generous to the Ladies, for whilst you are proclaiming peace and good will to Men, Emancipating all Nations, you insist upon retaining an absolute power over Wives. But you must remember that Arbitary power is like most other things which are very hard, very liable to be broken—and notwithstanding all your wise Laws and Maxims we have it in our power not only to free ourselves but to subdue our Masters, and without violence throw both your natural and legal authority at our feet—

169

[Abigail Adams to John Adams]   July 31, 1777

I have nothing new to entertain you with, unless it is an account of a New Set of Nobility which have lately taken the Lead in B[osto]n. You must know that there is a great Scarcity of Sugar and Coffe, articles which the Female part of the State are very loth to give up, expecially whilst they consider the Scarcity occasioned by the merchants having secreted a large Quantity. There has been much rout and Noise in the Town for several weeks. Some Stores had been opend by a number of people and the Coffe and Sugar carried into the Market and dealt out by pounds. It was rumourd that an eminent, wealthy, stingy Merchant (who is a Batchelor) had a Hogshead of Coffe in his Store which he refused to sell to the committee under 6 shillings per pound. A Number of Females some say a hundred, some say more assembled with a cart and trucks, marched down to the Ware House and demanded the keys, which he refused to deliver, upon which one of them seazd him by his Neck and tossd him into the cart. Upon his finding no Quarter he deliverd the keys, when they tipd up the cart and dischargd him, then opend the Warehouse, Hoisted out the Coffe themselves, put it into the trucks and drove off.

It was reported that he had a Spanking among them, but this I believe was not true. A large concourse of Men stood amazd silent Spectators of the whole transaction.

Conscious Dignity That Ought
Rather to Be Cherish'd

Mercy Otis Warren expressed her ardent patriotism by composing satirical anti-British dramas, which were popular reading in revolutionary Boston. She also produced an important three-volume *History of the Rise, Progress, and Termination of the American Revolution*. Writing to her young niece, she discussed women's roles with the assertive confidence of many women of her era. In her satirical prologue to "The Group," Warren proclaimed that she would expose the wrongdoing of all "knaves": "Yes, while I live, no rich or noble knave / Shall walk the world in credit to his grave; / To virtue only, and her friends, a friend, / The world beside may murmur or commend."

From letter of Mercy Otis Warren in Alice Brown, *Mercy Warren* (New York: Charles Scribner's Sons, 1896), pp. 241–42.

❖

It is my Opinion that that Part of the human Species who think Nature (as well as the infinitely wise & Supreme Author thereof) has given them the Superiority over the other, mistake their own Happiness when they neglect the Culture of Reason in their Daughters while they take all possible Methods of improving it in their sons.

The Pride you feel on hearing Reflections indiscriminately Cast on the Sex, is laudable if any is so.—I take it, it is a kind of Conscious Dignity that ought rather to be cherish'd, for while we own the appointed Subordination (perhaps for the sake of Order in Families) let us by no Means Acknowledge such an Inferiority as would Check the Ardour of our endeavours to equal in all Accomplishments the most masculine Heights, that when these temporary Distinctions subside we may be equally qualified to taste the full Draughts of Knowledge & Happiness prepared for the Upright of every Nation & Sex; when Virtue alone will be the Test of Rank, & the grand Œconomy for an Eternal Duration will be properly Adjusted.

Our Republican and Laborious Hands

The daughter of a prominent English merchant with colonial sympathies, Esther DeBerdt Reed (1746–80) had married a Philadelphia lawyer and come to America in 1770. Within five years she was a leader of the Daughters of Liberty while her husband became adjutant general to George Washington and later "president" of Pennsylvania.

One of Reed's activities was to organize a women's fund drive for revolutionary soldiers, setting a new precedent for public activity among patriotic mothers of the Republic. She wrote a pamphlet citing heroines of history as exemplars, with directions for an efficient county fund-raising organization. Tories in Philadelphia groaned with disgust at the "unladylike" behavior of female rebels knocking on every door for contributions. The women raised three hundred thousand dollars in Continental currency.

Knowing that the new nation's inflated paper currency made soldiers' pay almost worthless and that taxes in each colony were supposed to pay for the basic needs of the ragtag army, Reed's organization stipulated that their donation could not "be employed to procure to the army, the objects of subsistence, arms or clothing, which are due them by the Continental Congress. It is an extraordinary bounty intended to render the condition of the Soldier more pleasant, and not to hold place of the things which they ought to receive from the Congress or the States." Yet General Washington objected to cash bonuses, insisting that the money be deposited in the national bank to shore up the shaky economy. He thought the women should make shirts instead. They reluctantly acquiesced (after Reed's letter of protest was ignored) and produced over two thousand shirts before winter. But Esther Reed, recently recovered from smallpox and childbirth and with five children under eight years old, died that September of acute dysentery, at thirty-four, before the sewing was finished.

From Esther DeBerdt Reed, "The Sentiments of an American Woman," pamphlet reprinted in *Pennsylvania Magazine of History and Biography* 17 (1894): 361–66; William Bradford Reed, ed., *The Life of Esther DeBerdt Reed* (Philadelphia: C. Sherman, 1853; reprint, New York: Arno Press, 1971), pp. 322–24.

❖

On the commencement of actual war, the Women of America manifested a firm resolution to contribute as much as could depend on them, to the deliverance of their country. Animated by the purest patriotism they are sensible of sorrow at this day, in not offering more than barren wishes for the success of so glorious a Revolution. They aspire to render themselves more really useful; and this sentiment is universal from the north to the south of the Thirteen United States. Our ambition is kindled by the fame of those heroines of antiquity, who . . . have been seen forgeting the weakness of their sex, building new walls, digging trenches with their feeble hands; furnishing arms to their defenders, they themselves darting the missile weapons on the enemy, resigning the ornaments of their apparel, and their fortunes to fill the public treasury, and to hasten the deliverance of their country; burying themselves under its ruins; throwing themselves into the flames rather than submit to the disgrace of humiliation before a proud enemy. . . . [She lists and describes numerous great women in history.]

Who, amongst us, will not renounce with the highest pleasure, those vain ornaments, when she shall consider that the valiant defenders of America will be able to draw some advantage from the money which she may have laid out in these; that they will be better defended from the rigours of the seasons, that after their painful toils, they will receive some extraordinary and unexpected relief; that these presents will perhaps be valued by them at a greater price, when they will have it in their power to say: *This is the offering of the Ladies.* The time is arrived to display the same sentiments which animated us at the beginning of the Revolution, when we renounced the use of teas, however agreeable to our taste, rather than receive them from our persecutors; when we made it appear to them that we placed former necessaries in the rank of superfluities, when our liberty was interested; when our republican and laborious hands spun the flax, prepared the linen intended for the use of our soldiers; when [as] exiles and fugitives we supported with courage all the evils which are the concomitants of war.

Letter to General Washington

Banks of Schuylkill, July 31st, 1780.

Sir,

Ever since I received your Excellency's favour the 20th of this month, I have been endeavouring to procure the linen for the use of the soldiers, and it was not till Saturday last I have been able to meet with any fit for the purpose, it being unavoidably delayed so long. I have been informed of some circumstances, which I beg leave to mention and from which perhaps the necessity for shirts may have ceased; one is the supply of 2000 sent from this State to their line, and the other, that a considerable number is arrived in the French fleet, for the use of the army in general. Together with these an idea prevails among the ladies, that the soldiers will not be so much gratified, by bestowing an article to which they are entitled from the public, as in some other method which will convey more fully the idea of a reward for past services, and an incitement to future duty. Those who are of this opinion propose the whole of the money to be changed into hard dollars, and giving each soldier two, to be entirely at his own disposal. This method I hint only, but would not, by any means wish to adopt it or any other, without your full approbation. If it should meet with your concurrence, the State of Pennsylvania will take the linen I have purchased, and, as far as respects their own line, will make up any deficiency of shirts to them, which they suppose will not be many after the fresh supplies are received. If, after all, the necessity for shirts, which, though it may cease, as to the Pennsylvania Troops, may still continue to other parts of the army, the ladies will immediately make up the linen we have, which I think can soon be effected, and forward them to camp, and procure more as soon as possible, having kept in hand the hard money I have received, until I receive your reply. . . . 173

> I have the honour to be, dear Sir,
> With the highestest esteem,
> Your obedient servant,
>
> E. Reed.

I Would Be Happy in Spite of Them

The daughter of a wealthy Philadelphia doctor, Grace Growden apparently failed to make an antenuptial agreement regarding her inheritance when she married Joseph Galloway, a Pennsylvania politician and Loyalist. According to her journal and poetry, Galloway mistreated her and mismanaged her property. During the Revolution he fled Philadelphia with their daughter, Betsy. Grace stayed behind to try, for their daughter's sake, to save her property from confiscation. Grace's journal reveals the sufferings of an unhappy marriage, as did some of her earlier poetry, in which she advised, "Never get tyed to a Man / for when once you are yoked / Tis all a mere joke / of seeing your freedom again." These journal excerpts also describe some of the problems of a Loyalist woman during the American Revolution. Rebels confiscated Galloway's house, her carriage, and some of her other property. She died, depressed and impoverished, in 1779 without seeing her daughter again. Betsy finally recovered most of her mother's property in 1803.

From "Journal of Grace Growden Galloway" in Elizabeth Evans, *Weathering the Storm: Women of the American Revolution* (New York: Charles Scribner's Sons, 1975), pp. 185–244. Paragon House Publishers paperback, 1989. Copyright © Elizabeth Evans. Reprinted with her permission.

❖

July 9, 1778: Israel Pemberton advised me to see lawyers, as men were nominated to seize our estate. I sent for Lewis [William Lewis, lawyer] and gave him ten guineas. He promised to consult Abel James and Mr. Chew [Benjamin Chew, lawyer] to see if I could have dower [rights to the property she owned before marriage].

July 21: About 2 o'clock they came—one Smith (a hatter), Col. Will, one Schreiner, and a dutchman (I know not his name). They took an inventory of everything, even to broken china and empty bottles. I left nurse with them, called Sidney Howell, and sat at the door with her. Mrs. Erwin and Mrs. Jones went about with them. I had such spirits that I appeared not uneasy. They told me they must advertise the house. I told them they may do as they pleased, but 'till it was decided by a court I would not go out unless by the force of a bayonet. . . .

He [her lawyer] tells me I can't stay in the house. Yet on my saying "Where should I go?" never offered to take me in; nor did Molly Craig, who was here, and Peggy Johns. Not one has offered me a house to shelter me; but Betsy Jones behaves the best of all. Oh God, what shall I do? There is no dependence on the arm of flesh; nor have I one hope in this world nor anything to rely on. I am afraid how my child and husband came out of New York. All hope is over.

August 1: I was pretty cheerful. In the afternoon Mrs. Wharton sent to know if I would take a ride. She called on me just before sunset. She seemed very reserved, but when she found I was not like to trouble them she cleared up. We went all the back ways of the town and rode three miles round. Just as we came to Second Street she ordered the man to go to our house. I then said I was in hopes I should have seen friend [Thomas] Wharton, as I wanted to speak to him and had no way of coming. She said "I tell thee, friend Galloway, thee can't go now, as it is like to be a gust [windstorm]." I said there was no prospect of a gust. She then said "I left Rachel and Suky Hudson at our house and promised to take them home." I then said I was sorry I should take her from her company, but I wanted to see her husband if it was but for five minutes, as I had no other opportunity of seeing him. She then told me she did not know of Hudsons coming when she sent to me, and thought I wanted to ride. I replied the only inducement I had for coming today was to see her husband, but since it was so disagreeable, my going to her house, I wished he would call on me and, if I had known I could not see him I would not have come. She replied "Why was thee not glad of the ride. I thought thee would be glad to ride out." I told her that such rides as this I would not give a pin for, and the exercise of riding three miles and being out half an hour would contribute but little to my health.

Aug. 13: A rainy day. Very unwell when I got up. Mrs. Erwin here, begged her ask her husband and Billy Gray to be security for me if they will let me have the house. Mr. Erwin called afterwards and said they will. Peggy Johns here but I was taken ill and was on the bed 'till night. These villains will kill me. Owen Jones and Lewis here in the evening and Lewis says he will take care they shall not trouble me tomorrow. I am very ill and low. After they went I sat down and wrote. My hopes and spirits are quite gone. They will kill me if I am harassed much more.

August 19: I heard Peale had been there to inform me I must go out of my house tomorrow at 10 o'clock. I was much shocked, as I expected the Council had put a stop to it.

Aug. 20: Lewis sent me word that I must shut my doors and windows and, if they would come, to let them make a forcible entry. Accordingly, I did so, and a little after 10 o'clock they knocked violently at the door three times. The third time I sent nurse, and I called out to tell them I was in possession of my own house and would keep so, and that they should gain no admittance. Here upon which they went round in the yard and tried every door, but could none open. Then they went to the kitchen door and with a scrubbing brush, which they broke to pieces, they forced that open—we women standing in the entry in the dark. They made repeated strokes at the door, and I think it was eight or ten minutes before they got it open. When they came in I had the windows open. They looked very mad. There was Peale, Smith, and a Col. Will. I spoke first and told them I was used ill, and I showed them the opinion of the lawyers. Peale read it; but they all despised it, and Peale said he had studied the law and knew they did right.

Nov. 13: I went with nurse to Mr. Craig's. Major Franks overtook us and told me he heard I was in great trouble at a report that Mr. G. was taken and carried into Boston, but that it was false. I told him I had not heard of it before, but I did not believe it, as Mr. G. went under the care of a man-of-war. The man-of-war would be taken too. When I got to Craig's I was more uneasy. But they all assured me it was a lie. They had made inquiry into it. In the evening came on a storm and it rained very hard, but I would come home, and I leaned on Johnny Commins. He held an umbrella over me; but I was so wet in my feet and petti-coats, as if I had been dipped in water; I was so frightened that we went into Owen Jones's. They told me to be easy, for Mr. G. was not taken. I came home from there in better spirits, and as I was walking in the rain my own chariot drove by. I own that I then thought it hard, but kept up pretty well; but when

I turned into the alley my dear child came into my mind, and what she would say to see her mamma walking five squares in the rain at night like a common woman, and go to rooms in an alley for her home. I dare not think, and when I got in shifted all my clothes, for I was dripping wet.

176 *Nov. 25:* I supped by myself. I want to write to my dearest child but cannot. Have such dreadful thoughts of her being dead that I have no peace, and am determined to go to her in the spring. As to myself, I am happy and the liberty of doing as I please makes even poverty more agreeable than any time I ever spent since I married. But my child is dearer to me than all nature, and if she is not happy, or anything should happen to her, I am lost. Indeed, I have no other wish in life than her welfare. Indeed I am concerned for her father; but his unkind treatment makes me easy, nay, happy not to be with him. If he is safe I want not to be kept so like a slave as he always made me, in preventing every wish of my heart.

April 20 [1779]: I went to Billy Turner's. The two Mrs. Bonds were there. I got my spirits at command and laughed at the whole Whig party. I told them I was the happiest woman in town, for I had been stripped and turned out of doors, yet I was still the same and must be J.G.'s wife and Lawrence Growdon's daughter, and that it was not in their power to humble me, for I should be Grace Growdon Galloway to the last, and as I had now suffered all that they can inflict upon me . . . That I would never let these people pull me down, for while I had splendid shilling left I would be happy in spite of them. My borrowed bed, I told them, was down and I could lay me down and sleep composedly on it without feeling one thorn, which was more than the creatures could do who had robbed me. But all that vexed me was that I should be so far humbled as to be ranked as a fellow creature with such brutes, for I could not think they could be called men. So I ran on and was happy, tho' Madam Bond seemed sometimes to wince.

It Was a Glorious Victory

It was women who nursed the wounded after the revolutionary war battles. Mary Hooks Slocumb (1760–1836), the sixteen-year-old wife of a troop commander in North Carolina's Light Horse Rangers, was at the crucial Battle of Moore's Creek Bridge on February 27, 1776, one of the bloodiest of the Revolution. Her spirited action matched her fervor; note her riding ability and her knowledge of curative leaves despite her youth. For the rest of her life, Mary

Slocumb boycotted British goods, always wearing homespun cloth for the sake of political principle.

From Elizabeth F. Ellet, *The Women of the American Revolution,* vol. 1 (1850; reprint, New York: Haskell House, 1969), pp. 316–21.

❖

The men all left on Sunday morning. More than eighty went from this house with my husband. . . . I kept thinking where they had got to—how far; where and how many of the regulars and tories they would meet; and . . . I had a dream. . . . I saw distinctly a body wrapped in my husband's guard-cloak—bloody—dead; and others dead and wounded on the ground about him. . . . If ever I felt fear it was at that moment . . . I told the woman I could not sleep and would ride down the road. She appeared in great alarm; but I merely told her to lock the door after me, and look after the child. I went to the stable, saddled my mare—as fleet and easy a nag as ever travelled; and in one minute we were tearing down the road at full speed. . . . When day broke I was some thirty miles from home. . . .

The sun must have been well up, say eight or nine o'clock, when I heard a sound like thunder, which I knew must be cannon. It was the first time I ever heard a cannon. . . . I spoke to my mare and dashed on in the direction of the firing and the shouts, now louder than ever. The blind path I had been following brought me into the Wilmington road leading to Moore's Creek Bridge, a few hundred yards below the bridge. A few yards from the road, under a cluster of trees were lying perhaps twenty [wounded] men. . . . In an instant my whole soul was centred in one spot; for there, wrapped in his bloody guard-cloak, was my husband's body! . . . I remember uncovering his head and seeing a face clothed with gore from a dreadful wound across the temple. I put my hand on the bloody face; 'twas warm; and an *unknown voice* begged for water. A small camp-kettle was lying near, and a stream of water was close by. I brought it; poured some in his mouth; washed his face; and behold—it was Frank Cogdell. He soon revived and could speak. I was washing the wound in his head. Said he, "It is not that; it is that hole in my leg that is killing me." A puddle of blood was standing on the ground about his feet. I took his knife, cut away his trousers and stocking, and found the blood came from a shot-hole through and through the fleshy part of his leg. I looked about and could see nothing that looked as if it would do for dressing wounds but some heart-leaves. I gathered a handful and bound them tight to the holes; and the bleeding stopped. I then went to the others; and—Doctor! I dressed the wounds of many a brave fellow who did good fighting long after that day! . . . Just then I looked up, and my husband, as bloody as a butcher, and as muddy as a ditcher, stood before me.

"Why, Mary!" he exclaimed, "What are you doing there? Hugging Frank

Cogdell, the greatest reprobate in the army?" . . . I would not tell my husband what brought me there. I was so happy; and so were all! It was a glorious victory. . . . In the middle of the night I again mounted my mare and started for home. Caswell and my husband wanted me to stay till next morning and they would send a party with me; but no! I wanted to see my child, and I told them they could send no party who could keep up with me. What a happy ride I had back! and with what joy did I embrace my child as he ran to meet me!

178

Not Afraid of the Cannonballs

Women accompanied the Continental army throughout the war, and even generals' wives did necessary domestic work. Sarah Osborn Benjamin (1756–ca. 1854), however, was only a private's wife. She was a cook and washerwoman for several years, so close to the front lines that she even met General Washington near the trenches and noticed Lord Cornwallis's crossed eyes when he surrendered at Yorktown. She described her service fifty years later when she petitioned for her husband's veteran pension.

From John C. Dann, ed., *The Revolution Remembered: Eyewitness Accounts of the War for Independence* (Chicago: University of Chicago Press, 1980), pp. 241–48. Copyright © 1980 by the University of Chicago.

❖

That after deponent had married said Osborn, he informed her that he was returned during the war, and that he desired deponent to go with him. Deponent declined until she was informed by Captain Gregg that her husband should be put on the commissary guard, and that she should have the means of conveyance either in a wagon or on horseback. That deponent then in the same winter season in sleighs accompanied her husband and the forces under command of Captain Gregg. . . .

Deponent further says that she and her husband remained at West Point till the departure of the army for the South, a term of perhaps one year and a half, but she cannot be positive as to the length of time. While at West Point, deponent lived at Lieutenant Foot's, who kept a boardinghouse. Deponent was employed in washing and sewing for the soldiers. . . .

In their march for Philadelphia, they were under command of Generals Washington and Clinton. . . . They continued their march to Philadelphia, deponent on horseback through the streets, and arrived at a place towards the Schuylkill where the British had burnt some houses, where they encamped for the afternoon and night. Being out of bread, deponent was employed in baking the afternoon and evening. Deponent recollects no females but Sargeant Lamberson's and Lieutenant Forman's wives and a colored woman by the name of Letta. The Quaker ladies who came round urged deponent to stay, but her said husband said, "No, he could not leave her behind." . . . [They marched to Baltimore and then sailed to Virginia where] they had a fine time catching sea lobsters, which they ate.

They, however, marched immediately for a place called Williamsburg, as she thinks, deponent alternately on horseback and on foot. There arrived, they remained two days till the army all came in by land and then marched for Yorktown, or Little York as it was then called. . . . Deponent was on foot and the other females above named and her said husband still on the commissary's guard. Deponent's attention was arrested by the appearance of a large plain between them and Yorktown and an entrenchment thrown up. She also saw a number of dead Negroes lying round their encampment, whom she understood the British had driven out of the town and left to starve, or were first starved and then thrown out. Deponent took her stand just back of the American tents, say about a mile from the town, and busied herself washing, mending, and cooking for the soldiers, in which she was assisted by the other females; some men washed their own clothing. She heard the roar of the artillery for a number of days, and the last night the Americans threw up entrenchments, it was a misty, foggy night, rather wet but not rainy. Every soldier threw up for himself, as she understood, and she afterwards saw and went into the entrenchments. Deponent's said husband was there throwing up entrenchments, and deponent cooked and carried in beef, and bread, and coffee (in a gallon pot) to the soldiers in the entrenchment.

On one occasion when deponent was thus employed carrying in provisions, she met General Washington, who asked her if she "was not afraid of the canonballs?"

She replied, "No, the bullets would not cheat the gallows," that "It would not do for the men to fight and starve too."

They dug entrenchments nearer and nearer to Yorktown every night or two till the last. While digging that, the enemy fired very heavy till about nine o'clock next morning, then stopped, and the drums from the enemy beat excessively. Deponent was a little way off in Colonel Van Schaick's or the officers' marquee and a number of officers were present, among whom was Captain Gregg, who, on account of infirmities, did not go out much to do duty.

The drums continued beating, and all at once the officers hurrahed and swung their hats, and deponent asked them, "What is the matter now?"

One of them replied, "Are not you soldier enough to know what it means?" Deponent replied, "No."

They then replied, "The British have surrendered."

Deponent, having provisions ready, carried the same down to the entrenchments that morning, and four of the soldiers whom she was in the habit of cooking for ate their breakfasts.

Deponent stood on one side of the road and the American officers upon the other side when the British officers came out of the town and rode up to the American officers and delivered up [their swords, which the deponent] thinks were returned again, and the British officers rode right on before the army, who marched out beating and playing a melancholy tune, their drums covered with black handkerchiefs and their fifes with black ribbands tied around them, into an old field and there grounded their arms and then returned into town again to await their destiny. Deponent recollects seeing a great many American officers, some on horseback and some on foot, but cannot call them all by name. Washington, Lafayette, and Clinton were among the number. The British general at the head of the army was a large, portly man, full face, and the tears rolled down his cheeks as he passed along. She does not recollect his name, but it was not Cornwallis. She saw the latter afterwards and noticed his being a man of diminutive appearance and having cross eyes.

On going into town, she noticed two dead Negroes lying by the market house. She had the curiosity to go into a large building that stood nearby, and there she noticed the cupboards smashed to pieces and china dishes and other ware strewed around upon the floor, and among the rest a pewter cover to a hot basin that had a handle on it. She picked it up, supposing it to belong to the British, but the governor came in and claimed it as his, but said he would have the name of giving it away as it was the last one out of twelve that he could see, and accordingly presented it to deponent, and she afterwards brought it home with her to Orange County and sold it for old pewter, which she has a hundred times regretted.

180

REVOLUTIONARY DAYS

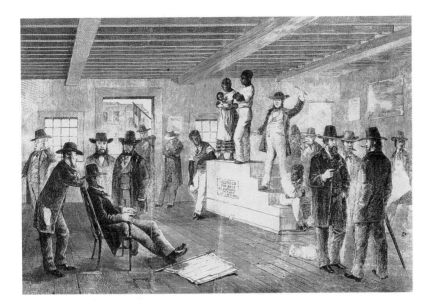

22. Slave Auction in Virginia

This picture was drawn by a New York newspaper illustrator, perhaps to indicate the growing northern abhorrence of slavery in the later colonial period. Clearly this family hopes to stay together, but their chances of being purchased as a group do not look promising if we note the lack of interest shown by the all-white, all-male prospective purchasers. Courtesy of Schomburg Center for Research in Black Culture, New York Public Library, Astor, Lenox, and Tilden Foundations.

23. *An Overseer Doing His Duty*

Notions about female weakness or delicacy did not spare black women from hard
field labor, watched by white overseers, on southern plantations. The noted contemporary architect and artist Benjamin Henry Latrobe captured such a scene in a
1798 watercolor-and-inkwash painting. Courtesy of Maryland Historical Society,
Baltimore.

24. Phillis Wheatley

Phillis Wheatley was hardly a typical eighteenth-century African-American woman. She was educated by her Quaker mistress, and her poems were published in 1773. She was invited to England soon after. Wheatley was freed when her mistress died, but freedom for a black woman in eighteenth-century Boston proved a mixed blessing. Her husband abandoned her, and she and her children died from poverty and disease in 1784. Engraving, September 1, 1773, from the frontispiece to Phillis Wheatley, *Poems on Various Subjects* (London, 1773). Courtesy of Schomburg Center for Research in Black Culture, New York Public Library, Astor, Lenox, and Tilden Foundations.

25. *A Society of Patriotic Ladies*

This British cartoon ridiculed the efforts of American women who were boycotting British goods to aid the cause of independence. Published on March 25, 1775, it depicted the signing of the Edenton Resolution by women in North Carolina. These women are caricatured as morally loose—drinking alcohol, flirting with bewigged gentlemen, and neglecting their children, one of whom is sitting on the floor and being licked by a dog that is not even housebroken. The slave in the background also has a rebellious expression on her face; "uppity" women might encourage all kinds of rebellion! Courtesy of the Library of Congress, Washington, D.C.

After the Storm

THOMAS JEFFERSON wrote in the Declaration of Independence that "all men are created equal," but he meant only white propertied males; he did not consider women, the poor, and black and Indian minorities. In a letter to a woman friend, on one occasion, Jefferson explained his view of appropriate female roles. He described the politically active women of France during the 1780s as "Amazons" and compared them with American "Angels." He seems to have been quite unaware of the contributions and political passions of American women during this era.

In spite of Jefferson's myopia, some brief legal and political gains were made after the Revolution. For example, in New Jersey, widows and spinsters with property voted in a number of local elections until 1807, when a politician they had opposed introduced legislation banning blacks and women from suffrage rights in that state. Claiming that "female reserve and delicacy are incompatible with the duties of a free elector," conservative New Jersey politicians repealed the voting rights of single tax-paying women, rights that had been granted without controversy in that state's 1790 constitution. (Women did not have the vote at all in other states.) Rhetoric about women's rights made its way into popular magazines and best-selling works such as Charles Brockden Brown's feminist tract *Alcuin* (1798). But as the century drew to a close, anxiety that potentially changing roles would endanger the family, fear that women would compete in business and political realms reserved for men, and concern that the French Revolution had unleashed dangerously democratic influences all combined to bring about more conservative definitions of women's "traditional" sphere.

These were political times, but the ideology of the Enlightenment, which dominated both revolutionary thinking and the doctrines of the new Republic, could lead in divergent directions: toward traditional thinking about women as well as toward more openness. Liberal Enlightenment thought separated individuals from their social contexts and therefore considered each person solely responsible for her/his own fate; no social or political circumstances accounted for the oppressive lives of many individuals. Additionally, this brand of individualism discouraged identifying oneself with a subgroup. Ideals of sisterhood, which had flourished earlier in the century, were frowned upon as divisive during this tumultuous time. Finally, the liberal philosophy of this era venerated reason above all other characteristics. For women, who had been identified as more emotional than men, this was another justification for male superiority. And without an equivalent education, women could hardly assert the equality of their untrained minds.

It was, however, in the area of education that women made some of their most impressive gains during the period after 1770. Early feminists, like Mary Wollstonecraft in England and Judith Sargent Murray in Gloucester, Massachusetts, argued that women needed a better education in order to discover their rational potential. Written in the 1780s and 1790s, Murray's widely read essays asserted that only education could confer dignity and a degree of equality on American women. The playwright and historian Mercy Otis Warren had argued a decade earlier that women needed education in order to develop their own intellects and teach the children entrusted to them.

The statesmen John Adams and Benjamin Franklin and the distinguished physician Benjamin Rush agreed that women needed to be better educated but emphasized that they should use this training to help with their husband's business and social concerns and to teach future male citizens. In 1787 Rush applied his very practical view of female education in the founding of the Philadelphia Female Academy, the first institution to implement ideas about female schooling that reached beyond the ornamental education offered by earlier dame schools or girl's boarding schools. Other teachers, like Susanna Rowson and Sarah Pierce in New England, followed this lead and established their own academies in the last years of the eighteenth century. But few of these early theorists envisioned the use that women would make of improved educational options. Academies emphasized self-respect for women, and the female networks that emerged often lasted throughout women's lives. Most important, the more education women received, the better able they were to recognize and articulate their own concerns.

Like middle-class women, working-class women were also measuring some gains during this period. In the interests of building a strong U.S. economy, like women all over the country, the women of Hartford continued to boycott imports and promote home industry after the Revolution. The nation's new secretary of the treasury, Alexander Hamilton, quickly recognized the potential of women's labor for the development of a manufacturing economy at a time when manpower was in short supply. Many of his advisers' reports on local industries and household manufacturing had shown that women's production in their homes was essential to the nation's economic survival and growth. But Hamilton's first *Report on Manufactures,* promoting industrial growth as a crucial factor in the new national economy, did not stress the value of women's work as much as it emphasized the idea that factory labor would make good use of women's and children's "idle" time. His report is one of the first denigrations of unpaid household labor in comparison with wage labor. Thus Hamilton contributed to the process of devaluing "women's work" whether it was done within or outside the home; the results can be seen in women's lower wages to this day.

Living on western frontiers presented other unusual challenges. Ann Bailey aided the U.S. Army in its battles against the Native Americans in the trans-Appalachian valley of the Kenhawha River. Bailey built a reputation for herself as a hardy individualist who was unafraid of the wilderness. On the other hand, Mary Jemison, captured during the French and Indian War, chose to live out her life among the Senecas of western New York State. Her description of life with her adoptive Indian family helps us understand the attractiveness of the more egalitarian Native American life-style for women at a time when gender hierarchies were solidifying in American society.

Many middle-class "ladies" read a controversial new book written by England's Mary Wollstonecraft and first published in 1792. She advocated freedom and equal rights for all women, but like Alice Izard, most Americans expressed dismay over and disapproval of both her radical ideas and her life-style, which included having a child out of wedlock. Philadelphia's Elizabeth Drinker wrote in her diary in 1796, "In very many of her sentiments she . . . *speaks my mind.*" Yet Wollstonecraft's unorthodox sexual behavior, publicly revealed when she died in 1797, made her anathema. Her ideas did not bear fruit until the next generation; Margaret Fuller and Elizabeth Cady Stanton, among others, viewed her with sympathy and often expressed their admiration for her ideas.

This section includes two diary accounts written by white middle-class Philadelphia women after the Revolution. For Ann Warder, little had changed in the social and working responsibilities of an urban woman whose genteel life was made possible by commercial wealth in the nation's leading city. Elizabeth Drinker's account of her daughter's childbirth experience is a reminder that even for wealthy women, who could afford to pay for a private doctor, the experience of giving birth remained a difficult and primarily female responsibility. For both women, strong ties with women relatives and friends remained the greatest source of comfort.

Of Amazons and Angels

Even the most radical statesmen of the new American Republic had no intention of giving women political equality. Thomas Jefferson, the author of the Declaration of Independence, governor of Virginia, and third president of the United States, was America's representative in France during the 1780s. In a letter to a woman friend, during the "political fever" just before the French Revolution and just after America's Constitutional Convention in Philadelphia, he praised "good" domestic American "Angels" in contrast to worldly "Amazons," legendary usurpers and destroyers of male prerogatives. Jefferson thought gossip was the only news worth sharing with a woman.

From "Letter to Anne Willing Bingham," May 11, 1788, in Julian P. Boyd, ed., *The Papers of Thomas Jefferson,* vol. 13 (Princeton, N.J.: Princeton University Press, 1956), pp. 151–52. Copyright © 1956 by Princeton University Press. Reprinted by permission of Princeton University Press.

Dear Madam ❖ Paris May 11. 1788.

A gentleman going to Philadelphia furnishes me the occasion of sending you some numbers of the Cabinet des modes and some new theatrical pieces. These last have had great success on the stage, where they have excited perpetual applause. We have now need of something to make us laugh, for the topics of the times are sad and eventful. The gay and thoughtless Paris is now become a furnace of Politics. All the world is run politically mad. Men, women, children talk nothing else; and you know that naturally they talk much, loud and warm. Society is spoilt by it, at least for those who, like myself, are but lookers on.— You too have had your political fever. But our good ladies, I trust, have been too wise to wrinkle their foreheads with politics. They are contented to soothe and calm the minds of their husbands returning ruffled from political debate. They have the good sense to value domestic happiness above all other, and the art to cultivate it beyond all others. There is no part of the earth where so much of this is enjoyed as in America. You agree with me in this: but you think that the pleasures of Paris more than supply it's want: in other words that a Parisian is happier than an American. You will change your opinion, my dear Madam, and come over to mine in the end. Recollect the women of this capital, some on foot, some on horses, and some in carriages hunting pleasure in the streets, in routs and assemblies, and forgetting that they have left it behind them in their nurseries; compare with our own countrywomen occupied in the tender and tranquil amusements of domestic life, and confess that it is a comparison of

Amazons and Angels.—You will have known from the public papers that Monsieur de Buffon, the father, is dead: and you have known long ago that the son and his wife are separated. They are pursuing pleasure in opposite directions. Madame de Rochambeau is well; so is Madame de la Fayette. I recollect no other Nouvelles de societé interesting to you, and as for political news of battles and sieges, Turks and Russians, I will not detail them to you, because you would be less handsome after reading them.

A New Source of Profit

Alexander Hamilton was the powerful treasury secretary during George Washington's two terms as the first president. He promoted industrial progress for the new nation by encouraging the employment of "idle" women and children in factories, claiming that farmers and communities would thus have a new source of profit and support. He wanted to emulate the "immense progress" of Great Britain, which he attributed to the cotton mill labor of women and children. Hamilton was establishing policy for coming generations, and he made women's labor a major component of that policy—a fact conveniently forgotten by those who would attribute America's economic greatness to the labor of men.

From Alexander Hamilton, "Report on Manufactures to the U.S. House of Representatives," Dec. 5, 1791, in *The Works of Alexander Hamilton,* vol. 4, ed. Henry Cabot Lodge (New York: G. P. Putnam's Sons, 1885–86), pp. 90–91.

❖

The cotton-mill, invented in England, within the last twenty years, is a signal illustration of the general proposition which has been just advanced. In consequence of it, all the different processes for spinning cotton are performed by means of machines, which are put in motion by water, and attended chiefly by women and children—and by a smaller number of persons, in the whole, than are requisite in the ordinary mode of spinning. . . . The prodigious effect of such a machine is easily conceived. To this invention is to be attributed, essentially, the immense progress which has been so suddenly made in Great Britain, in the various fabrics of cotton. . . .

In places where those institutions prevail, besides the persons regularly engaged in them, they afford occasional and extra employment to industrious individuals and families, who are willing to devote the leisure resulting from the intermissions of their ordinary pursuits to collateral labors, as a resource for multiplying their acquisitions or their enjoyments. The husbandman himself experiences a new source of profit and support from the increased industry of his wife and daughters, invited and stimulated by the demands of the neighboring manufactories.

Besides this advantage of occasional employment to classes having different occupations, there is another, of a nature allied to it, and of a similar tendency. This is the employment of persons who would otherwise be idle, and in many cases a burthen on the community, either from the bias of temper, habit, infirmity of body, or some other cause, indisposing or disqualifying them for the toils of the country. It is worthy of particular remark that, in general, women and children are rendered more useful, and the latter more early useful, by manufacturing establishments, than they would otherwise be.

The Mechanism of a Pudding

One of America's earliest women essayists was Judith Sargent Murray (1751–1820), whose pen name was "Constantia." She began publishing essays in 1784, and as this excerpt shows, she reflected the increasing interest in education and self-respect among women of the rising middle class in the new Republic. Her assertion of the equality of men's and women's minds is similar to the ideas of her English contemporary Mary Wollstonecraft, whose *Vindication of the Rights of Women* (1792) Murray later read. The belief that women should not humbly accept the limitations of the women's sphere foreshadows the more explicit feminist assertions of women like Elizabeth Cady Stanton over fifty years later, making Murray the first American feminist in print. Like Stanton, Murray found much in her own life to encourage her early feminism. Her first husband, a Gloucester, Massachusetts, sea captain whom she married at eighteen, died after seventeen difficult years of marriage. They had no children. She then married John Murray, a founder of the Universalist church in America. They had two children, but only their daughter survived. Murray spent most of her married life in the Gloucester mansion pictured in this section. As "Constantia," she had a long-standing interest in the education of young ladies, an interest matched only by her determination to be a writer and to prove that, with similar educational opportunities, women could reason as well as men.

From Judith Sargent Murray, "On the Equality of the Sexes," *Massachusetts Magazine,* March 1790, pp. 132–35.

❖

Is it upon mature consideration we adopt the idea, that nature is thus partial in her distributions? Is it indeed a fact, that she hath yielded to one half of the human species so unquestionable a mental superiority? I know that to both sexes elevated understandings, and the reverse, are common. But suffer me to ask, in what the minds of females are so notoriously deficient, or unequal? May not the intellectual powers be ranged under their four heads—imagination, reason, memory and judgment. The province of imagination has long since been surrendered up to us, and we have been crowned undoubted sovereigns of the regions of fancy. Invention is perhaps the most arduous effort of the mind; this branch of imagination hath been particularly ceded to us. . . . Observe the variety of fashions (here I bar the contemptuous smile) which distinguish and adorn the female world; how continually are they changing. . . . Now, what a playfulness, what an exhuberance of fancy, what strength of inventive imagination, doth this continual variation discover? . . . Another instance of our creative powers, is our talent for slander; how ingenious are we at inventive scandal? what a formidable story can we in a moment fabricate merely from the force of a prolifick imagination? how many reputations, in the fertile brain of a female, have been utterly despoiled? . . . Perhaps it will be asked if I furnish these facts as instances of excellency in our sex. Certainly not; but as proofs of a creative faculty, of a live imagination. Assuredly great activity of mind is thereby discovered, and was this activity properly directed, what beneficial effects would follow. Is the needle and kitchen sufficient to employ the operations of a soul thus organized? I should conceive not. Nay, it is a truth that those very departments leave the intelligent principle vacant, and at liberty for speculation. Are we deficient in reason? We can only reason from what hath been denied us, the inferiority of our sex cannot fairly be deduced from thence.

"But our judgment is not so strong—we do not distinguish so well." Yet it may be questioned, from what doth . . . superiority in this discriminating faculty of the soul, proceed. May we not trace its source in the difference of education, and continued advantages? Will it be said that the judgment of a male of two years old, is more sage than that of a female's of the same age? I believe the reverse is generally observed to be true. But from that period, what partiality! how is the one exalted and the other depressed, by the contrary modes of education which are adopted! the one is taught to aspire, and the other is early confined and limited. As their years increase, the sister must be wholly domesticated, while the brother is led by the hand through all the flowery paths of science. Grant that their minds are by nature equal, yet who shall wonder at the *apparent* superiority, if indeed custom becomes *second nature;* nay if it taketh the place of nature, and that it doth the experience of each day will evince. At length arrived at womanhood, the uncultivated fair one feels a void, which the employments allotted to her are by no means capable of filling. What can she do? to books, she may not apply; or if she doth, *to those only of the novel kind,* lest she merit the appellation of a *learned lady,* and what ideas have been affixed to this term, the observation of many can testify. Fashion, scandal and sometimes

187

what is still more reprehensible, are then called to her relief. . . . Meantime she herself is most unhappy; she feels the want of a cultivated mind. Is she single, she in vain seeks to fill up time from sexual employments or amusements. Is she united to a person whose soul nature made equal to her own, education has set him so far above her, that in those entertainments which are productive of such rational felicity, she is not qualified to accompany him. She experiences a mortifying consciousness of inferiority which embitters every enjoyment. . . .

188

Now, was she permitted the same instructors as her brother, (with an eye however to their particular departments) for the employment of a rational mind an ample field would be opened. In astronomy she might catch a glimpse of the immensity of the Deity. . . . In geography she would admire Jehovah in the midst of his benevolence. . . . In natural philosophy she would adore the infinite majesty of heaven, clothed in condescension; and as she traversed the reptile world, she would hail the goodness of a creating God. A mind, thus filled, would have little room for the trifles with which our sex are, with too much justice, accused of amusing themselves, and they would thus be rendered fit companions for those, who should one day wear them as their crown. Fashions . . . would then give place to conjectures, . . . and there would be no leisure for slander or detraction. Reputation would not then be blasted, but serious speculations would occupy the lively imaginations of the sex. Unnecessary visits would be precluded, and that custom would only be indulged by way of relaxation, or to answer the demands of consanguinity and friendship. Females would become discreet, their judgments would be invigorated, and their partners for life being circumspectly chosen, an unhappy Hyman [marriage] would then be as rare, as is now the reverse.

Will it be urged that those acquirements would supersede our domestick duties, I answer that every requisite in female economy is easily attained; and, with truth I can add, that once attained, they require no further *mental attention*. Nay, while we are pursuing the needle, or the superintendency of the family, I repeat, that our minds are at full liberty for reflection; that imagination may exert itself in full vigor; and that if a just foundation [is] early laid, our ideas will then be worthy of rational beings. . . . Should it still be vociferated, "Your domestick employments are sufficient"—I would calmly ask, is it reasonable, that a candidate for immortality, for the joys of heaven, an intelligent being, who is to spend an eternity in contemplating the works of the Deity, should at present be so degraded, as to be allowed no other ideas, than those which are suggested by the mechanism of a pudding, or the sewing of the seams of a garment?

Yes, ye lordly, ye haughty sex, our souls are by nature *equal* to yours; the same breath of God animates, enlivens, and invigorates us; . . . from the observations I have made in the contracted circle in which I have moved, I dare confidently believe, that from the commencement of time to the present day, there hath been as many females, as males who by *mere force of natural powers* have merited the crown of applause; who *thus unassisted,* have seized the wreath of fame. . . .

I know there are [those] who assert, that as the animal powers of the one sex are superior, of course their mental facilities also must be stronger. . . . But if this reasoning is just, man must be content to yield the palm to many of the brute creation, since by not a few of his brethen of the field, he is far surpassed in bodily strength. . . . Besides, were we to grant that animal strength proved anything, taking into consideration the accustomed impartiality of nature, we should be induced to imagine, that she had invested the female mind with superior strength as an equivalent for the bodily powers of man. But waving this however palpable advantage, for *equality* only, we wish to contend.

189

Constantia

Eve Was the Stronger Vessel

Judith Sargent Murray's early letters show that her independent thinking had been taking shape for years before her essays were published. Late in her life, Murray made copies of the letters and wrote, "Upon the whole, I commend these volumes of letters to affectionate posterity, and thus patronized, I am assured I have little to fear." The first three letters, addressed to young friends, discuss the female "virtue" that was beginning to define the mothers of the new Republic. Demonstrating the breadth of her reading, Murray argues for the biblical Eve's superiority against John Milton's famous line in *Paradise Lost:* "He [Adam] for God, and she for God in him." A letter to her cousin laments her lack of education (although she did attend sessions with her brother's tutor) and describes the hopeful confidence she discovered in religious faith. Writing to her brother, a major in the American Army, Murray argues that women have a special concern in matters of war and peace. During the horrible winter of 1778 spent by Washington's forces at Valley Forge, Murray seems to deplore the persecution of Loyalists, the desertions by American troops, and the sentiment—prevalent during this time among some Americans—to give up the fight for independence. She encourages her brother and other "admired Heroes" to fight on.

From Mississippi Department of Archives and History, Jackson, Mississippi. Transcription by Marianne Dunlop, Sargent-Murray-Gilman-Hough House Association, Independent Christian Church, Gloucester, Massachusetts, from the letterbooks discovered by the Reverend Gordon Gibson in 1986.

❖

To Miss Palfrey   Gloucester November 24th 1776

Thank you my good Girl for your care in sending me the card, and for your wishes, expressed with so much duteous ardour, and [so] marked by affection. . . . May you rank high in the esteem of those worthy individuals, to whom you are known, and with whom you stand connected. May Virtue be the guide of your every action—and if you are conscious of rectitude, do not over much lament the [censure] of those who are often misjudging. Let the opinion of the World obtain only second place in your estimation. . . .

Chastity is one of the most essential ornament[s] of female life—and it appears to me, that Chastity is, in an important sense violated, when those decorums which may be regarded as requisite barriers, are sacrificed. Yes, all beauteous, all potent virtue, and every rule which she hath benignly instituted, should ever obtain the most scrupulous observance, and filial reverence. I have then, my dear Girl, to wish that you would make it your first care, to approve yourself to the eye of Omniscience, when the plaudit of your own Conscience will become a natural consequence—and next, that you would endeavour to entitle your self to the respect of your fellow Creatures—and should you, in an attempt so praiseworthy, be ultimately unsuccessful, should censorious envy refuse its fairest hopes, be not too much depressed, but let the requittal of your own bosom, outweigh every other condemnation. Fame, we know, is a Time Server, ready to answer the purpose of every base employer; she lifts on high her trumpet, and the fairest reputation is wounded by her malignant shafts. Meantime, let the World condemn, or acquit, assure your self, my dear Girl, that in me you shall ever find a sympathizing friend.

To [Miss Goldthwait, a cousin]   Gloucester June 6th 1777

. . . Do you not know, my dear Girl, that every man is not an Adam—"True" you reply "but surely they ought to be unto their own Eves." Perhaps they ought—yet I must confess that my aspiring soul, would hang with most rapturous delight upon the seraphic sounds which we may suppose . . . would be attained by an angel of the Most High, [rather] than upon the tongue of any mortal, however dignified, however beloved, and this, I imagine, will more especially be my choice, were my senses divested of that density, in which our first Parents, by their heedless wandering hath so wrapped them about. It is a delicate hint of the inferiority of our sex, given by Milton in the passage to which you refer, but [even] had it been more severely [painted], it could no more than unveil the opinion of the Poet, as it respects the inferiority of our sex, but by no means established his hypothesis. This [compliment] upon the conjugal affection of our general Mother is, I confess, poetry. . . .

That Eve was the weaker Vessel, I boldly take upon me to deny—Nay, it should seem she was abundantly the stronger vessel since all the deep laid Art, of the most subtle fiend that inhabited the infernal regions, was requisite to draw her from her allegiance, while Adam was overcome by the softer passions, merely by his attachment to a female—a fallen female—in whose cheek "Distemper flushing glowed" and you know, my dear, that by resisting the aberrating Fair One, Adam would have given the highest proof of firmness. But forgive this levity, it is seldom I allow my pen thus to wander.

To Miss Goldthwait   Gloucester Jan. 5, 1778
    . . . . Nature my dear hath not been bounteous to me, she hath dealt her favours with a step Dame's hand. The circumstances of my life and the place of my residence hath contributed to contrasting ideas. My education hath been upon a very narrow scale. I was early committed to the care of an ill taught old Woman, which hopeful preceptress was to form me for my future part! How hard is the destiny of the generality of our sex. A few light romances, which tend rather to corrupt than to instruct a young mind, were all the helps which chance presented to me. Unless, indeed, I were to account the solemn lectures which I received from a superstitious, gloomy pastor, as such. Thus accomplished almost in the dawn of my being, reason but just budding, I was placed at the head of an encumbered family, and although children have not blest my marriage, yet, I assure you, I have not been exempt from care. "But to what purpose is this tedious harangue." Patience, good Cousin, I am coming to the point. In the very commencement of my career, I was seized by an alarming disposition, in the course of which, I became more intimately acquainted with that best of women, my Aunt E.S., from her I received the most elevated [understanding] of the Great First Cause—the Deity cloathed in humanity. The Deity united to the Sinner. . . . By a messenger from the Most High, I have since been led to trace "truths of sovereign aid to peace" through the volume of revelation and through the Universal page of Nature. These unmistakably point out an all Bountiful, an all gracious, a redeeming God. This stupendous Theme, like some mighty Virtue, seemed for a time to swallow up every inferior consideration. . . .

To my brother [Winthrop]   Gloucester Feb 25 1778
    . . . How shall I presume to detain your attention? I say presume, for e'er you receive this letter, the vernal season will be at the door[,] the skies will resume a serene aspect, and all Nature will be preparing to put on the most gay attire—in consequence of which, the military æra will commence, and contrasted to the mild atmosphere, and its peace inspiring azure, hostile fields will be displayed. Men will array themselves in all the dreadful habiliments of War!

Eagerly they will seize the deathful weapon, and prepare for the destruction of their fellow Man! What a sight for those guardian spirits by whom it is said we are surrounded! Surely they must turn with ineffable disgust from a scene so replete with horror—Did you ever read Swift's Gulliver? If you have not, I wish you would seize the first opportunity of devoting a small portion of your time to its perusal. But whither am I wandering—I meant merely to observe that as you will (to adopt my language to your feelings) e'er this letter can reach you, be engaged in the most momentous of temporal concerns, [a]ctively engaged in struggling for the sacred rights of Mankind, you will hardly be able to lend your ear to the prattle of a female fan.

192

. . . You will receive from my Father, domestic, and commercial intelligence accounts of Captures, etc., etc. What then remains for me to write? The welfare of my Country, the interests of this extensive Continent [then], I do assure you, are subjects very near my heart. I am persuaded you do not yield your reason to the tide of vulgar prejudice, you will not say a female is out of her sphere, although . . . she should venture to express her solicitude, for are not our sex interested as wives, as Mothers and as friends? Shall we not rise or fall with those to whom, by this the most [endearing], we are eternally bound—questionless we shall, and is it not natural for the susceptible heart to inquire where will these things end? Permit me then to ask—what are our prospects? A letter written, not long since, by you to my Father filled me with the most corroding apprehension. Alas! for us Moderation hath fled from our borders, she hath retired to climes more congenial with the benignity of her temperature. It is truly distressing, truly wonderful, to see those individuals, who were heretofore bound in bonds of consanguinity, and united in the most endearing friendship, now kindle into the most portentous rage, upon every discovery of opposite sentiments. Those in whose bosoms once flowed the milk of human kindness, who appeared uniformly calm, uniformly benevolent, are at this fearful period, actuated by the most baleful passions. Mistrust, and malevolence mark their conduct, and, not content with forging adamantine chains for the actions of their brethren, they aspire by their text, acts etc., etc. to fetter the free born Mind! Goddess of Liberty [armed] in all the Majesty of thy mighty power—shine upon this benighted World[,] [assert] thy genuine sway, and let a ray of thy divinity illume the chaos [now] so fearfully pervading. [Bind] us in thy silken bands, and let every heart enamoured with thy beauty feel that from confidence and unison, they can only derive real safety. Say, my dearest, are not our prospects [dreary]—Our Fortifications, while defended by men who must rank with the bravest Veterans, have yet fallen before the tools of arbitrary power. Does not oppression, with brazen front [stalk] forth gigantic[?] What spirit apparently influences our Senators—Are not our officers daily resigning? . . . I protest, I respond the few brave men, who remain with that General, so worthy of veneration, and whose name shall live upon the historic page, with peerless, and imperishable honour, I regard, I say those never enough admired Heroes . . . ye exalted, disinterested Patriots, my bosom swells with the most candid sentiments of your noble perseverance.

A Duty They Owe Their Country

Patriotic women continued their endeavors to aid their new country's economy after the Revolution. Their calls for frugality and home manufactures anticipated Secretary of the Treasury Alexander Hamilton's famous writings and speeches on this subject. In Hartford, Connecticut, the Ladies Association criticized extravagant fashions because their wearers relied on luxuries imported from Europe. They also counseled wearing clothing manufactured in this country in order to conserve and wisely invest the new nation's wealth. The newspaper reported that this association had begun with one hundred members but had rapidly grown to include "a majority of other ladies." Reprinted in the national magazine *American Museum, or Repository* in 1787, the association's boycott had widespread influence.

From *Hartford Courant,* November 6, 1786.

❖

The Ladies of the City of Hartford, taking into serious consideration the unhappy situation of their country, and being fully sensible that our calamities are in a great measure occasioned by the luxury and extravagance of individuals; are of opinion, that it is a duty they owe their country as well as their families, to retrench as far as possible all unnecessary expenses—that while the Gentlemen are anxiously devising other and more extensive plans of policy for the salvation of this and the United States, the Ladies may unite their influence in effecting the same desirable purpose by a strict attention to domestic economy and frugality.

Those Ladies that used to excel in dress, it is hoped will endeavour to set the best examples, by laying aside their richest silks and superfluous decorations, and as much as possible, distinguish themselves by their perfect indifference to those ornaments and superfluities which in happier times might become them.

Hoping for the concurrence of the ladies in every part of the State, and confident of the assistance and approbation of every Gentleman of sense and patriotism, they have subscribed to the following articles:

1. That from the date hereof, until the 25th of June next, they will not purchase any Gauze, Ribbons, Lace, Feathers, Beaver-Hats, Silks, Muslins and Chintzes, except only for weddings and for mourning.

2. They will dress their persons in the plainest manner, and encourage indus-

try, frugality, and neatness—giving all due preference to the manufactures of their own country.

3. That when they receive visits, and make entertainments, it will be their study to avoid unnecessary expense, especially in foreign articles.

194

4. During the above term, as they will have time to observe the operation of their plan, they will endeavour to turn their attention to the forming of a more systematic and extensive method of domestic economy, suited to the circumstances of their country, and continue the same by agreement to a greater length of time.—Hartford, Nov. 6. 1786.

Ann Bailey of the Kenhawha

Life after the Revolution beyond the Appalachian Mountains required very different skills from those needed by city dwellers like Judith Sargent Murray. Women like Ann Bailey, who had come with many other poor emigrants from England to America in the 1760s (note her working-class accent), faced wilderness living and understandable Indian hostility. Bailey's reknown was such that she became known as "the white squaw of the Kanawha" after her husband's death in 1774. One of her feats was riding one hundred miles alone to bring ammunition to besieged Fort Lee during Indian attacks in 1791. Anne Royall, a notable woman journalist, described Bailey after meeting her in 1823.

From Anne Royall, *Sketches of History, Life, and Manners in the United States* (New Haven, Conn.: Printed for the Author, 1826), pp. 59–60.

❖

This female is a Welch woman, and is now very old. At the time General Lewis's army lay at the Point, a station on Kenhawha River, Ann would shoulder her rifle, hang her shotpouch over her shoulder, and lead a horse laden with ammunition to the army, two hundred miles distant, when not a man could be found to undertake the perilous task—the way thither being a perfect wilderness, and infested with Indians. I asked her if she was not afraid—she replied "No, she was not; she trusted in the Almighty—she knew she could only be killed, and she had to die some time." I asked her if she never met with the Indians in her various journies, (for she went several times.) "Yes, she once met with two, and one of them said to the other let us kill her, (as she supposed, from the answer of the other,) no, said his companion, God dam, too good a soger [soldier], and let her pass:" but how, said I, did you find the way,—"Steered by the trace of Lewis's army, and I had a pocket compass too." "Well, but how did you get over the water courses?"—Some she forded, and some she swam, on others she made a raft: she "halways carried a hax and a hauger, and she could chop as well as hany man;" such was her dialect. This is a fact that hundreds can attest. A gentleman informed, that while the army was stationed near the mouth of the Elk, he walked down that river to where it intersects with the Kenhawha, for the purpose of fishing; he had not remained long there before he heard a plunge in the water, and upon looking up, he discovered Ann on horseback swimming toward him; when the horse gained the landing, she observed, "cod, I'd like to a swum." She was quite a low woman in height, but very strongly made, but had the most pleasing countenance I ever saw, and for her, very affable. "And what would the General say to you, when you used to get safe to camp with your ammunition." "Why he'd say, you're a brave soldier, Ann, and tell some of the men to give me a dram." She was fond of a dram. . . . I shall never forget Ann Bailey.

With Them Was My Home

Mary Jemison (1743–1833), one of many captive women who lived among Native Americans during the colonial and revolutionary eras, found the work of Indian women to be less burdensome than that of white women. She especially liked having "no master to oversee or drive us." Captured when she was fifteen, during the French and Indian War in frontier Pennsylvania, Jemison was adopted by the Senecas. After the Revolution she refused redemption, preferring to continue living with the Senecas, though she did retain her English name. Her biographer was amazed that she even insisted on sitting on the floor Indian-style when he interviewed her in her old age.

From James Seaver, ed., *A Narrative of the Life of Mrs. Mary Jemison* (Canandaigua, N.Y.: J. D. Bemis and Co., 1823), pp. 46–49.

❖

I had then been with the Indians four summers and four winters, and had become so far accustomed to their mode of living, habits and dispositions, that my anxiety to get away, to be set at liberty, and leave them, had almost subsided. With them was my home; my family was there, and there I had many friends. . . . Our labor was not severe; and that of one year was exactly similar, in almost every respect, to that of the others, without that endless variety that is to be observed in the common labor of the white people. Notwithstanding the Indian women have all the fuel and bread to procure, and the cooking to perform, their task is probably not harder than that of white women, who have those articles provided for them; and their cares certainly are not half as numerous, nor as great. In the summer season, we planted, tended and harvested our corn, and generally had all our children with us; but had no master to oversee or drive us, so that we could work as leisurely as we pleased. We had no ploughs on the Ohio; but performed the whole process of planting and hoeing with a small tool that resembled, in some respects, a hoe with a very short handle.

Our cooking consisted in pounding our corn into samp or hommany, boiling the hommany, making now and then a cake and baking it in the ashes, and in boiling or roasting our venison. As our cooking and eating utensils consisted of a hommany block and pestle, a small kettle, a knife or two, and a few vessels of bark or wood, it required but little time to keep them in order for use.

Spinning, weaving, sewing, stocking knitting, and the like, are arts which have never been practised in the Indian tribes generally. After the revolutionary war, I learned to sew, so that I could make my own clothing after a poor fashion; but the other domestic arts I have been wholly ignorant of the application of, since my captivity. In the season of hunting, it was our business, in addition to our cooking, to bring home the game that was taken by the Indians, dress it, and carefully preserve the eatable meat, and prepare or dress the skins. Our clothing was fastened together with strings of deer skin, and tied on with the same.

Gossiping About

Ann Warder's daily accounts present a picture of urban affluence and its impact on women's roles after the American Revolution. Although a Quaker and therefore opposed to ostentatious materialism, Warder obviously enjoyed the prosperity provided by her husband's fortune. Her daily visiting and entertaining may appear to be leisure activities, but performing these social obligations, along with managing a household, were hard work and were the major responsibilities of middle-class women of this period. Because there was little or no paid employment open to women, their station in life depended almost entirely on their fathers or husbands; for this reason, one will note the enormous importance of courtship and marriage in their lives. Quakers were expected to shun anyone who married a non-Quaker. Warder also refers to Grace Growden Galloway, "Betsy Galloway's mother," whose misfortunes were described earlier in this book by Galloway herself.

From "The Diary of Ann Warder," *Pennsylvania Magazine of History and Biography* 18 (1894): 51–63.

❖

9th mo. 22d. [1786]—After dinner prepared for a general ramble among my friends. First called on Hessy Fisher, who was rather unwell; then to Abijah Dawes, where I saw Sally; then to my much valued friend Sally Waln who was sitting very comfortably with Nicholas, who has not long returned from New England. After calling on Tommy Fisher went to James Pemberton's, whose wife has lately met with so severe loss in the death of Robert Morton. On the way home stopped at Uncle Head's, where was much company, and was given four bunches of grapes, with some of his best plums and peaches. I darned a place in my light calico gown torn some weeks ago, have had no time before to darn it, in which situation I have now a great heap of work that decreases very slowly through gossiping about, which is unavoidable without giving my kind friends offense, for the great number before I have got once around renders it necessary to begin again. . . .

9th mo. 23d.—Just as we dined brother and sister Vaux came in, but the afternoon being wet prevented us going to cousin Richard's. Johnny treated me today with a very friendly satin, the general wear in this country for young women. . . .

10th mo. 9th.—After dinner Lydia, Sally and Becky and myself were conducted by my husband, Jerry Parker and Dr. Parke to the public library, which is an humble imitation of our British Museum. However, there were some things I was much pleased with, remarkable snakeskins and a medal of William Penn; we also viewed the books of paintings and other curiosities. From there we proceeded to the Hospital, which is chiefly inhabited by lunatics in cells on the lower floor of the house. . . .

11th mo. 4th.—Early in the forenoon Cousin Nelly Parker and self went shopping and visiting—called at Tommy Fisher's, Nicholas Wain's and Hessy Fisher's, which nearly finished the morning and we had only time before dinner to go to Richard Vaux's for some purple gloves. He has a very neat store much like our wholesale warehouses, only it contains a greater variety of goods. . . .

11th mo. 8th.—We dined with Anne Giles, daughter to friend Clifford, her father and mother, with Tommy, John and wife, and brother and sister Warder. First rock fish, next mock turtle, ducks, ham and boiled turkey, with plenty of vegetables, and after these were removed, we had floating island, several kinds of pies with oranges and preserves. When we were well satisfied, left the men to their pipes and went up stairs to our chat. . . .

11th mo. 10th.—This morning most of the family busy preparing for a great dinner, two green turtles having been sent by Forbes & Stevens, of New Providence, to Johnny and to the firm. We concluded to dress them both together here and invited the whole family in. Aunt and uncle Hootton, uncle and aunt Baker, Uncle Head, Aunt Emlen, brother Jerry and wife, Caleb and wife, Billy Morris and wife, Jimmy Vaux and friend Sykes. We had a black woman to cook and an elegant entertainment it was—having three tureens of soup, the two shells baked besides several dishes of stew, with boned turkey, roast ducks, veal and beef. After these were removed the table was filled with two kinds of jellies, and various kinds of puddings, pies and preserves; and then almonds, raisins, nuts, apples and oranges. Twenty-four sat down at the table. I admired the activity of the lusty cook, who prepared everything herself, and charged for a day and a half but three dollars. . . .

11th mo. 27th.—My husband passed a restless night [with gout]; I had waited on him closely all day. While I was down stairs a sweet looking young woman called to see the girls, who in a few days is to be married out of the Society to the great Dr Hutchinson, many years older than herself and a widower with one son. Evident it is here that girls feel the scarcity of men or they would not sacrifice themselves. . . .

12th mo. 2d.—Our family reduced by Billy Parker going to Vaux Hill with brother James. Dr Parke called. Jerry, Lydia and Sally invited to dine with Dr Hutchinson and wife, which as they had been married by a priest would be hardly orthodox with us, but here much too many make no distinction, paying them just the same respect—calling the first three mornings to drink punch with the groom and the next week drinking tea with the bride. I think the evil consequences of mixed marriages are reduced in the view of some young minds, who perhaps become entangled in this improper way at some of these places. They had a large company and superb entertainment. In the evening sister M_____ came in when we had a long conversation on this subject, to which dress was introduced, when I warmly reprobated the too general practice of people here making such figures in the morning and when out such a show you scarcely know them. This being exactly *her* case; she pretended as an excuse, that it was very extravagant wearing long gowns to go about the house. I told her if my husband's circumstances would not afford me a good long gown, I had rather wear a common worsted one always, than like her sit at home not fit to be seen by man sometimes, and when out a Duchess could not be finer. She finding the whole company against her, the subject closed—my husband never goes to the house without giving her a rub. She wanted to retort upon Sally Morris, who she said dressed more than anybody. . . .

12th mo. 6th.—My best beloved able to walk with a little assistance to the window. Little Billy Morris last night had convulsions and continued in them for several hours, but today he is recovering fast. The cause proved to be from eating too many raw cranberries, many of which he swallowed whole. People here are not half attentive to children's food, they eat too many high seasoned and rich things themselves and the dear babes partake with them. After dinner Jerry Parker took Sally, Lydia, with myself and son, out sleighing, which I found much more agreeable than expected. We met several parties starting out as we returned. This pastime is abused; large parties collect and riotly go together to taverns where they sup and return at all hours of the night.

12th mo. 21st.—On coming home to dinner found sister Morris had desired my company to dinner, therefore went there and dined on nice partridge pie, soon after which Lydia and I went out shopping. I had better success than on a former occasion—wanting a piece of purple ribbon to let out a mitt, went to fifteen shops before obtaining it. Bought silk for a new light bonnet, gloves and Barcelona handkerchiefs, having an intimation that we were to be invited to Elliston Perot's wedding, and I may also want them to pay visits to several brides. . . .

199

2 mo. 19th. [1789]—Called on Debby Morris, who though an old maid has had her portion of care and trouble, being seldom without some one at her house who requires much of her, among them that much to be lamented woman Betsy Galloway's mother, who in all probability fell a victim to disappointment and distress. When her husband was driven from this city, she was prevailed upon by her friends not to stir, with the hope this would prove the means of securing her property. But alas! this was a mistaken idea, for the opposite party came and drove her out of her house by main force, she resolutely objecting to walk. A Friend having a carriage ready at the door took her to his house where she continued about three months and then came here. . . .

10th mo. 5th. [In 1788, Ann Warder's husband had presented her with a new house on the outskirts of Philadelphia.]—Anxious to see my destined habitation, we arose and went before breakfast—It is just about half a mile from mother's; too great a distance in some respects. The house pleased me, being exceedingly convenient, though larger than I wished, it having four rooms on a floor—Kitchen, counting house and two parlors on the first floor, eight bed rooms and two garrets. Many handy closets. A small yard and beyond it another with grass plot, good stable and chaise house, so that I see every prospect of our being comfortable. Came home to dinner; after tea Alithea and her husband called, and later William Savery to smoke a pipe with our beloved.

Sally's Birth Day

One of the most prominent women in America's leading city during the revolutionary war era was Elizabeth Drinker. Throughout much of her life, she kept a diary, from which comes the following description of the confinement of her daughter Sally. This birth of a new grandchild in 1799 vividly reveals the community of social concern and involvement that surrounded such an event, at least in the upper classes. Births took place at home, with a competent midwife and, if possible, one's mother always available. For the wealthy, a doctor was also on hand, though Sally's mother worried about the danger of his using instruments, known sometimes to lacerate the mother or damage the infant. Difficult childbirth might even require the destruction of the baby to remove it and save the mother's life; cesarean section was not feasible in the era before anesthesia, unless the mother was already dead. In Sally's case, Dr. William Shippen was the foremost doctor in the country, having studied in England to learn the use of forceps. It is notable that Drinker refers to the practice of deliberate birth control by means of long-continued breast-feeding to decrease the likelihood of conception. The practice of bloodletting and the use of laudanum, which contained opium, were remedies for all ailments, as common as aspirin is today.

From Elizabeth Drinker, Diary, October 23, 1799, ms. 94. By permission of the Historical Society of Pennsylvania, Philadelphia.

❖

October 23. My poor dear Sally was taken unwell last night. Dan [her servant] came for us early this morn'g Sister is gone there—I stay to see D'r Kuhn when he visits William who has not yet this morn'g had a return of the disorder—he is in bed and I hardly know how he is as yet—Sally has always been very lingering, how it will be this time, the Lord only knows. I am to be sent for if she should grow worse—this is her birth-day. . . .

Nancy Skyrin came in, she had been to see Sally. I believe she dont intend, if she can help it, to be with Sally at the extremity, she says that I need not leave William yet, that they will let me know when I ought to come, but having my cloak on and ready to go, and all things in order at home, I went—found D'r Shippen half asleep in the back parlor by himself—I question'd him relative to Sallys situation, he s'd she was in the old way, and he thinks she don't require bleeding by her pulse—. . . . went into Sallys Cham'r. she is in pain at times, forerunning pains of a lingering labour, a little low Spirited, poor dear Child—This day is 38 years since I was in agonies bringing her into this world of trouble: she told me with tears that this was her birth day, I endeavour'd to talk her into better Spirits, told her that the time of her birth was over by some hours, she was now in her 39'th year, and that this might possibly be the last trial of this sort, if she could suckle her baby for 2 years to come, as she had several times done heretofore &c.—I came home to dinner, found W.D. neither better or worse, brought little Henry home with me,—O dear! only to think that I have eat my dinner almost as heartily as usual, my Son pale and poorly up stairs, tho' on the recovery, and my Eldest daughter in actual labour, tho' not yet come to the extremity, could I have done so once? I think not; I believe that as we grow in years, we become more callous, or in some measure loose that quick sense of feeling, that attends us in our more youthful days: not that I have lost my sinsibility, oh no! by no means, but do not quite as much anticipate; 'tis a favour, granted to declining life:—If it was not for some moments of seeming forgetfullness, we might, perhaps sink under Troubles that we are often supported through. . . .

I went again afternoon left John James with H D—found no change had taken place: Sally in almost continual pain, I came home again in the even'g. William better . . . 'twas near 11 oClock when I got there—Sally was all night in great distress, the pain never quit off, sometimes on the bed, but most of the night in the Easy Chair as it is called,—between two and 3 oClock in the morn'g D'r Shippen desired Jacob to call up a John Perry, who lives near them, to open a vein, 'tho it is a opperation she very much dreads, she gave up to it without saying a word: he perform'd with great care and dexterity as I thought, he took twelve or 14 ounces. Sally had two smart, or rather hard pains while the bleeder was there, he is a married man; she has taken 80 or 90 drops liquid laudanum during the day and night but has not had many minutes sleep for 48 hours—the D'r says the Child is wedg'd on or near the shear bone and he cannot get at it, to alter the position of its head, I came home between 7 and 8 in the morning of the 24'th. after breakfast, and giving orders for dinner &c. W.D. up stairs, I went again to Sally, the Doc'r had given her an Opium pill three grains he said, in order to ease her pain, or to bring it on more violently: neither appear'd to happen—in the afternoon the Doc'r saw, the Child must be brought forward—he went out, which he had not done before, that he was going for instruments occur'd to me but I was afraid to ask him, least he should answer in the affirmative—towards evening I came home as usual, and after seeing all things in order, was getting ready to depart, when little Dan enter'd the sight of him flutter'd me, yet I had a secret hope that it was over, when Dan told us that his mistress had a fine boy and was as well as could be expected. . . . This joyfull intelligence quite changed my feelings, I was apprehensive that the Child would not be born alive;—my husband went with me there, they were at supper, very chearful, like Sailors after a storm—I went up to Sally, would not suffer her to talk.—I was thankful, that I happend to be absent at the time, tho' I intended otherwise. D'r Shippen told me that he thought he should have had occasion for instruments, which s'd he I have in my pocket, claping his hand on his side, when I heard them rattle, but some time after you went away, I found matters were chang'd for the better, the Child, said he, is a very large one for Sally.—It is a very fine lusty fatt boy, the same countenance as little Sally. . . . The Doctor was very kind and attentive during the whole afflicting scene, was there two nights and 2 days and sleep't very little—my husband, Nancy and self came home about 11 oClock—as I had not had my cloaths off for two days and one night, going backwards and forwards, with my mind disturbed, I felt exceedingly weary when I went to bed.

On Reading Mary Wollstonecraft

Like most other American ladies of their era, Alice Izard and her daughter Margaret Manigault, of Charleston, South Carolina, were familiar with Mary Wollstonecraft's *Vindication of the Rights of Women*. The book was first published in the United States in 1792. And most women would have agreed with Izard's righteous disapproval. That Izard was reading the book to her husband is one proof of the notoreity of Wollstonecraft's work. An English woman living "in sin" with French Revolution sympathizers, Wollstonecraft gained a controversial reputation, which contributed to suspicion of her carefully reasoned argument for women's equal rights. The book nevertheless influenced a whole generation to think about the legal conditions and education of women.

From Alice Izard letter to Margaret Manigault, May 29, 1801, Manigault Family Papers, South Caroliniana Library, University of South Carolina, Columbia.

❖

. . . I have just finished reading the rights of Woman to your Father, i.e. as much of it as I could read, for I was often obliged to stop, & pass over, & frequently to cough & stammer it. He is as much disgusted with the book as I am, & calls the author a vulgar, impudent Hussy. Certainly our Jes will never be improved by following her precepts or example. It is not by being educated with Boys, or imitating the manners of Men that we shall become more worthy beings. The great author of Nature has stamped a different character on each sex, that character ought to be cultivated in a distinct manner to make each equally useful, & equally amiable. The rank of a good Woman in society leaves her little to complain of. She frequently guides, where she does not govern, & acts like a guardian angel by preventing the effects of evil desires, & strong passions & leading them to worthy pursuits. An Author of merit remarks that many of the great events in life would never have taken place had not some men been married to some Women. Their names are not brought forward, but they enjoy the internal sense of their own abilities. "In which consists Woman's domestic honor, & true praise."

The Inconveniences of Allowing Females to Vote

The New Jersey Constitution of 1790 specifically allowed all inhabitants worth fifty monetary pounds of property, both male and female, to exercise the right to vote. But when women turned out to be a major factor in the victory of Thomas Jefferson over the Federalists in 1800, conservative opinion decried the "hideous" development of dangerous "party spirit" and the danger to female "reserve and delicacy" as women became "passive tools" of campaigning candidates. Such "inconveniences" far outrode the principle of justice, said the "Friend to the Ladies" who wrote the following letter. New Jersey repealed female suffrage in 1807.

From *True American,* October 18, 1802, quoted in Mary Philbrook, "Woman's Suffrage in New Jersey Prior to 1807," *Proceedings of the New Jersey Historical Society* 57 (1939): 95–96.

❖

For the True American:

Among the striking scenes which our election presents to the disinterested observer, none is more amusing than the sight of whole wagon loads of those "privileged fair", who for the lucky circumstance of being possessed of 50 pounds, and of being disengaged at the age of 21, are entitled to vote.

What a blissful week has the preceding one been for them! How respectfully attentive each young Federalist and Republican has been to the fair elector! How ready to offer them his horses, his carriages, to drag them in triumph to the election ground! Oh sweet week! Why do you not last the whole year round!

However pleasing these reflections may be to the Ladies it must be owned that the inconvenience attending the practice far outweighs the benefits derived from it. We may well be allowed to answer, without being accused of detraction, that those votes are rarely, if ever unbiased. Timid and pliant, unskilled in politics, unacquainted with all the real merits of the several candidates, and almost always placed under the dependence or care of a father, uncle or brother &c, they will of course be directed or persuaded by them. And the man who brings his two daughters, his mother and his aunt to the elections, really gives five votes instead of one. How will an obedient daughter dare to vote against the sentiments of her father and how can a fair one refuse her lover, who on his knees beseeches her by her beauty, by his passion, to give her vote to Lambert or Anderson!

When our Legislature passed the act by which the females are entitled to share in our elections they were not aware of its inconveniences, and acted from a principle of justice, deeming it right that every free person who pays a tax should have a vote. But from the moment when party spirit began to rear its hideous head the female vote became its passive tools, and the ill consequences of their admission have increased yearly. This year their number arose to an alarming height; in some townships I am told they made up almost one fourth of the total number of votes, and we cannot blame the apprehensions of an old farmer who feared that the next election would be entirely left to the ladies.

This defect in our Constitution certainly deserves the notice of our Government, and if not attended to may in a few years cause the most fatal confusion; for until it is amended, each party will of course muster all its female champions, from an apprehension that its antagonists will do the same.

Let not our fair conclude that I wish to see them deprived of their rights. Let them rather consider that female reserve and delicacy are incompatible with the duties of a free elector, that a female politician is often subject of ridicule and they will recognize in the writer of this a sincere

Friend to the Ladies.

Dated Oct. 18, 1802.

AFTER THE STORM

26. Abigail Adams
This portrait, said to be Abigail Adams as an older woman, testifies to her strength of character. Her dignified apparel and thoughtful expression suggest her role as a foremother of the new American Republic and wife of America's second president. By an unknown artist. Courtesy of New York State Historical Association, Cooperstown.

27. Home of Judith Sargent Murray

This beautiful New England frame house was built for Judith Sargent by her father in 1768–69 when, at age eighteen, she married her first husband, John Stevens, a sea captain. Judith Sargent Murray, regarded today as America's first feminist writer, lived there with her second husband, John Murray, from 1788 to 1793. In the eighteenth century, the house overlooked Gloucester's busy wharves and was surrounded by pleasant gardens. Its large and gracious rooms were decorated elaborately; by this date, the kitchen in middle-class homes had been relegated to a back room, where servants did most of the work. Today the house is a museum honoring Judith Sargent Murray, John Murray, the founder of Universalism, and her famous descendent, the painter John Singer Sargent. Photo courtesy of Sargent-Murray-Gilman-Hough House Association Board of Managers, Gloucester, Massachusetts.

PART THREE

The Nineteenth Century

Home and Marketplace

COMMERCIAL and industrial development accompanied massive terri-
torial expansion in the ambitious new United States of the nineteenth
century. Home and marketplace gradually became separate entities,
though even more dependent on one another; the self-sufficient household or
farm gradually became both unattainable and obsolete. Money replaced barter
as a means of exchange, and disparities of wealth, social status, education, and
economic development created growing divisions between regions and groups
as well as between the sexes.

Women like Roxanna Beecher decorated their floors by hand at the beginning of the century. Her daughter appreciated the cheaper textiles and changing
standards of cleanliness that were among the many aspects of nineteenth-century
progress. However, such progress had a dual effect on women's lives; the welcome improvements also necessitated more changes of clothing and increased
the burden of doing laundry. The intricacies of the clothes-washing process were
explained in a best-selling how-to book by Catharine Beecher, who assumed
that her middle-class readers would be supervising servants, rather than doing
the heavy labor themselves. But her directions for washing and starching different materials, as well as for doing many other household tasks, were also needed
by uprooted frontier women. Christiana Holmes Tillson's memoir about life on
the Illinois frontier in the 1820s shows how this transplanted New Englander
needed to relearn preindustrial skills like candlemaking and butchery in order
to survive.

Industrialization affected eastern and urban women first, eliminating some
tasks but increasing responsibilities in other ways. Community involvement in
such processes as cornhusking or flax preparation remained essential. Abigail
Scott Duniway tells what a difference it made in frontier Illinois when factory
production relieved her mother of some stages in cloth making, although a new
stove led to more complicated methods of cooking. Later, however, in 1850s
Oregon, Duniway was still cooking over a fire and making things by hand,
without any of the household help or amenities that many eastern or urban

women could take for granted. In addition, although urban birthrates were falling throughout the century, rural women like Duniway's mother produced the many children (twelve in her case) who became consumers of industry's products and provided labor power for frontier development. For example, every Oregon farm woman had at least one child under five in 1850—a significantly higher birthrate than that of India in 1961.

Women's household industry was a major source of cash income for hard-pressed families. Butter, eggs, woven cloth, or bread and pies found ready markets even if a farmer's crop failed or a miner could find no gold. Makeshift kitchens or a laundress's skill was the most reliable source of income in any gold-mining camp or newly settled town. Quilts made of textile scraps were cold-weather necessities for every household. But arranging those scraps into complex designs, and sewing them together with friends at a quilting bee, could also satisfy artistic urges and the need for female companionship. Indeed, a carpet like Zeruah Caswell's (see illustration) was a cherished artistic luxury, requiring years of her own labor.

As industrial development swept the nation, mills were established in every village where small or large rivers could be harnessed for power. Some companies used a "putting out" system, consigning certain processes to women in their homes at piece rates, to be returned to the factory for finishing. Women became silkworm growers, glove makers, seamstresses, or shoe stitchers to obtain cash to buy other products no longer made at home. They were usually poorly paid for long hours of labor, but sometimes their enterprises, like Mrs. Williston's button making, provided the foundation for a thriving family business.

In newly established factories from Maryland and Ohio to Maine, women were the indispensable work force. The logic of their recruitment was that industrialists were organizing and mechanizing the kind of work that women had previously performed at home. Everyone took it for granted that women had always worked and should continue to work. Furthermore, male workers were frequently unavailable; both ideology and the agrarian reality of the time required most men to tend independent farms or else move westward and establish new farms. However, some mill owners contracted for the labor of an entire family, with family wages paid to a man for himself, his wife (at a lower rate), and his children (at still lower rates). In a pattern not entirely dissimilar to the exploitative economy of southern slavery, these contracts plus company-owned housing and shops made for powerful paternalistic control of workers.

The Lowell Corporation in Massachusetts promoted a new method of recruiting women workers in the 1820s and 1830s. Hailed by contemporaries as a model of benevolence and efficiency, the carefully laid out new city of Lowell provided a "home-like" atmosphere of regulated boardinghouses and cultural opportunities for farmers' daughters. These "advantages" were supposed to mitigate the rigors of operating complicated looms thirteen or fourteen hours a day in noisy, lint-filled factory spaces. Harriet Farley's slightly fictionalized "Letters from Susan," published in a company-sponsored literary magazine, described the difficult working conditions as well as the pleasures of earned wages and other opportunities in a factory town.

Manufacturers began lowering wages and increasing work loads during and after the financial panic of 1837. They welcomed a mid-century influx of work-hungry immigrants from Germany and Ireland, who gradually replaced earlier workers. Factory women organized to petition against unhealthful conditions and fourteen-hour workdays and even led coordinated strikes in New England and Pennsylvania. Similar unrest swept urban centers like New York and Philadelphia. Even pieceworkers in rural villages felt the exploitation. A significant number of those who attended the first Women's Rights Convention in 1848 were local glove makers who felt underpaid by their employers.

Conditions continued to deteriorate, accentuating status differences between "millgirls," who had to work (but generally only until they married), and "ladies," for whom work outside the home was said to be "beyond their sphere." In New York, burgeoning commercial development took place in a city where cows and hogs still roamed the streets. Many impoverished immigrants could not afford to leave the city; women were particularly vulnerable to exploitation and misery. The Ladies' Moral Reform Association, focusing on individuals only, attempted to rescue and rehabilitate "fallen women," but the city health officer, Dr. William Sanger, documented the exploitative conditions of labor that oppressed so many working women and drove some of them into prostitution.

Industrialization, while accumulating wealth from female labor in northern factories, increased the leisure and cultural opportunities of middle- and upper-class white women in all sections of the country. But the economic transformation that moved so much work out of the home and into a cash-based marketplace also led to the undervaluing of the work of all women—whether enslaved in the South or employed in the North, whether at home or in the workplace. Earning pin money was not the same as breadwinning, and the distinction has remained in the American vocabulary. Still, most American women in the nineteenth century continued to do a prodigious amount of work for their expanding families and the expanding economy.

A Carpet for Her Parlor

Carpets and other luxuries were too scarce and expensive for most families in the early American Republic. Ordinary people left their floors bare or covered them with sand, swept into patterns and later swept away along with accumulated dirt. The mother of the educator Catharine Beecher, however, was more ambitious; in her first home on Long Island around 1800, Roxanna Beecher designed and made a carpet of her own, starting with a raw bale of cotton and doing all the labor herself except the weaving, which she hired out.

From Catharine Beecher, *Educational Reminiscences and Suggestions* (New York: J. B. Ford, 1874), pp. 10–12.

❖

. . . At one time my father bought a bale of cotton simply because it was cheap, without the least idea or plan for its use. On its arrival, my mother projected a carpet for her parlor, such an article being unused through the whole primitive town, where in place of carpet were lumps of wet sand evenly trodden down, and then stroked with a broom into zig-zag lines. So she carded and spun the cotton, hired it woven, cut and sewed it to fit the parlor, stretched and nailed it to the garret floor, and brushed it over with thin paste. Then she sent to her New York brother for oil-paints, learned how to prepare them from an Encyclopedia, and then adorned the carpet with groups of flowers, imitating those in her small yard and garden. In like manner she painted a set of old wooden chairs, adorned them with gilt paper cut in pretty figures, and varnished them. This illustrates the aesthetic element of her character directed to practical usefulness, while her beautiful specimens of needlework, her remarkable paintings of fruits, flowers and birds, her miniature likenesses of friends on ivory, accomplished when the mother of four and five young children, a housekeeper and a teacher of a boarding school, are all illustrations of her high ideals and her perseverance in attaining excellence in most unfavorable circumstances.

On Washing

Forty years later, Catharine Beecher described even more complex methods of housekeeping. Her *Treatise on Domestic Economy,* frequently reprinted for decades, was one of the most popular how-to books of the nineteenth century. Her advice reveals, however, that she assumed household work would be done by a domestic servant supervised by the lady who was her mistress. The chapter on washing also assumes a great many articles of clothing and types of cloth, widely available from factories. Comparing her detailed instructions for an urban housewife with the facilities available to frontier women like Abigail Duniway or Christiana Tillson shows how rising standards could complicate the lives of less-affluent women. Even the simplest washing required sorting, boiling, and stirring the heavy clothes and carrying all the necessary water by hand from a well. Such heavy labor would later become a women's rights issue when Duniway and other feminists argued that doing laundry ought not to be a housewife's work at all.

From Catharine Beecher, *A Treatise on Domestic Economy for the Use of Young Ladies at Home and at School,* 3d rev. ed. (New York: Harper and Brothers, 1858), pp. 284–89. ❖

There is nothing, which tends more effectually to secure good washing, than a full supply of all conveniences; and among these, none is more important, than an abundance of warm and cold water: but, if this be obtained, and heated, at a great expense of time and labor, it will be used in stinted measure. . . .

A plenty of soft water is a very important item. When this cannot be had, ley or soda can be put in hard water, to soften it; care being used not to put in so much, as to injure the hands and clothes. Two wash-forms are needed; one for the two tubs in which to put the suds, and the other for blueing and starching tubs. Four tubs, of different sizes, are necessary; also a large *wooden* dipper, (as metal is apt to rust;) two or three pails; a grooved wash-board; a clothes-line, (sea-grass, or horse-hair is best;) a wash-stick to move clothes, when boiling, and a wooden fork to take them out. Soap-dishes, made to hook on the tubs, save soap and time. Provide, also, a clothes-bag, in which to boil clothes; an indigo-bag, of double flannel; a starch-strainer, of coarse linen; a bottle of ox-gall for calicoes; a supply of starch, neither sour nor musty; several dozens of clothes-pins, which are cleft sticks, used to fasten clothes on the line; a bottle of dissolved gum Arabic; two clothes-baskets; and a brass or copper kettle, for boiling clothes, as iron is apt to rust. A closet, for keeping all these things, is a great convenience. It may be made six feet high, three feet deep, and four feet wide. The tubs and pails can be set on the bottom of this, on their sides, one within another. Four feet from the bottom, have a shelf placed, on which to put the basket of clothes-pins, the line, soap-dishes, dipper, and clothes-fork. Above this, have another shelf, for the bottles, boxes, &c. The shelves should reach out only half way from the back and nails should be put at the sides, for hanging the wash-stick, clothes-bag, starch-bag, and indigo-bag. The ironing conveniences might be kept in the same closet, by having the lower shelf raised a little, and putting a deep drawer under it to hold the ironing-sheets, holders, &c. A lock and key should be put on the closet. If the mistress of the family requests the washer-woman to notify her, when she is through, and then ascertains if all these articles are put in their places, it will prove useful. Tubs, pails, and all hooped wooden ware, should be kept out of the sun, and in a cool place, or they will fall to pieces.

Common Mode of Washing.

Assort the clothes, and put them in soak, the night before. Never pour hot water on them, as it sets the dirt. In assorting clothes, put the flannels in one lot, the colored clothes in another, the coarse white ones in a third, and the fine clothes in a fourth lot. Wash the fine clothes in one tub of suds; and throw them, when wrung, into another. Then wash them, in the second suds, turning them wrong side out. Put them in the boiling-bag, and boil them in strong suds, for half an hour, and not much more. Move them, while boiling, with the clothes-stick. Take them out of the boiling-bag, and put them into a tub of water, and rub the dirtiest places, again, if need be. Throw them into the rinsing-water, and then wring them out, and put them into the blueing-water. Put the articles to be stiffened, into a clothes-basket, by themselves, and just before hanging out, dip them in starch, clapping it in, so as to have them equally stiff, in all parts. Hang white clothes in the sun, and colored ones, (wrong side out,) in the shade. Fasten them with clothes-pins. Then wash the coarser white articles, in the same manner. Then wash the colored clothes. These must not be soaked, not have ley or soda put in the water, and they ought not to lie wet long before hanging out, as it injures their colors. Beef's-gall, one spoonful to two pailfuls of suds, improves calicoes. Lastly, wash the flannels, in suds as hot as the hand can bear. Never rub on soap, as this shrinks them in spots. Wring them out of the first suds, and throw them into another tub of hot suds, turning them wrong side out. Then throw them into hot blueing-water. Do not put blueing into suds, as it makes specks in the flannel. Never leave flannels long in water, nor put them in cold or lukewarm water. Before hanging them out, shake and stretch them. Some housekeepers have a close closet, made with slats across the top. On these slats, they put their flannels, when ready to hang out, and then burn brimstone under them, for ten minutes. It is but little trouble, and keeps the flannels as white as new. Wash the colored flannels, and hose, after the white, adding more hot water. Some persons dry woollen hose on stocking-boards, shaped like a foot and leg with strings to tie them on the line. This keeps them from shrinking, and makes them look better than if ironed. It is also less work, than to iron them properly.

Bedding should be washed in long days, and in hot weather. Pound blankets in two different tubs or barrels of hot suds, first well mixing the soap and water. Rinse in hot suds; and, after wringing, let two persons shake them thoroughly, and then hang them out. If not dry, at night, fold them, and hang them out the next morning. Bedquilts should be pounded in warm suds; and, after rinsing, be wrung as dry as possible. Bolsters and pillows can be pounded in hot suds, without taking out the feathers, rinsing them in fair water. It is usually best, however, for nice feathers, to take them out, wash them, and dry them on a garret floor. Cotton comforters should have the cases taken off and washed. Wash bedticks, after the feathers are removed, like other things. Empty straw beds once a year.

The following cautions, in regard to calicoes, are useful. Never wash them in very warm water; and change the water, when it appears dingy, or the light parts will look dirty. Never rub on soap; but remove grease with French chalk, starch, magnesia, or Wilmington clay. Make starch for them, with coffee-water, to prevent any whitish appearance. Glue is good for stiffening calicoes. When laid aside, not to be used, all stiffening should be washed out, or they will often be injured. Never let calicoes freeze, in drying. Some persons use bran-water, (four quarts of wheat-bran to two pails of water,) and no soap, for calicoes; washing and rinsing in the bran-water. Potato-water is equally good. Take eight peeled and grated potatoes to one gallon of water.

Clothes-pins Were Not Known There

Christiana Holmes Tillson (1796–1872), the newly married wife of a young land agent, reluctantly left New England for southern Illinois in 1822. The memoir she later wrote for her children included many vivid vignettes of western life. Washing, meat butchering, and candlemaking were doubly hard for Tillson because she had never done such work before. In the absence of established markets and with the continuing shortage of available labor, women of all classes had to work hard. Growing their own food and making their own clothes, soap, and candles, women were more than glad when markets and industry caught up with expanding settlement. The ability to purchase goods instead of making one's own would become an important mark of social status.

From Christiana Holmes Tillson, *A Woman's Story of Pioneer Illinois,* ed. Milo Milton Quaife (Chicago: Lakeside Press, 1919), pp. 25–26, 147–50.

❖

You may feel that I have attached undue notice to the meals given and the calls on our hospitality, but could you know the labor of bringing from raw materials anything at all presentable for family use, you would understand why the impression was so lasting. Besides the burden of cooking, there were many others. Every Monday morning, instead of pumping out a boiler of soft water, the kettle had to be suspended over the fire by means of pot-hooks fastened to a trammel that was suspended from a bar in the chimney. The getting the kettle hung was too severe for a woman's muscle, and a man had to be called into the performance. Then a small kettle containing ashes and water must also be put on the fire; when the small kettle boiled and the water became lye, it was taken off and settled as you would a pot of coffee; not with egg, but with cold water. When the large kettle of water boiled, the water from the small kettle must be dipped into it and stirred until flakes like snowflakes came up, and then, as Mother Seward—who instructed me in the process—would say, "the water was broke." The scum was then taken off from the top and the water dipped into tubs to cool, a thick sediment would fall to the bottom of the tubs, leaving the water clean and pure, ready for use. As several kettles full had to pass through this process, it would occupy the first half of washing day, thereby bringing everything wrong. When the clothes were washed I, contrary to all rule among my neighbors, hung them on a line instead of the fence, but as clothes-pins were not known there, had to wait until I could find Loomis in the right mood to whittle some out, which, after about three months, he accomplished. The first time they were used I was attracted to the window to see what was the source of such jollification as was being shown by two of our backwoods neighbors. They were looking at the clothes yard, and calling to the third, who was on his way to join them, "See here, ain't that jest the last Yankee fixin'? jest see them ar little boys ridin' on a rope."

We had no market and must live as did our neighbors on corn bread and "flitch." "Flitch" was the fat portion of the hog, which would be laid on the floor in one corner of their smoke-house, and salt sprinkled over it; it was a filthy process, and when cooked (fried) was a disgusting food; so in order to have more comfortable fare ourselves, and to have something in readiness for the visitors that so unceremoniously came upon us, I had recourse to all the poor wits I possessed. We usually had a quarter of beef—nothing less—brought at a time; sometimes a whole animal. Your father knew nothing about cutting and dividing meat, so by the help of directions laid down in a cookery book and a little saw I attempted this art. When I could not manage among the big bones I would enlist your Uncle Robert, and we performed wonderfully. A part would be salted down to be used for corn beef when the fresh had been eaten; the pieces for roast and steak set apart; the fat about the kidneys carefully picked out and put to dry for suet, and the remainder of the fat melted, strained, and put away for candles; a part made into "collared" or "pressed beef;" the round made into "hunter's beef," and the shins hung up in a cool place for soup; so in attending to the different ways of disposing of these things I had plenty to do, to say nothing of the care required in warm weather to keep the flies from leaving a deposit whereby animal life was engendered.

But the most tedious thing was candlemaking. Each desk in the office must be supplied with two candles, and with what was necessary for other parts of the house not less than three dozen would suffice for a week. Unfortunately for my own comfort I had experimented and made improvements in dipped candles until I had succeeded in getting them of such brilliancy that no others were to be used in the office. I used to dip sixteen dozen in the fall and twenty dozen in the spring. For the spring candles I boiled the tallow in alum water to harden it for summer use. Were I to attempt to tell you the process, or the labor bestowed on these "nocturnal luminaries," you would not comprehend it, and as the day is past for making them, being a part of housekeeping, it will not be worth while to expatiate further on their merits. But oh! I can fancy my poor, tired shoulder and strained arm are now in sympathy with the toil of tallow. Not like practicing two hours on the piano, which when you are tired you can stop, but from three to four mortal hours the right arm must be in constant movement. If a rest is given to the arm the candles become too hard and break, and the tallow in the pot gets too cool, so dip, dip, dip, six candles at a time; each time the candles grow heavier and heavier, and the shoulder more rebellious. Besides the dipped candles I had moulds in which I could mould two dozen at once, and all the accumulations from the beef that we weekly cooked was turned into moulded candles, which your father said looked well, but did not give as clear a light as his office candles. I sometimes bought a cake of deer's tallow; it was harder than beef, but not as white; the natives used to put beeswax in their tallow. I tried it, but found they emitted an unpleasant smoke.

A Woman's Lot Is So Hard!

When the suffragist and editor Abigail Scott Duniway (1834–1915), of Oregon, remembered her frontier Illinois childhood, she vividly recalled the work done by her mother and sisters and herself. Frequent childbearing accompanied heavy labor of all sorts; children cared for babies as their mother toiled at the weaving loom. It was an unusual luxury, requiring new skills, to cook on a stove rather than over a fireplace in 1844, though eastern women had started using stoves a generation earlier. Mrs. Scott rejoiced as industrialization removed some aspects of textile production from her domestic responsibilities, but her daughter was to face equally heavy labor on the Oregon frontier. In fact, it was Abigail's farm production that kept the entire family solvent.

216

From Abigail Scott Duniway, *Path Breaking* (Portland, Ore.: James, Kerns and Abbott, 1914), pp. 3–10.

❖

I was born October 22, 1834, just four years after my parents' wedding day, I being the third of their rapidly increasing family of a dozen, the eldest of whom had died in infancy, before the second child, a daughter, had seen the light. Their disappointment, when this second child was born a daughter, was severe; and when, about seventeen months after, I was born, I remember that my mother informed me on my tenth birthday that her sorrow over my sex was almost too grievous to be borne.

I must have been 9 or 10 years old when my father brought home the first cooking stove I had ever seen. It was a huge, awkward affair, and my mother said it was more trouble to keep it in order for baking than it was to do her cooking by the fireplace, as her neighbors did. . . .

. . . One day when my mother was busy at the loom in an adjoining cabin, our little sister Catherine, afterwards known to fame in many useful ways, . . . toppled forward from her chair and fell into the fire. I remember my sister and I trying to catch her as she fell, and, failing, joined a chorus of children's screaming voices and brought our agonized mother to the scene. To this day I cannot recall that incident without a shudder. My baby sister, too young to remember it, did not suffer after all, as we older ones did, who always felt that we ought to have known enough to have kept her away from the fire. . . .

Work in the maple sugar camp was one of the annual employments of my childhood's days. . . . I and my sister, seventeen months older, collected the sap, gathered branches from fallen trees, built the fires and boiled the syrup, which we carried to the house in pails for mother to "sugar-off." . . .

Then, too, I recall many hot Summer days, of seemingly interminable length, when we were kept busy at picking wool by hand, or paring and coring apples, stringing the quarters on twine for drying in the sun; such monotonous occupations often confining us from daylight until dark. When the "rolls" came home from the woolen mill, spinning by hand was next in order; then "spooling," "reeling" and "hanking" had also to be done, and our dear mother experienced great relief when the yarn was sent to the factory to be dyed and woven into cloth and blankets for household use, relieving her from much of her former labor as a manufacturer in the home. . . .

I remember standing at the bedside, when another little sister came to our crowded home, and my mother said, through her tears: "Poor baby! She'll be a woman some day! Poor baby! A woman's lot is so hard!"

. . . [In Oregon] I met my fate in the person of Mr. Ben C. Duniway, a young rancher of Clackamas County, who took me, a bride [of eighteen], to his bachelor ranch, where we lived for four years. . . . It was a hospitable neighborhood composed chiefly of bachelors, who . . . seemed especially fond of congregating at the hospitable cabin home of my good husband, who was never quite so much in his glory as when entertaining them at his fireside, while I, if not washing, scrubbing, churning, or nursing the baby, was preparing their meals in our lean-to kitchen. To bear two children in two and a half years from my marriage day, to make thousands of pounds of butter every year for market, not including what was used in our free hotel at home; to sew and cook, and wash and iron; to bake and clean and stew and fry; to be, in short, a general pioneer drudge, with never a penny of my own, was not pleasant business for an erstwhile school teacher, who had earned a salary that had not gone before marriage, as did her butter and eggs and chickens afterwards, for groceries, and to pay taxes or keep up the wear and tear of horseshoeing, plow-sharpening and harness-mending. My recreation during those monotonous years was wearing out my wedding clothes, or making over for my cherished babies the bridal outfit I had earned as a school teacher.

217

Piecin' a Quilt's Like Livin' a Life

Making bed quilts was both a practical and an artistic necessity, a form of productivity that almost every nineteenth-century woman learned at an early age. Quilts kept families warm, whether sleeping in log cabins or mansions. They utilized precious scrap materials. They enabled women to express a sense of beauty even in the most drab circumstances. And quilting bees provided opportunities for a sociable exchange of information and companionship.

From letter quoted in Ruth Finley, *Old Patchwork Quilts and the Women Who Made Them* (Newton Center, Mass.: Charles T. Branford Co., 1929, 1957), p. 37; Caroline R. Clarke, *Diary of Caroline Cowles Richards, 1852–1872* (New York: N.p., 1908), p. 102; Eliza Calvert Hall, *Aunt Jane of Kentucky* (Boston: Little, Brown, 1907), pp. 58–59, 64–65, 73–77.

❖

Ohio, February 7, 1841. . . . We have had deep snow. No teams passed for over three weeks, but as soon as the drifts could be broken through Mary Scott sent her boy Frank around to say she was going to have a quilting. Everybody turned out. Hugh drove to the Center where he and several other men stayed at the Tavern until it was time to come back to the Scotts for the big supper and the evening. There were papers at the Tavern, and Hugh says they are full of the New Whig President [William Henry Harrison]. . . . I took six squash pies for Mary's supper. My pumpkins all froze. She had two big turkeys and her famous bar le duc [a dessert of current jam and cream cheese]. What wouldn't I give to taste some real cranberry sauce again—and oysters. But of course we don't have anything like that here. One of Mary's quilts she called "The Star and Crescent." I had never seen it before. She got the pattern from a Mrs. Lefferts, one of the new Pennsylvania Dutch families, and pieced it this winter. A lot of Dutch are taking up land here in the Reserve. . . . Her other quilt was just an old fashioned "Nine-Patch."

❖

March 26, 1862. I have been up at Laura Chapin's from 10 o'clock in the morning until 10 at night, finishing Jennie Howell's bed quilt, as she is to be married very soon. Almost all of the girls were there. We finished it at 8 P.M. and when we took it off the frames we gave three cheers. Some of the youth of the village came up to inspect our handiwork and see us home. Before we went Julia Phelps sang and played on the guitar and Captain Barry also sang and we all sang together, "O, Columbia, the gem of the ocean, three cheers for the red, white and blue."

❖

". . . There never was any time wasted on my quilts, child. I can look at every one of 'em with a clear conscience. I did my work faithful; and then, when I might 'a' set and held my hands, I'd make a block or two o' patchwork, and before long I'd have enough to put together in a quilt. I went to piecin' as soon as I was old enough to hold a needle and a piece o' cloth, and one o' the first things I can remember was settin' on the back door-step sewin' my quilt pieces, and mother praisin' my stitches. Nowadays folks don't have to sew unless they want to, but when I was a child there warn't any sewin'-machines, and it was about as needful for folks to know how to sew as it was for 'em to know how to eat; and every child that was well raised could hem and run and backstitch and gether and overhand by the time she was nine years old. Why, I'd pieced four quilts by the time I was nineteen years old, and when me and Abram set up housekeepin' I had bedclothes enough for three beds.

"I've had a heap o' comfort all my life makin' quilts, and now in my old age I wouldn't take a fortune for 'em. . . . You see, some folks has albums to put folks' pictures in to remember 'em by, and some folks has a book and writes down the things that happen every day so they won't forget 'em; but, honey, these quilts is my albums and my di'ries. . . .

"Now this quilt, honey," she said, "I made out o' the pieces o' my children's clothes, their little dresses and waists and aprons. . . .

"Here's a piece o' one o' Sally Ann's purple caliker dresses. Sally Ann always thought a heap o' purple caliker. Here's one o' Milly Amos' ginghams—that pink-and-white one. And that piece o' white with the rosebuds in it, that's Miss Penelope's. She give it to me the summer before she died. Bless her soul! That dress jest matched her face exactly. Somehow her and her clothes always looked alike. . . .

"Here's a piece o' one o' my dresses," she said; "brown ground with a red ring in it. Abram picked it out. And here's another one, that light yeller ground with the vine runnin' through it. I never had so many caliker dresses that I didn't want one more, for in my day folks used to think a caliker dress was good enough to wear anywhere. Abram knew my failin', and two or three times a year he'd bring me a dress when he come from town. And the dresses he'd pick out always suited me better'n the ones I picked. . . .

"Did you ever think, child," she said, presently, "how much piecin' a quilt's like livin' a life? And as for sermons, why, they ain't no better sermon to me than a patchwork quilt, and the doctrines is right there a heap plainer'n they are in the catechism. Many a time I've set and listened to Parson Page preachin' about predestination and free-will, and I've said to myself, 'Well, I ain't never been through Centre College up at Danville, but if I could jest git up in the pulpit with one of my quilts, I could make it a heap plainer to folks than parson's makin' it with all his big words.' You see, you start out with jest so much caliker; you don't go to the store and pick it out and buy it, but the neighbors will give you a piece here and a piece there, and you'll have a piece left every time you cut out a dress, and you take jest what happens to come. And that's like predestination. But when it comes to the cuttin' out, why, you're free to choose your own pattern. You can give the same kind o' pieces to two persons, and one'll make a 'nine-patch' and one'll make a 'wild-goose chase,' and there'll be two quilts made out o' the same kind o' pieces, and jest as different as they can be. And that is jest the way with livin'. The Lord sends us the pieces, but we can cut 'em out and put 'em together pretty much to suit ourselves, and there's a heap more in the cuttin' out and the sewin' than there is in the caliker. . . .

"The same trouble'll come into two people's lives, and one'll take it and make one thing out of it, and the other'll make somethin' entirely different. There was Mary Harris and Mandy Crawford. They both lost their husbands the same year; and Mandy set down and cried and worried and wondered what on earth she was goin' to do, and the farm went to wrack and the children turned out bad, and she had to live with her son-in-law in her old age. But Mary, she got up and went to work, and made everybody about her work, too; and she managed the farm better'n it ever had been managed before, and the boys all come up steady, hard-workin' men, and there wasn't a woman in the county better fixed up than Mary Harris. Things is predestined to come to us, honey, but we're jest as free as air to make what we please out of 'em. . . . You can spoil the prettiest quilt pieces that ever was made jest by puttin' 'em together with the wrong color, and the best sort o' life is miserable if you don't look at things right and think about 'em right.

A Wife of the Right Sort

Gold miners of every sort have been immortalized in American myth, but the real gold in western mining towns was quite likely to be "mined" by women rather than men. As both of the following narratives indicate, the ability to do washing or run a boardinghouse (no matter how rudimentary) was far more lucrative than the search for mineral wealth. Louise Amelia Knapp Smith Clappe (1819–1906) wrote twenty-three letters to her sister in "the States" in 1851–52 describing life in the Rich Bar mining camp of California's Feather River canyon. She also published the letters under the pseudonym "Dame Shirley" in a local newspaper. Mary Ballou and her husband joined the California gold rush, leaving her children at home in Connecticut in the care of her oldest son, with the intent of making money from her cooking skills.

From Carl I. Wheat, ed., *The Shirley Letters from the California Mines, 1851–1852* (New York: Alfred A. Knopf, 1949), pp. 45–46; Mary Bean Ballou, "Journal of Her Voyage to California," Yale Collection of Western Americana, Beinecke Rare Book and Manuscript Library, Yale University, ms. #S-681.

❖

To-day I called at the residence of Mrs. R. It is a canvas house, containing a suite of three "apartments,"—as Dick Swiveller would say—which, considering that they were all on the ground-floor, are kept surprisingly neat. There is a barroom, blushing all over with red calico, a dining-room, kitchen and a small bedcloset. The little sixty-eight-pounder woman is queen of the establishment. By the way, a man who walked home with us, was enthusiastic in her praise. "Magnificent woman that, sir," he said, addressing my husband; "a wife of the right sort, *she* is. Why," he added, absolutely rising into eloquence as he spoke, "she earnt her *old man*," (said individual twenty-one years of age, perhaps,) "nine hundred dollars in nine weeks, clear of all expenses, by washing! Such women ain't common, I tell *you*; if they were, a man might marry, and make money by the operation." I looked at this person with somewhat the same kind of *inverted* admiration, wherewith Leigh Hunt was wont to gaze upon that friend of his, "who used to elevate the common-place to a pitch of the sublime;" and he looked at *me* as if to say, that, though by no means gloriously arrayed, I was a mere cumberer of the ground; inasmuch as I toiled not, neither did I wash. Alas!

I hung my diminished head; particularly when I remembered the eight dollars a dozen, which I had been in the habit of paying for the washing of linen-cambric pocket-handkerchiefs while in San Francisco. But a lucky thought came into my mind. As all men cannot be Napoleon Bonapartes, so all women cannot be *manglers;* the majority of the sex must be satisfied with simply being *mangled.* Re-assured by this idea, I determined to meekly and humbly pay the amount per dozen required to enable this really worthy and agreeable little woman "to lay up her hundred dollars a week, clear of expenses." But is it not wonderful, what femininity is capable of? To look at the tiny hands of Mrs. R., you would not think it possible, that they could wring out anything larger than a doll's night-cap. But, as is often said, nothing is strange in California. I have known of sacrifices, requiring, it would seem, superhuman efforts, made by women in this country, who at home were nurtured in the extreme of elegance and delicacy.

❖

My Dear Selden

. . . Well I suppose you would like to know what I am doing in this gold region. well I will try to tell you what my work is here in this muddy Place. All the kitchen that I have is four posts stuck down into the ground and covered over the top with factory cloth no floor but the ground. this is a Boarding House kitchen. there is a floor in the dining room and my sleeping room covered with nothing but cloth. we are at work in a Boarding House.

Oct 27 [1852] this morning I awoke and it rained in torrents. well I got up and I thought of my House. I went and looket into my kitchen. the mud and water was over my Shoes I could not go into the kitchen to do any work to day but kept perfectly dry in the Dining so I got along verry well. your Father put on his Boots and done the work in the kitchen. . . .

now I will try to tell you what my work is in this Boarding House. well somtimes I am washing and Ironing sometimes I am making mince pie and Apple pie and squash pies. Somtimes frying mince turnovers and Donuts. I make Buiscuit and now and then Indian jonny cake and then again I am making minute puding filled with rasons and Indian Bake pudings and then again a nice Plum Puding and then again I am Stuffing a Ham of pork that cost forty cents a pound. Somtimes . . . I am making gruel for the sick now and then cooking oisters sometimes making coffee for the French people strong enough for any man to walk on that has Faith as Peter had. three times a day I set my Table which is about thirty feet in length and do all the little fixings about it such as filling pepper boxes and vinegar cruits and mustard pots and Butter cups. somtimes I am feeding my chickens and then again I am scareing the Hogs out of my kitchen and Driving the mules out of my Dining room. you can see by the description of that I have given you of my kitchen that anything can walk into the kitchen that chooses to walk in and there being no door to shut from the kitchen into the Dining room you see that anything can walk into the kitchen and then from kitchen into the Dining room so you see the Hogs and mules can walk in any time day or night if they choose to do so. somtimes I am up all times a night scaring the Hogs and mules out of the House. last night there a large rat came down pounce down onto our bed in the night. sometimes I take my fan and try to fan myself but I work so hard that my Arms pain me so severely that I kneed some one to fan me so I do not find much comfort anywhere. I made a Bluberry puding to day for Dinner. Somtimes I am making soups and cramberry tarts and Baking chicken that cost four Dollars a head and cooking Eggs at three Dollars a Dozen. Somtimes boiling cabbage and Turnips and frying fritters and Broiling stake and cooking codfish and potatoes. I often cook nice Salmon trout that weigh from ten to twenty pound apiece. somtimes I am taking care of Babies and nursing at the rate of Fifty Dollars a week but I would not advise any Lady to come out here and suffer the toil and fatigue that I have suffered for the sake of a little gold neither do I advise any one to come. Clarks Simmon wife . . . came in here last night and said, "Oh dear I am so homesick that I must die," and then again my other associate came in with tears in her eyes and said that she had cried all day. . . . My own heart was two sad to cheer them much. . . .

there I hear the Hogs in my kitchen turning the Pots and kettles upside down so I must drop my pen and run and drive them out. so you this is the way that I have to write—jump up every five minutes for somthing and then again I washed out about a Dollars worth of gold dust the fourth of July in the cradle so you see that I am doing a little mining in this gold region but I think it harder to rock the cradle to wash out gold than it is to rock the cradle for the Babies in the States. . . .

Oh my Dear Selden I am so Home sick I will say to you once more to see that Augustus has every thing that he kneeds to make him comfortable and by all means have him Dressed warm this cold winter. I worry a great deal about my Dear children. it seems as though my heart would break when I realise how far I am from my Dear Loved ones this from your affectionate mother

Mary B. Ballou

Every Village Had Its *Curandera*

In the southwestern areas of the United States, which were still Mexican territories during the early nineteenth century, Spanish-American women were indispensable workers and caregivers within the still mostly feudal patriarchal system. Here Fabiola Cabeza de Baca describes her grandmother's experience, arguing that the frontier llano (the high plateau of what is now northwestern

Texas and northeastern New Mexico) broke down class distinctions and encouraged women's resourcefulness. However, like most colonizers, she overlooked the probable contributions of generations of Indian women to the Spanish knowledge of medicinal plants. With the transfer of the llano to a market economy and U.S. control in the latter half of the century, Hispanics in general, as well as women, gradually lost much of their autonomy.

From Fabiola Cabeza de Baca, *We Fed Them Cactus* (Albuquerque: University of New Mexico Press, 1954), pp. 59–61.

❖

The women on the Llano and Ceja played a great part in the history of the land. It was a difficult life for a woman, but she had made her choice when in the marriage ceremony she had promised to obey and to follow her husband. It may not have been her choice, since parents may have decided for her. It was the Spanish custom to make matches for the children. Whether through choice or tradition, the women had to be a hardy lot in order to survive the long trips by wagon or carriage and the separation from their families, if their families were not among those who were settling on the Llano.

The women had to be versed in the curative powers of plants and in midwifery, for there were no doctors within a radius of two hundred miles or more.

The knowledge of plant medicine is an inheritance from the Moors and brought to New Mexico by the first Spanish colonizers. From childhood, we are taught the names of herbs, weeds and plants that have curative potency; even today when we have doctors at our immediate call, we still have great faith in plant medicine. Certainly this knowledge of home remedies was a source of comfort to the women who went out to the Llano, yet their faith in God helped more than anything in the survival.

Every village had its *curandera* or *medica* and the ranchers rode many miles to bring the medicine woman or the midwife from a distant village or neighboring ranch.

Quite often, the wife of the *patron* was well versed in plant medicine. I know that my grandmother, Dona Estefana Delgado de Baca, although not given the name of *medica,* because it was not considered proper in her social class, was called every day by some family in the village, or by their *empleados* [employers], to treat a child or some other person in the family. In the fall of the year, she went out to the hills and valleys to gather her supply of healing herbs. When she went to live in La Liendre, there were terrible outbreaks of smallpox and she had difficulty convincing the villagers that vaccination was a solution. Not until she had a godchild in every family was she able to control the dreaded disease. In Spanish tradition, a godmother takes the responsibility of a real mother, and in that way grandmother conquered many superstitions which the people had. At least she had the power to decide what should be done for her godchildren.

From El Paso, Texas, she secured vaccines from her cousin, Doctor Samaniego. She vaccinated her children, grandchildren and godchildren against the disease. She vaccinated me when I was three years old and the vaccination has passed many doctors' inspections.

As did my grandmother, so all the wives of the *patrones* held a very important place in the villages and ranches on the Llano. The *patron* ruled the *rancho*, but his wife looked after the spiritual and physical welfare of the *empleados* and their families. She was the one called when there was death, illness, misfortune or good tidings in a family. She was a great social force in the community—more so than her husband. She held the purse strings, and thus she was able to do as she pleased in her charitable enterprises and to help those who might seek her assistance.

There may have been class distinction in the larger towns, but the families on the Llano had none; the *empleados* and their families were as much a part of the family of the *patron* as his own children. It was a very democratic way of life.

The women in these isolated areas had to be resourceful in every way. They were their own doctors, dressmakers, tailors and advisers.

The settlements were far apart and New Mexico was a poor territory trying to adapt itself to a new rule. The Llano people had no opportunity for public schools, before statehood, but there were men and women who held classes for the children of the *patrones* in private homes. . . . Dona Luisa Gallegos de Baca, who herself had been educated in a convent in the Middle West, served as teacher to many of the children on the Llano territory.

Without the guidance and comfort of the wives and mothers, life on the Llano would have been unbearable, and a great debt is owed to the brave, pioneer women who ventured into the cruel life of the plains, far from contact with the outside world. Most of them have gone to their eternal rest and God must have saved a very special place for them to recompense them for their contribution to colonization and religion in an almost savage country.

A Sempstress Wanted

In well-to-do families, the housewife's skills were supplemented by those of various domestic workers, of whom a good seamstress was perhaps most in demand. A single or widowed woman could obtain room, board, and wages, as indicated in the following advertisement. Other women might go from household to household, spending a few days at each place, fitting and sewing for the entire family.

From *National Intelligencer* (Washington, D.C.), July 1818.

❖

A Sempstress Wanted: One who can come well recommended for orderly deportment and good temper as well as skill and experience in her business, may have a good situation and very good monthly wages, in a family residing on Capitol Hill, and may engage for a year at a time. She must be skilled in cutting out and making boys' garments as well as the common plain needlework of a family. None need apply but those who show unquestionable testimonials. Inquire of William A. Scott, on Capitol Hill, or Mrs. Ann Sawyer on Pennsylvania Avenue.

A Button Business

Many early American industries had their foundations in the ingenious enterprise of a wife or mother. A "putting out system," practiced in Europe and America for several hundred years and still common in the nineteenth century, involved assigning specific stages of production to women in their homes. The following story, told by Samuel Williston to Caroline Dall, details the beginnings in 1825 of a significant Easthampton, Massachusetts, button company. One should remember that before the invention of zippers, buttons were virtually indispensable to every item of clothing.

From Caroline Dall, *College, Market, and Court; or, Woman's Relation to Education, Labor, and Law* (1867; reprint, New York: Arno Press, 1972), pp. 469–70.

❖

This great industry was founded by a woman. . . . I found Samuel Williston . . . very willing to tell his wife's story if it would "encourage other women."

"My wife's father . . . was a Mr. Graves. He was a poor man, with a large family of children. His wife and daughters used to go over to Northampton to get knitting from the stores. One day all the knitting had been given out; and Mrs. Graves showed her disappointment so plainly that the shopman asked her to take some buttons to cover. In those days, all the buttons came from England, where they were made by hand; but our tailor had got out, and wanted some for coats and vests in a hurry. Mrs. Graves made about a gross, all her daughters helping, and did it so well that the work was continued. Then my wife took it up. She got some of the work from her mother. That was in 1825–26,—forty years ago. I had invested in merino sheep, but I . . . found it hard to get along. It looked as though this business would help. My wife wanted to control the work. She hired girls to help her, and took all the orders that came. J. D. Whitney and Hayden & Whitney sold all she could make. When she had had the business a year, I went to Boston, Providence, Hartford, New Haven, New York,—in short, I went all around,—with samples. I got my orders at first hand, and from that the business began.

"When we heard that machine-made buttons had been introduced into England, we sent over to buy the right to make them, and Mr. Hayden introduced them here.

"Every man must have his small beginning," added Mr. Williston, with an embarrassed blush, "but, when a man has such a wife as mine, he is lucky."

Working in the Mill

This semifictional "letter," published in the *Lowell Offering* by its "millgirl" editor, Harriet Farley (1813–1907), purports to depict pleasurable work in one of New England's earliest factories. The magazine, subsidized by management, was one aspect of the company's active recruitment of women workers and the company's promotion of its image as a model of enlightened, benevolent industrial organization. But these women workers in newly industrialized America put in long hours of tedious labor. Though wages were high when the New England farmers' daughters first came to the factories in the 1830s, conditions soon deteriorated. A depressed economy and then an influx of cheaper immigrant labor enabled employers to cut wages and require more production, such as assigning one woman to three or four looms instead of one. The workers are seen in this excerpt enduring excessive heat, disagreeable smells, deafening noise, swollen feet and hands, and the pressures of piecework quotas—all of it "not disagreeable . . . when one is accustomed to it."

From Benita Eisley, ed., *The Lowell Offering: Writings by New England Mill Women (1840–1845)* (Philadelphia, Pa.: J. B. Lippincott, 1977), pp. 51–53.

❖

Dear Mary: In my last I told you I would write again, and say more of my life here; and this I will now attempt to do.

I went into the mill to work a few days after I wrote to you. It looked very pleasant at first, the rooms were so light, spacious, and clean, the girls so pretty and neatly dressed, and the machinery so brightly polished or nicely painted. The plants in the windows, or on the overseer's bench or desk, gave a pleasant aspect to things. You will wish to know what work I am doing. I will tell of the different kinds of work.

There is, first, the carding-room, where the cotton flies most, and the girls get the dirtiest. But this is easy, and the females are allowed time to go out at night before the bell rings—on Saturday night at least, if not on all other nights. Then there is the spinning-room, which is very neat and pretty. In this room are the spinners and doffers. The spinners watch the frames; keep them clean, and the threads mended if they break. The doffers take off the full bobbins, and put on the empty ones. They have nothing to do in the long intervals when the frames are in motion, and can go out to their boarding-houses, or do anything else that they like. In some of the factories the spinners do their own doffing, and when this is the case they work no harder than the weavers. These last have the hardest time of all—or can have, if they choose to take charge of three or four looms, instead of the one pair which is the allotment. And they are the most constantly confined. The spinners and dressers have but the weavers to keep supplied, and then their work can stop. The dressers never work before breakfast, and they stay out a great deal in the afternoons. The drawers-in, or girls who draw the threads through the harnesses, also work in the dressing-room, and they all have very good wages—better than the weavers who have but the usual work. The dressing-rooms are very neat, and the frames move with a gentle undulating motion which is really graceful. But these rooms are kept warm, and are disagreeably scented with the "sizing," or starch, which stiffens the "beams," or unwoven webs. There are many plants in these rooms, and it is really a good green-house for them. The dressers are generally quite tall girls, and must have pretty tall minds too, as their work requires much care and attention.

I could have had work in the dressing-room, but chose to be a weaver; and I will tell you why. I disliked the closer air of the dressing-room, though I might have become accustomed to that. I could not learn to dress so quickly as I could to weave, nor have work of my own so soon, and should have had to stay with Mrs. C. two or three weeks before I could go in at all, and I did not like to be "lying upon my oars" so long. And, more than this, when I get well learned I can have extra work, and make double wages, which you know is quite an inducement with some.

Well, I went into the mill, and was put to learn with a very patient girl—a clever old maid. I should be willing to be one myself if I could be as good as she is. You cannot think how odd every thing seemed to me. I wanted to laugh at every thing, but did not know what to make sport of first. They set me to threading shuttles, and tying weaver's knots, and such things, and now I have improved so that I can take care of one loom. I could take care of two if I only had eyes in the back part of my head, but I have not got used to "looking two ways of a Sunday" yet.

At first the hours seemed very long, but I was so interested in learning that I endured it very well; and when I went out at night the sound of the mill was in my ears, as of crickets, frogs, and jewsharps, all mingled together in strange discord. After that it seemed as though cotton-wool was in my ears, but now I do not mind at all. . . .

It makes my feet ache and swell to stand so much, but I suppose I shall get accustomed to that too. The girls generally wear old shoes about their work, and you know nothing is easier; but they almost all say that when they have worked here a year or two they have to procure shoes a size or two larger than before they came. The right hand, which is the one used in stopping and starting the loom, becomes larger than the left; but in other respects the factory is not detrimental to a young girl's appearance. . . .

You wish to know minutely of our hours of labor. We go in at five o'clock; at seven we come out to breakfast; at half-past seven we return to our work, and stay until half-past twelve. At one, or quarter-past one four months in the year, we return to our work, and stay until seven at night. Then the evening is all our own, which is more than some laboring girls can say, who think nothing is more tedious than a factory life. . . .

You ask if the girls are contented here: I ask you, if you know of *any one* who is perfectly contented. . . . The girls here are not contented; and there is no disadvantage in their situation which they do not perceive as quickly, and lament as loudly, as the sternest opponents of the factory system do. They would scorn to say they were contented, if asked the question; for it would compromise their Yankee spirit—their pride, penetration, independence, and love of "freedom and quality" to say that they were *contented* with such a life as this. Yet, withal, they are cheerful. I never saw a happier set of beings. They appear blithe in the mill, and out of it. If you see one of them, with a very long face, you may be sure that it is because she has heard bad news from home, or because her beau has vexed her. But, if it is a Lowell trouble, it is because she has failed in getting off as many "sets" or "pieces" as she intended to have done; or because she had a sad "break-out," or "break-down," in her work, or something of that sort.

You ask if the work is not disagreeable. Not when one is accustomed to it. It tried my patience sadly at first, and does now when it does not run well; but, in general, I like it very much. It is easy to do, and does not require very violent exertion, as much of our farm work does.

The Factory Bell

This poem by an anonymous factory worker in Exeter, New Hampshire, speaks of the changes in women's work brought about by industrialization. No longer did sunrise and sunset mark the beginning and end of a day's labor, as they had on the farm. And no longer did the worker work primarily for herself and her family. As the poem indicates, workers now labored according to the boss's bell, for small wages, so that owners could make profits. For some "Yankee millgirls," factory work meant independence, their own money, an opportunity to learn new things, and sisterly relationships with fellow workers. For others, millwork was oppressive.

From *The Factory Girls' Garland* (Exeter, N.H., ca. 1843).

❖

Loud the morning bell is ringing,
    Up, up sleepers, haste away;
Yonder sits the redbreast singing,
    But to list we must not stay.

Not for us is morning breaking,
    Though we with Aurora rise;
Not for us is nature waking,
    All her smiles through earth and skies.

Sisters, haste, the bell is tolling.
    Soon will close the dreadful gate;
Then alas! we must go strolling,
    Through the counting room, too late.

Now the sun is upward climbing,
    And the breakfast hour has come;
Ding, dong ding, the bell is chiming,
    Hasten, Sisters, hasten home.

Quickly now we take our ration,
    For the bell will babble soon;
Each must hurry to her station,
    There to toil till weary noon.

Mid-day sun in heaven is shining,
    Merrily now the clear bell rings,

And the grateful hour of dining,
    To us weary sisters brings.

Now we give a welcome greeting,
    To those viands cooked so well;
Horrors! oh! not half done eating—
    Rattle, rattle goes the bell!

Sol behind the hills descended,
    Upward throws his ruby light;
Ding, dong ding,—our toil is ended,
    Joyous bell, good night, good night.

A Factory Strike

Women factory workers began to protest their working conditions by organized strikes as early as 1828. Harriet Hanson Robinson (1825–1911) was only a child at the time of the first strike at Lowell Mills in 1836. Despite its failure, she remained proud of her participation. In 1844 Sarah Bagley established the Lowell Female Labor Reform Association, which petitioned the Massachusetts legislature for a ten-hour day, without success. Wage cuts and work increases, along with immigration, soon made factory labor far less appealing to the farm girls of New England.

From Harriet Hanson Robinson, *Loom and Spindle* (New York: Thomas Y. Crowell, 1898), pp. 83–86.   ❖

One of the first strikes of cotton-factory operatives that ever took place in this country was that in Lowell, in October, 1836. When it was announced that the wages were to be cut down, great indignation was felt, and it was decided to strike, *en masse*. This was done. The mills were shut down, and the girls went in procession from their several corporations to the "grove" on Chapel Hill, and listened to "incendiary" speeches from early labor reformers.

One of the girls stood on a pump, and gave vent to the feelings of her companions in a neat speech, declaring that it was their duty to resist all attempts at cutting down the wages. This was the first time a woman had spoken in public in Lowell, and the event caused surprise and consternation among her audience.

Cutting down the wages was not their only grievance, nor the only cause of this strike. Hitherto the corporations had paid twenty-five cents a week towards the board of each operative, and now it was their purpose to have the girls pay the sum; and this, in addition to the cut in the wages, would make a difference of at least one dollar a week. It was estimated that as many as twelve or fifteen hundred girls turned out, and walked in procession through the streets. They had neither flags nor music, but sang songs, a favorite (but rather inappropriate) one being a parody on "I won't be a nun."

> "Oh! isn't it a pity, such a pretty girl as I—
> Should be sent to the factory to pine away and die?
> > Oh! I cannot be a slave,
> > I will not be a slave,
> > For I'm so fond of liberty
> > That I cannot be a slave."

My own recollection of this first strike (or "turn out" as it was called) is very vivid. I worked in a lower room, where I had heard the proposed strike fully, if not vehemently, discussed; I had been an ardent listener to what was said against this attempt at "oppression" on the part of the corporation, and naturally I took sides with the strikers. When the day came on which the girls were to turn out, those in the upper rooms started first, and so many of them left that our mill was at once shut down. Then, when the girls in my room stood irresolute, uncertain what to do, asking each other, "Would you?" or "Shall we turn out?" and not one of them having the courage to lead off, I, who began to think they would not go out, after all their talk, became impatient, and started on ahead, saying, with childish bravado, "I don't care what you do, *I* am going to turn out, whether any one else does or not;" and I marched out, and was followed by the others.

As I looked back at the long line that followed me, I was more proud than I have ever been since at any success I may have achieved, and more proud than I shall ever be again until my own beloved State gives to its women citizens the right of suffrage.

The agent of the corporation where I then worked took some small revenges on the supposed ringleaders; on the principle of sending the weaker to the wall, my mother was turned away from her boarding-house, that functionary saying, "Mrs. Hanson, you could not prevent the older girls from turning out, but your daughter is a child, and *her* you could control."

It is hardly necessary to say that so far as results were concerned this strike did no good. The dissatisfaction of the operatives subsided, or burned itself out, and though the authorities did not accede to their demands, the majority returned to their work, and the corporation went on cutting down the wages.

And after a time, as the wages became more and more reduced, the best portion of the girls left and went to their homes, or to the other employments that were fast opening to women, until there were very few of the old guard left; and thus the *status* of the factory population of New England gradually became what we know it to be to-day.

A Platoon of Women

In the mid-1840s, petition movements and then strikes spread through the factories of New England, upper New York State, and Pennsylvania. Factory operatives from as far away as Manchester, New Hampshire, and Massachusetts organized fund-raising and child care for striking women in western Pennsylvania's Pittsburgh and Allegheny mills. In one instance, Pittsburgh employers locked out their workers unless they agreed to continue the twelve-hour work schedule. One hundred women, desperately in need of wages, agreed to return to work, so the machines were started again on July 30, 1846. A reporter described the resulting confrontation.

From *Pittsburgh Daily Commercial Journal,* July 30, 1846.

❖

We visited the scene of excitement at about 12 o'clock, M. . . . A dense mass of men, and children were collected around the front gate of the factory—facing toward the Allegheny—with the avowed intention of taking summary vengeance on the delinquents who had gone to work, so soon as they should get out for dinner.

Tired of waiting, and their passions constantly becoming more excited—demonstrations toward breaking open the gate were at last made.

An axe was procured, and a woman seizing hold of it commenced hewing away with true Amazonian vehemence and vigor.

The gate was of pine, and would soon have yielded to the energetic exertions of this young woman but for the protection afforded by an iron bar, which we were told secured it on the inside.

She at length desisted, wearied with the labor, and a man took the axe and threw it over the fence into the yard of the factory. . . .

At this juncture, a loud shout on Isabella street announced the occurrence of a new subject for excitement in that quarter. . . .

A portion of the crowd remaining, as if to guard the main gate, the greater number of them immediately proceeded to the new scene of action. The whole street . . . was soon densely thronged. . . .

Suddenly a cry arose that several women and children had been scalded from the engine room, and yells of vengeance were heard on all sides. . . .

As if by common consent, a rush was made to storm the factory. A platoon of women were in front as a sort of forlorn hope, followed by a storming party of men, who kept up a continuous cheer as the whole column moved on to the assault.

The scene at this moment was exciting in the extreme. The girls in front acted for the time as pioneers and commenced tearing away the boards from the fence so as to make a breach, through which their storming columns could enter.

Protected by a hurricane of brickbats, mud, and stones, these warriors made great progress, and in a short time a breach was made which the general in command (whoever he was) pronounced practicable, "Now, men!" "hurra!" "Give 'em h-ll!" and yells utterly indescribable by any combination of letters, announced the onset upon this second Molina del Rey.

The sheriff of the county, John Forsyth, esq.; the owners of the mill, clerks, and a detachment of the Allegheny police were inside and they prepared manfully to resist the attack.

Placing themselves opposite the breach they awaited the charge.

One moment of calm preceded the bursting of the storm, and then a general volley of brickbats and bludgeons commenced the grand movement of the day.

The authorities made a gallant stand, but in vain. In a minute they began to waver, and finally broke and retired from the disastrous encounter. . . .

The scene of uproar and confusion inside the yard now baffled description.

Stones and brickbats were flying in every direction and the windows in that part of the building were soon entirely destroyed. . . .

At this juncture it is said a man, who was on the fence, reached and struck a girl with a stick. In an instant the man was surrounded, and although he attempted escape he was very badly bruised and beaten. . . .

The battle was now over. No further resistance was attempted, and the insurgents held undisputed sway over the captured fortress; the works were silenced, the machinery stopped, and "Warsaw was conquered."

The operatives who had been employed abandoned their work.

At this moment a woman raised on the point of a pole a hat, which it was alleged had been captured from Mr. Kennedy, one of the owners, who was present with the sheriff when he attempted to resist the storming party. Loud cheers greeted this trophy of victory. . . .

We left the ground about 3 o'clock, when it appeared that the operatives had completely triumphed. The sheriff had abandoned the ground, as had also the police. The factory appeared to be completely in the power of the operatives, and they had it all their own way.

Working Women of New York in 1857

Dr. William Sanger was health officer for the city of New York during the 1850s, when he closely examined the medical and social reality of prostitution in the city. He prepared a questionnaire, answered by over two thousand women, to learn their backgrounds, living conditions, and medical problems. He also examined police reports, treated victims of syphilis and gonorrhea, and listened sympathetically to individual stories. Though his report, included within his lengthy and scholarly history of prostitution throughout the world, had little immediate effect, it is a rich source for knowledge about the poor women of New York in his time. Most of Sanger's conclusions are still relevant to the world's women today. This brief excerpt describes the working conditions that drove women into sexual servitude. Low wages, an oversupply of labor due to immigration and hard times, the hazards of domestic service, the "putting out" system among seamstresses, and the limited types of jobs available to women all contributed to their victimization.

From William W. Sanger, *The History of Prostitution* (1857; reprint, New York: Eugenics Publishing Co., 1937), pp. 524–34.

❖

Question. What trade or calling did you follow before you became a prostitute?

Occupations	Numbers	Occupations	Numbers
Artist	1	Shoe-binders	16
Nurse in Bellevue		Vest-makers	21
Hospital, N.Y.	1	Cap-makers	24
School-teachers	3	Book-folders	27
Fruit-hawkers	4	Factory girls	37
Paper-box-makers	5	Housekeepers	39
Tobacco-packers	7	Milliners	41
Attended stores or bars	8	Seamstresses	59
Attended school	8	Tailoresses	105
Embroiderers	8	Dress-makers	121
Fur-sewers	8	Servants	933
Hat-trimmers	8	Lived with parents	
Umbrella-makers	8	or friends	499
Flower-makers	9	Total	2000

Wherever the social condition of woman has been considered, one fact has always been painfully apparent, namely, the difficulties which surround her in any attempt to procure employment beyond the beaten track of needlework or domestic service. Numerous light or sedentary employments now pursued by men might with much greater propriety be confided to women, but custom seems to have fixed an arbitrary law which can not be altered. If a lady enters a dry goods store, she is waited upon by some stalwart young man, whose energy and muscle would be far more useful in tilling the ground, or in some other out-door employment. If she wishes to make a purchase of jewelry, she is served by the same class of attendants. Why should not females have this branch of employment at their command? . . .

In the list of occupations pursued by the women who are now prostitutes in New York, a most lamentable monotony is visible. Domestic service and sewing are the two principal resources. From the gross number of two thousand deduct those who lived with their parents or friends, children attending school, domestic servants and housekeepers, amounting in the aggregate to 1322, and there is a balance of 678, nearly six hundred of whom depend upon needles and thread for an existence. In the total number reported there are *only four, or exactly one in every five hundred,* who relied for support upon any occupation requiring mental culture, that is, one artist and three school-teachers. This fact in itself sustains the theories that mental cultivation and sufficient employment are restrictions to the spread of prostitution.

If women are compelled to undergo merely the slavery of life, no moral advancement can ever be expected from them. If every approach to remunerative employment is systematically closed against them, nothing but degradation can ensue, and the moralist who shuddered with horror at the bare possibility of a woman being allowed to earn a competent living in a respectable manner will ejaculate, "What awful depravity exists in the female sex!" He and others of his class drive a woman to starvation by refusing to give her employment, and then condemn her for maintaining a wretched existence at the price of virtue.

But to notice more particularly the employments which the courtesans of New York have followed. The domestic servants amount to 931. No modern fashion has yet been introduced to deprive females of this sphere of labor, but so progressive is the age that even that may be accomplished within a few years, and the advertising columns of the newspapers teem with announcements of some newly-invented "scrubbing-machine." . . . While allowing that many employers treat their servants as human beings gifted with the same sensibilities and feelings as themselves, it must be regretted that there are others who use them in a manner which would bring a blush to the cheek of a southern slave-driver. With such mistresses the incapacity of servants is a constant theme, nor do they ever ask themselves if they have learned the science of governing. Assuming that they themselves are right, they conclude that the "help" is, of course, wrong. Is it any wonder that girls are driven to intoxication and disgrace by this conduct? Another reason which forces servant-girls to prostitution is the excessive number who are constantly out of employment, estimated at one fourth of those resident in the city, an evil which would be diminished were there more opportunities for female labor.

236

What is the position of the needle-woman? Far worse than that of the servant. The latter has a home and food in addition to her wages; the former must lodge and keep herself out of earnings which do not much exceed in amount the servant's pay. . . . Working from early dawn till late at night, with trembling fingers, aching head, and very often an empty stomach, the poor seamstress ruins her health to obtain a spare and insufficient living. There is no variety in her employment; it is the same endless round of stitches, varied only by a wearisome journey once or twice a week to the store whence she receives her work, and where the probabilities are that a portion of her scanty wages will be deducted for some alleged deficiency in the work. She has no redress, but must submit or be discharged.

Nor is the position of a milliner or dress-maker much superior to this. She has a room provided for her in the employer's establishment, and there she must remain so long as the inexorable demands of fashion, or the necessity of preparing bonnets or dresses for some special occasion require. It matters not if she faint from exhaustion and fatigue; Mrs. _____ wants her ball-dress to-morrow, and the poor slave (we use this word advisedly) must labor as if her eternal salvation rested on her nimble fingers. But the gay robe which is to deck the form of beauty is completed; the hour of release has come at last; and, as at night the wearied girl walks feebly through the almost deserted streets, she meets some of the frail of her own sex, bedecked in finery, with countenances beaming from the effects of their potations, and the thought flashes across her mind, "They are better off than I am." Her human nature can scarcely repress such an exclamation, which is too often but the precursor of her own ruin.

Paper-box-makers, tobacco-packers, and book-folders are no better off. They must work in crowded shops, must inhale each other's breath during the whole day (for such work-shops are not the best-ventilated buildings in New York, generally speaking), and receive, as their remuneration, barely sufficient to find them food, clothes, and shelter. . . .

Question. What were your average weekly earnings at your trade?

Average Earnings	Numbers	Average Earnings	Numbers
1 dollar	534	7 dollars	8
2 dollars	336	8 dollars	5

3 dollars	230	20 dollars	1
4 dollars	127	50 dollars	1
5 dollars	68	Unascertained	663
6 dollars	27	Total	2000

Our cities are overcrowded; remove some of their inhabitants to the country. In our cities work can not be obtained; in the country both male and female laborers are urgently required. In cities an unemployed woman is exposed to innumerable temptations; in the country she need never be unemployed, and consequently would escape such dangers. . . .

In the city of New York one fourth part of the domestic servants are constantly out of employment; remove them, and, while the wants of the community will be amply supplied, the market value of a faithful servant would increase to a living rate. Send away a number of needle-women, reducing the supply of labor to meet the actual demand; tailors, shirt-makers, and dress-makers must employ seamstresses, and in such cases they could not obtain them without paying remunerative wages. The prices of our wearing apparel would probably be advanced five per cent., with a saving of fifteen per cent. taxation in the reduced expenses of police, judiciary, prisons, hospitals, and charitable institutions. . . .

The competition which keeps wages at starvation point is aggravated by a notion entertained by many native women, and by some foreigners who have been long in the country, that domestic service is ungenteel. This idea drives them to needlework to maintain their respectability, and thus, while service is abandoned, the ranks of seamstresses are augmented. By decreasing the number of the employed, and consequently advancing their wages and insuring better treatment from their employers, the servant's life would be divested of many of its objections, and old-fashioned house-work would once more be deemed respectable. This consummation rests more with mistresses than servants. The former give tone to the manners of the latter. It can not be denied that many young women date their ruin from unkind or unwomanly treatment by their mistresses, who have given a free rein to their caprices, confident that if a girl left them they could soon supply her place. This . . . would be an important step toward reducing prostitution. . . .

It can not be expected that this vice will decrease in New York when five hundred and thirty-four, out of a total of two thousand, earn only one dollar weekly. No economist, however closely he may calculate, will pretend that fourteen cents a day will supply any woman with lodging, food, and clothes. She who should attempt to exist on such a sum would starve to death in less than a month, and yet it is a notorious fact that many are expected to support themselves upon it. . . .

Thus far manufacturers have been blamed for the depression of wages, but is not the consumer equally open to censure? He purchases an article of dress from A, because it is a trifle cheaper than in B's store. The cost of the raw material is the same to each, and each uses the same quantity in every article; but if A can find customers for three times the amount of goods which B can sell, on account of the saving he effects through paying lower wages, it is scarcely in human nature, decidedly not in commercial nature, to be expected that he will refuse the opportunity. . . . The public sanction a system which enforces starvation or crime, and, for the sake of saving a few cents, add their influence to swell the ranks of prostitutes, and condemn many a poor woman to eternal ruin.

. . . Apart from the low rate of wages paid to women, thus causing destitution which forces them to vice, the associations of most of the few trades they are in the habit of pursuing are prejudicial to virtue. The trade of tailoress or seamstress may be cited as a case in point. . . . The woman leaves either a cash deposit or the guarantee of some responsible person at the store, and receives a certain amount of materials to be made up by a specified time: when she returns the manufactured goods she is paid, and has more work given her to make up. This may seem a very simple course . . . but one feature in it gives rather a sinister aspect. The person who delivers the materials, receives the work, and pronounces on its execution, is almost invariably a man, and upon his decision rests the question whether the operative shall be paid her full wages, or whether any portion of her miserable earnings shall be deducted because the work is not done to his satisfaction. In many cases he wields a power the determinations of which amount to this: "Shall I have any food to-day, or shall I starve?"

It is reasonable . . . to imagine that her necessities will force her to use every means to accomplish her task in a satisfactory manner . . . but there are instances where lubricity has exacted farther concessions, and the sacrifice of a woman's virtue been required as an equivalent for the privilege of sewing at almost nominal prices. . . . If the outrageous request is denied, she will get no more work from the shop, and may seek other employment with almost a certainty of meeting the same indignity elsewhere. That this is a frequent occurrence, unfortunately, can not be denied: that it exercises much influence on public prostitution can not be doubted.

HOME AND MARKETPLACE

28. *Embroidered Carpet*

This 1835 hand-embroidered wool carpet, about thirteen by twelve feet in size, consists of seventy-six squares and a removable rectangular section that covered the fireplace hearth during the summer. Zeruah Caswell, of Castleton, Vermont, sheared, spun, and dyed the wool for her creation. In a square directly in front of the hearth, she depicted the couple who would live with the carpet. Her initials and the date are at the top. She married Mr. Caswell in 1846, more than ten years after completing the carpet. It was her most prized possession for the rest of her life, about which nothing else is known. Zeruah Higley Guernsey Caswell. Courtesy of the Metropolitan Museum of Art, New York City. Gift of Katherine Keyes, 1938, in memory of her father, Homer Eaton Keyes. No. 38,157.

29. *The Quilting Party*

In this painting of a quilting bee, the unknown artist has shown the mix of generations as well as of sexes. While the women sew, the men serve the food and hold
the baby. There is a little romance developing in the righthand corner; perhaps
the quilt was being made for that couple's forthcoming wedding. Anonymous oil
painting on wood, ca. 1854, West Virginia. Courtesy of Abby Aldrich Rockefeller
Folk Art Center, Colonial Williamsburg Foundation, Williamsburg, Virginia.

30. *Flax-Scutching Bee*

Flax scutching was the first stage in the complicated linen-making process. It was often carried out at a community gathering, a "bee," where everyone enjoyed mutual companionship as well as work. This painting by a frontier artist shows the bundles, or "strikes," of flax at the left and the dagger-shaped wooden swingling knives used to beat the bundles to release the usable pith from the reluctant fibers. Romance was portrayed as one side effect of such community gatherings; the event was supervised by the pipe-smoking mistress of the homestead. Men and women worked together on such occasions, making the work somewhat easier and much more fun. Linton Park, painting. Gift of Edgar, William, and Bernice Chrysler Garbisch. © 1993 National Gallery of Art, Washington, D.C.

31. *Woman Spinning*

Although this photograph was taken later in the nineteenth century, the woman at
the spinning wheel had been doing such work all her life, transforming raw wool
into thread and then, as we can see at her feet, knitting the yarn into clothing
for her family. The photographer, Chansonetta Stanley Emmons, grew up in rural
Maine and used her art to capture the details of rural life which women shared
throughout the country. Note the large washtub in the background and the rain
barrel close at hand to collect pure water. Photograph by Chansonetta Stanley
Emmons in Emmons Collection. Courtesy of Colby College Museum of Art,
Waterville, Maine.

32. *Lowell Offering*—Title Page

This title-page engraving for the Lowell Mills literary magazine in 1845 attempts
to reconcile women's domesticity with the factory workplace. A demure young girl
holding a book and a market bag is surrounded by homelike vines and an industrious beehive. In the distant background, the church steeple symbolizes protection of her virtue and approval of the neighboring factory building. Photo from
Lowell Offering, 1845.

33. Power Loom Weaving

Women worked long hours at large power looms under strict supervision in the many new factories established throughout the Northeast in the 1830s. Women began by being responsible for one loom but were soon required to manage three or four at a time without any increase in pay. From "Power Loom Weaving," in George White, *Memoir of Samuel Slater* (1836; reprint, New York: A.M. Kelley, 1967). Courtesy of Merrimack Valley Textile Museum, Lowell, Massachusetts.

Women's Sphere

ONE OF THE ironies of the nineteenth century was its growing emphasis on the importance and moral superiority of the "woman's sphere," even as that sphere was increasingly separated from the "worldly" political and economic activities supposedly reserved to men. The rhetoric of separate spheres ignored the fact that women filled factories and worked diligently in frontier households or as slaves on southern plantations or as servants for the well-to-do; it stressed only the importance of women's innate virtue, mainly as wives and mothers supporting the Republic. Women themselves often used the same rhetoric as a means to justify expansion of their influence within its boundaries. Others made fun of the rhetoric and expanded their horizons regardless of sphere.

Throughout the century, conservatives like the editor of *Harper's New Monthly Magazine* in 1856 defined "the sentiment of home" as "the main-spring of our industry and enterprise" and did all they could to keep middle-class housewives inside those symbolic havens. For more than a hundred years, women were denied participation in the universal suffrage that national expansion had brought to white American men, even though ideologists continued to affirm the political significance of women's virtue. A mother's daily activities were thought to sanctify her existence as the symbolic center of family life. The *Harper's* editor continued:

> Home is the great power that rules the civilized man. . . . It is the main secret of our prosperity. It has done more to expand the territory, develop the resources, and enrich the wealth of our nation than any thing else. . . . Woman, its central figure . . . is a great moral and social power in our country. No people defer more to her than ourselves. She gives law to our households. (p. 554)

Pillared classical temples became the most popular architectural style of the time, while "pseudo-Gothic" villas built in the 1850s provided castle-like refuge in wealthy new suburbs (see illustration). Artists and poets depicted women as guardian angels of national expansion—Madonnas in sunbonnets or floating goddesses far above the turmoil of westward-moving wagon trains, as in John Gast's painting (see illustration).

Though women as well as men built new enterprises and communities, trekked across mountains and prairies, endured "primitive" frontier living conditions, and sought the personal freedom that was America's promise, concern about financial independence was seen as a man's prerogative. A "true woman" was supposed to be pious, obedient, and submissive to her husband's will and circumstances, devoting herself entirely to the physical and emotional care of her family, in accordance with the "subordinate but equal" notions articulated by Catharine Beecher and others. Gradually it became unseemly for women of "the better sort" to sell their labor for wages, though thousands of women of all sorts continued to do so out of family and personal necessity. The astute English sociologist Harriet Martineau traveled throughout the United States and claimed, in an 1837 essay, that American gentlemen indulged their women "as a substitute for justice" and that telling about "the condition of the female working classes" would make "emotions of horror and shame . . . tremble through the whole of society."

When Angelina Grimké spoke out in 1837 about the evils of slavery, especially in regard to women, the Congregational ministers of New England issued a pastoral letter saying that women's moral power should be exercised only through dependency and in private. When a woman "assumes the place and tone of man as a public reformer," they said, "she yields the power which God has given her for protection, and her character becomes unnatural." They used a metaphor about a woman's proper role as a clinging vine, which was repeated by men and repudiated by women for the rest of the century. (Later in the century, the feminist Abigail Scott Duniway sarcastically remarked that if a tree in the forest is well entwined by a vine, it will most likely be dead.)

Among the many reformers who penned witty rejoinders to the pastoral letter was the abolitionist poet and activist Maria Weston Chapman. Margaret Fuller pointed out that women's primary allegiance in conscience was to God, not men. The editor Amelia Bloomer was particularly incensed that the Tennessee legislature in 1849 solemnly agreed that married women did not have independent souls and could therefore not own property. The writer Caroline Kirkland denounced the notion of a woman's sphere "to which she is supposed to be fastened, as a door to its hinges; fulfilling her destiny if she be always at her *post* and never *ajar*." And the poet Emily Dickinson recognized and disdained the snobbish "Dimity Convictions" of conventional ladies.

In the nineteenth century as in the twentieth, there were differences among women about how best to achieve their goals. The educator Catharine Beecher thought that American women would always be protected and respected because men justly recognized women's moral superiority. The antislavery journalist Lydia Maria Child, on the other hand, in her *Letters from New York*, frequently expressed the idea that "gallantry" was "an odious word to every sensible woman" because it was merely "the flimsy veil which foppery throws over sensuality." Child preferred to concentrate on her writing and on personal actions against slavery. Some women preferred organizational and religious activism, whereas Emily Dickinson became a recluse in order to maintain her independence. Women disagreed about principles as well as about tactics, but they read each other's books, corresponded, visited, and helped one another with a strong sense of sisterhood. Few nineteenth-century women denied that there was need for much improvement in their condition.

By 1848, when Elizabeth Cady Stanton and Lucretia Mott organized the first Women's Rights Convention in Seneca Falls, New York, a groundswell of concern about a woman's right to legal control of her own property, to good health and comfortable clothing, to marital equality, and to the pursuit of education and of justice was coalescing into desire for political equality too. And women were becoming increasingly aware of the parallel injustices of slavery. The mothers of the American Republic were about to demand their share of the fruits of American citizenship. It would be a long time coming.

Subordinate but Equal

The writer-educator Catharine Beecher (1800–1878) was perhaps the most influential promoter of the doctrine of a "woman's sphere" in nineteenth-century America. The oldest daughter of Lyman Beecher, a notable Calvinist minister, and the sister of the novelist Harriet Beecher Stowe and the popular preacher Henry Ward Beecher, Catharine trained schoolteachers, lectured and wrote for female audiences, and argued for the systemization of housework, as in her analysis of clothes washing in the previous section of this book.

The opening chapter of her popular household manual expressed Beecher's admiration for Alexis de Tocqueville's new book and her belief in the interrelationship of democracy, Christianity, and a woman's separate sphere. She advocated a kind of trade-off: women should accept domestic and political subordination in order to guarantee respect for their moral superiority. They should exercise power only indirectly, for society's sake, believing that all decent men would do a good woman's bidding. Because of her affluent, middle-class, Protestant viewpoint, Beecher opposed woman suffrage as immoral, but her ideas provided a theoretical foundation for strong-minded assertiveness among women reformers, who would extend their "blessed influences" over the whole world in order to "renovate degraded man" and shape the earth into a temple of God.

From Catharine Beecher, *A Treatise on Domestic Economy for the Use of Young Ladies at Home and at School*, 3d rev. ed. (New York: Harper and Brothers, 1858), pp. 3–38.

242

❖

The tendencies of democratic institutions, in reference to the rights and interests of the female sex, have been fully developed in the United States; and it is in this aspect, that the subject is one of peculiar interest to American women. In this Country, it is established, both by opinion and by practice, that woman has an equal interest in all social and civil concerns; and that no domestic, civil, or political, institution, is right, which sacrifices her interest to promote that of the other sex. But in order to secure her the more firmly in all these privileges, it is decided, that, in the domestic relation, she take a subordinate station, and that, in civil and political concerns, her interests be intrusted to the other sex, without her taking any part in voting, or in making and administering laws. . . .

It appears, then, that it is in America, alone, that women are raised to an equality with the other sex, and that, both in theory and practice, their interests are regarded as of equal value. They are made subordinate in station, only where a regard to their best interests demands it, while, as if in compensation for this, by custom and courtesy, they are always treated as superiors. Universally, in this Country, through every class of society, precedence is given to woman, in all the comforts, conveniences, and courtesies, of life.

In civil and political affairs, American women take no interest or concern, except so far as they sympathize with their family and personal friends; but in all cases, in which they do feel a concern, their opinions and feelings have a consideration, equal, or even superior, to that of the other sex.

In matters pertaining to the education of their children, in the selection and support of a clergyman, in all benevolent enterprises, and in all questions relating to morals or manners, they have a superior influence. In such concerns, it would be impossible to carry a point, contrary to their judgement and feelings; while an enterprise, sustained by them, will seldom fail of success.

If those who are bewailing themselves over the fancied wrongs and injuries of women in this Nation, could only see things as they are, they would know, that whatever remnants of a barbarous or aristocratic age may remain in our civil institutions, in reference to the interests of women, it is only because they are ignorant of them, or do not use their influence to have them rectified; for it is very certain that there is nothing reasonable, which American women would unite in asking, that would not readily be bestowed.

The preceding remarks, then, illustrate the position that the democratic institutions of this Country are in reality no other than the principles of Christianity carried into operation, and that they tend to place woman in her true position in society, as having equal rights with the other sex; and that, in fact, they have secured to American women a lofty and fortunate position, which, as yet, has been attained by the women of no other nation. . . .

But the part to be enacted by American women, in this great moral enterprise, is the point to which special attention should here be directed.

The success of democratic institutions as is conceded by all, depends upon the intellectual and moral character of the mass of the people. If they are intelligent and virtuous, democracy is a blessing; but if they are ignorant and wicked, it is only a curse, and as much more dreadful than any other form of civil government, as a thousand tyrants are more to be dreaded than one. It is equally conceded, that the formation of the moral and intellectual character of the young is committed mainly to the female hand. The mother forms the character of the future man; the sister bends the fibres that are hereafter to be the forest tree; the wife sways the heart, whose energies may turn for good or for evil the destinies of a nation. Let the women of a country be made virtuous and intelligent, and the men will certainly be the same. The proper education of a man decides the welfare of an individual; but educate a woman, and the interests of a whole family are secured.

If this be so, as none will deny, then to American women, more than to any others on earth, is committed the exalted privilege of extending over the world those blessed influences, which are to renovate degraded man, and "clothe all climes with beauty."

No American woman, then, has any occasion for feeling that hers is an humble or insignificant lot. The value of what an individual accomplishes, is to be estimated by the importance of the enterprise achieved, and not by the particular position of the laborer. The drops of heaven which freshen the earth, are each of equal value, whether they fall in the lowland meadow, or the princely parterre. The builders of a temple are of equal importance, whether they labor on the foundations, or toil upon the dome.

Thus, also, with those labors which are to be made effectual in the regeneration of the Earth. And it is by forming a habit of regarding the apparently insignificant efforts of each isolated laborer, in a comprehensive manner, as indispensable portions of a grand result, that the minds of all, however humble their sphere of service, can be invigorated and cheered. The woman, who is rearing a family of children; the woman, who labors in the schoolroom; the woman, who, in her retired chamber, earns, with her needle, the mite, which contributes to the intellectual and moral elevation of her Country; even the humble domestic, whose example and influence may be moulding and forming young minds, while her faithful services sustain a prosperous domestic state;—each and all may be animated by the consciousness, that they are agents in accomplishing the greatest work that ever was committed to human responsibility. It is the building of a glorious temple, whose base shall be coextensive with the bounds of the earth, whose summit shall pierce the skies, whose splendor shall beam on all lands; and those who hew the lowliest stone, as much as those who carve the highest capital, will be equally honored, when its top-stone shall be laid, with new rejoicings of the morning stars, and shoutings of the sons of God.

Of Chivalry and Justice

Harriet Martineau (1802–76) was one of the most astute European observers of American society during the Jacksonian era. She toured the country from 1834 to 1836, visiting and talking with many American women shortly after Alexis de Tocqueville's similar journey. While she was still in America, her forthright disapproval of slavery and endorsement of abolitionism severely dampened her welcome, and the publication of her book made her even less popular. She took a view opposite of Catharine Beecher's and argued against Tocqueville's opinion that America's democracy and greatness was directly related to its deferential treatment of women; one of Martineau's major criticisms concerned America's subordination of women. Her critique encouraged the nascent women's rights movement of her time and still sounds relevant today.

From Harriet Martineau, *Society in America,* vol. 3 (London: Saunders and Otley, 1837), pp. 105–51.   ❖

If a test of civilisation be sought, none can be so sure as the condition of that half of society over which the other half has power,—from the exercise of the right of the strongest. Tried by this test, the American civilisation appears to be of a lower order than might have been expected from some other symptoms of its social state. The Americans have, in the treatment of women, fallen below, not only their own democratic principles, but the practice of some parts of the Old World.

The unconsciousness of both parties as to the injuries suffered by women at the hands of those who hold the power is a sufficient proof of the low degree of civilisation. . . . While woman's intellect is confined, her morals crushed, her health ruined, her weaknesses encouraged, and her strength punished, she is told that her lot is cast in the paradise of women: and there is no country in the world where there is so much boasting of the "chivalrous" treatment she enjoys. That is to say,—she has the best place in stage-coaches: when there are not chairs enough for everybody, the gentlemen stand: she hears oratorical flourishes on public occasions about wives and home, and apostrophes to women: her husband's hair stands on end at the idea of her working, and he toils to indulge her with money: she has liberty to get her brain turned by religious excitements, that her attention may be diverted from morals, politics, and philosophy; and, especially, her morals are guarded by the strictest observance of propriety in her presence. In short, indulgence is given her as a substitute for justice. Her case differs from that of the slave, as to the principle, just so far as this; that the indulgence is large and universal, instead of petty and capricious. In both cases, justice is denied on no better plea than the right of the strongest. In both cases, the acquiescence of the many, and the burning discontent of the few of the oppressed, testify, the one to the actual degradation of the class, and the other to its fitness for the enjoyment of human rights. . . .

245

The intellect of woman is confined by an unjustifiable restriction of . . . education. . . . As women have none of the objects in life for which an enlarged education is considered requisite, the education is not given. . . . There is a profession of some things being taught which are supposed necessary because everybody learns them. They serve to fill up time, to occupy attention harmlessly, to improve conversation, and to make women something like companions to their husbands, and able to teach their children somewhat. But what is given is, for the most part, passively received; and what is obtained is, chiefly, by means of memory. There is rarely or never a careful ordering of influences for the promotion of clear intellectual activity. Such activity, when it exceeds that which is necessary to make the work of the teacher easy, is feared and repressed.

. . . Nothing is thus left for women but marriage.—Yes, Religion, is the reply. . . . [But] American women have not the requisites for the study of theology. . . . It is religion which they pursue as an occupation; and hence its small results upon the conduct, as well as upon the intellect. . . . The sum and substance of female education in America . . . is training women to consider marriage as the sole object in life, and to pretend that they do not think so.

The morals of women are crushed. . . . The whole apparatus of opinion is brought to bear offensively upon individuals among women who exercise freedom of mind in deciding upon what duty is, and the methods by which it is to be pursued. There is nothing extraordinary to the disinterested observer in women being so grieved at the case of slaves,—slave wives and mothers, as well as spirit-broken men,—as to wish to do what they could for their relief: there is nothing but what is natural in their being ashamed of the cowardice of such white slaves of the north as are deterred by intimidation from using their rights of speech and of the press, in behalf of the suffering race. . . . A family of ladies, whose talents and conscientiousness had placed them high in the estimation of society as teachers, have lost all their pupils since they declared their anti-slavery opinions. . . . The incessant outcry about the retiring modesty of the sex proves the opinion of the censors to be, that fidelity to conscience is inconsistent with retiring modesty. . . . The brave American wives and daughters of half a century ago are honoured, while the intrepid moralists of the present day, worthy of their grandmothers, are made the confessors and martyrs of their age. . . .

How fearfully the morals of women are crushed, appears from the prevalent persuasion that there are virtues which are peculiarly masculine, and others which are peculiarly feminine. It is amazing that a society which makes a most emphatic profession of its Christianity, should almost universally entertain such a fallacy. . . . It is not only that masculine and feminine employments are supposed to be properly different. No one in the world, I believe, questions this. But it is actually supposed that what are called the hardy virtues are more appropriate to men, and the gentler to women. . . .

. . . The consequences are [that] . . . Men are ungentle, tyrannical. They abuse the right of the strongest, however they may veil the abuse with indulgence. They want the magnanimity to discern woman's human rights; and they crush her morals rather than allow them. Women are, as might be anticipated, weak, ignorant and subservient, in as far as they exchange self-reliance for reliance on anything out of themselves. . . .

One consequence, mournful and injurious, of the "chivalrous" taste and temper of a country with regard to its men is that it is difficult, where it is not impossible, for women to earn their bread. Where it is a boast that women do not labour, the encouragement and rewards of labour are not provided. It is so in America. . . . The lot of poor women is sad. Before the opening of the factories, there were but three resources; teaching, needle-work, and keeping boarding-houses or hotels. Now, there are the mills; and women are employed in printing-offices; as compositors, as well as folders and stitchers.

I dare not trust myself to do more than touch on this topic . . . for the mischief lies in the system by which women are depressed, so as to have the greater number of objects of pursuit placed beyond their reach. . . . The condition of the female working classes is such that if its sufferings were but made known, emotions of horror and shame would tremble through the whole of society. . . .

. . . On the whole, the scanty reward of female labour in America remains the reproach to the country which its philanthropists have for some years proclaimed it to be. I hope they will persevere in their proclamation, though special methods of charity will not avail to cure the evil. It lies deep; it lies in the subordination of the sex. . . . All women should inform themselves of the condition of their sex, and of their own position.

An Odious Word to Every Sensible Woman

Lydia Maria Child (1802–80) was one of the earliest proponents of women's rights. She also published America's first history of slavery, in 1833—for which she was shunned by proper Bostonians. She was a successful novelist and the editor of the *Juvenile Miscellany,* America's first children's magazine, which later folded because her subscribers disapproved of her antislavery reputation. One of her last books was *An Appeal for the Indians,* and she actively supported all human rights throughout her lifetime. In this 1843 newspaper "letter" from New York, she castigates prevalent opinions and customs about true womanhood.

From Lydia Maria Child, *Letters from New York* (New York: Charles S. Francis and Co., 1843), pp. 232, 234, 238.

❖

You ask what are my opinions about "Women's Rights." I confess a strong distaste to the subject, as it has been generally treated. On no other theme, probably, has there been uttered so much of false, mawkish sentiment, shallow philosophy, and sputtering, farthing-candle wit. If the style of its advocates has often been offensive to taste, and unacceptable to reason, assuredly that of its opponents have been still more so. College boys have amused themselves with writing dreams, in which they saw women in hotels, with their feet hoisted, and chairs tilted back, or growling and bickering at each other in legislative halls, or fighting at the polls, with eyes blackened by fisticuffs. But it never seems to have occurred to these facetious writers, that the proceedings which appear so ludicrous and improper in women, are also ridiculous and disgraceful in men. . . .

That the present position of women in society is the result of physical force, is obvious enough; whosoever doubts it, let her reflect why she is afraid to go out in the evening without the protection of a man. What constitutes the danger of aggression? Superior physical strength, uncontrolled by the moral sentiments. If physical strength were in complete subjection to moral influence, there would be no need of outward protection. . . .

This sort of politeness to women is what men call gallantry; an odious word to every sensible woman, because she sees that it is merely the flimsy veil which foppery throws over sensuality, to conceal its grossness. So far is it from indicating sincere esteem and affection for women, that the profligacy of a nation may, in general, be fairly measured by its gallantry. This taking away rights, and condescending to grant privileges, is an old trick of the physical force principle; and with the immense majority, who only look on the surface of things, this mask effectually disguises an ugliness, which would otherwise be abhorred. The most inveterate slaveholders are probably those who take most pride in dressing their household servants handsomely, and who would be most ashamed to have the name of being unnecessarily cruel. And profligates, who form the lowest and most sensual estimate of women, are the very ones to treat them with an excess of outward deference. . . .

The nearer society approaches to divine order, the less separation will there be in the characters, duties, and pursuits of men and women. Women will not become less gentle and graceful, but men will become more so. Women will not neglect the care and education of their children, but men will find themselves ennobled and refined by sharing those duties with them; and will receive, in return, co-operation and sympathy in the discharge of various other duties, now deemed inappropriate to women. The more women become rational companions, partners in business and in thought, as well as in affection and amusement, the more highly will men appreciate home.

To One Master Only Are They Accountable

The Massachusetts writer Margaret Fuller (1810–50) was a member of the prestigious Transcendentalist intellectual movement, which included Ralph Waldo Emerson and Henry David Thoreau. Editor of the literary journal *The Dial* from 1840 to 1844, she next became literary critic for Horace Greeley's influential *New York Tribune.* Her *Woman in the Nineteenth Century,* published in 1845, provided welcome ammunition for the women's movement and became a classic text for generations. She herself became a tragic and controversial public figure when, as foreign correspondent for the *Tribune* in Europe, she became involved in the Italian Revolution of 1849 and married a young Italian revolutionary— who was already the father of her child. They all sailed to America in 1850, but their ship was wrecked off Fire Island, New York. As the ship was breaking up on a sandbar, she refused to be rescued without her husband; their bodies were never found.

From Margaret Fuller Ossoli, *Woman in the Nineteenth Century* (1845; reprint, Boston: Roberts Brothers, 1893), pp. 31–38.

❖

The numerous party, whose opinions are already labeled and adjusted too much to their mind to admit of any new light, strive, by lectures on some model-woman of bride-like beauty and gentleness, by writing and lending little treatises, intended to mark out with precision the limits of Woman's sphere, and

Woman's mission, to prevent other than the rightful shepherd from climbing the wall, or the flock from using any chance to go astray. . . .

It may well be an Anti-Slavery party that pleads for Woman, if we consider merely that she does not hold property on equal terms with men; so that, if a husband dies without making a will, the wife, instead of taking at once his place as head of the family, inherits only a part of his fortune, often brought him by herself, as if she were a child, or ward only, not an equal partner.

We will not speak of the innumerable instances in which profligate and idle men live upon the earnings of industrious wives; or if the wives leave them, and take with them the children, to perform the double duty of mother and father, follow from place to place, and threaten to rob them of the children, if deprived of the rights of a husband, as they call them, planting themselves in their poor lodgings, frightening them into paying tribute by taking from them the children, running into debt at the expense of these otherwise so overtasked helots. Such instances count up by scores within my own memory. I have seen the husband who had stained himself by a long course of low vice, till his wife was wearied from her heroic forgiveness, by finding that his treachery made it useless, and that if she would provide bread for herself and her children, she must be separate from his ill fame—I have known this man come to install himself in the chamber of a woman who loathed him, and say she should never take food without his company. I have known these men steal their children, whom they knew they had no means to maintain, take them into dissolute company, expose them to bodily danger, to frighten the poor woman, to whom, it seems, the fact that she alone had borne the pangs of their birth, and nourished their infancy, does not give an equal right to them. . . .

. . . The public opinion of their own sex is already against such men, and where cases of extreme tyranny are made known, there is private action in the wife's favor. But she ought not to need this, nor, I think, can she long. Men must soon see that as, on their own ground, Woman is the weaker party, she ought to have legal protection, which would make such oppression impossible. But I would not deal with "atrocious instances," except in the way of illustration, neither demand from men a partial redress in some one matter, but go to the root of the whole. If principles could be established, particulars would adjust themselves aright. Ascertain the true destiny of Woman; give her legitimate hopes, and a standard within herself; marriage and all other relations would by degrees be harmonized with these.

But to return to the historical progress of this matter. Knowing that there exists in the minds of men a tone of feeling toward women as toward slaves, such as is expressed in the common phrase, "Tell that to women and children;" . . . that the gift of reason, Man's highest prerogative, is allotted to them in much lower degree; that they must be kept from mischief and melancholy by being constantly engaged in active labor, which is to be furnished and directed by those better able to think, &c, &c,—we need not multiply instances, for who can review the experience of last week without recalling words which imply, whether in jest or earnest, these views, or views like these,—knowing this, can we wonder that many reformers think that measures are not likely to be taken in behalf of women, unless their wishes could be publicly represented by women?

"That can never be necessary," cry the other side. "All men are privately influenced by women; each has his wife, sister, or female friends, and is too much biased by these relations to fail of representing their interests; and, if this is not enough, let them propose and enforce their wishes with the pen. The beauty of home would be destroyed, the delicacy of the sex be violated, the dignity of halls of legislation degraded, by an attempt to introduce them there. Such duties are inconsistent with those of a mother;" and then we have ludicrous pictures of ladies in hysterics at the polls, and senate-chambers filled with cradles.

But if, in reply, we admit as truth that Woman seems destined by nature rather for the inner circle, we must add that the arrangements of civilized life have not been, as yet, such as to secure it to her. Her circle, if the duller, is not the quieter. If kept from "excitement," she is not from drudgery. Not only the Indian squaw carries the burdens of the camp, but the favorites of Louis XIV. accompany him in his journeys, and the washerwoman stands at her tub, and carries home her work at all seasons, and in all states of health. Those who think the physical circumstances of Woman would make a part in the affairs of national government unsuitable, are by no means those who think it impossible for negresses to endure field-work, even during pregnancy, or for sempstresses to go through their killing labors. . . .

If men look straitly to it, they will find that, unless their lives are domestic, those of the women will not be. A house is no home unless it contain food and fire for the mind as well as for the body. . . . For human beings are not so constituted that they can live without expansion. If they do not get it in one way, they must in another, or perish.

As to men's representing women fairly at present, . . . when not one man, in the million, shall I say? no, not in the hundred million, can rise above the belief that Woman was made *for Man,*—when such traits as these are daily forced upon the attention, can we feel that Man will always do justice to the interests of Woman? . . . The lover, the poet, the artist, are likely to view her nobly. The father and the philosopher have some chance of liberality; the man of the world, the legislator for expediency, none.

. . . We would have every arbitrary barrier thrown down. We would have every path laid open to Woman as freely as to Man. Were this done, and a slight temporary fermentation allowed to subside, we should see crystallizations more pure and of more various beauty. We believe the divine energy would pervade nature to a degree unknown in the history of former ages, and that no discordant collision, but a ravishing harmony of the spheres, would ensue.

Yet, then and only then will mankind be ripe for this, when inward and outward freedom for Woman as much as for Man shall be acknowledged as a *right,* not yielded as a concession. As the friend of the negro assumes that one man cannot by right hold another in bondage, so should the friend of Woman assume that Man cannot by right lay even well-meant restrictions on Woman. If the negro be a soul, if the woman be a soul, apparelled in flesh, to one Master only are they accountable. . . . What Woman needs is not as a woman to act or rule, but as a nature to grow, as an intellect to discern, as a soul to live freely and unimpeded, to unfold such powers as were given her when we left our common home.

Pastoral Letter of the Congregational Ministers of Massachusetts

Conservative clergymen in New England were appalled by Angelina Grimké's public "promiscuous" lectures (to mixed-sex audiences) against slavery in 1837. Thus the issue of women's right to speak and act according to conscience was joined to the still unpopular abolitionist movement. Urging for women the same sort of ignorance of "things 'which ought not to be named'" as had the Marquis of Halifax in the eighteenth century, the ministers' appeal to women's piety, modesty, and weakness was of obvious political significance.

From the *Liberator,* Boston, Massachusetts, August 11, 1837.

❖

We invite your attention to the dangers which at present seem to threaten the female character with wide-spread and permanent injury.

The appropriate duties and influence of women are clearly stated in the New Testament. Those duties and that influence are unobtrusive and private, but the source of mighty power. When the mild, dependent, softening influence of woman upon the sternness of man's opinions is fully exercised, society feels the effects of it in a thousand forms. The power of women is in her dependence, flowing from the consciousness of that weakness which God has given her for her protection, and which keeps her in those departments of life that form the character of individuals and of the nation. There are social influences which females use in promoting piety and the great objects of Christian benevolence which we cannot too highly commend. We appreciate the unostentatious prayers and efforts of woman in advancing the cause of religion at home and abroad; in Sabbath-schools; in leading religious inquirers to the pastors for instruction; and in all such associated effort as becomes the modesty of her sex; and earnestly hope that she may abound more and more in these labors of piety and love.

252   But when she assumes the place and tone of man as a public reformer, our care and protection of her seem unnecessary; we put ourselves in self-defence against her; she yields the power which God has given her for protection, and her character becomes unnatural. If the vine, whose strength and beauty is to lean upon the trellis-work and half conceal its clusters, thinks to assume the independence and the overshadowing nature of the elm, it will not only cease to bear fruit, but fall in shame and dishonor into the dust. We cannot, therefore, but regret the mistaken conduct of those who encourage females to bear an obtrusive and ostentatious part in measures of reform, and countenance any of that sex who so far forget themselves as to itinerate in the character of public lecturers and teachers.—We especially deplore the intimate acquaintance and promiscuous conversation of females with regard to things "which ought not to be named"; by which that modesty and delicacy which is the charm of domestic life, and which constitutes the true influence of woman in society, is consumed, and the way opened, as we apprehend, for degeneracy and ruin. We say these things, not to discourage proper influences against sin, but to secure such reformation as we believe is Scriptural, and will be permanent.

The Times That Try Men's Souls

Described by the suffragist Elizabeth Cady Stanton as "one of the grand women in Boston" leading the antislavery struggle, the writer Maria Weston Chapman (1806–85) helped William Lloyd Garrison edit the *Liberator* and encouraged Angelina and Sarah Grimké to give their abolition lectures in 1837, thus prompting the Congregational ministers' outrage. "The Times That Try Men's Souls," Chapman's satirical ten-stanza poem (from which we reprint four stanzas), was originally published in the *Liberator* as a specific reply to the ministers. It was read at the Rochester Women's Convention (two weeks after the Seneca Falls meeting) in August 1848.

From Maria Weston Chapman in Elizabeth Cady Stanton, Susan B. Anthony, and Matilda Joslyn Gage, *History of Woman Suffrage,* 2d ed., vol. 1 (Rochester, N.Y.: Charles Mann, 1889), pp. 82–83.

❖

Confusion has seized us, and all things go wrong,
    The women have leaped from "their spheres,"
And, instead of fixed stars, shoot as comets along,
    And are setting the world by the ears!
In courses erratic they're wheeling through space,
In brainless confusion and meaningless chase.

In vain do our knowing ones try to compute
    Their return to the orbit designed;
They're glanced at a moment, then onward they shoot,
    And are neither "to hold nor to bind;"
So freely they move in their chosen ellipse,
The "Lords of Creation" do fear an eclipse.

They've taken a notion to speak for themselves,
    And are wielding the tongue and the pen;
They've mounted the rostrum; the termagent elves,
    And—oh horrid!—are talking to men!
With faces unblanched in our presence they come
To harangue us, they say, in behalf of the dumb.

. . . .

Our grandmothers' learning consisted of yore
    In spreading their generous boards;
In twisting the distaff, or mopping the floor,
    And *obeying the will of their lords.*
Now, misses may reason, and think, and debate,
Till unquestioned submission is quite out of date.

Women Have No Souls?

Amelia Jenks Bloomer (1818–94) attended the Seneca Falls Women's Rights Convention in 1848 but was so undecided about the movement that she did not sign her name to the resulting declaration. A year later, the Tennessee legislature formally debated and concluded that married women did not have free and independent souls and therefore had no right to own property. This was, in fact, the legal position in most states and territories; in the nineteenth century, laws as well as common practice increasingly denied women even the property rights they had exercised in the colonial era. Amelia Bloomer was so incensed that she wrote an editorial for her temperance journal, the *Lily,* which helped open the discussion of women's rights to a larger, nationwide audience. Later, Bloomer became president of the Iowa Woman Suffrage Society and an inspiration to suffragists all over the country.

From Amelia Bloomer, in the *Lily*, March 1849.

❖

Wise men these, and worthy to be honoured with seats in the halls of legislation in a Christian land. Women no souls! Then, of course, we are not accountable beings, and if not accountable to our Maker, then surely not to man. Man represents, legislates for us, and now holds himself accountable for us! How kind in him, and what a weight is lifted from us! We shall no longer be subject to punishment for breaking them, no longer be responsible for any of our doings. Man in whom iniquity is perfected has assumed the whole charge of us and left us helpless, soulless, defenceless creatures dependent on him for leave to speak or act.

We suppose the wise legislators consider the question settled beyond dispute, but we fear they will have some trouble with it yet. Although it may be an easy matter for them to arrive at such a conclusion, it will be quite another thing to make women believe it. We are not so blind to the weakness and imperfection of man as to set his word above that of our Maker, or so ready to yield obedience to his laws as to place them before the laws of God. However blindly we may be led by them, however much we may yield to his acquired power over us, we cannot yet fall down and worship him as our superior. Some men even act as though women had no souls, but it remained for the legislature of Tennessee to speak it to the world.

A Great Clacking among the Sisterhood

Caroline Kirkland (1801–64) launched her career as a popular writer with an autobiographical novel, *A New Home—Who'll Follow?*, about a frontier Michigan village. Published in 1839, it was the first such realistic novel, in an age of romanticism and sentiment. The following excerpt is taken from the introduction to the American edition of an English feminist's book. Her analogy about chickens in a basket exemplifies her down-to-earth, woman-to-woman rhetoric. There is, even today, a restaurant in Waterville, Maine, bearing the name and illustrated sign "The Headless Woman."

From Caroline M. Kirkland, "General Introduction" to Mrs. Hugo Reid, *Woman, Her Education and Influence* (New York: Fowlers and Wells, 1848), pp. 9–10.

❖

The condition of the women of the present day seems to bear no little resemblance to that of the unfortunate hens in the basket of the poulterer;—restless, crowded and uncomfortable; evincing, ever and anon, by a faint, uneasy chirping, a desire for wider bounds, and occasionally risking strangulation by a spasmodic effort, which only forces the aspiring head through a mesh in the strong netting, occasions a great clacking among the sisterhood, and earns a rap on the pate from the hard-hearted owner. This has been so universally the fate of all who have ventured upon any thing like a plea for woman, that to venture at all, bespeaks a courage which deserves, at least, better fortune. . . . 255

We doubt not the very mention of [women's rights] has already brought to the mind of the reader a little, kitten-faced person, disputing with her husband the possession of his wardrobe; or perhaps a whole host of Amazons, in helmets and plate-armor, ready to do battle for the right (or wrong), and to drink the blood of the slain.

At the very least, he has represented to himself the women who dare, like poor Oliver Twist, to "ask for more," as a great party, whose interests are wholly opposed to those of men; angry claimants who must be kept at bay; perverse disputants who are clamoring for they know not what; and who, if they gained one point where they were probably right, would insist on some others where they were clearly wrong. Just demands are to be refused, lest they should lead to others that are not just; real grievances are not to be redressed, because unreal ones may be alleged; and acknowledged abuses are to be maintained, because unavoidable evils may be placed in the same rank, and made the ground for renewed complaint. All this is not very philosophical; but men cannot afford to be philosophers where women are concerned. . . .

Women have been thoroughly imbued with the idea that their vocation is to persuade, not to command; to ask as a boon, rather than to claim as a right, any thing beyond the "meat, clothes and fire," which they share with "insane persons and idiots." . . . We object also to the tendency of certain time-worn, we will not say time-honored phrases and sentences;—conventionalisms, fair-sounding enough, but covering a mass of folly and injustice. Such are "woman's sphere," a term which is understood to imply a certain round of household duties, to which she is supposed to be fastened, as a door to its hinges; fulfilling her destiny if she be always at her *post* and never *ajar*. "The Good Woman" is aptly pictured upon sundry signposts in England, as a woman without a head, and a kindred notion is naturalized in this country.

Dimity Convictions

Emily Dickinson (1830–86) is now acknowledged as one of America's greatest poets, but her work remained unpublished and unknown during her lifetime. Dickinson lived as a recluse in Amherst, Massachusetts, but she corresponded with many feminist and reformist women of her day, and she read the books of women such as Margaret Fuller and Lydia Maria Child with great pleasure. Her life-style seems to have been her way of obtaining personal and intellectual freedom to devote herself to poetry. She hated the weakness, hypocrisy, and snobbery of conventional women with "dimity convictions."

From Thomas H. Johnson, ed., *The Complete Poems of Emily Dickinson* (Boston: Little, Brown and Co., 1960), p. 191.

❖

What Soft – Cherubic Creatures –
These Gentlewomen are –
One would as soon assault a Plush –
Or violate a Star –

Such Dimity Convictions –
A horror so refined
Of freckled Human Nature –
Of Deity – ashamed –

It's such a common – Glory –
A Fisherman's – Degree –
Redemption – Brittle Lady –
Be so – ashamed of Thee –

To Be Free as Man Is Free

The year 1848 marks a turning point in the history of American women. In that summer, Elizabeth Cady Stanton (1815–1902) and her Quaker friend Lucretia Mott (1793–1880) placed a small ad in the Seneca Falls, New York, newspaper to convene the first Women's Rights Convention. To their surprise, three hundred women and some men gathered in the Methodist meetinghouse to discuss women's legal problems and the need for change. In Stanton's opening speech to the assemblage, she demanded the right to vote.

From Elizabeth Cady Stanton, *Address Delivered at Seneca Falls and Rochester, N.Y.* (1870), reprinted in Ellen Carol DuBois, ed., *Elizabeth Cady Stanton / Susan B. Anthony: Correspondence, Writing, Speeches* (New York: Schocken, 1981), pp. 28–33, 35. ❖

I should feel exceedingly diffident to appear before you at this time, having never before spoken in public, were I not nerved by a sense of right and duty, did I not feel the time had fully come for the question of woman's wrongs to be laid before the public, did I not believe that woman herself must do this work; for woman alone can understand the height, the depth, the length, and the breadth of her own degradation. Man cannot speak for her, because he has been educated to believe that she differs from him so materially, that he cannot judge of her thoughts, feelings, and opinions by his own. Moral beings can only judge of others by themselves. The moment they assume a different nature for any of their own kind, they utterly fail. . . .

Let us consider . . . man's superiority, intellectually, morally, physically.

Man's intellectual superiority cannot be a question until woman has had a fair trial. When we shall have had our freedom to find out our own sphere, when we shall have had our colleges, our professions, our trades, for a century, a comparison then may be justly instituted. When woman, instead of being taxed to endow colleges where she is forbidden to enter—instead of forming sewing societies to educate "poor, but pious," young men, shall first educate herself, when she shall be just to herself before she is generous to others; improving the talents God has given her, and leaving her neighbor to do the same for himself, we shall not hear so much about this boasted superiority. . . .

. . . God's commands rest upon man as well as woman. It is as much his duty to be kind, self-denying and full of good works, as it is hers. As much his duty to absent himself from scenes of violence as it is hers. . . . The false ideas that prevail with regard to the purity necessary to constitute the perfect character in woman, and that requisite for man, has done an infinite deal of mischief in the world. I would not have woman less pure, but I would have man more so. I would have the same code of morals for both. . . .

Let us now consider man's claim to physical superiority. Methinks I hear some say, surely, you will not contend for equality here. Yes, we must not give an inch, lest you take an ell. We cannot accord to man even this much, and he has no right to claim it until the fact has been fully demonstrated. . . . We cannot say what the woman might be physically, if the girl were allowed all the freedom of the boy in romping, climbing, swimming, playing whoop and ball.

Among some of the Tartar tribes of the present day, women manage a horse, hurl a javelin, hunt wild animals, and fight an enemy as well as a man. The Indian women endure fatigues and carry burdens that some of our fair-faced, soft-handed, moustached young gentlemen would consider quite impossible for them to sustain. . . . It is no uncommon sight in our cities, to see the German immigrant with his hands in his pockets, walking complacently by the side of his wife, whilst she bears the weight of some huge package or piece of furniture upon her head. Physically, as well as intellectually, it is use that produces growth and development. . . .

We have met here to-day to discuss our rights and wrongs, civil and political, and not, as some have supposed, to go into the detail of social life alone. We do not propose to petition the legislature to make our husbands just, generous and courteous, to seat every man at the head of a cradle, and to clothe every woman in male attire. None of these points, however important they may be considered by leading men, will be touched in this Convention. . . .

We are assembled to protest against a form of government, existing without the consent of the governed—to declare our right to be free as man is free, to be represented in the government which we are taxed to support, to have such disgraceful laws as give man the power to chastise and imprison his wife, to take the wages which she earns, the property which she inherits, and, in case of separation, the children of her love; laws which make her the mere dependent on his bounty. It is to protest against such unjust laws as these that we are assembled to-day, and to have them, if possible, forever erased from our statute-books, deeming them a shame and a disgrace to a Christian republic in the nineteenth century. . . .

And, strange as it may seem to many, we now demand our right to vote according to the declaration of the government under which we live. . . . We have no objection to discuss the question of equality, for we feel that the weight of argument lies wholly with us, but we wish the question of equality kept distinct from the question of rights, for the proof of the one does not determine the truth of the other. All white men in this country have the same rights, however they may differ in mind, body or estate. The right is ours. The question now is, how shall we get possession of what rightfully belongs to us. We should not feel so sorely grieved if no man who had not attained the full stature of a Webster, Clay, Van Buren, or Gerrit Smith could claim the right of the elective franchise. But to have drunkards, idiots, horse-racing, rumselling rowdies, ignorant foreigners, and silly boys fully recognized, while we ourselves are thrust out from all the rights that belong to citizens, it is too grossly insulting to the dignity of woman to be longer quietly submitted to. The right is ours. Have it we must. Use it we will. The pens, the tongues, the fortunes, the indomitable wills of many women are already pledged to secure this right. The great truth, that no just government can be formed without the consent of the governed, we shall echo and re-echo in the ears of the unjust judge, until by continual coming we shall weary him. . . .

But what would woman gain by voting? Men must know the advantages of voting, for they all seem very tenacious about the right. Think you, if woman had a vote in this government, that all those laws affecting her interests would so entirely violate every principle of right and justice? Had woman a vote to give, might not the office-holders and seekers propose some change in her condition? Might not Woman's Rights become as great a question as free soil?

"But you are already represented by your fathers, husbands, brothers and sons?" Let your statute book answer the question. We have had enough of such representation. In nothing is woman's true happiness consulted. Men like to call her an angel—to feed her on what they think sweet food—nourishing her vanity; to make her believe that her organization is so much finer than theirs, that she is not fitted to struggle with the tempests of public life, but needs their care and protection!! Care and protection—such as the wolf gives the lamb— such as the eagle the hare he carries to his eyrie!! Most cunningly he entraps her, and then takes from her all those rights which are dearer to him than life itself— rights which have been baptized in blood—and the maintenance of which is even now rocking to their foundations the kingdoms of the Old World.

The most discouraging, the most lamentable aspect our cause wears is the indifference, indeed, the contempt, with which women themselves regard the movement. Where the subject is introduced, among those even who claim to be intelligent and educated, it is met by the scornful curl of the lip, and by expression of ridicule and disgust. But we shall hope better things of them when they are enlightened in regard to their present position. When women know the laws and constitutions under which they live, they will not publish their degradation by declaring themselves satisfied, nor their ignorance, by declaring they have all the rights they want. . . .

Let woman live as she should. Let her feel her accountability to her Maker. Let her know that her spirit is fitted for as high a sphere as man's, and that her soul requires food as pure and exalted as his. Let her live *first* for God, and she will not make imperfect man an object of reverence and awe. Teach her her responsibility as a being of conscience and reason, that all earthly support is weak and unstable, that her only safe dependence is the arm of omnipotence, and that true happiness springs from duty accomplished. Thus will she learn the lesson of individual responsibility for time and eternity. . . .

. . . We do not expect our path will be strewn with the flowers of popular applause, but over the thorns of bigotry and prejudice will be our way, and on our banners will beat the dark storm-clouds of opposition from those who have entrenched themselves behind the stormy bulwarks of custom and authority, and

259

who have fortified their position by every means, holy and unholy. But we will steadfastly abide the result. Unmoved we will bear it aloft. Undaunted we will unfurl it to the gale, for we know that the storm cannot rend from it a shred, that the electric flash will but more clearly show to us the glorious words inscribed upon it, "Equality of Rights."

260

Declaration of Sentiments

Elizabeth Cady Stanton also drew up a "Declaration of Sentiments" eloquently modeled on Jefferson's Declaration of Independence. Stanton's fiery rhetoric established a new direction for American women—a public campaign and political challenge by an organized suffrage movement.

From Elizabeth Cady Stanton, "Declaration of Sentiments," in Elizabeth Cady Stanton, Susan B. Anthony, and Matilda Joslyn Gage, *History of Woman Suffrage,* vol. 1 (Rochester, N.Y.: Charles Mann, 1881), pp. 70–71.

❖

When, in the course of human events, it becomes necessary for one portion of the family of man to assume among the people of the earth a position different from that which they have hitherto occupied, but one to which the laws of nature and of nature's God entitle them, a decent respect to the opinions of mankind requires that they should declare the causes that impel them to such a course.

We hold these truths to be self-evident: that all men and women are created equal; that they are endowed by their Creator with certain inalienable rights; that among these are life, liberty, and the pursuit of happiness; that to secure these rights governments are instituted, deriving their just powers from the consent of the governed. Whenever any form of government becomes destructive of these ends, it is the right of those who suffer from it to refuse allegiance to it, and to insist upon the institution of a new government, laying its foundation on such principles, and organizing its powers in such form, as to them shall seem most likely to affect their safety and happiness. . . . Such has been the patient sufferance of the women under this government, and such is now the necessity which constrains them to demand the equal station to which they are entitled.

The history of mankind is a history of repeated injuries and usurpations on the part of men toward women, having in direct object the establishment of an absolute tyranny over her. To prove this, let facts be submitted to a candid world.

He has never permitted her to exercise her inalienable right to the elective franchise.

He has compelled her to submit to laws, in the formation of which she had no voice.

He has withheld from her rights which are given to the most ignorant and degraded men—both natives and foreigners.

Having deprived her of this first right of a citizen, the elective franchise, thereby leaving her without representation in the halls of legislation, he has oppressed her on all sides.

He has made her, if married, in the eye of the law, civilly dead.

He has taken from her all rights in property, even to the wages she earns.

He has made her, morally, an irresponsible being, as she can commit many crimes with impunity, provided they be done in the presence of her husband. In the covenant of marriage, she is compelled to promise obedience to her husband, he becoming, to all intents and purposes, her master—the law giving him power to deprive her of her liberty, and to administer chastisement.

He has so framed the laws of divorce, as to what shall be the proper causes, and in case of separation, to whom the guardianship of the children shall be given, as to be wholly regardless of the happiness of women—the law, in all cases, going upon a false supposition of the supremacy of man, and giving all power into his hands.

After depriving her of all rights as a married woman, if single, and the owner of property, he has taxed her to support a government which recognizes her only when her property can be made profitable to it.

He has monopolized nearly all the profitable employments, and from those she is permitted to follow, she receives but a scanty remuneration. He closes against her all the avenues to wealth and distinction which he considers most honorable to himself. As a teacher of theology, medicine, or law, she is not known.

He has denied her the facilities for obtaining a thorough education, all colleges being closed against her.

He allows her in Church, as well as State, but a subordinate position, claiming Apostolic authority for her exclusion from the ministry, and, with some exceptions, from any public participation in the affairs of the Church.

He has created a false public sentiment by giving to the world a different code of morals for men and women, by which moral delinquencies which exclude women from society, are not only tolerated, but deemed of little account in men.

He has usurped the prerogative of Jehovah himself, claiming it as his right to assign for her a sphere of action, when that belongs to her conscience and to her God.

He has endeavored, in every way that he could, to destroy her confidence in her own powers, to lessen her self-respect, and to make her willing to lead a dependent and abject life.

Now, in view of this entire disfranchisement of one-half the people of this country, their social and religious degradation—in view of the unjust laws above mentioned, and because women do feel themselves aggrieved, oppressed, and fraudulently deprived of their most sacred rights, we insist that they have immediate admission to all the rights and privileges which belong to them as citizens of the United States.

In entering upon the great work before us, we anticipate no small amount of misconception, misrepresentation, and ridicule; but we shall use every instrumentality within our power to effect our object. We shall employ agents, circulate tracts, petition the State and National legislatures, and endeavor to enlist the pulpit and the press in our behalf. We hope this Convention will be followed by a series of Conventions embracing every part of the country.

WOMEN'S SPHERE

34. *A Greek Revival House*
Houses designed like Greek temples, and even small one-story cottages with classical columns, were built all over the country during the nineteenth century. They symbolized not only the republican values derived from Greek and Roman history but also the domestication of women. Women were now the new nation's "goddesses" of the home, sequestered within on ideological pedestals. Photo by Emil Lorch, of Gordon Hall, Dexter, Michigan, in Talbot Hamlin, *Greek Revival Architecture in America* (New York: Oxford University Press, 1944), plate 84.

RESIDENCE OF N. P. WILLIS AT IDLEWILD, ON THE HUDSON.

PLAN OF PRINCIPAL FLOOR.

35. A "Pseudo-Gothic" Villa

Growing urbanization and wealth in the nineteenth century led to America's first suburbs, ostentatious homes on the outskirts of cities, where women reigned over the domestic establishment and where men returned to a "peaceful haven" from their commercial occupations. Many of the houses were "villas" and "cottages" designed by Calvert Vaux, whose 1857 book of house plans was one of the first of that genre. The homes usually had basement kitchens, where the mundane domestic work was relegated to servants. No longer did a mistress work alongside her helpers; she now gave directions, organized household efficiency, and pursued benevolence and culture. Useless balconies on these houses were supposed to appeal to feminine sentimentality, and extensive space was allotted for entertaining in dining and drawing rooms. From Calvert Vaux, "Residence of N.P. Willis at Idlewild, on the Hudson," frontispiece, *Villas and Cottages* (New York: Harper and Brothers, 1857).

36. *Westward the Course of Empire*

This painting by John Gast took its title from an eighteenth-century poem by
Bishop George Berkeley. The figure in flowing drapery, occupying the center of the
painting and suggesting the female figureheads on the prows of ships, is symbolic
of the nineteenth-century ideological belief in woman as the carrier of civilization, the inspiration for progress. She strings out telegraph wire as she moves, thus
also symbolizing communication, which holds old and new together. Larger than
life and perfect in beauty, she hovers *above* the real world—where all the action
is apparently being performed by men. The painting thus exemplifies nineteenth-
century attitudes toward the separate spheres of male and female behavior. Painting
by John Gast, in Harry T. Peters Collection. Courtesy of the Library of Congress,
Washington, D.C.

Expanding Horizons

WOMEN OF ALL classes and races were deeply moved by waves of religious revivalism known as the Second Great Awakening at the turn of the nineteenth century and lasting through the 1830s. The fervor of religious reform swept all parts of the country. There were decorous prayer meetings in New England churches, evangelical preaching in rural Baptist and Methodist meetinghouses, and huge open-air camp meetings on the western frontier. The first such camp meeting, in 1799 in Kentucky, drew twenty-five thousand people—almost the entire population of the state. There was one constant factor: women were prime targets of the preachers' zeal, and they were constantly urged to be the means of salvation for the men of their families. Peter Cartwright, one of the frontier's most famous preachers, testified in his *Autobiography* (New York: Carlton and Porter, 1856) that many women often "felt greatly attached to [him] as the instrument, in the hands of God, of their salvation" (p. 66). Old churches expanded and new denominations thrived, often amid great friction about what was true and what was false doctrine.

For Rebecca Jackson, a Shaker eldress, faith provided a modicum of power to resist an abusive husband and become a leader in her African-Methodist-Episcopal community. The prominent New Yorker Elizabeth Bayley Seton, after a conversion to Catholicism bitterly opposed by her relatives and friends, founded the first American community of teaching nuns in 1808. Her Sisters of Charity continued to expand their teaching and nursing activities throughout the country, while Elizabeth Seton herself became the first American to be canonized. Other Catholic nuns escaped from antireligious persecution in postrevolutionary France to establish schools in both urban and rural locations. They faced the hostility of anti-Catholic prejudice, but their communities also served as havens for abused wives or women seeking education.

Fervent Protestant women, like Ellen Lee, were also encouraged to become teachers or missionaries. Significant numbers of nineteenth-century women even went to Burma, China, Africa, and the Middle East. Others shared in various utopian experiments, both religious and "free-thinking," which emphasized improvements in women's lives and health. In the numerous Shaker communities, both men and women practiced celibacy and cared for homeless children. Oneida Perfectionists advocated "complex-marriage" (each is married to all) and "stirpiculture" (eugenic procreation). Socialist and Fourierist communities were established at New Harmony, Indiana, Brook Farm, Massachusetts, and Redbank, New Jersey. A "Free Love" community flourished on Long Island, while Swedish Jansenists and other religious groups settled in the Midwest.

In almost every city and town, philanthropic women established church societies, orphanages, and various types of aid societies. Rebecca Gratz started a Sunday school movement among American Jewish congregations, much like similar schools taught by Protestant women throughout the country. In a letter about the arrangement of a child's adoption, Gratz disgustedly notes the prevalence of religious prejudice—in this case, among Presbyterians against Unitarians. Gratz's Jewish faith was more highly respected than the Catholic or dissident, nontrinitarian Christian faiths.

Women met regularly in prayer groups, sewing circles, or cultural organizations. Like Susan Huntington, they joined maternal societies and prayed over their newly articulated responsibilities, sometimes sounding very modern complaints about the time demands of so many worthwhile organizations. Women created charitable societies for the care of widows and orphans, for reforming prostitutes, and for abolishing slavery. Health and dress reform became major women's issues. In a discussion on "voluntary motherhood," Sarah Grimké explains what many women were thinking and saying about the right of a woman to control her husband's sexual behavior and thus restrict excessive childbearing. Dr. Harriot Hunt organized the first of many "physiological societies," where women could exchange information with one another. As male doctors gradually took over childbirth care and the treatment of women's diseases, previously handled by midwives, their women patients were frequently victims of men's practical ignorance and theoretical, by-the-book education.

Women like Emma Willard demanded or took advantage of new educational opportunities; Willard's school at Troy, New York, educated a number of nineteenth-century women leaders, including Elizabeth Cady Stanton. Women were gradually welcomed into the profession of teaching, in an expanding system of public education, partly because they were paid much less than men. And literary women flourished, singing the praises of motherhood and home even as they managed their highly professional careers. But women were deliberately excluded from the developing legal and medical professions. The forty-year-old Dr. Hunt was finally admitted to Harvard Medical School, but she could not take courses because the university's male students successfully petitioned against her attendance, claiming her presence would be contrary to feminine "delicacy" and would be distracting to men. No wonder she became one of the earliest suffragists!

A Community of Women

When a wave of religious fervor swept the country at the beginning of the nineteenth century, converts were to be found in all churches. Elizabeth Bayley Seton (1774–1821) was the daughter of a prominent New York doctor who died treating immigrant patients in a 1797 yellow fever epidemic and was the wife of a prosperous merchant who died of tuberculosis in Italy, where she had taken him in hopes of a cure. Already a devout Episcopalian, she became a convert to Roman Catholicism, a step that alienated her relatives and left her almost destitute of means for herself and her five children. In 1809 she founded a small community of teaching nuns, the Sisters of Charity of St. Joseph, in Emmitsburg, Maryland. Among others, her niece Harriet Seton broke an engagement to Elizabeth Seton's profligate brother in order to join the community. The order grew quickly, from ten to one hundred in the thirteen years before she died. It soon expanded to Philadelphia and New York and eventually across the country. In addition to her work, she had to endure the death of her daughter and two sisters from tuberculosis; at age forty-six, she died from the same disease after several years of illness. Mother Seton was the first native-born American Catholic to be canonized, in recognition of the sanctity of her life.

From Ellin Kelly and Annabelle Melville, eds., *Elizabeth Seton: Selected Writings* (New York: Paulist Press, 1987), pp. 277–80.

❖

To Antonio Filicchi

St. Joseph's Valley 8th November 1809

My dearest Antonio

It is eighteen months since I have a line from Leghorn until a few days ago your letter of 30th November 1808. . . .

Now then you will laugh when I tell you that your wicked little Sister is placed at the head of a Community of Saints, ten of the most pious Souls you could wish, considering that some of them are young and all under thirty. Six more postulents are daily waiting till we move into a larger place to receive them, and we might be a very large family if I received half who desire to come, but your Reverend Mother is obliged to be very cautious for fear we should not have the means of earning our living during the Winter. Yet as Sisters to Charity we should fear nothing. Your thousand Dollars will greatly relieve us

dear Antonio may you be blessed
to give more, for your generosity has already been too great, and
whose sake and to whom you have given in the person of a Widow, and the
Orphan can alone repay you. But that you might find it proper after consulting
proper persons to invest some of your property in establishing us who have now
been called to the service of God in a religious state, and many others whose
vocation is undoubted, I have proposed to you without fear since He seemed
to open this door for us in your generous benevolence, my only fear is that perhaps my intention was not sufficiently expressed to you.

May 20th 1810

Since the above was written, my Brother, I have never been able to hear of
a good occasion to write, and have besides been so beset with difficulties that
having but a few moments and nothing but trouble to tell you of, was not very
anxious to write. Yet do I speak of trouble before the boundless joy of having
received another most dear Sister in our holy Church.

Perhaps you may remember Harriet Seton who was engaged to marry my
Brother, the Doctor Bayley. She was in the top of fashion, amusement and the
Belle of New York, when making us a visit while I was in Baltimore for the
recovery of Cecelia's health, she followed us to the mountain, where our Community is established, became a fervent convert approached Communion twice
a week and exercised every mark of faithful Souls. In the midst of this happiness
after having received the reproachful letters of her friends and the learned ones
of Controvertists, renouncing them and the engagement to my Brother (unless
he joined her intentions) she was taken ill and died singing a Salutation to the
blessed Sacrament. Since that, Cecilia too has departed, the admiration and triumph of all who know her in our Faith. Your poor Sister to be sure is called the
pest of Society, and all the lovely names of Hypocrite, Bigot etc. etc. which you
know are all music to the spirit longing only to be conformed to Him who was
despised and rejected by men.

In our house we have had continual sickness too, all the Winter, and I have
been obliged to incur many expences, and to go thro' every difficulty natural to
such an undertaking as I have engaged in. You know the enemy of all good will of
course make his endeavours to destroy it, but it seems our Adored is determined
on its full success by the excellent subjects he has placed in it. We are now twelve,
and as many again are waiting for admission. I have a very very large school to
superintend every day, and the entire charge of the religious instruction of all the
country round. All happy to [be with] the Sisters of Charity who are night and
day devoted to the sick and ignorant. Our blessed Bishop intends removing a
detachment of us to Baltimore to perform the same duties there. We have here a

very good house tho' a [ ] Building and it will be the Mother house, and retreat. In all cases a portion of the Sisterhood will always remain in it to keep the spinning, weaving and knitting and school for country people regularly progressing. Our blessed Bishop is so fond of our establishment that it seems to be the darling part of his charge and this consoles me for every difficulty and embarassment. All the Clergy in America support it by their prayers and there is every hope that it is the seed of an immensity of future good. You must admire how Our Lord should have chosen such a one as *I* to preside over it, but you know he loves to show his strength in weakness, and his wisdom in the ignorant, his blessed name be adored forever, it is in the humble poor and helpless he delights to number his greatest mercies and set them as marks to encourage poor Sinners. . . .

22nd of May

. . . I forgot, and it is almost useless to tell you that the New Yorkers have given me up altogether and entirely, Mr. Wilkes and Mrs. Startin, before Harriet's conversion had ceased correspondance and looked upon me as one of the evils of Society but since that, from what Sam Seton one of our younger Brothers has written to Cecilia before her death I find my name cannot be mentioned before them.

They Also Pelt Us with Snowballs

In many parts of the country, Catholic nuns were the first to establish schools for girls, both in cities and on the frontier. Evangelical Protestants who promoted teaching as a way of civilizing the West frequently remarked that they were seeking to emulate and counteract the nuns' influence. Sisters of St. Joseph in Bardstown, Kentucky, educated girls from many of Kentucky's leading families in the 1820s, as did other Sisters in Texas, Louisiana, Maryland, Oregon, and elsewhere. Often, however, nativist mobs and anti-Catholic zealots denounced nuns for their foreign language, customs, and religion. For example, in 1834, the Ursuline Convent in Boston was burned to the ground. This mid-century letter from a nun to her family in France mentions a similar event in Indiana. The virtues most extolled for pious Protestant matrons—"their sweet and engaging manners, their knowledge, and their attractions"—were cited as the reason Catholic nuns were dangerous. Apparently, however, many women, regardless of religious affiliation, perceived convents as places of refuge and female community.

From Clementine De La Corbiniere, *The Life and Letters of Sister St. Francis*

Xavier (St. Mary-of-the-Woods, Ind.: Providence Press, 1934), pp. 289–92. Courtesy of Sisters of Providence Archives, St. Mary-of-the-Woods, Indiana.

❖

This good news [of the conversion of a hardened sinner] will console you a little for the burning of the house of the Sisters of Charity at Fredericktown. The incendiaries, before enkindling the fire, disabled the fire engines so that the progress of the fire could not be arrested. The house was burned to the ground. We may, perhaps, have to endure a similar misfortune. A few days ago we received an anonymous letter warning us to be on our guard. For two or three nights our workmen have watched, armed with guns. Some men were found hiding in our fields, but God permitted one of our neighbors to see them. We trust that the Blessed Virgin, who has always been a mother to us, will continue to protect our poor community.

I have already told you that our mission at Madison is greatly exposed to the persecutions of the enemies of Catholicity. Not long since, our Sisters wrote that the Presbyterian minister assembled his congregation in the church, and then, transported by the *Spirit,* disclosed all the infamies perpetrated by priests and nuns since the beginning of the Church! He ended his harangue by hurling anathemas against the parents who sent their children to Catholic schools, and he predicted that they would not escape the divine vengeance. "When we go to Mass," wrote one of our Sisters at this time, "the little rogues of boys, seeing us with our pupils, run after us, screaming, 'Sheep, sheep, sheep.' They also pelt us with snowballs (but that does not hurt us), and sometimes even with eggs and stones."

The persecutions that our Sisters have been suffering at Madison are somewhat abated. Their most formidable adversary, however [Mr. Curtis], called together three hundred ministers last month, in order to devise in council some means of doing away with the *nuns.* But God laughs at the designs of men. Their ridiculous assembly inspired only contempt, and since that time the people are more favorably disposed toward our holy religion.

There is here an apostate monk from Italy, who goes from city to city giving lectures on the progress and danger of Catholicity. He was lately at Cincinnati, and I read a portion of his sixth discourse from which I quote: "When the demon wished to introduce evil into the world he made use of woman to corrupt man; now, to introduce Catholicism in America, he makes use of the nuns, true Eves, with their sweet and engaging manners, their knowledge, and their attractions. The Jesuits are dangerous, but the nuns are their agents, and are still more to be feared. Guard against sending your children to their schools, and even against placing among them servants trained by the Sisters, for they will instill their bad principles into the hearts of your children. The evil is greater than you think; and I know better than you that Catholicism is daily increasing," etc.

We do indeed remove the prejudices of our pupils. The parents have to choose between the inferiority of the other schools and what they call the *superstition* of ours; but, as many prefer having their children well instructed, they send them to us. Our boarding school is the best in Indiana, and would be considered very good even in France. We have about eighty pupils and several others are expected. I have never met young girls better taught than our first pupils. Mr. Pinatel, an old naval officer, was astonished at their knowledge of mathematics and astronomy. As these subjects and drawing were the ones to which he had principally devoted himself, this part of the examination pleased him best. The children especially excel, however, in Christian doctrine and in sacred and ecclesiastical history. They were highly commended, and with good reason, for the skill they show with the needle, particularly in plain sewing.

Every kind of absurdity and calumny finds acceptance with some of the people here. They were even so foolish as to believe that our chaplain had horns. One mischievous little woman, now a Catholic, told the villagers that if each of them would give her twenty-five cents, she would beg Father Corbe [*cor* in French means *horn*] to take off his hat and let them see the horns. Not seeing them on his head the people wanted to look in his hat, supposing he had left them there.

A solicitous friend wrote as follows to an old lady who had her daughter in our school at Terre Haute: "Dear Madam: Although I have not the honor of your acquaintance, the interest I take in your daughter prompts me to tell you that, if you leave her with the nuns, she will be lost. Twenty years from now she will remember the detestable principles she has imbibed there; and if she does not become a Catholic, she will at least defend the Sisters all her life and on all occasions."

The good lady replied that she was old enough to judge for herself and wise enough to know how to bring up her own children; that not only would she leave her daughter with the good Sisters, but that she herself, when her dear husband should be no more, would offer herself to the Sisters, not to teach in the boarding school, but to serve them in their houses, an office she would consider an honor. We have the strangest imaginable applications for admission. Some, like this lady, still have their dear husbands, and are not even baptized; others ask to be received for a year only, in the absence of their husbands; others would like to be Sisters, but have not yet decided to become Catholics, and so on.

I Can Read the Bible!

Rebecca Cox Jackson (1795–1871) was a free black woman of Philadelphia who became an extraordinary visionary and spiritual leader among her people. After experiencing "sanctification" within the African-Methodist-Episcopal church where her much-loved brother was a prominent preacher, she became a traveling preacher and then an eldress among the Shakers. Through her many visions and religious experiences, which she carefully wrote down in obedience to God's call, she gained personal certainty of her "gifts of power" and her calling to leave her husband and her household work in order to heal the sinful and preach the gospel. For this her husband frequently threatened to kill her, and ministers tried to silence her—until they discovered the quality of her eloquence and wisdom. In this excerpt, she describes a typical spiritual meeting and then the way in which God gave her the "gift" of reading.

From Jean McMahon Humex, ed., *Gifts of Power: The Writings of Rebecca Jackson, Black Visionary, Shaker Eldress* (Amherst: University of Massachusetts Press, 1981), pp. 105–7. Copyright © 1981 by The University of Massachusetts Press.

❖

The room was crowded and the stairs also. And as I saw that there was so many people, and as it was my night to lead, I opened the meeting in reading, then gave my views on the spiritual meaning of "the letter," showing how the letter killeth and how the spirit of God would make us alive through Jesus Christ our Lord, if we was willing. Then I gave place for speaking and I encouraged them as I had ability, and there was a warm time in the camp. . . .

The order of this little meeting was, after I opened it, we was to tell all we had done wrong—that is, if we had done any wrong—tell all our temptations, how we resisted them, and if we had yielded, we was to honestly confess it. Then all of us was to kneel down and pray for the one that was under sorrow, till they were released. Then we would go on holding our meeting. This meeting was a great strength to us all.

. . . When [sister A.B.] first began to come to see me, as seeking after spiritual light, I found her first work was to bring the sins of her friends. After she would lay them all before me, I would get up and lock the door. "Now, Sister, come. You must pray for them till you can feel that love and pity for their soul that you feel for your own soul. Without this you can never be saved." So when she found she had to pray for the people's sins when she brought them to me, she soon quit bringing them. This I done to her and everybody else that brought the sins of others. But when they felt to tell their own, I always had words given me for them, and encouragement. For when they would begin to tell me, I would begin to pray to God to give me understanding and give me suitable answers, and to give me a discerning eye, that I might know when I heard the truth. And I can truly say that my prayers have been answered again and again, for which I give the glory to that God to whom it belongs. I am only a pen in His hand. Oh, that I may prove faithful to the end.

. . . After I received the blessing of God, I had a great desire to read the Bible. I am the only child of my mother that had not learning. And now, having the charge of my brother and his six children to see to, and my husband, and taking in sewing for a living, I saw no way that I could now get learning without my brother would give me one hour's lesson at night after supper or before he went to bed. His time was taken up as well as mine. So I spoke to him about it. He said he would give me one or two lessons, I being so desirous to learn. . . . And my brother so tired when he would come home that he had not power so to do, and it would grieve me. Then I would pray to God to give me power over my feelings that I might not think hard of my brother. Then I would be comforted.

So I went to get my brother to write my letters and to read them. So he was awriting a letter in answer to one he had just read. I told him what to put in. Then I asked him to read. He did. I said, "Thee has put in more than I told thee." This he done several times. I then said, "I don't want thee to *word* my letter. I only want thee to *write* it." Then he said, "Sister, thee is the hardest one I ever wrote for!" These words, together with the manner that he had wrote my letter, pierced my soul like a sword. . . . I could not keep from crying. And these words were spoken in my heart, "Be faithful, and the time shall come when you can write." These words were spoken in my heart as though a tender father spoke them. My tears were gone in a moment.

One day I was sitting finishing a dress in haste and in prayer. This word was spoken in my mind, "Who learned the first man on earth?" "Why, God." "He is unchangeable, and if He learned the first man to read, He can learn you." I laid down my dress, picked up my Bible, ran upstairs, opened it, and kneeled down with it pressed to my breast, prayed earnestly to Almighty God if it was consisting to His holy will, to learn me to read His holy word. And when I looked on the word, I began to read. And when I found I was reading, I was frightened—then I could not read one word. I closed my eyes again in prayer and then opened my eyes, began to read. So I done, until I read the chapter. I came down. "Samuel, I can read the Bible." "Woman, you are agoing crazy!" Down I sat and read through. And it was in James. So Samuel praised the Lord with me. When my brother came to dinner I told him, "I can read the Bible! I have read a whole chapter!" "One thee has heard the children read, till thee has got it by heart." What a wound that was to me, to think he would make so light of a gift of God! But I did not speak. Samuel reproved him and told him all about it. He sat down very sorrowful. I then told him, "I had a promise, the day thee wrote my letter to sister Diges, that if I was faithful I would see the day when I can write." . . . So I tried, took my Bible daily and praying and read until I could read anywhere. The first chapter that I read I never could know it after that day. I only knowed it was in James, but what chapter I never can tell.

272

Oh how thankful I feel for this unspeakable gift of Almighty God to me! Oh may I make a good use of it all the days of my life!

To Improve Female Education

Emma Hart Willard (1787–1870) had a thirst for knowledge and a "visionary" longing to make women's education equal to men's. After growing up in Connecticut, she established her first school in Vermont after her marriage. She also became an organizer willing to lobby New York politicians in 1818 to ask for public funding for her school. No one seems to have impugned her femininity for doing so, perhaps because she was teaching daughters of some of the "best families." Although the legislators turned down her request, Willard's plan of study was praised by presidents and intellectuals. A predecessor of Mary Lyon, who founded Mount Holyoke in 1837, and of Catharine Beecher, who established Hartford Seminary in 1823, Emma Willard emphasized that educated women would be better mothers and more useful persons. She also insisted that women were capable of studying mathematics, science, and philosophy. The academy she founded in Troy, New York, in 1821 was attended by the suffragist Elizabeth Cady Stanton and many other influential nineteenth-century women. Willard's textbooks were widely used, and many of her graduates became teachers throughout the country.

From Emma Hart Willard, in Henry Barnard, ed., *Educational Biographies, Memoirs of Teachers, Educators, and Promoters and Benefactors of Education, Literature, and Science, Part I: Teachers and Educators,* 2d ed. (New York: F. C. Brownell, 1861), pp. 133–37. ❖

When I began my boarding school in Middlebury, in 1814, my leading motive was to relieve my husband from financial difficulties. I had also the further object of keeping a better school than those about me; but it was not until a year or two after, that I formed the design of effecting an important change in education, by the introduction of a grade of schools for women, higher than any heretofore known. My neighborhood to Middlebury College, made me bitterly feel the disparity in educational facilities between the two sexes; and I hoped that if the matter was once set before the men as legislators, they would be ready to correct the error. The idea that such a thing might possibly be effected by my means, seemed so presumptuous that I hesitated to entertain it, and for a short time concealed it even from my husband, although I knew that he sympathized in my general views. I began to write (because I could thus best arrange my ideas) "an address to the _____ Legislature, proposing a plan for improving Female Education." It was not till two years after that I filled up the blank. No one knew of my writing it, except my husband, until a year after it was completed, (1816), for I knew that I should be regarded as visionary, almost to insanity, should I utter the expectations which I secretly entertained in connection with it. But it was not merely on the strength of my arguments that I relied. I determined to inform myself, and increase my personal influence and fame as a teacher; calculating that in this way I might be sought for in other places, where influential men would carry my project before some legislature, for the sake of obtaining a good school.

My exertions meanwhile, became unremitted and intense. My school grew to seventy pupils. I spent from ten to twelve hours a day in teaching, and on extraordinary occasions, as preparing for examination, fifteen; besides, always having under investigation some one new subject which, as I studied, I simultaneously taught to a class of my ablest pupils. Hence every new term some new study was introduced; and in all their studies, my pupils were very thoroughly trained. In classing my school for the term of study, which was then about three months, I gave to each her course, (being careful not to give too much) with the certain expectation, that she must be examined on it at the close of the term. Then I was wont to consider that my first duty as a teacher, required of me that I should labor to make my pupils by explanation and illustration *understand* their subject, and get them warmed into it, by making them see its beauties and its advantages. During this first part of the process, I talked much more than the pupils were required to do, keeping their attention awake by frequent questions, requiring short answers from the whole class,—for it was ever my maxim, if attention fails, the teacher fails. Then in the *second* stage of my teaching, I made each scholar recite, in order that she might *remember*—paying special attention to the meaning of words, and to discern whether the subject was indeed understood without mistake. Then the *third* process was to make the pupil capable of *communicating*. And doing this in a right manner, was to prepare her for examination. At this time I personally examined all my classes.

This thorough teaching added rapidly to my reputation. Another important feature of a system, thus requiring careful drill and correct enunciation, was manifested by the examinations. The pupils there acquired character and confidence. Scholars thus instructed were soon capable of teaching; and here were now forming my future teachers; and some were soon capable of aiding me in arranging the new studies, which I was constantly engaged in introducing.

Here I began a series of improvements in geography—separating and first teaching what could be learned from maps—then treating the various subjects of population, extent, length of rivers, &c., by comparing country with country, river with river, and city with city,—making out with the assistance of my pupils, those tables which afterwards appeared in Woodbridge and Willard's Geographies. Here also began improvements in educational history. Moral Philosophy came next, with Paley for the author, and Miss Hemingway for the first scholar; and then the Philosophy of the Mind—Locke the author, and the first scholars, Eliza Henshaw, Katharine Battey, and Minerva Shipherd.

The professors of the college attended my examinations; although I was by the President advised, that it would not be becoming in me, not be a safe precedent, if I should attend theirs. So, as I had no teacher in learning my new studies, I had no model in teaching, or examining them. But I had full faith in the clear conclusions of my own mind. I knew that nothing could be truer than truth; and hence I fearlessly brought to examination, before the learned, the classes, to which had been taught the studies I had just acquired.

I soon began to have invitations to go from Middlebury. Gov. VanNess, wishing me to go to Burlington, I opened my views to him. The college buildings were then nearly vacant, and some steps were taken towards using them for a Female Seminary, of which I was to be Principal, but the negotiations failed. In the spring of 1818, I had five pupils from Waterford, of the best families. On looking over the map of the United States, to see where would be the best geographical location for the projected institution, I had fixed my mind on the State of New York, and thought, that the best place would be somewhere in the vicinity of the head of navigation on the Hudson. Hence, the coming of the Waterford pupils I regarded as an important event. I presented my views to Gen. Van Schornhoven, the father (by adoption,) of one of my pupils,—who was interested, and proposed to show my manuscript to the Hon. J. Cramer, of Waterford, and to De Witt Clinton, then Governor of New York; and if they approved it, then the "Plan" might go before the legislature with some chance of success. Thereupon I copied the manuscript with due regard to manner and chirography; having already rewritten it some seven times, and thrown out about three quarters of what it first contained—then sent it to Gov. Clinton with the following letter:

To his Excellency, De Witt Clinton,—

Sir,—Mr. Southwick will present to you a manuscript, containing a plan for improving the education of females, by instituting public seminaries for their use. Its authoress has presumed to offer it to your Excellency, because she believed you would consider the subject as worthy of your attention. . . .

Possibly your Excellency may consider this plan as better deserving your attention, to know that its authoress is not a visionary enthusiast, who has speculated in solitude without practical knowledge of her subject. For ten years she has been intimately conversant with female schools, and nearly all of that time she has herself been a preceptress. Nor has she written for the sake of writing, but merely to communicate a plan of which she fully believes that it is practicable; that, if realized, it would form a new and happy era in the history of her sex, and if of her sex, why not of her country, and of mankind? . . .

Your Obedient Servant, Emma Willard
Middlebury, Vt., February 5, 1818.

This treatise is in reality the foundation of the Troy seminary. It will not be thought surprising that I awaited with intense feeling Gov. Clinton's reply. It came before I expected it, expressing his accordance with my views in his happiest manner. His message to the legislature soon followed, in which, referring to my "Plan," (though not by its title or author's name,), he recommended legislative action in behalf of a cause heretofore wholly neglected. The Waterford gentlemen had made Gov. Clinton's opinion their guiding light. They were to present my "Plan" to the legislature; and advised that Dr. Willard and myself should spend a few weeks in Albany during the session, which we did. The Governor and many of his friends called on us; and I read my manuscript several times by special request to different influential members; and once to a considerable assemblage. The affair would have gone off by acclamation, could immediate action have been had. As it was, an act was passed incorporating the institution at Waterford; and another, to give to female academies a share of the literature fund. This law, the first whose sole object was to improve female education, is in force, and is the same by which female academies in the state now receive public money.

By Awakening Their Consciences

In 1839 the first normal school for teacher training was established in Massachusetts, and the movement for "common" grammar schools free to all comers began in earnest. Its purpose was to Americanize and Christianize (Protestant-style) the expanding populace, continuing the work of the many Sunday or Sabbath schools that zealous women had been establishing in new communities in the wake of the Second Great Awakening. Children were taught to read, write, and cipher—and to say their prayers and mind their morals. Women like the idealistic Ellen Lee, who wrote the following letter to her eastern sponsors, the National Board of Popular Education, gradually replaced men as teachers or established schools where none had been before. The board trained more than two hundred teachers in Hartford, Connecticut, during the 1840s and sent them as missionary educators to western communities.

276 From Ellen P. Lee, letter, January 6, 1852, from Hamilton County, Indiana, in National Board of Popular Education Collection, pp. 59–61, by permission of Connecticut Historical Society, Hartford.

❖

Hamilton County, Indiana
January 6, 1852

Dear Friends,

It is with pleasure that I comply with your request to write to you. I have just commenced the second term of my school here, so that I am able to judge pretty correctly of my prospects in this place.

It is a new settlement here, it being only fifteen years since the first person settled here. But the settlement is quite large, and thickly settled.

Nearly all live in log-houses. The people are kind to me, very kind; they are peaceful, honest, intelligent naturally, but have not had an opportunity for improving their minds; so that they are very ignorant. I have not seen a well-educated person; many of the adults can neither read nor write, and some cannot tell one letter from another, and do not care if the children cannot. There are nine preachers here, and scarcely one can read a chapter in the Bible correctly; and I have heard most of them preach; they are not at all like New England ministers and it is often a cross to hear them preach: but I hope some of them are good Christian men, who try to perform their duty, and not only preach, but practice what they preach. The religious societies here are United Brethren and New School or Antimason Methodist, the latter hold meetings in the house where I teach, and these I attend. They separated from the Episcopals on account of secret societies.

They have meetings every Sabbath, and preaching quite often; also meeting during the week evenings.

Just before I came here, a Sabbath School had been organized, and they had purchased a library of some more than 100 volumes; when I came they were on the point of giving it up. Those interested at first had got discouraged because they had failed to interest others. The school was conducted in a novel manner; no one here ever saw a school of the kind before, and considering this, and the qualifications of the teachers, they did well. I thought I could not get along without the Sabbath School, and they consented to try it longer.

We have now divided it into classes. I am obliged to take charge of all the females, there being no one else who can, and sometimes I have a great number, and of course can not do as I would: and beside they depend on me to assist the others, but I enjoy it much; in this way some can be taught, who can be taught in no other way. It now seems prosperous and the interest increasing; sometimes the house is nearly full of children. Some of the parents who at first felt no interest in it, say they would rather give up anything than the Sabbath School. I hope the interest will continue to increase, and that it will prove a blessing to the neighborhood.

I came here unexpected by the people, they not having heard from Gov. Slade, but I was received kindly. My school was not very large at first, but it has gradually increased, 'till I have now about 50 (?) pupils most of whom are between the ages of 14 and 22. There has been no school here before for more than a year, and they have never had a teacher who could do more than read, write and cipher a little; and these he did very imperfectly, so that my scholars are very backward but they are eager to learn, bright, active, attentive, and obedient, and learn very fast. I have a large number of young men between the ages of 18 and 21; they are very respectful, and obedient. I think I have gained the respect and affection of all my pupils, so that their obedience is cheerfully given. When I came here, there was a prejudice against female teachers; they had always employed men, and had never had a school six weeks without trouble, and they thought of course, if a man could not govern their boys, a woman could not; but I was allowed to take my own course, and I gave them only one rule, that was— Do right. And by awakening their consciences to a sense of right and wrong, and other similar influences, I have succeeded much better than I expected, and have had to use no other influences than kindness. The parents have been interested to visit the school, and I find this the best way, and the surest way to interest them. I commence school with devotional exercises which I think have a good effect on the school during the day; this is something which has never been done here before. In my school I am content, and happy for I hope I am doing good, but I am entirely deprived of sympathy, and good society. I have no human being here, in whom I can confide, or who possesses kindred feelings with mine. But there is one to whom I can go; were it not that I can cast all my care on God, and go to his Word for sympathy and consolation, I should be unhappy. I am also deprived of many New England comforts, and nearly all its privileges, but when I think that I am giving a privilege to others, which they have never enjoyed I think I ought not to complain. But although I sometimes sigh, and long for christian sympathy, and the privileges I once enjoyed, and feel lonely when I think of home, and friends, yet I am happy. I hope I have a friend who is always near and if I can in my way be useful I shall be happy. Pray for me, that my coming here may not be in vain. I should be pleased to hear from you.

Such an Illiberal Spirit

An outgrowth of the Second Great Awakening was the establishment of numerous women's benevolent organizations to alleviate poverty and provide public relief in growing cities and towns. Philadelphia's Rebecca Gratz (1781–1869), the daughter of a prominent Jewish merchant, was noted for her culture and philanthropy. She kept house for unmarried brothers and her sister's orphaned children and held office in several aid societies. Choosing to remain unmarried, she retained the legal right to handle money and business affairs, which a married woman could not do. At the age of twenty-one, she was the prime organizer of the Philadelphia Female Association for the Relief of Women and Children in Reduced Circumstances. She later became secretary of the Philadelphia Orphan Society for forty years, and she founded the Hebrew Sunday school movement in 1838. The following letters to her sister-in-law reveal the religious prejudices of her time as well as her role within the Orphan Society.

From Rabbi David Philipson, ed., *Letters of Rebecca Gratz* (Philadelphia: Jewish Publication Society of America, 1929), pp. 145–46, 289.

❖

April 13, 1832

I had my philosophy a little tried the other day by some good Christians, and as I dare not complain about it to anybody else (for I hate to set the subject in its true light at home)—I must make you my confidante—You know I promised our friend Mrs Furness to apply for a little girl out of the Asylum for her—well there is a good little girl I have kept my eye on and she is ready for a place—and my application is rejected because it is for a Unitarian—but "Ladies, said I, there are many children under my special direction—you all know my creed—suppose I should want one to bring up in my family?"—"you may have one, said a church woman—because the Jews do not think it a duty to convert"—but said a presbyterian "I should not consent to her being put under the influence of a Unitarian"—and so my dear after putting the question to vote—I could get nothing —and when the meeting broke up, had a mischievous pleasure in telling one of the most blue of the board that I construed their silence into consent—for only one lady voted in the affirmative—and they were all ashamed to vote no—but I do not mean to let Mrs F know how she is proscribed, because notwithstanding my own position, I am ashamed of such an illiberal spirit—I got into a long discussion on the subject of religion, with a lady after the meeting and though we have been more than twenty years acquainted—I expect she will look shy on me for the rest of our lives—what a pity that the best and holiest gift of God, to his most favoured creatures, should be perverted into a subject of strife—and that to seek to know and love the most High should not be the end and aim of all—without a jealous or persecuting feeling towards each other— . . . .

July 1841

I have just been called away on a business that interests me very much—application was made for the admission of a boy into the Orphan Asylum, by a person who had received him from his dying mother—had indentured him to be adopted as his own son, to change his name, educate & give him a trade—at this period the child was three years old—he is now five—and they brought him to me with such evil reports of his character that I thought it necessary to get the consent of the Board—this was obtained but thinking the man who had taken him with such promises ought to pay some consideration, he was told so—and while I supposed he was making preparations to relinquish the child—found he had (perhaps to save the fee) placed him in the house of Refuge—a child 5 yrs old to be brought up among convicts!! this appears so shocking that we intend to get him out and take him to the Asylum—It is impossible that such an infant can deserve to be punished to such a degree, and if not, what must he become living among old offenders?—you shall know the result if we succeed, and make him a good boy.

So Many Charitable Societies

There is a modern ring to Susan Mansfield Huntington's complaint about being censured for being both too active and not active enough in public affairs. She had helped establish the Boston Maternal Association to discuss child rearing with other mothers, and her editor lists her membership in an impressive number of other benevolent organizations. Susan Huntington (1791–1823) took very seriously the task of educating her children for moral excellence. Whereas such education had been a father's responsibility in colonial times, the changing roles of men and women in the nineteenth century helped reverse parental roles. Well-to-do fathers were now absent at work, and mothers were expected to give much more time and energy to child rearing.

From Benjamin B. Wisner, ed., *Memoirs of the Late Mrs. Susan Mansfield Huntington* (Boston: Crocker and Brewster, 1826), pp. 122–24, 127–29.

❖

January 5, [1815] How difficult, how hopeless is the task of pleasing every body! A fortnight since a lady said to me, with a tone and manner which gave peculiar emphasis to the words, "How is it possible you can go out so much, visit your people so frequently, and be engaged in so many charitable societies, without neglecting your family?" This week a different imputation has been attached to my conduct. I am censured for doing so little in a public way, and confining myself so much to my family. I am accused of want of interest in public charities, because I give to them so little of my time and attention. Such different opinions are formed of the same conduct! But the voice of wisdom bids me, cease from man whose breath is in his nostrils, and study to approve myself to God—As to my conduct, I am very sensible that I do little good in the world, in comparison with what I might do. But whether I could, with propriety, devote more time to the active duties of public charities, I have serious doubts. More of the charity of prayer, to Him who can effectually ameliorate the calamities of the world by subduing its corruptions, I might, I ought, to bestow. Alas! here how far I fall short! But my opinion is, that her own family has the first claim to the attention and active exertions of a married lady. So much time as can be redeemed, (and she should feel it her duty to redeem as much as possible,) from the ordering of domestic affairs, the care and culture of children, the duties of personal religion, the improvement of her own mind, and the perusal of works from which assistance may be derived in the all-important business of education, may be, and much of it ought to be, devoted to the duties of public charity.

I feel that I do very wrong in suffering myself to be so much affected by the opinions of my fellow creatures. A person must form his own rules of conduct; and having judiciously formed, must pursue them, and not be continually fluctuating according to the sentiments of every one with whom he happens to meet. Oh that God would give me grace to redeem my time, so that I may render my account of it with joy!

[Original editor's note: It may be well to state in this place, that, at the time of her death, Mrs. Huntington was a life member of the Female Orphan Asylum, and of the Fragment Society; a life member, and the Vice President, of the Graham Society; a life member, and a director, of the Corban Society, and of the Female Society of Boston and Vicinity for promoting Christianity among the Jews; a life member, and the Corresponding Secretary, and one of the visiting and distributing Committee, of the Female Bible Society of Boston and Vicinity; an annual subscriber to the Widows' Society, and to the Boston Female Education Society; an annual subscriber to, and the Vice President of, the Old South Charity School Society; an annual subscriber to, and a Director of, the Boston Female Tract Society; and a member of the Boston Maternal Association.]

April 4 [1815] This subject of education is one that lies nearer my heart than any other merely temporal concern. It is easy to speculate about it, and to prescribe rules to others. It is easy to form a correct and most judicious system; and to say with Foster's man of indecision, "this is a good plan, a plan which would be very useful in its results," and after all, make shipwreck of the disposition and minds of our children by mismanagement. All this is easy, for the same reason that it is easy to acquire correct opinions on any subject. But acting, practice; here, here is the difficulty. The truth is, no one can govern a family of children well, without much reflection and, what the world calls, trouble. There must be an accurate judgment formed respecting the character of each child, and a *regular* and *consistent* method, adapted to each, pursued. And, what is more difficult still, the parent must uniformly govern herself. This, certainly, is not easy; it calls for the unremitted exertion of several most eminent and rare Christian graces.

281

It appears to me that three simple rules, steadily observed from the very germ of active existence, would make children's tempers much more amiable than we generally see them. *First.* Never to give them any thing improper for them, because they strongly and passionately desire it: and even to withhold proper things, until they manifest a right spirit. *Second.* Always to gratify every reasonable desire, when a child is pleasant in its request; that your children may see that you love to make them happy. *Third.* Never to become impatient and fretful yourself, but proportion your displeasure exactly to the offence. If parents become angry, and speak loud and harsh, upon every slight failure of duty, they may bid a final adieu to domestic subordination, unless the grace of God interposes to snatch the little victims of severity from destruction. I feel confident, from what observation I have made, that, although more children are injured by excessive indulgence than by the opposite fault, yet the effects of extreme rigor are the most hopeless. And the reason is, associations of a disagreeable nature, as some of the ablest philosophers have stated, are the strongest. This may account for the melancholy fact, that the children of some excellent people grow up more strenuously opposed to every thing serious, than others. They have been driven, rather than led, to observe the forms and outward duties of religion, and its claims upon their hearts have been too commonly presented to their minds, in the imperative, and not in the inviting form.

For my own part, I find myself falling so far short, that I am, sometimes, overwhelmed with the distressing apprehension of erring fatally. Dear children! I tremble for you, when I reflect how dangerous is the path in which you are to tread, and how difficult the task of directing you in safety.

A Visit to Margaret Fuller

The journalist Lydia Maria Child visited the writer Margaret Fuller while both were living in New York in 1845, and Child was glad to help promote Fuller's work. Here she describes Fuller's home and thus also provides a unique description of long-ago New York. Such "networking" has always been important among women writers and reformers.

From Milton Meltzer and Patricia G. Holland, eds., *Lydia Maria Child: Selected Letters, 1817–1880* (Amherst: University of Massachusetts Press, 1982), pp. 217–18. By permission of Child Papers, William L. Clements Library, University of Michigan, Ann Arbor (first letter); Child Papers, A/C 536, folder 1, Schlesinger Library, Radcliffe College, Cambridge, Massachusetts (second letter).

❖

To Anna Loring

New York Feb. 6th, 1845

Dear Anna,

. . . A little while ago, I set forth to make our friend Margaret Fuller a visit. It was an undertaking for *me,* I assure you; for we live three miles apart, and the roads were one mass of mud. I went out in the Harlem omnibus to *forty ninth street,* where she told me she lived. But instead of a street, I found a winding zigzag cart-track. It was as rural as you can imagine, with moss-covered rocks, scraggly bushes, and a brook that came tumbling over a little dam, and ran under the lane. After passing through three great swinggates, I came to the house, which stands all alone by itself, and is as inaccessible, as if I had chosen it, to keep people off. It is a very old house, with a very old porch, and very old vines, and a very old garden, and very old summer-houses dropping to pieces, and a very old piazza at the back, overgrown with very old rosebushes, which at that season were covered with red berries. The piazza is almost *on* the East river, with Blackwell's Island in full view before it. Margaret's chamber looks out upon a little woody knoll, that runs down into the water, and boats and ships are passing her window all the time. How anything so old and picturesque has been allowed to remain standing near New York so long, I cannot imagine. I spent three or four delightful hours with Margaret, and then trudged home in the mud, afoot and alone. . . .

To Louisa Loring

New York, Feb. 8'th 1845

Dearest Louise,

. . . I have read Margaret's book, Woman in the Nineteenth Century, and I like it much. I procured it in proof-sheet, and sent a brief notice of it to the Boston Courier, thinking it might possibly help the sale a little. It is a bold book, I assure you. I should not have dared to have written some things in it, though it would have been safer for me, being married. But they need to be said, and she is brave to do it. She bears a noble testimony to anti slavery principles in several places. She is a great woman, and no mistake. I like her extremely.

283

Social Architects of Modern Times

The Shakers were one of the most notable of the utopian communities established during the nineteenth century. Founded by Mother Ann Lee when she and her followers came to America in 1774, the group thrived in numerous affiliated settlements, some of which survived into the late twentieth century. This description is by a contemporary observer.

From William Alfred Hines, *American Communities* (1878; reprint, Secaucus, N.J.: Citadel Press, 1961), pp. 94–95, 97, 101–2, 104, 105.

❖

The world is more indebted to the Shakers than to all other social architects of modern times. . . . Their example has, indeed encouraged every effort at Communism in this country and in Europe which has been attempted since the walls of their Zion were laid at Mt. Lebanon in 1787. . . .

And of persecution, for the first half century of their existence at least, they had their full share. At Lebanon, Ohio, their houses were beset at night; their windows broken; their persons assaulted with clubs and stones; their fences thrown down; cattle were turned into their grain-fields; their fruit-trees cut and mangled; their horses cropped and otherwise disfigured; their barns and stables, containing their stores of hay and grain, burned, as also their place of worship. . . .

Intense religious earnestness has been the distinguishing characteristic of the Shakers, as a body, during their entire history. . . . It is a rule in all Shaker Societies that the members shall rise simultaneously at the ringing of the bell, which in the summer is at half-past four, and in the winter at five; and that breakfast shall be an hour and a half after rising; dinner at twelve; supper at six, except on Sunday, when the Shakers rise and breakfast half an hour later, dine lightly at twelve, and sup at four. A large bell always rings a few moments before meal-time. The brothers and sisters eat apart from each other. . . .

It is a common charge against the Shaker system that its regulations and restrictions are unfavorable to individual development. . . . The conditions of communal life existing in Shaker Societies do certainly tend to the development of some high qualities of character, such as obedience, resignation, loyalty, earnestness. Moreover, they are favorable to the development of the talents which are exercised in mechanical invention; and the Shakers claim, and apparently with good reason, to have contributed to general society quite a number of its most useful inventions and mechanical improvements, such as the corn broom, tongue-and-groove machinery, cut nails, Babbitt-metal, an improved washing-machine, an improved lathe, a pea-sheller, mowing- and reaping-machines, etc. . . .

Except as revivals occasionally bring them converts, the Shakers have to depend for their members, in great part, upon the unfortunate people who flock to them for homes when they find the struggle for existence too hard for them; and upon orphans and the children of poor people, glad to put their little ones where they will have enough to eat and wear, and be brought up in habits of strict morality. . . .

The women of the Shaker Societies claim to be fully emancipated—to have equal rights with the men in all respects. The Shaker government is dual in all its departments and offices. The women appear to have as much influence and voice as the men; a woman founded the organization, and a woman held its first office for twenty-five years during its greatest period of prosperity; women are as free as men to speak in their meetings; women are as free as men to write for their paper; women manage their own departments of industry independently of the men.

The Shakers themselves are persuaded that the celibate condition is superior to any other and raises them above the worldly or generative plane. . . . Celibacy is thought by many to be less favorable to health than marriage. If this be true it only proves that the general conditions of Communism are greatly superior to those of common society, for the Shakers are unusually long-lived even for Communists. The eightieth year is often reached, and some live far past the ninetieth.

Of Corsets and Health

Health problems were common among nineteenth-century women, due not only to overwork or excessive childbearing but also to the physical burden of tight-laced corsets. Young girls were corseted well before puberty, so that their bone and internal structures were affected for life. The health reformer Orson Fowler wrote and lectured throughout America on the ill effects of wasp-waist fashions and lack of exercise on women's health. Distortion of the ribs and spine, along with displacement of internal organs, was comparable to the horrors of Chinese foot-binding, he said. Women reformers agreed, and dress reform was a significant part of the women's rights agenda.

From Orson S. Fowler, *Intemperance and Tight Lacing* (New York: Fowler and Wells, 1848), p. 6.

❖

Lacing prevents that expansion of the chest which is natural in breathing, and by means of which alone air can be admitted into the lungs. . . . Tight-lacing prevents breathing, and thus literally *suffocates* its fashionable victim. And I now appeal to every corseted woman, whether she does not experience a sinking faintness, a choking for want of breath, a suffocating sensation, as though she should die; a panting for breath, which, carried much farther, would destroy life on the spot. It is this which occasions so many laced women to faint at church, or on occasions where the house is full, and the air therefore less pure. They obtain but little breath at all events, and that little being impure, they faint from mere want of it, including also that want of circulation, caused by cramping the heart and arteries. And how quick a woman comes to, when her girt-strings are cut!

Tight lacing violates another important physiological principle. Digestion is greatly facilitated by *motion* in the stomach. Indeed, without this motion, its functions soon become enfeebled, its conditions diseased, its product corrupt, and life itself consequently enfeebled, by the disease thereby engendered in the whole system. To render this motion constant, and thus perpetually to assist digestion, it is so arranged that every breath we draw presses downward upon all the organs below the lungs, and thus imparts this much needed motion to the digestive apparatus. But tight-lacing *girts in* the lower portion of the lungs, and cuts off all that downward movement naturally imparted by breathing to the organs of digestion; and confines all the motion occasioned by breathing to the upper portion of the lungs. By noticing the motion made in breathing, it is easy to see who is laced, for those who *are* laced, will heave the upper part of their chests greatly, but the entire region of the abdomen will be motionless; the consequence of which is a most fatal torpor of the whole digestive apparatus, that gradually but effectually stops the manufactory and flow of vitality at its fountain head, weakening the powers of life while we live, and bringing them the sooner to a fatal cessation.

286

Of Voluntary Motherhood

Among nineteenth-century reformers, notions about the "natural laws" of sexual abstinence (based on observations of animal mating behavior) laid the foundations of the future birth-control movement. Emphasizing a woman's right to determine whether or not she should become pregnant, and her right to resist a man's "ungoverned passion," even in marriage, this essay by Sarah Grimké expressed ideas that were widespread at the time. Women's rights advocates perceived "voluntary motherhood" through abstinence a necessity for personal freedom, not a restriction (as twentieth-century women would later claim). Prominent doctors wrote textbooks and warned their patients that marital intercourse should not occur more than once or twice a month in order to preserve male as well as female health. "Sexual excess," even within marriage, was considered contrary to the laws of nature.

Sarah Grimké (1792–1873), one of fourteen children, never married. Instead, she devoted herself to caring for the three children of her sister, Angelina Grimké Weld. Angelina (1805–79) suffered poor health most of her married life, apparently from a prolapsed uterus caused by childbirth difficulties. Thus Sarah's ideas on marriage also had a pragmatic basis.

From Sarah Grimké, "Marriage," 1855, Weld-Grimké Papers, William L. Clements Library, University of Michigan, Ann Arbor, pp. 4–9, 18–19, 21.

❖

An eminent physician of Boston once remarked that if in the economy of nature, the sexes alternated in giving birth to children no family would ever have more than three, the husband bearing one & the wife two. But the *right* to decide this matter has been almost wholly denied to woman. How often is she forced into an untimely motherhood which compels her to wean her babe, thus depriving it of that nutriment provided by nature as the most bland & fitting, during the period of dentition. Thousands of deaths from this cause, in infancy, are attributed by superstition & ignorance to the dispensations of Divine Providence. How many thousands, too, of miscarriages are forced upon woman by the fact that man lives down that law of his being which would protect her from such

terrible consequences just as animal instinct protects the female among brutes.
To save woman from legalized licentiousness is then one of the reasons why we
plead for *equality of rights*.

No one can fail to see that this condition of things results from several causes:

1st Ignorance of those physical laws which every man & woman *ought* to
know before marriage, the knowledge of which has been withheld from the
young, under a false & fatal idea of delicacy. Many a man ruins his own health
& that of his wife & his children too, thro' ignorance. A diffusion of knowledge
respecting these laws would greatly defuse existing evils.

2 A false conception in man & woman of *his* nature & necessities. The
great truth that the most concentrated fluid of the body has an office to perform
in the product of *great tho'ts & original ideas,* as well as in the reproduction of
the species is known to few & too little appreciated by all. The prodigal waste
of this by legalized licentiousness has dwarfed the intellect of man. . . .

3d The fact that many legal marriages are not love marriages. In a pure,
true relation between the sexes, no difficulties can ever arise, but a willing
recognition of each other's rights & mutual wants, naturally & spontaneously
resulting in voluntary motherhood, a joyful appreciation of the blessedness of
parentage, the birth of healthy, comely children & a beautiful home.

But it may be asked, what is to be done in cases of uncongenial marriages.
Are not such men & women to follow their attractions outside of the legal relation. I unhesitatingly answer No! Where two persons have established a false
marriage relation, *they are bound to abide by the consequences* of the mistake they
have made. Perhaps they did love each other, but a nearer intimacy has frozen
this love or changed it into disgust. Or, theirs may have been a marriage of *convenience,* or one for the sake of obtaining a house, a fortune, a position in life: or
it may have been a mere act of obedience to parents, or of gratitude, or a means
of canceling a monied obligation. Multiform are the *unworthy* motives which
seduce men & women into this sacred relation. In all these cases, let them abide
the consequences of their own perversion of marriage, in exchanging personal
chastity for the pride of life, vanity in dress, position or a house to live in, without that *love* which alone can make that house a *home.*

In some cases, it may be duty for the parties to separate, but let both keep
themselves pure, so long as both are living. Let them accept the discipline thus
afforded, & spiritual strength & growth will be their reward.

The Doctrine that human beings are to follow their attractions, which lies at
the base of that miscalled "free love" system, is fraught with infinite danger. We
are too low down to listen for one moment to its syren voice. . . .

Let me then exculpate "the woman's rights movement," from the charge of
"tending directly and rapidly to the Free Love system, & nullifying the very idea

of Marriage as anything more than a partnership at will." On the contrary our great desire is to purify & exalt the marriage relation & destroy *all* licentious-ness. . . .

288

. . . Man seems to feel that Marriage gives him the control of Woman's person just as the Law gives him the control of her property. Thus are her most sacred rights destroyed by that very act, which, under the laws of Nature should en-large, establish & protect them. In marriage is the origin of Life—in it woman finds herself endowed with a creative energy she never possessed before. In it new aspirations take possession of her, an indescribable longing after mother-hood as the felt climax of her being. She joyfully gives herself away, that she may receive the germ of a new being, & true to nature, would fain retire within herself & absorb & expend all her energies in the development of this precious germ. But alas! How few are permitted, unmolested to pursue that end, which for the time being, has become the great object of life. How often is she com-pelled by various considerations to yield to the *unnatural* embraces of her hus-band, & thus to endanger the very existence of her embryo babe. How often is it sacrificed to the ungoverned passion of its own father, & the health of the mother serious impaired. Every unnatural process is deleterious, hence abor-tions are destructive to the constitution & many women are broken down in the prime of life by them alone, & their haggard countenances too plainly re-veal their secret sorrows. A lady once said to me I have but one child, but I have had 12 miscarriages—another had 4 children & 15 abortions. And why I would ask this untimely casting of her fruit? Do the beasts of the field miscarry? Why not? *They* are governed by instinct. Are the *brutes* safe during the period of ges-tation whilst *Woman* is not! . . .

. . . Again—look at the burdens imposed upon her by the care of many children following in quick succession. How can any mother do her duty to her family, if in 8 years she have 6 children. Look at the unnatural tug upon her constitution, her night watches, her sore vexations & trials & causes nameless & numberless, that wear away her life. If men had to alternate with their wives, the duties of the nursery, fewer & further between would be its inmates.

A Ladies' Physiological Society

The ill health of nineteenth-century women was a topic of concern to many reformers. They claimed that middle-class women were less healthy than their mothers and grandmothers. Doctors agreed that gynecological disorders and psychosomatic illnesses were common. Reformers blamed the troubles on a "proper" lady's lack of exercise, her fashionable clothes, the hothouse atmosphere of wood-stove heating at eighty degrees, a lack of bathing, and too many drugs. Above all, midwives and women physicians were being replaced by male professionals, whose only training was by lectures and books and who were hampered in practice by prudery and embarrassment. Boston's Harriot Hunt (1805–75) had a long and successful medical practice, specializing in the treatment of women. The meetings she describes here were emulated by numerous other women reformers in the following decades.

From Harriot Hunt, *Glances and Glimpses* (Boston: John P. Jewett, 1856), pp. 177–79.

❖

But to come at once to the Charlestown Ladies' Physiological Society:—I had watched some time for a circle of women, well acquainted with each other, that might be induced to meet, commence a course of physiological reading, bring their experiences to enlighten each other, and develop thoughts and reflections which were embryotic. The opportunity had come at last, and my soul was gladdened.

The Circle first met, April 25th, 1843, at the house of Mrs. Curtis in Charlestown. . . . In the following year, . . . our numbers had increased from less than a dozen, to fifty.

We had lectures twice a month:—I call them lectures, though they rather had the character of conversations. Meanwhile, the ladies were occupied in knitting stockings for the poor children of the "Charlestown Infant School Society."

During the second year of the Society the lectures were continued once a fortnight, the infant school children were not forgotten . . . . We were cheered and instructed by lectures from Horace Mann, Dr. Smith, and others.

I have given this outline of its general course of proceeding, in the hope that it may awaken my country friends to form similar associations. If no one is prepared to lecture, read Combe's "Constitution of Man," Combe on Infancy, etc. Such works will furnish conversation, and stimulate thought. . . .

The interest manifested by the members of this society gave me great satisfaction and encouragement. Social life thus connected with the acquisition of knowledge, assumed a new and more important aspect. I would here express my thanks to every lady composing that Circle, and gratefully recognize their charity for my short-comings, and their tenderness to me when I was in affliction. They are constantly kept in memory more by these things than by the tangible souvenirs they generously gave me—the desk they presented me, in which I found a case of sewing utensils, was doubly valued as a testimony of their womanly interest in me.

. . . If every little village throughout the country would commence a similar society, with even five persons as a nucleus, they would be richly repaid by the acquisition of useful knowledge.

The freedom with which we conversed about diseases peculiar to women, proved the utility of such associations. I can truthfully say that some members of this society told me that their doctor's bills were one half reduced in consequence of their obedience to physical laws.

No Women at Harvard

After twenty years of medical experience, Harriot Hunt applied to Harvard to seek more "scientific light." The Harvard trustees considered it "inexpedient" to admit her because her presence would be distracting to men. Only one college in the country, Geneva College in western New York State, then admitted women medical students; few others would do so throughout the rest of the century.

From Harriot Hunt, *Glances and Glimpses* (Boston: John P. Jewett, 1856), pp. 214–18, 270–71.

❖

General and special anatomy,—shall I ever forgive the Harvard Medical College for depriving me of a thorough knowledge of that science, a knowledge only to be gained by witnessing dissections in connection with close study and able lectures? Physiology, with all its thousand ramifications, had a fascination for me beyond all other branches—use, abuse—cause, effect—beginning, and end—all were significant in the light of a science undarkened by technicalities, doubtful assumptions, tedious dissertations, controversies, and contradictions. My mind was greedy for knowledge, the more I investigated, the more I was delighted, wonderstruck;—and I was often startled by the rays of light that unexpectedly shone during my research. Setting aside medication, we endeavored to trace diseases to violated laws, and learn the science of prevention. That word—preventive—seemed a great word to me; curative, was small beside it. . . .

About this time queries were often put to me respecting my attending medical lectures, which many of my patients knew I was very anxious to do. "Why," I was asked, "do you not apply to Harvard College for permission to attend the lectures there; you have been in practice so many years in Boston, that such a request could not be refused?" "Physicians speak well of you as a woman—Dr. _____ knows the class of patients that sustain you." "I have no doubt Harvard would open its doors to you; your age, your birthright as a Bostonian, must have weight with them." These and many similar interrogatories strengthened my purpose, although I differed from them. I well knew that the conservatism of Harvard would blind the trustees, professors, etc., to the importance of recognizing woman as a physician. I knew they would have a childish fear of looking truth in the face, and establishing a precedent which might bring into comparison, if not into conflict, masculine and feminine minds. I knew it required more magnanimity, more freedom, more generosity, and a deeper sense of justice, than I supposed existed at Harvard, to acknowledge by such a step, that mind was not sexual. Still while I did not participate in the sanguine hopes of my friends, that application would insure admission, the feeling that it was a duty to *try* became stronger and stronger and stronger, and resulted in the following letter. When I sat down to write, it really seemed to me farcical, to ask whether a woman, who had been practicing medicine many years—a mind thirsting for knowledge, lavishly bestowed on all sensible and unsensible male applicants, *might be allowed* to share the privilege of drinking at the fountains of science, a privilege which would not impoverish them, but make me rich indeed. I well knew through my practice the quality of young men, who with M.D. attached, put up their sign in some country village, and as well did I know the determination to avoid them. . . . Instances of malpractice often presented themselves. . . . I was sometimes thunderstruck at the egregious blunders made by doctors, yet I can safely say I have never interfered with family physicians. . . .

[The reply to Dr. Hunt's application was dated January 5, 1845]:

"At a stated meeting of the President and Fellows of Harvard College, in Boston, Dec. 27, 1844, the President submitted to the board a letter from Dr. Holmes, transmitting an application from Miss Harriot Kezia Hunt, to be permitted to attend the lectures at the Medical College. Whereupon it was voted, that it is *inexpedient* to reconsider the vote of the corporation, of the 14th of August, relative to a similar request."

A true copy of record.—Attest,
James Walker, *Sec.*

It is said to be dangerous to tell tales out of school. *"Inexpedient"* it certainly is when you wish to keep all hush—but as one is not hung for thoughts, I will tell mine. Having a conversation with one of the professors I told him my intention. I think he informed the clique, and that law was passed to meet my application—but no matter. The facts are on record—when civilization is further advanced, and the great doctrine of human rights is acknowledged, this act will be recalled, and wondering eyes will stare, and wondering ears be opened, at the semi-barbarism of the middle of the nineteenth century. . . .

[In 1850 Harriot Hunt again applied to Harvard. This time she was actually given permission to attend lectures, but without the promise of a degree. This led to a] series of resolutions passed at a meeting of the medical class with but *one* dissenting vote, and afterwards respectfully presented to the Faculty of the Medical College.

Whereas, it has been ascertained that permission has been granted to a female to attend the Medical Lectures of the present winter, therefore

Resolved, That we deem it proper both to testify our disapprobation of said measure, and to take such action thereon as may be necessary to preserve the dignity of the school, and our own self-respect.

Resolved, That no woman of true delicacy would be willing in the presence of men to listen to the discussion of the subjects that necessarily come under the consideration of the student of medicine.

Resolved, That we object to having the company of any female forced upon us, who is disposed to unsex herself, and to sacrifice her modesty, by appearing with men in the medical lecture room.

Resolved, That we are not opposed to allowing woman her rights, but do protest against her appearing in places where her presence is calculated to destroy our respect for the modesty and delicacy of her sex.

Resolved, That the medical professors be, and hereby are, respectfully entreated to do away forthwith an innovation expressly at variance with the spirit of the introductory lecture, with our own feelings, and detrimental to the prosperity, if not to the very existence of the school.

Resolved, That a copy of these resolutions be presented to the Medical Faculty.
Scalpel.

. . . The class at Harvard in 1851, have purchased for themselves a notoriety they will not covet in years to come.

EXPANDING HORIZONS

37. *A Methodist Camp Meeting*

Evangelical revival meetings drew enthusiastic crowds of worshipers all over the country during the "Second Great Awakening" of religious fervor in the early nine-teenth century. In rural areas, people camped in wagons or tents for days, inspired by many preachers and enjoying the company of fellow believers. From Richard N. Current and Gerald J. Goodwin, *A History of the United States* (New York: Alfred A. Knopf, 1980), p. 272.

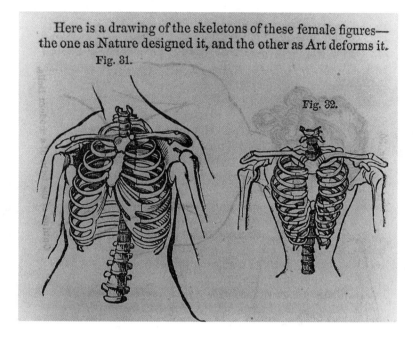

Here is a drawing of the skeletons of these female figures— the one as Nature designed it, and the other as Art deforms it. Fig. 31.

Fig. 32.

38. Effects of Tight Lacing

Sixteen- or eighteen-inch waistlines, formed by tight corsets from prepuberty on, did indeed deform the rib cage and crowd the interior organs as decried by nineteenth-century medical books and many women reformers, like Catharine Beecher. She wrote: "So long as it is the fashion to admire, as models of elegance, the wasp-like figures which are presented at the rooms of mantuamakers and milliners, there will be hundreds of foolish women, who will risk their lives and health to secure some resemblance of these deformities of the human frame. . . . Such female figures as our print-shops present, are made, not by the hand of the Author of all grace and beauty, but by the murderous contrivances of the corset-shop; and the more a woman learns the true rules of grace and beauty for the female form, the more her taste will revolt from such ridiculous distortions. The folly of the Chinese belle, who totters on two useless deformities, is nothing, compared to that of the American belle, who impedes all the internal organs in the discharge of their functions, that she may have a slender waist." From Catharine Beecher, *A Treatise on Domestic Economy for the Use of Young Ladies at Home and at School*, 3d rev. ed. (New York: Harper and Brothers, 1858), p. 116. Illustration from Catharine Beecher, *Letters to the People on Health and Happiness* (New York: Harper and Brothers, 1855), p. 178.

39. *The Bloomer Dress*

Though cartoonists and traditionalists made merciless mockery of women wearing trousers, the new comfortable fashion of "bloomer" pants under a loose-fitting tunic was popular with many American women during the 1850s. Named after Amelia Bloomer, the first to publicize it in her magazine the *Lily,* the costume hardly seems as daring as its reputation. It even inspired this sheet-music song. From Charles Nelson Gattey, *The Bloomer Girls* (New York: Coward-McCann, 1967), p. 65.

40. *Ad for Clarke's Female Pills*

Abortifacient medicines were commonly advertised in nineteenth-century newspapers and apparently were widely used. Neither mothers nor moralists could
confirm pregnancies until quickening, at about the fifth month, which was then
generally defined as the beginning of life. Advertisement, Middletown, Connecticut, *Constitution,* 1858. Photo courtesy of the Connecticut Historical Society.

Enslavement and Abolition

ALL REFORM activities increased women's awareness of the need for equal rights, but the issue of slavery provided a particularly important impetus. Abolitionists recognized that the treatment of slave women was in direct contrast to the pious ideology of superior female virtue. Slavery became a paradigm of the condition of women in general, deprived of their rights to property, suffrage, and personal freedom. Many prominent leaders of the nascent women's rights movement began their work within the antislavery movement. The public opposition they felt as abolitionists fueled their awareness of gender inequality as well as racial injustice.

The invention of the cotton gin in 1793, which enabled one slave to produce as much cotton for market as had ten slaves before, also commercialized cotton agriculture on expanding plantations, especially in the fertile lower Mississippi Valley. Although small southern farms like the one Nicey Kinney describes remained self-sufficient and somewhat less exploitative, large plantations were market-oriented communities dependent on slave labor for their rapidly accumulating wealth. African-American slaves in the Old South were transferred or sold to plantations in Alabama, Mississippi, or Arkansas. Such moves frequently shattered family relationships, as illustrated by the letter from two slaves begging not to be sent to Texas without their husbands. Thousands of enslaved Americans passed through the New Orleans market, described by a Swedish traveler, Fredrika Bremer.

Among the many narratives depicting slavery, the autobiographies of former slaves provide compelling testimony about the evils of the system, though most of them were not published until the 1860s or later. One moving early account was that of a northern free black man who was kidnapped and enslaved for thirteen years. His description of the tragedy of Patsey and other slaves he encountered provided a voice for their voicelessness. We see also the interaction between Patsey's misery and the misery-induced cruelty of her jealous white mistress; both women were, in a sense, victimized by the system—as women abolitionists so frequently pointed out.

Another powerful voice for the voiceless was that of Sojourner Truth, a six-foot-tall former slave from New York whose religious convictions and charismatic personality impressed everyone she met. Her impact on the writer Harriet Beecher Stowe, and the subtle authority that Sojourner Truth exercised even over strangers, can be seen in Stowe's description of their first meeting. Stowe also wrote *Uncle Tom's Cabin,* an antislavery book that inflamed the entire nation. President Abraham Lincoln later claimed that the book was a major factor leading to the Civil War.

A religious conversion in Hartford, Connecticut, led the newly widowed black spokeswoman Maria Miller Stewart to become the first female public speaker to oppose slavery before "promiscuous" (mixed-gender) audiences. But she was silenced by the disapproval of black men who wanted her to act like a lady. Prudence Crandall, a white educator, was hounded out of Canterbury, Connecticut, for establishing an academy for well-to-do, free "young ladies of color." The American husband of the English actress Fanny Kemble divorced her and kept her children away from her because of her concern for the slaves on his Georgia plantation. The Grimké sisters, from one of South Carolina's most prestigious slave-owning families, were accused of immodesty and indecency by New England's Congregationalist ministers when they lectured publicly about the cruelty and sexual double standard of slavery. Hundreds of women collected thousands of signatures on so many antislavery petitions (the only form of political action allowed to women by the U.S. Constitution) that in 1836 Congress passed an unprecedented and aptly named "Gag Rule" to avoid having to accept and read them.

But no matter how strong the convictions and heartfelt the concern, women who opposed slavery faced tremendous difficulties in offering practical help to their enslaved sisters. The writer-abolitionist Lydia Maria Child, writing to her friend Angelina Grimké about their mutual friend Rosa, a slave visiting Massachusetts with her white mistress, describes the legal and personal impediments that made this particular injustice impossible to resolve. National laws, not just good intentions, were needed to eliminate the slave system altogether, and these did not come until after the Civil War. American women, however, were prime movers in the effort.

He Was Sho Mighty Good to Us

The work on the average small plantation was not entirely oppressive for all slave women, despite the lack of freedom. Such farms, with only one or two slaves and their children, constituted the majority of slaveholding establishments, and 80 percent of white southerners owned no slaves at all. On a small farm, whites and blacks often worked together, and humane owners might love and be loved by their slaves. Nicey Kinney was an aged survivor of the system when she told the story of her childhood, colored perhaps by a bit of nostalgia. She remembered that neither the homes nor the work of "Mistess" and "Mammy" were very different from one another. The children spun the cotton thread for clothing, and the mistress knew how to make dyes from wild plants and to weave all their cloth.

From Nicey Kinney, Georgia Narratives, ca. 1930, Manuscript Slave Narrative Collection, Federal Writers' Project, Library of Congress, Washington, D.C., pt. 3, pp. 24–28.

❖

Marse Gerald Sharp and his wife, Miss Annie, owned us and, child, dey was grand folks. Deir old home was 'way up in Jackson Country 'twixt Athens and Jefferson. Dat big old plantation ran plumb back down to de Oconee River. Yes, mam, all dem rich river bottoms was Marse Gerald's.

Mammy's name was Ca'line and she b'longed to Marse Gerald, but Marse Hatton David owned my daddy—his name was Phineas. De David place warn't but 'bout a mile from our plantation and daddy was 'lowed to stay wid his fambly most evvy night; he was allus wid us on Sundays. Marse Gerald didn't have no slaves but my mammy and her chillun, and he was sho mighty good to us.

Marse Gerald had a nice four-room house wid a hall all de way through it. It even had two big old fireplaces on one chimbly. No, mam, it warn't a rock chimbly; dat chimbly was made out of home-made bricks. Marster's fambly had deir cookin' done in a open fireplace lak evvybody else for a long time and den jus' 'fore de big war he bought a stove. Yes, mam, Marse Gerald bought a cook stove and us felt plumb rich 'cause dere warn't many folks dat had stoves back in dem days.

Mammy lived in de old kitchen close by de big house 'til dere got to be too many of us; den Marse Gerald built us a house jus' a little piece off from de big house. It was jus' a log house, but Marster had all dem cracks chinked tight wid red mud, and he even had one of dem franklin-back chimblies built to keep our little cabin nice and warm. Why, Child, ain't you never seed none of dem old chimblies? Deir backs sloped out in de middle to throw out de heat into de room and keep too much of it from gwine straight up de flue. Our beds in our cabin was corded jus' lak dem up at de big house, but us slept on straw ticks and, let me tell you, dey sho slept good atter a hard day's wuk. . . .

I never done much field wuk 'til de war come on, 'cause Mistess was larnin' me to be a housemaid. Marse Gerald and Miss Annie never had no chillun 'cause she warn't no bearin' 'oman, but dey was both mighty fond of little folks. On Sunday mornin's mammy used to fix us all up nice and clean and take us up to de big house for Marse Gerald to play wid. Dey was good christian folks and tuk de mostest pains to larn us chillun how to live right. Marster used to 'low as how he had done paid $500 for Ca'line but he sho wouldn't sell her for no price.

Evrything us needed was raised on dat plantation 'cept cotton. Nary a stalk of cotton was growed dar, but jus' de same our clothes was made out of cloth dat Mistess and my mammy wove out of thread us chillun spun, and Mistess tuk a heap of pains makin' up our dresses. Durin' de war evvybody had to wear home-spun, but dere didn't nobody have no better or prettier dresses dan ours, 'cause Mistess knowed more'n anybody 'bout dyein' cloth. When time come to make up a batch of clothes Mistess would say, "Ca'line help me git up my things for dyein'," and us would fetch dogwood bark, sumach, poison ivy, and sweetgum bark. That poison ivy made the best black of anything us ever tried, and Mistess could dye the prettiest sort of purple wid sweetgum bark. Cop'ras was used to keep de colors from fadin', and she knowed so well how to handle it dat you could wash cloth what she had dyed all day long and it wouldn't fade a speck.

Marster was too old to go to de war, so he had to stay home and he sho seed dat us done our wuk raisin' somepin t'eat. He had us plant all our cleared ground, and I sho has done some hard wuk down in dem old bottom lands, plowin', hoein', pullin' corn and fodder, and I'se even cut cordwood and split rails. Dem was hard times and evvybody had to wuk.

It Required So Much Labor

Emily Burke was a northern schoolteacher who lived in Georgia during the 1830s and 1840s as a family tutor. She recognized the economic significance of slave labor in preparing cotton for market, and she sympathized with both the field workers' and house servants' hard physical labor. In fact, she particularly noted the harsh conditions of women's work.

From Emily P. Burke, *Reminiscences of Georgia* (N.p.: James M. Fitch, 1850), pp. 112–14.

❖

During the greater part of the winter season the negro women are busy in picking, ginning, and packing the cotton for market.

In packing the cotton, the sack is suspended from strong spikes, and while one colored person stands in it to tread the cotton down, others throw it into the sack. I have often wondered how the cotton could be sold so cheap when it required so much labor to get it ready for the market, and certainly it could not be if all their help was hired at the rate of northern labor.

The last of January the servants began to return to the plantation to repair the fences and make ready for planting and sowing. The fences are built of poles arranged in a zigzag manner, so that the ends of one tier of poles rests upon the ends of another. In this work the women are engaged as well as the men. They all go into the woods and each woman as well as man cuts down her own pine sapling, and brings it upon her head. It certainly was a most revolting sight to see the female form scarcely covered with one old miserable garment, with no covering for the head, arms, or neck, nor shoes to protect her feet from briers and thorns, employed in conveying trees upon her head from one place to another to build fences. When I beheld such scenes I felt culpable in living in ease and enjoying the luxuries of life, while so many of my own sex were obliged to drag out such miserable existences merely to procure these luxuries enjoyed by their masters. When the fences were completed, they proceeded to prepare the ground for planting. This is done by throwing the earth up in ridges from one side of the field to the other. This work is usually executed by hand labor, the soil is so light, though sometimes to facilitate the process a light plough, drawn by a mule, is used. The ground there is reckoned by tasks instead of acres. If a person is asked the extent of a certain piece of land, he is told it contains so many tasks, accordingly so many tasks are assigned for a day's work, in hoeing corn, three tasks are considered a good day's work for a man, two for a woman and one and a half for a boy or girl fourteen or fifteen years old. . . .

I have, in a previous letter, spoken of the slaves grinding corn; this is done by hand-mills constructed of two round flat stones, the upper one being turned around upon the other by hand labor. One person can, though, with a good deal of difficulty, grind corn alone, but it is customary for two at a time to engage in this labor. This mill is probably the same in kind with those used in Oriental countries, respecting which our Savior said, "Two women shall be grinding at the mill, the one shall be taken the other left." The time for the grinding of corn was always in the evening after the daily tasks were done.

About seven o'clock, in the summer season, the colored people would generally begin to assemble in the yard belonging to the planter's residence. Here they would kindle little bonfires, not only to ward off the mosquitoes, but because they are considered essential in the hot season to purify the air when it is filled with feverish vapors that arise from decayed vegetable matter. Then while two of their number are engaged at the mill, all the rest join in a dance around the burning fagots. In this manner were spent the greater part of the summer evenings. . . . Slaves from adjoining plantations would often come to spend an evening with their acquaintances, and bring their corn with them to grind. The grinding generally commences at about six in the evening, and the hoarse sound of the mill seldom ceased much before midnight.

Though the slaves in general, notwithstanding all their hard toils and sorrows, had their happy hours, there was one old woman on the plantation who always looked cast down and sorrowful, and never appeared to take any interest in what caused the joy and mirth of those around her. She was one of Afric's own home born daughters, and she had never forgotten those who nursed her in infancy, nor the playmates of her childhood's happy hours. She told me she was stolen one day while gathering shells into a little basket on the sea shore, when she was about ten years old, and crowded into a vessel with a good many of her own race, who had also been stolen and sold for slaves, and from that hour when she left her mother's hut to go out to play she had never seen one of her own kindred. . . .

Of all the house-servants, I thought the task of the cook was the most laborious. Though she did no other housework she was obliged to do every thing belonging to the kitchen department, and that, too, with none of those conveniences without which a Northern woman would think it was impossible for her to prepare a meal of victuals. After having cooked the supper and washed the dishes she goes about making preparations for the next morning's meal. In the first place she goes into the woods to gather sticks and dried limbs of trees, which she ties in bundles and brings to the kitchen on her head, with which to kindle the morning fire; to get as much fuel as she will want to use in preparing the breakfast she is often obliged to go into the woods several times. When this is done she has all the corn to grind for the hommony and bread, then the evening's preparations are completed. In the morning she is obliged to rise very early, for she has every article of food that comes on to the table to cook, nothing ever being prepared till the hour it is needed. When she has gone through with all the duties connected with the morning's repast, then she goes about the dinner, bringing fuel from the woods, grinding corn, etc. In this manner the cook spends her days, for in whatever department the slaves are educated, they are generally obliged to wear out their lives.

A Letter from Sukey and Ersey

Two slave women wrote this letter to their master, Tucker, at his home in Virginia from one of his other plantations in Missouri. At the time of this letter, Texas was an independent republic outside of U.S. jurisdiction, but Americans had been colonizing there for twenty years. Apparently Tucker was an absentee landowner in Texas as well as Missouri, and the "Mr. Bundlett" mentioned here was his plantation overseer. With careful deference (probably helped by a friend who wrote "their humble request"), these women begged their master to sell them to a Missouri neighbor rather than transfer them away from their husbands and friends. There is no available information about the results.

From letter to Master Beverley Tucker, October 24, 1842, in Mrs. George P. Coleman, ed., *Virginia Silhouettes* (Richmond, Va.: Dietz Publishing Co., 1934), pp. 38–40.

❖

St. Louis, Oct 24th 1842

Dear Master [Beverley Tucker]—

We, two of your humble Servants have come to the conclusion to write you a few lines upon a subject that has given us much pain, which will be more keenly felt if you will not grant their humble request. We hope and pray that you will not think hard of us in so doing, as we are in much distress, and write the very feelings of our hearts.

About two weeks ago Mr Jones, a neighbour of Mr Bundlett in Texas, called with a letter from Mr Bundlett saying that we must come on with Mr Jones. As we had been here a long time and had become much attached to the place (our Husbands being here) and as we hated the idea of going to Texas, Mr Jones was kind enough to let us remain till March, before which time he expected to hear from you on the subject. Our object in writing dear Master is this: We can't bear to go to Texas with a parcel of strangers—if you were there we should go without saying a word, but to be separated from our husbands forever in this world would make us unhappy for life. We have a great many friends in this place and would rather be sold than go to Texas.

In making this request, dear Master, we do not do it through any disrespect (for you have always been kind to us) but merely because we shall be happier here with our friends and Husbands. We don't think there will be the least difficulty in getting ourselves sold, together with our children from whom we hope you will not separate us. Ersey has six children, the youngest of which is about six weeks old, a fine little Girl. Susan has two Boys, the eldest nearly three years old, and the youngest eight months.

We hope dear Master and Mistress that you will not let us go to Texas, but grant us our humble petition. We are both well, also our children. If you conclude to sell us, please write to any of the following gentlemen, with your terms, with whom you are acquainted. Edward Bates, Andrew Elliott, R. H. Graham or Wm G. Pettus Remember us kindly to Mistress and her children and the Servants & children.

300

Yours truly
Susan (Sukey)
& Ersey

Sold for Seven Hundred Dollars

The well-known Swedish novelist Fredrika Bremer (1801–65) was one of numerous European travelers to America during the nineteenth century. She wrote two volumes about her impressions, with special emphasis on slavery and on the condition of women. White women were generally banned from viewing slave markets, but she persuaded a doctor friend to take her there.

From Fredrika Bremer, *The Homes of the New World: Impressions of America*, vol. 2, trans. Mary Howitt (New York: Harper and Bros., 1853), pp. 202–8.

❖

And now, while the weather is bad, and the great world is paying visits and compliments, and polite gentlemen are sunning themselves in the beautiful smiles of elegant ladies, in gas-lighted drawing-rooms, I will, at my ease, converse with you about the occurrences of the last few days, about the slave-market and a slave-auction at which I have been present.

I saw nothing especially repulsive in these places excepting the whole thing; and I can not help feeling a sort of astonishment that such a thing and such scenes are possible in a community calling itself Christian. It seems to me sometimes as if it could not be reality—as if it were a dream.

The great slave-market is held in several houses situated in a particular part of the city. One is soon aware of their neighborhood from the groups of colored men and women, of all shades between black and light yellow, which stand or sit unemployed at the doors. Accompanied by my kind doctor, I visited some of these houses. We saw at one of them the slave-keeper or owner—a kind, good-tempered man, who boasted of the good appearance of his people. The slaves were summoned into a large hall, and arranged in two rows. They were well fed and clothed, but I have heard it said by the people here that they have a very different appearance when they are brought hither, chained together two and two, in long rows, after many day's fatiguing marches. . . .

Among the women, who were few in number in comparison with the men (there might be from seventy to eighty of them), there were some very pretty light mulattoes. A gentleman took one of the prettiest of them by the chin, and opened her mouth to see the state of her gums and teeth, with no more cere- mony than if she had been a horse. Had I been in her place, I believe that I should have bitten his thumb, so much did I feel myself irritated by his behavior, in which he evidently, no more than she, found any thing offensive. Such is the custom of the place. . . .

On the 31st of December I went with my kind and estimable physician to witness a slave-auction, which took place not far from my abode. It was held at one of the small auction-rooms which are found in various parts of New Orleans. The principal scene of slave-auctions is a splendid rotunda, the magnificent dome of which is worthy to resound with songs of freedom. . . .

Dr. D. and I entered a large and somewhat cold and dirty hall, on the basement story of a house, and where a great number of people were assembled. About twenty gentlemenlike men stood in a half circle around a dirty wooden platform, which for the moment was unoccupied. On each side, by the wall, stood a number of black men and women, silent and serious. The whole assembly was silent, and it seemed to me as if a heavy gray cloud rested upon it. One heard through the open door the rain falling heavily in the street. The gentlemen looked askance at me with a gloomy expression, and probably wished that they could send me to the North Pole.

. . . A tall, stout man, with a gay and good-tempered aspect, evidently a *bon vivant,* ascended the auction platform. . . . He took the auctioneer's hammer in his hand, and addressed the assembly much as follows:

"The slaves which I have now to sell, for what price I can get, are a few home-slaves, all the property of one master. This gentleman having given his bond for a friend who afterward became bankrupt, has been obliged to meet his responsibilities by parting with his faithful servants. These slaves are thus sold, not in consequence of any faults which they possess, or for any deficiencies. They are all faithful and excellent servants, and nothing but hard necessity would have compelled their master to part with them. They are worth the highest price, and he who purchases them may be sure that he increases the prosperity of his family."

After this he beckoned to a woman among the blacks to come forward, and he gave her his hand to mount upon the platform, where she remained standing beside him. She was a tall, well-grown mulatto, with a handsome but sorrowful countenance, and a remarkably modest, noble demeanor. She bore on her arm a young sleeping child, upon which, during the whole auction ceremonial, she kept her eyes immovably riveted, with her head cast down. She wore a gray dress made to the throat, and a pale yellow handkerchief, checked with brown, was tied round her head.

The auctioneer now began to laud this woman's good qualities, her skill, and her abilities, to the assembly. He praised her character, her good disposition, order, fidelity; her uncommon qualifications for taking care of a house; her piety, her talents, and remarked that the child which she bore at her breast, and which was to be sold with her, also increased her value. After this he shouted with a loud voice, "Now, gentlemen, how much for this very superior woman, this remarkable, &c., &c., and her child?"

He pointed with his outstretched arm and fore-finger from one to another of the gentlemen who stood around, and first one and then another replied to his appeal with a short silent nod, and all the while he continued in this style:

"Do you offer me five hundred dollars? Gentlemen, I am offered five hundred dollars for this superior woman and her child. It is a sum not to be thought of! She, with her child, is worth double that money. Five hundred and fifty, six hundred, six hundred and fifty, six hundred and sixty, six hundred and seventy. My good gentlemen, why do you not at once say seven hundred dollars for this uncommonly superior woman and her child? Seven hundred dollars—it is downright robbery! She would never have been sold at that price if her master had not been so unfortunate," &c., &c.,

The hammer fell heavily; the woman and her child were sold for seven hundred dollars to one of those dark, silent figures before her. Who he was; whether he was good or bad; whether he would lead her into tolerable or intolerable slavery—of all this, the bought and sold woman and mother knew as little as I did, neither to what part of the world he would take her. And the father of her child—where was he?

With eyes still riveted upon that sleeping child, with dejected but yet submissive mien, the handsome mulatto stepped down from the auction-platform to take her stand beside the wall, but on the opposite side of the room. . . .

Next, a very dark young negro girl stepped upon the platform. She wore a bright yellow handkerchief tied very daintily round her head, so that the two ends stood out like little wings, one on each side. Her figure was remarkably trim and neat, and her eyes glanced round the assembly both boldly and inquiringly.

The auctioneer exalted her merits likewise, and then exclaimed,

"How much for this very likely young girl?"

She was soon sold, and, if I recollect rightly, for three hundred and fifty dollars. . . .

Patsey

Solomon Northup was a free black man from New York State with a wife and three children when he was kidnapped in 1841, sold by a slave trader in Washington, D.C., and taken to a frontier cotton plantation near the Red River in northwestern Louisiana. After he was finally rescued in 1853, he wrote a long memoir published with the help of northern abolitionists. Names and events have been verified by historians, and Northup's account remains one of the most vivid and literate accounts of the slave experience. His description of what happened to the high-spirited Patsey, and also to her jealous mistress, shows how the institution of slavery combined with the biological dimension of sex to shape some women's lives into total tragedy.

From Solomon Northup, *Twelve Years a Slave: Narrative of Solomon Northup, a Citizen of New-York, Kidnapped in Washington City in 1841, and Rescued in 1853, from a Cotton Plantation near the Red River in Louisiana* (Auburn: Derby and Miller; Buffalo: Derby, Orton and Mulligan, 1853), pp. 166, 186, 188–89, 197–200, 253–59.

❖

An ordinary day's work [cotton picking] is two hundred pounds. . . . Patsey . . . was known as the most remarkable cotton picker of Bayou Boeuf. She picked with both hands and with such surprising rapidity that five hundred pounds a day was not unusual for her. . . .

Patsey is twenty-three. . . . She . . . glories in the fact that she is the offspring of a "Guinea nigger," brought over to Cuba in a slave ship, and in the course of trade transferred to Buford, who was her mother's owner. . . .

Patsey was slim and straight. She stood erect as the human form is capable of standing. There was an air of loftiness in her movement, that neither labor, nor weariness, nor punishment could destroy. Truly, Patsey was a splendid animal, and were it not that bondage had enshrouded her intellect in utter and everlasting darkness, would have been chief among ten thousand of her people. She could leap the highest fences, and a fleet hound it was indeed, that could outstrip her in a race. No horse could fling her from his back. She was a skillful teamster. She turned as true a furrow as the best, and at splitting rails there were none that could excel her. When the order to halt was heard at night, she would have her mules at the crib, unharnessed, fed and curried, before uncle Abram had found his hat. Not, however, for all or any of these, was she chiefly famous. Such lightning-like motion was in her fingers as no other fingers ever possessed, and therefore it was, that in cotton picking time, Patsey was queen of the field.

She had a genial and pleasant temper, and was faithful and obedient. Naturally, she was a joyous creature, a laughing, light-hearted girl, rejoicing in the mere sense of existence. Yet Patsey wept oftener, and suffered more, than any of her companions. She had been literally excoriated. Her back bore the scars of a thousand stripes; not because she was backward in her work, nor because she was of a unmindful and rebellious spirit, but because it had fallen her lot to be the slave of a licentious master and a jealous mistress. She shrank before the lustful eye of the one, and was in danger even of her life at the hands of the other, and between the two, she was indeed accursed. In the great house, for days together, there were high and angry words, poutings and estrangement, whereof she was the innocent cause. Nothing delighted the mistress so much as to see her suffer, and more than once, when Epps had refused to sell her, has she tempted me with bribes to put her secretly to death, and bury her body in some lonely place in the margin of the swamp. Gladly would Patsey have appeased this unforgiving spirit, if it had been in her power, but not like Joseph, dared she escape from Master Epps, leaving her garment in his hand. Patsey walked under a cloud. If she uttered a word in opposition to her master's will, the lash was resorted to at once, to bring her to subjection; if she was not watchful when about her cabin, or when walking in the yard, a billet of wood, or a broken bottle perhaps, hurled from her mistress' hand, would smite her unexpectedly in the face. The enslaved victim of lust and hate, Patsey had no comfort of her life. . . .

. . . Patsey . . . had been getting deeper and deeper into trouble. The poor girl was truly an object of pity. "Old Hogjaw," the name by which Epps was called, when the slaves were by themselves, had beaten her more severely and frequently than ever. As surely as he came from Holmesville, elated with liquor—and it was often in those days—he would whip her, merely to gratify the mistress; would punish her to an extent almost beyond endurance, for an offence of which he himself was the sole and irresistible cause. In his sober moments he could not always be prevailed upon to indulge his wife's insatiable thirst for vengeance.

To be rid of Patsey—to place her beyond sight or reach, by sale, or death, or in any other manner, of late years, seemed to be the ruling thought and passion of my mistress. Patsey had been a favorite when a child, even in the great house. She had been petted and admired for her uncommon sprightliness and pleasant disposition. She had been fed many a time, so Uncle Abram said, even on biscuit and milk, when the madam, in her younger days, was wont to call her to the piazza, and fondle her as she would a playful kitten. But a sad change had come over the spirit of the woman. Now, only black and angry fiends ministered in the temple of her heart, until she could look on Patsey but with concentrated venom.

Mistress Epps was not naturally such an evil woman, after all. She was possessed of the devil, jealousy, it is true, but aside from that, there was much in

her character to admire. Her father, Mr. Roberts, resided in Cheneyville, an influential and honorable man, and as much respected throughout the parish as
any other citizen. She had been well educated at some institution this side the
Mississippi; was beautiful, accomplished and usually good-humored. She was
kind to all of us but Patsey—frequently, in the absence of her husband, sending
out to us some little dainty from her own table. In other situations—in a different society from that which exists on the shores of Bayou Boeuf, she would
have been pronounced an elegant and fascinating woman. An ill wind it was
that blew her into the arms of Epps.

He respected and loved his wife as much as a coarse nature like his is capable
of loving, but supreme selfishness always overmastered conjugal affection. . . .
He was ready to gratify any whim—to grant any request she made, provided it
did not cost too much. Patsey was equal to any two of his slaves in the cotton
field. He could not replace her with the same money she would bring. The idea
of disposing of her, therefore, could not be entertained. The mistress did not
regard her at all in that light. The pride of the haughty woman was aroused; the
blood of the fiery southern boiled at the sight of Patsey, and nothing less than
trampling out the life of the helpless bondwoman would satisfy her.

Sometimes the current of her wrath turned upon him whom she had just
cause to hate. But the storm of angry words would pass over at length, and there
would be a season of calm again. At such times Patsey trembled with fear, and
cried as if her heart would break, for she knew from painful experience, that if
mistress should work herself to the red-hot pitch of rage, Epps would quiet her
at last with a promise that Patsey should be flogged—a promise he was sure to
keep. Thus did pride, and jealousy, and vengeance war with avarice and brute-
passion in the mansion of my master, filling it with daily tumult and contention.
Thus, upon the head of Patsey . . . the force of all these domestic tempests spent
itself at last.

. . . The most cruel whipping that ever I was doomed to witness—one I can
never recall with any other emotion than that of horror—was inflicted on the
unfortunate Patsey.

It has been seen that the jealousy and hatred of Mistress Epps made the daily
life of her young and agile slave completely miserable. I am happy in the belief that on numerous occasions I was the means of averting punishment from
the inoffensive girl. In Epps' absence the mistress often ordered me to whip her
without the remotest provocation. I would refuse, saying that I feared my master's displeasure, and several times ventured to remonstrate with her against the
treatment Patsey received. I endeavored to impress her with the truth that the
latter was not responsible for the acts of which she complained, but that she
being a slave, and subject entirely to her master's will, he alone was answerable.

At length "the green-eyed monster" crept into the soul of Epps also, and

305

then it was that he joined with his wrathful wife in an infernal jubilee over the girl's miseries.

On a Sabbath day in hoeing time, not long ago, we were on the bayou bank, washing our clothes, as was our usual custom. Presently Patsey was missing. Epps called aloud, but there was no answer. No one had observed her leaving the yard, and it was a wonder with us whither she had gone. In the course of a couple of hours she was seen approaching from the direction of Shaw's. This man, as has been intimated, was a notorious profligate, and withal not on the most friendly terms with Epps. Harriet, his black wife, knowing Patsey's troubles, was kind to her, in consequence of which the latter was in the habit of going over to see her every opportunity. Her visits were prompted by friendship merely, but the suspicion gradually entered the brain of Epps, that another and a baser passion led her thither—that it was not Harriet she desired to meet, but rather the unblushing libertine, his neighbor. Patsey found her master in a fearful rage on her return. His violence so alarmed her that at first she attempted to evade direct answers to his questions, which only served to increase his suspicions. She finally, however, drew herself up proudly, and in a spirit of indignation boldly denied his charges.

"Missus don't give me soap to wash with, as she does the rest," said Patsey, "and you know why. I went over to Harriet's to get a piece," and saying this, she drew it forth from a pocket in her dress and exhibited it to him. "That's what I went to Shaw's for, Massa Epps," continued she; "the Lord knows that was all."

"You lie, you black wench!" shouted Epps.

"I *don't* lie, massa. If you kill me, I'll stick to that."

"Oh! I'll fetch you down. I'll learn you to go to Shaw's. I'll take the starch out of ye," he muttered fiercely through his shut teeth.

Then turning to me, he ordered four stakes to be driven into the ground, pointing with the toe of his boot to the places where he wanted them. When the stakes were driven down, he ordered her to be stripped of every article of dress. Ropes were then brought, and the naked girl was laid upon her face, her wrists and feet each tied firmly to a stake. Stepping to the piazza, he took down a heavy whip, and placing it in my hands, commanded me to lash her. Unpleasant as it was, I was compelled to obey him. Nowhere that day, on the face of the whole earth, I venture to say, was there such a demoniac exhibition witnessed as then ensued.

Mistress Epps stood on the piazza among her children, gazing on the scene with an air of heartless satisfaction. The slaves were huddled together at a little distance, their countenances indicating the sorrow of their hearts. Poor Patsey prayed piteously for mercy, but her prayers were vain. Epps ground his teeth, and stamped upon the ground, screaming at me, like a mad fiend, to strike *harder*.

"Strike harder, or *your* turn will come next, you scoundrel," he yelled.

"Oh, mercy, massa!—oh! have mercy, *do*. Oh, God! pity me," Patsey exclaimed continually, struggling fruitlessly, and the flesh quivering at every stroke.

When I had struck her as many as thirty times, I stopped, and turned round towards Epps, hoping he was satisfied; but with bitter oaths and threats, he ordered me to continue. I inflicted ten or fifteen blows more. By this time her back was covered with long welts, intersecting each other like net work. Epps was yet furious and savage as ever; demanding if she would like to go to Shaw's again, and swearing he would flog her until she wished she was in h——l. Throwing down the whip, I declared I could punish her no more. He ordered me to go on, threatening me with a severer flogging than she had received, in case of refusal. My heart revolted at the inhuman scene, and risking the consequences, I absolutely refused to raise the whip. He then seized it himself, and applied it with ten-fold greater force than I had. The painful cries and shrieks of the tortured Patsey, mingling with the loud and angry curses of Epps, loaded the air. She was terribly lacerated—I may say, without exaggeration, literally flayed. The lash was wet with blood, which flowed down her sides and dropped upon the ground. At length she ceased struggling. Her head sank listlessly on the ground. Her screams and supplications gradually decreased and died away into a low moan. She no longer writhed and shrank beneath the lash when it bit out small pieces of her flesh. I thought that she was dying!

It was the Sabbath of the Lord. The fields smiled in the warm sunlight— the birds chirped merrily amidst the foliage of the trees—peace and happiness seemed to reign everywhere, save in the bosoms of Epps and his panting victim and the silent witnesses around him. The tempestuous emotions that were raging there were little in harmony with the calm and quiet beauty of the day. I could look on Epps only with unutterable loathing and abhorrence, and thought within myself—"Thou devil, sooner or later, somewhere in the course of eternal justice, thou shalt answer for this sin!"

Finally, he ceased whipping from mere exhaustion, and ordered Phebe to bring a bucket of salt and water. After washing her thoroughly with this, I was told to take her to her cabin. Untying the rope, I raised her in my arms. She was unable to stand, and as her head rested on my shoulder, she repeated many times, in a faint voice scarcely perceptible, "Oh, Platt—oh, Platt!" but nothing further. Her dress was replaced, but it clung to her back, and was soon stiff with blood. We laid her on some boards in the hut, where she remained a long time, with eyes closed and groaning in agony. At night Phebe applied melted tallow to her wounds, and so far as we were able, all endeavored to assist and console her. Day after day she lay in her cabin upon her face, the sores preventing her resting in any other position.

A blessed thing it would have been for her—days and weeks and months of misery it would have saved her—had she never lifted her head in life again. Indeed, from that time forward she was not what she had been. The burden of a deep melancholy weighed heavily on her spirits. She no longer moved with that buoyant and elastic step—there was not that mirthful sparkle in her eyes that formerly distinguished her. The bounding vigor—the sprightly laughter-loving spirit of her youth, were gone. She fell into a mournful and desponding mood, and oftentimes would start up in her sleep, and with raised hands, plead for mercy. She became more silent than she was, toiling all day in our midst, not uttering a word. A care-worn, pitiful expression settled on her face, and it was her humor now to weep, rather than rejoice. If ever there was a broken heart—one crushed and blighted by the rude grasp of suffering and misfortune—it was Patsey's.

Sojourner Truth: A Sign unto This Nation

Among the women reformers and religious believers of mid-nineteenth-century America, Sojourner Truth (1797–1883) early became a living legend. She traveled throughout the country in the 1840s and 1850s, preaching at churches and abolitionist meetings and women's rights conventions, often facing ridicule and suspicion along with awed admiration. A slave in New York State until slavery was outlawed in 1827, most of her thirteen children had been sold away from her at an early age. Despite her illiteracy and wandering unconventionality, or perhaps partly because of them, Sojourner Truth's eloquence educated many about the evils of slavery and the importance of Christian love. Her nonviolent message reminds one of Martin Luther King, Jr.'s, more than a hundred years later.

Sojourner had already created a stir among women at the 1851 National Woman's Rights Convention, a year before meeting Harriet Beecher Stowe. She had countered an anti–woman's rights preacher with her famous "And a'n't I a woman" speech, concluding: "Den dat little man in black dar, he say women can't have as much rights as men, 'cause Christ wan't a woman! Whar did your Christ come from? From God and a woman! Man had nothin' to do wid Him." She went to see Harriet Beecher Stowe (1811–96) in 1852, shortly after Stowe's *Uncle Tom's Cabin* had become an all-time best-seller, inflaming and popularizing antislavery convictions throughout America. Stowe's description of their meeting is amusing in the way it reveals subtle status conflict between the illiterate itinerant and the "celebrated" white lady and gentlemen who greeted her. Sojourner's faith in Jesus had given her the unshakable confidence, determination, and authority to shape her world for the better.

From Harriet Beecher Stowe, "Sojourner Truth: The Libyan Sibyl," *Atlantic Monthly* 11 (April 1863): 473–78. ❖

On one occasion, when our house was filled with company, several eminent clergymen being our guests, notice was brought up to me that Sojourner Truth was below, and requested an interview. Knowing nothing of her but her singular name, I went down, prepared to make the interview short, as the pressure of many other engagements demanded.

When I went into the room, a tall, spare form arose to meet me. She was evidently a full-blooded African, and though now aged and worn with many hardships, still gave the impression of a physical development which in early youth must have been as fine a specimen of the torrid zone as Cumberworth's celebrated statuette of the Negro Woman at the Fountain. . . .

I do not recollect ever to have been conversant with any one who had more of that silent and subtle power which we call personal presence than this woman. In the modern spiritualistic phraseology, she would be described as having a strong sphere. Her tall form, as she rose up before me, is still vivid to my mind. She was dressed in some stout, grayish stuff, neat and clean, though dusty from travel. On her head she wore a bright Madras handkerchief, arranged as a turban, after the manner of her race. She seemed perfectly self-possessed and at her ease; in fact, there was almost an unconscious superiority, not unmixed with a solemn twinkle of humor, in the odd, composed manner in which she looked down on me. Her whole air had at times a gloomy sort of drollery which impressed one strangely.

"So this is *you*," she said.

"Yes," I answered.

"Well, honey, de Lord bless ye! I jes' thought I'd like to come an' have a look at ye. You's heerd o' me, I reckon?" she added.

"Yes, I think I have. You go about lecturing, do you not?"

"Yes, honey, that's what I do. The Lord has made me a sign unto this nation, an' I go round a-testifyin', an' showin' on em' their sins agin my people."

So saying, she took a seat, and, stooping over and crossing her arms on her knees, she looked down on the floor, and appeared to fall into a sort of reverie. . . .

By this time I thought her manner so original that it might be worth while to call down my friends; and she seemed perfectly well pleased with the idea. An audience was what she wanted—it mattered not whether high or low, learned or ignorant. She had things to say, and was ready to say them at all times, and to any one.

I called down Dr. Beecher, Professor Allen, and two or three other clergymen, who, together with my husband and family, made a roomful. No princess could have received a drawing-room with more composed dignity than Sojourner her audience. She stood among them, calm and erect, as one of her own native palm-trees waving alone in the desert. I presented one after another to her, and at last said—

"Sojourner, this is Dr. Beecher. He is a very celebrated preacher."

"*Is* he?" she said, offering her hand in a condescending manner, and looking down on his white head. "Ye dear lamb, I'm glad to see ye! De Lord bless ye! I loves preachers. I'm a kind o' preacher myself."

"You are?" said Dr. Beecher. "Do you preach from the Bible?"

"No, honey, can't preach from de Bible—can't read a letter."

"Why, Sojourner, what do you preach from, then?"

Her answer was given with a solemn power of voice, peculiar to herself, that hushed every one in the room.

"When I preaches, I has jest one text to preach from, an' I always preaches from this one. *My* text is, 'When I Found Jesus!'"

"Well, you couldn't have a better one," said one of the ministers.

She paid no attention to him, but stood and seemed swelling with her own thoughts, and then began this narration:—

"Well, now, I'll jest have to go back an' tell ye all about it. Ye see we was all brought over from Africa, father, an' mother an' I, an' a lot more of us; an' we was sold, up an' down, an' hither an' yon; an' I can 'member, when I was a little thing, not bigger than this 'ere,' pointing to her grandson, 'how my ole mammy would sit out o' doors in the evenin,' an' look up at the stars an' groan. She'd groan, an groan, an' says I to her,

"'Mammy, what makes you groan so?'

"An' she'd say,

"'Matter enough, chile! I'm groanin' to think o' my poor children: they don't know where I be, an' I don't know where they be; they looks up at the stars, an' I looks up at the stars, but I can't tell where they be.

"'Now,' she said, 'chile, when you're grown up, you may be sold away from your mother an' all your old friends, an' have great troubles come on ye; an' when you has these troubles come on ye, ye jes' go to God, an' he'll help ye.' . . .

"At last I got sold away to a real hard massa an' missis. Oh, I tell you they *was* hard! 'Peared like I couldn't please 'em nohow. An' then I thought o' what my old mammy told me about God; an' I thought I'd got into trouble, sure enough, an' I wanted to find God, an' I heerd some one tell a story about a man that met God on a threshin'-floor, an' I thought, well an' good, I'll have a threshin'-floor, too. So I went down in the lot, and I threshed down a place real hard, an' I used to go down there every day, an' pray an' cry with all my might, a-prayin' to the Lord to make my massa an' missis better, but it didn't seem to do no good; and so says I, one day,

"'O God, I been a askin' ye, an' askin' ye, an askin' ye, for all this long time, to make my massa an' missis better, an' you don't do it, an' what *can* be the reason? Why, maybe you *can't*. Well, I shouldn't wonder if you couldn't. Well, now, I tell you, I'll make a bargain with you. Ef you'll help me to git away from my massa an' missis, I'll agree to be good; but ef you don't help me, I really don't think I can be. Now,' says I, 'I want to git away; but the trouble's jest here; ef I try to git away in the night, I can't see; an' ef I try to git away in the day-time, they'll see me an' be after me.'

"Then the Lord said to me, 'Git up two or three hours afore daylight, an' start off.'

"An' says I, 'Thank'ee Lord! that's a good thought.'

"So up I got about three o'clock in the mornin', an' I started an' traveled pretty fast, till, when the sun rose, I was clear away from our place an' our folks, an' out o'sight. An' then I begun to think I didn't know nothin' where to go. So I kneeled down, and says I,

" 'Well, Lord, you've started me out, an' now please to show me where to go.'

"Then the Lord made a house appear to me, an' he said to me that I was to walk on till I saw that house, an' then go in an' ask the people to take me. An' I traveled all day, an' didn't come to the house till late at night; but when I saw it, sure enough, I went in, an' I told the folks that the Lord sent me; an' they was Quakers, an' real kind they was to me. . . .

"Well, ye see, honey, I stayed an' lived with 'em. An' now jes' look here: instead o' keepin' my promise an' bein' good, as I told the Lord I would, jest as soon as everything got a-goin' easy, *I forgot all about God.*

"Pretty well don't need no help; an' I gin up prayin'. I lived there two or three years, an' then the slaves in New York were all set free, 'an ole massa came to our house to make a visit, an' he asked me ef I didn't want to go back an' see the folks on the ole place. An' I told him I did. So he said, ef I'd jes' git into the wagon with him, he'd carry me over. Well, jest as I was goin' out to get into the wagon, *I met God!* an' says I, 'O God, I didn't know as you was so great!' An' I turned right round an' come into the house, an' set down in my room; for 't was God all around me. . . . An' I begun to feel sech a love in my soul as I never felt before—love to all creatures. An' then, all of a sudden, it stopped, an' I said, 'Dar's de white folks that have abused you, an' beat you, an' abused your people—think o' them!' But then there came another rush of love through my soul, an' I cried out loud—'Lord, Lord, I can love *even de white folks!*' . . .

"Well, den ye see, after a while I thought I'd go back an' see de folks on de ole place. Well, you know de law had passed dat de culled folks was all free; an' my old missis, she had a daughter married about dis time who went to live in Alabama—an' what did she do but give her my son, a boy about de age of dis yer, for her to take down to Alabama? When I got back to de ole place, they told me about it, an' I went right up to see ole missis, an' says I,

" 'Missis, have you been an' sent my son away down to Alabama?'

" 'Yes, I have,' says she; 'he's gone to live with your young missis.'

" 'Oh, Missis,' says I, 'how could you do it?'

" 'Poh!' says she, 'what a fuss you make about a little nigger! Got more of 'em now than you know what to do with.'

"I tell you, I stretched up. I felt as tall as the world!

" 'Missis,' says I, *I'll have my son back agin!*'

"She laughed.

" '*You* will, you nigger? How you goin' to do it? You ha'n't got no money.'

" 'No, Missis—but *God* has—an' you'll see he'll help me!'—an' I turned round an' went out.

"Oh, but I *was* angry to have her speak to me so haughty an' so scornful, as ef my chile wasn't worth anything. I said to God, 'O Lord, render unto her double!' It was a dreadful prayer, an' I didn't know how true it would come.

"Well, I didn't rightly know which way to turn; but I went to the Lord, an' I said to him, 'O Lord, ef I was as rich as you be, an' you was as poor as I be, I'd help you—you *know* I would; and, oh, do help me!' An' I felt sure then that he would.

"Well, I talked with people, an' they said I must git the case before a grand jury. So I went into the town when they was holdin' a court, to see ef I could find any grand jury. An' I stood round the courthouse, an' when they was a-comin' out, I walked right up to the grandest lookin' one I could see, an' says I to him:—

" 'Sir, be you a grand jury?'

"An' then he wanted to know why I asked, an' I told him all about it; an' he asked me all sorts of questions, an' finally he says to me:—

" 'I think, ef you pay me ten dollars, that I'd agree to git your son for you.' An' says he, pointin' to a house over the way, 'You go 'long an' tell your story to the folks in that house, an' I guess they'll give you the money.'

"Well, I went, an' I told them, an' they gave me twenty dollars; an' then I thought to myself, 'Ef ten dollars will git him, twenty dollars will git him *sartin.*' So I carried it to the man all out, an' said,

" 'Take it all—only be sure an' git him.'

"Well, finally they got the boy brought back; an' then they tried to frighten him, an' to make him say that I wasn't his mammy, an' that he didn't know me; but they couldn't make it out. They gave him to me, an' I took him and carried him home; an' when I came to take off his clothes, there was his poor little back all covered with scars an' hard lumps, where they'd flogged him.

"Well, you see, honey, I told you how I prayed the Lord to render unto her double. Well, it came true; for I was up at ole missis' house not long after, an' I heerd 'em readin' a letter to her how her daughter's husband had murdered her—how he'd thrown her down an' stamped the life out of her, when he was in liquor; an' my ole missis, she giv a screech, an fell flat on the floor. Then says I, 'O Lord, I didn't mean all that! You took me up too quick.'

"Well, I went in an' tended that poor critter all night. She was out of her mind —a cryin', an' callin' for her daughter; an' I held her poor ole head on my arm, an' watched for her as ef she'd been my babby. An' I watched by her, an' took care on her all through her sickness after that, an' she died in my arms, poor thing!" 313

"Well, Sojourner, did you always go by this name?"

"No, 'deed! My name was Isabella; but when I left the house of bondage, I left everything behind. I wa'n't goin' to keep nothin' of Egypt on me, an' so I went to the Lord an' asked him to give me a new name. And the Lord gave me Sojourner, because I was to travel up an' down the land, showin' the people their sins, an' bein' a sign unto them. Afterward I told the Lord I wanted another name, 'cause everybody else had two names; and the Lord gave me Truth, be-cause I was to declare the truth to the people."

Let Us Make a Mighty Effort, and Arise

Maria Stewart (1803–79) was the first American woman to lecture in public, five years before the more famous Grimké sisters. Orphaned at five and brought up as a servant in a Hartford clergyman's family, she married a Boston shipping agent who died three years later. Both were involved with the Massachusetts General Colored Association to improve African-American conditions and agi-tate against slavery, but after his death and that of the "incendiary" black pam-phleteer David Walker, she experienced a profound "awakening" and a call to devote her life to the cause of God and freedom. In Boston, she wrote essays and gave speeches, which the abolitionist William Lloyd Garrison then published in his *Liberator;* she urged black people to demand education and rights and op-pose the "false promise" of the Liberia colonization movement. But even her own people condemned her for such "unfeminine" lecturing, and in 1833, she gave it up, spending the rest of her life as a teacher. It was probably Stewart's words in the *Liberator* that inspired Prudence Crandall's educational efforts.

From Maria Miller Stewart, "Religion and the Pure Principles of Morality" (1831), reprinted in Marilyn Richardson, ed., *Maria W. Stewart: America's First Black Woman Political Writer, Essays and Speeches* (Bloomington: Indiana Univer-sity Press, 1987), pp. 36–40. ❖

Finally, my heart's desire and prayer to God is that there might come a thorough reformation among us. Our minds have too long grovelled in ignorance and sin. Come, let us incline our ears to wisdom, and apply our hearts to understanding; promote her, and she will exalt thee; she shall bring thee honor when thou dost embrace her. An ornament of grace shall she be to thy head, and a crown of glory shall she deliver to thee. Take fast hold of instruction; let her not go; keep her, for she is thy life (Proverbs 4:13). Come, let us turn unto the Lord our God, with all our heart and soul, and put away every unclear and unholy thing from among us, and walk before the Lord our God, with a perfect heart, all the days of our lives: then we shall be a people with whom God shall delight to dwell; yea, we shall be that happy people whose God is the Lord.

I am of a strong opinion that the day on which we unite, heart and soul, and turn our attention to knowledge and improvement, that day the hissing and reproach among the nations of the earth against us will cease. And even those who now point at us with the finger of scorn, will aid and befriend us. It is of no use for us to sit with our hands folded, hanging our heads like bulrushes, lamenting our wretched condition; but let us make a mighty effort, and arise; and if no one will promote or respect us, let us promote and respect ourselves.

The American ladies have the honor conferred on them, that by prudence and economy in their domestic concerns, and their unwearied attention in forming the minds and manners of their children, they laid the foundation of their becoming what they now are. The good women of Wethersfield, Conn., toiled in the blazing sun, year after year, weeding onions, then sold the seed and procured enough money to erect them a house of worship; and shall we not imitate their examples, as far as they are worthy of imitation? Why cannot we do something to distinguish ourselves, and contribute some of our hard earnings that would reflect honor upon our memories, and cause our children to arise and call us blessed? Shall it any longer be said of the daughters of Africa, they have no ambition, they have no force? By no means. Let every female heart become united, and let us raise a fund ourselves; and at the end of one year and a half, we might be able to lay the corner stone for the building of a High School, that the higher branches of knowledge might be enjoyed by us; and God would raise us up, and enough to aid us in our laudable designs. Let each one strive to excel in good housewifery, knowing that prudence and economy are the road to wealth. Let us not say we know this, or we know that, and practise nothing; but let us practise what we do know.

How long shall the fair daughters of Africa be compelled to bury their minds and talents beneath a load of iron pots and kettles? Until union, knowledge and love begin to flow among us. How long shall a mean set of men flatter us with their smiles, and enrich themselves with our hard earnings; their wives' fingers sparkling with rings, and they themselves laughing at our folly? Until we begin to promote and patronize each other. Shall we be a by-word among the nations any longer? Shall they laugh us to scorn forever? Do you ask, what can we do? unite and build a store of your own, if you cannot procure a license. Fill one side with dry goods, and the other with groceries. Do you ask where is the money? We have spent more than enough for nonsense, to do what building we should want. We have never had an opportunity of displaying our talents; therefore the world thinks we know nothing. And we have been possessed by far too mean and cowardly a disposition, though I highly disapprove of an insolent or impertinent one. Do you ask the disposition I would have you possess? Possess the spirit of independence. The Americans do, and why should not you? Possess the spirit of men, bold and enterprising, fearless and undaunted. Sue for your rights and privileges. Know the reason that you cannot attain them. Weary them with your importunities. You can but die if you make the attempt; and we shall certainly die if you do not. The Americans have practised nothing but head-work these 200 years, and we have done their drudgery. And is it not high time for us to imitate their examples, and practise head-work too, and keep what we have got, and get what we can? We need never to think that anybody is going to feel interested for us, if we do not feel interested for ourselves. That day we, as a people, hearken unto the voice of the Lord, our God, and walk in his ways and ordinances, and become distinguished for our ease, elegance and grace, combined with other virtues, that day the Lord will raise us up, and enough to aid and befriend us, and we shall begin to flourish.

Did every gentleman in America realize, as one, that they had got to become bondmen, and their wives, their sons, and their daughters, servants forever, to Great Britain, their very joints would become loosened, and tremblingly would smite one against another; their countenance would be filled with horror, every nerve and muscle would be forced into action, their souls would recoil at the very thought, their hearts would die within them, and death would be far more preferable. Then why have not Afric's sons the right to feel the same? Are not their wives, their sons, and their daughters, as dear to them as those of the white man's? Certainly God has not deprived them of the divine influences of his Holy Spirit, which is the greatest of all blessings, if they ask him. Then why should man any longer deprive his fellow-man of equal rights and privileges? Oh, America, America, foul and indelible is thy stain! Dark and dismal is the cloud that hangs over thee, for thy cruel wrongs and injuries to the fallen sons of Africa. The blood of her murdered ones cries to heaven for vengeance against thee. Thou art almost become drunken with the blood of her slain; thou hast enriched thyself through her toils and labors, and now thou refuseth to make even a small return. And thou hast caused the daughters of Africa to commit whoredoms and fornications; but upon thee be their curse.

O, ye great and mighty men of America, ye rich and powerful ones, many of you will call for the rocks and mountains to fall upon you, and to hide you from the wrath of the Lamb (Revelation 6:16), and from him that sitteth upon the throne; whilst many of the sable-skinned Africans you now despise will shine in the kingdom of heaven as the stars forever and ever. Charity begins at home, and those that provide not for their own are worse than infidels. We know that you are raising contributions to aid the gallant Poles; we know that you have befriended Greece and Ireland, and you have rejoiced with France, for her heroic deeds of valor. You have acknowledged all the nations of the earth, except Hayti; and you may publish, as far as the East is from the West, that you have two millions of negroes, who aspire no higher than to bow at your feet, and to court your smiles. You may kill, tyrannize, and oppress as much as you choose, until our cry shall come up before the throne of God; for I am first persuaded, that he will not suffer you to quell the proud, fearless and undaunted spirits of the Africans forever; . . . but we will tell you that our souls are fired with the same love of liberty and independence with which your souls are fired. We will tell you that too much of your blood flows in our veins, too much of your color in our skins, for us not to possess your spirits. We will tell you that it is our gold that clothes you in fine linen and purple, and causes you to fare sumptuously every day (Luke 16:19); and it is the blood of our fathers, and the tears of our brethren that have enriched your soils. AND WE CLAIM OUR RIGHTS.

To Serve the People of Color

Prudence Crandall (1803–90) was a Quaker schoolteacher in the village of Canterbury, Connecticut, when she made the "mistake" of admitting a local black girl to her female academy. White parents protested and removed their daughters, so she reopened the school in 1833 for black girls only, advertising in the New York and Boston papers with the backing of leading abolitionists. Townspeople petitioned the legislature against her, harassed her by throwing dead animals and manure into her well and onto her property, refused to sell food to her, had her arrested, and finally, on the night of September 9, 1834, broke all the windows in her house and set a fire nearby. She closed the school and moved west with her new husband. In 1885, the town of Canterbury again petitioned the legislature, to grant her a pension. When the author Mark Twain heard of her destitution, he offered, anonymously, to lease her house for her to return; she was very grateful but preferred to stay in Kansas. The 1885 pension petition was signed by the nephew of the judge who had led her initial persecution.

From Prudence Crandall, letter to Editor, *Windham County Advertiser*, May 7, 1833; Petition to Legislature, 1885; and letter to *Hartford (Conn.) Courant*, 1886. All reprinted in Marvis Olive Welch, *Prudence Crandall: A Biography* (Manchester, Conn.: Jason Publishers, 1983), pp. 51–53, 205, 208.

❖

Windham County Advertiser May 7, 1833

Mr. Holbrook: Whatever reluctance I may feel to appear before the public, circumstance requires that I should do so. After all that has been said in various newspapers, about me and my school and my friends it seems that I owe it to them and to myself to make a simple statement that you and others may know the object of my present school and also what first induced me to establish it; and to exonerate my friends and myself from several unreasonable censures and misrepresentations that are in circulation.

A colored girl of respectability—a professor of religion—and daughter of honorable parents called on me sometime during the month of September last and said in a very earnest manner "Miss Crandall, I want to get a little more learning, if possible enough to teach colored children and if you will admit me to your school, I shall forever be under greatest obligation to you. If you think it will be the means of injuring you, I will not insist on the favor."

I did not answer her immediately, as I thought if I gave her permission some of my scholars might be disturbed. In further conversation with her however I found she had great anxiety to improve in learning.

Her repeated solicitations were more than my feelings could resist and I told her if I was injured on her account I would bear it—she might enter as one of my pupils. The girl had not been long under my instruction before I was informed by several persons that she must be removed or my school would be greatly injured.

This was unpleasant news for me to hear but I continued her in my school. Previous to any excitement concerning her there fell in my way several publications that contained many facts relative to the people of color of which I was entirely ignorant. My feelings began to awaken. I saw that the prejudice of whites against color was deep and inveterate. In my humble opinion it was the strongest if not the only chain that bound those heavy burdens on the wretched slaves, which we ourselves are not willing to touch with one of our fingers. I felt in my heart to adopt the language of the Sacred Preacher when He said—"So I turned to consider all the oppressions that are done under the sun and behold the tears of such as were oppressed, and they had no comforter; and on the side of their oppression there was power but they had no comforter. Therefore I praised the dead that are already dead more than the living which are yet alive."

I said in my heart, here are my convictions. What shall I do? Shall I be inactive and permit prejudice, "The mother of abominations" to remain undisturbed? Or shall I venture to enlist in the ranks of those who with the Sword of Truth dare hold combat with prevailing iniquity? I contemplated for a while the manner in which I might best serve the people of color. As wealth was not mine, I saw no other means of benefitting them, than by imparting to those of my own sex that were anxious to learn, all the instruction I might be able to give, however small the amount. This I deem my duty, how to perform it, I knew not. With the friends of the people of color, called "Abolitionists" I was entirely unacquainted save by reputation.

318   Having for some time wished to visit New York or some other places of schools and also to purchase for the benefit of my scholars, school apparatus, I came to the conclusion that I would perform my long contemplated journey and visit the schools in Boston while at the same time the most prominent object of my tour was to visit William L. Garrison—to obtain his opinion respecting the propriety of establishing a school for colored females—and the prospect of success should I attempt it. Being an entire stranger in Boston previous to my journey, I took the liberty to enquire of several of my neighbors, if they had any friends in Boston to whom they would be willing to give me a line of introduction. Rev. Mr. Kneeland and Rev. Mr. Platt were the only persons I found who had any acquaintances in the place. These gentlemen very kindly gave me letters to distinguished clergymen in that city. Neither to these gentlemen, my neighbors nor my scholars did I make known all my business. And I felt perfectly justified in telling them I was going to visit schools, which I did and to purchase the before mentioned apparatus which was at that time my determination and the want of money was the only reason why I did not purchase.

Now because I did not see fit to expose my business before I knew whether I could obtain a sufficient number of colored pupils to sustain my school and also did not purchase the apparatus, I am charged that too in a public manner of falsehood or at least willful prevarication. False and scandalous reports about me and my friends are in constant circulation, some of which are dispersed by the papers far and near. In the piece signed "A friend of the Colonization Cause" that first appeared in the Norwich Republican, which you have copied into your paper, the author upon his own authority has declared that there are a few men in Boston and Providence who have laid the foundation of this school which is entirely false as I was wholly self moved in the plan, though I gratefully acknowledge their kind approbation. Furthermore, he asks "and what do they intend to do with this institution?" After making several ungenerous and detestable replies the sentence is closed with this remark—"In a word they hope to force the races (black and white) to amalgamate." This is utterly false—the object, the sole object, at this school is to instruct the ignorant and fit and prepare teachers for the people of color that they may be elevated and their intellectual and moral wants supplied. . . .

Respectfully yours,
Prudence Crandall

Petition to the Connecticut Legislature, 1885

We, the undersigned citizens of the State and of the town of Canterbury, mindful of the dark blot that rests upon our fair fame and name for the cruel outrages inflicted upon a former citizen of our Commonwealth, a noble Christian woman (Miss Prudence Crandall, now Mrs. Philleo) at present in straightened circumstances and far advanced in years, respectfully pray your Honorable Body to make such late reparation for the wrong done her as your united wisdom, your love of justice and an honorable pride in the good name of our noble state, shall dictate.

It will be remembered that she stands in the Records of the Court as a convicted criminal for the offense of teaching colored girls to read and suffered unnumbered outrages in person and property for a benevolent work that now to its great honor the general government is enjoined in.

We respectfully suggest that you make a fair appropriation in her behalf which shall at once relieve her from any anxiety for the future and from the official stigma that rests upon her name and purge our own record from its last remaining stain in connection with the colored race.

And your petitioners will ever pray. Signed

Thomas J. Clark (and many others)

[To the Editor, *Hartford Courant*] 1886

What an amount of obligation I am under to the press generally and above all to those notable progressive persons who got up the petition at the first to be presented to their Legislature in my behalf.

I wish to express my gratitude and thankfulness to that worthy body for their appropriation with which I am more than satisfied. In 1833 when the law was passed by which my life prospects were destroyed, it was celebrated by ringing the bell in the church into which we were not allowed to enter. And by firing a cannon 13 times, placed upon an elevation a few rods from my door: and today when your telegram arrived the only jubilant display I wished to make was to have a private nook where my tears of gratitude and joy could flow unobserved for the change that has been wrought in the views and feelings of the mass of the people.

Mrs. Prudence C. Philleo

I Had My Cry out for Them

Slave women did heavy field labor even during pregnancy and after childbirth, and they were frequently victims of malnutrition and untreated gynecological injuries. Fanny Kemble (1809–93) was an illustrious English actress who married a wealthy southern planter, Pierce Butler, during her acclaimed tour of America in the 1830s. She was shocked by the slavery on his rice and cotton plantations in Georgia and quickly tried to alleviate conditions. He in turn was disgusted with her "unladylike" meddling and forbade her from talking to him on behalf of his slaves. She discovered that she too was enslaved by the system. For this, and his infidelity, she left him. He accused her of desertion and, in accordance with the prevailing divorce laws, refused her access to her children until they became adults.

From Frances Anne Kemble, *Journal of a Residence on a Georgian Plantation in 1838–39* (New York: Harper and Brothers, 1863), pp. 174, 182–83, 189–92.

❖

This morning I had a visit from two of the women, Charlotte and Judy, who came to me for help and advice for a complaint, which it really seems to me every other woman on the estate is cursed with, and which is a direct result of the conditions of their existence; the practice of sending women to labor in the fields in the third week after their confinement is a specific for causing this infirmity, and I know no specific for curing it under these circumstances. As soon as these poor things had departed with such comfort as I could give them, and the bandages they especially begged for, three other sable graces introduced themselves, Edie, Louisa, and Diana; the former told me she had had a family of seven children, but had lost them all through "ill luck," as she denominated the ignorance and ill-treatment which were answerable for the loss of these, as of so many other poor little creatures their fellows. . . .

The women who visited me yesterday evening were all in the family-way, and came to entreat of me to have the sentence (what else can I call it?) modified which condemns them to resume their labor of hoeing in the fields three weeks after their confinement. They knew, of course, that I cannot interfere with their appointed labor, and therefore their sole entreaty was that I would use my influence with Mr. [Butler] to obtain for them a month's respite from labor in the field after childbearing. Their principal spokeswoman, a woman with a bright sweet face, called Mary, and a very sweet voice, which is by no means an uncommon excellence among them, appealed to my own experience; and while she spoke of my babies, and my carefully tended, delicately nursed, and tenderly watched confinement and convalescence, and implored me to have a kind of labor given to them less exhausting during the month after their confinement, I held the table before me so hard in order not to cry that I think my fingers ought to have left a mark on it. At length I told them that Mr. [Butler] had forbidden me to bring him any more complaints from them, for that he thought the ease with which I received and believed their stories only tended to make them discontented, and that, therefore, I feared I could not promise to take their petitions to him; but that he would be coming down to "the Point" soon, and that they had better come then sometime when I was with him, and say what they had just been saying to me; and with this, and various small bounties, I was forced, with a heavy heart, to dismiss them; and when they were gone, with many exclamations of, "Oh yes, missis, you will, you will speak to massa for we; God bless you, missis, we sure you will!" I had my cry out for them, for myself, for us. All these women had had large families, and *all* of them had lost half their children, and several of them had lost more. How I do ponder upon the strange fate which has brought me here. . . .

Before closing this letter, I have a mind to transcribe to you the entries for today recorded in a sort of daybook, where I put down very succinctly the number of people who visit me, their petitions and ailments, and also such special particulars concerning them as seem to me worth recording. You will see how miserable the physical condition of many of these poor creatures is; and their physical condition, it is insisted by those who uphold this evil system, is the only part of it which is prosperous, happy, and compares well with that of Northern laborers. Judge from the details I now send you; and never forget, while reading them, that the people on this plantation are well off, and consider themselves well off, in comparison with the slaves on some of the neighboring estates.

Fanny has had six children; all dead but one. She came to beg to have her work in the field lightened.

Nanny has had three children; two of them are dead. She came to implore that the rule of sending them into the field three weeks after their confinement might be altered.

Leah, Caesar's wife, has had six children; three are dead.

Sophy, Lewis's wife, came to beg for some old linen. She is suffering fearfully; has had ten children; five of them are dead. The principal favor she asked was a piece of meat, which I gave her.

Sally, Scipio's wife, has had two miscarriages and three children born, one of whom is dead. She came complaining of incessant pain and weakness in her back. This woman was a mulatto daughter of a slave called Sophy, by a white man of the name of Walker, who visited the plantation.

Charlotte, Renty's wife, had had two miscarriages, and was with child again.

She was almost crippled with rheumatism, and showed me a pair of poor swollen knees that made my heart ache. I have promised her a pair of flannel trowsers, which I must forthwith set about making.

Sarah, Stephen's wife—this woman's case and history were alike deplorable. She had had four miscarriages, had brought seven children into the world, five of whom were dead, and was again with child. She complained of dreadful pains in the back, and an internal tumor which swells with the exertion of working in the fields; probably, I think, she is ruptured. She told me she had once been mad and had ran into the woods, where she contrived to elude discovery for some time, but was at last tracked and brought back, when she was tied up by the arms, and heavy logs fastened to her feet, and was severely flogged. After this she contrived to escape again, and lived for some time skulking in the woods, and she supposes mad, for when she was taken again she was entirely naked. She subsequently recovered from this derangement, and seems now just like all the other poor creatures who come to me for help and pity. I suppose her constant childbearing and hard labor in the fields at the same time may have produced the temporary insanity.

Sukey, Bush's wife, only came to pay her respects. She had had four miscarriages; had brought eleven children into the world, five of whom are dead.

Molly, Quambo's wife, also only came to see me. Hers was the best account I have yet received; she had had nine children, and six of them were still alive.

This is only the entry for today, in my diary, of the people's complaints and visits. Can you conceive a more wretched picture than that which it exhibits of the conditions under which these women live? Their cases are in no respect singular, and though they come with pitiful entreaties that I will help them with some alleviation of their pressing physical distresses, it seems to me marvelous with what desperate patience (I write it advisedly, patience of utter despair) they endure their sorrow-laden existence. Even the poor wretch who told that miserable story of insanity, and lonely hiding in the swamps, and scourging when she was found, and of her renewed madness and flight, did so in a sort of low, plaintive, monotonous murmur of misery, as if such sufferings were all "in the day's work."

I ask these questions about their children because I think the number they bear as compared with the number they rear a fair gauge of the effect of the system on their own health and that of their offspring. There was hardly one of these women, as you will see by the details I have noted of their ailments, who might not have been a candidate for a bed in a hospital, and they had come to me after working all day in the fields.

Appeal to Southern Women

Angelina Grimké Weld (1805–79) and her sister Sarah Grimké (1792–1873) both rebelled against the slavery they had witnessed within their prominent Charleston, South Carolina, family. They came north, joined the Quakers, and became active in the Female Anti-Slavery Society. Angelina, a gifted speaker, began lecturing on abolition in 1837, thus inspiring the censure of Congregationalist ministers for her "unladylike" attention to "politics." Grimké's 1836 "Appeal to the Christian Women of the South" argued that the prevailing ideology of women's superior morality justified and required such public action. The pamphlet was confiscated by postmasters in the South, where laws forbade the circulation of antislavery "propaganda"; southern women were forbidden to organize or protest as their northern sisters were doing.

From Angelina Emily Grimké, "Appeal to the Christian Women of the South," *Anti-Slavery Examiner* 1, no. 2 (September 1836): 16–26.

❖

I have thus, I think, clearly proved to you seven propositions, viz.: First, that slavery is contrary to the declaration of our independence. Second, that it is contrary to the first charter of human rights given to Adam, and renewed to Noah. Third, that the fact of slavery having been the subject of prophecy, furnishes *no* excuse whatever to slavedealers. Fourth, that no such system existed under the patriarchal dispensation. Fifth, that *slavery never* existed under the Jewish dispensation; but so far otherwise, that every servant was placed under the *protection of law,* and care taken not only to prevent all *involuntary* servitude, but all *voluntary perpetual* bondage. Sixth, that slavery in America reduces a *man* to a *thing,* a "chattel personal," *robs him* of *all* his rights as a *human being,* fetters both his mind and body, and protects the *master* in the most unnatural and unreasonable power, whilst it *throws him out* of the protection of law. Seventh, that slavery is contrary to the example and precepts of our holy and merciful Redeemer, and of his apostles.

But perhaps you will be ready to query, why appeal to *women* on this subject? *We* do not make the laws which perpetuate slavery. *No* legislative power is vested in *us; we* can do nothing to overthrow the system, even if we wished to do so. To this I reply, I know you do not make the laws, but I also know that *you are the wives and mothers, the sisters and daughters of those who do;* and if you really suppose *you* can do nothing to overthrow slavery, you are greatly mistaken. You can do much in every way: four things I will name. 1st. You can read on this subject. 2d. You can pray over this subject. 3d. You can speak on this subject. 4th. You can *act* on this subject. I have not placed reading before praying because I regard it more important, but because, in order to pray aright, we must understand what we are praying for; it is only then we can "pray with the understanding and the spirit also." . . .

But you will perhaps say, such a course of conduct would inevitably expose us to great suffering. Yes! my christian friends, I believe it would, but this will *not* excuse you or any one else for the neglect of *duty*. If Prophets and Apostles, Martyrs, and Reformers had not been willing to suffer for the truth's sake, where would the world have been now? If they had said, we cannot speak the truth, we cannot do what we believe is right, because the *laws of our country or public opinion are against us,* where would our holy religion have been now? . . .

But you may say we are *women,* how can our hearts endure persecution? And why not? Have not women stood up in all the dignity and strength of moral courage to be the leaders of the people, and to bear a faithful testimony for the truth whenever the providence of God has called them to do so? . . .

Already are there sixty female Anti-Slavery Societies in operation. These are doing just what the English women did, telling the story of the colored man's wrongs, praying for his deliverance, and presenting his kneeling image constantly before the public eye on bags and needle-books, card-racks, pen-wipers, pin-cushions, &c. Even the children of the north are inscribing on their handy work, "May the points of our needles prick the slaveholder's conscience." Some of the reports of these Societies exhibit not only considerable talent, but a deep sense of religious duty, and a determination to persevere through evil as well as good report, until every scourge, and every shackle, is buried under the feet of the manumitted slave.

The Ladies' Anti-Slavery Society of Boston was called last fall, to a severe trial of their faith and constancy. They were mobbed by "the gentlemen of property and standing," in that city at their anniversary meeting, and their lives were jeopardized by an infuriated crowd; but their conduct on that occasion did credit to our sex, and affords a full assurance that they will *never* abandon the cause of the slave. The pamphlet, Right and Wrong in Boston, issued by them in which a particular account is given of that "mob of broad cloth in broad day," does equal credit to the head and the heart of her who wrote it. I wish my Southern sisters could read it; they would then understand that the women of the North have engaged in this work from a sense of *religious duty,* and that nothing will ever induce them to take their hands from it until it is fully accomplished. They feel no hostility to you, no bitterness or wrath; they rather sympathize in your trials and difficulties; but they well know that the first thing to be done to help you, is to pour in the light of truth on your minds, to urge you to reflect on, and pray over the subject. This is all *they* can do for you, *you* must work out your own deliverance with fear and trembling, and with the direction and blessing of God, *you can do it*. Northern women may labor to produce a correct public opinion at the North, but if Southern women sit down in listless indifference and criminal idleness, public opinion cannot be rectified and purified at the South. It is manifest to every reflecting mind, that slavery must be abolished; the era in which we live, and the light which is overspreading the whole world on this subject, clearly show that the time cannot be distant when it will be done. Now there are only two ways in which it can be effected, by moral power or physical force, and it is for *you* to choose which of these you prefer. Slavery always has, and always will produce insurrections wherever it exists, because it is a violation of the natural order of things, and no human power can much longer perpetuate it. . . .

325

The *women of the South can overthrow* this horrible system of oppression and cruelty, licentiousness and wrong. Such appeals to your legislatures would be irresistible, for there is something in the heart of man which *will bend under moral suasion*. There is a swift witness for truth in his bosom, which *will respond to truth* when it is uttered with calmness and dignity. If you could obtain but six signatures to such a petition in only one state, I would say, send up that petition, and be not in the least discouraged by the scoffs and jeers of the heartless, or the resolution of the house to lay it on the table. It will be a great thing if the subject can be introduced into your legislatures in any way, even by *women,* and *they* will be the most likely to introduce it there in the best possible manner, as a matter of *morals* and *religion,* not of expediency or politics. You may petition, too, the different ecclesiastical bodies of the slave states. Slavery must be attacked with the whole power of truth and the sword of the spirit. You must take it up on *Christian* ground, and fight against it with Christian weapons, whilst your feet are shod with the preparation of the gospel of peace. And *you are now* loudly called upon by the cries of the widow and the orphan, to arise and gird yourselves for this great moral conflict, with the whole armour of righteousness upon the right hand and on the left.

Petition to Congress against Slavery

Abolitionist women in the 1830s gathered signatures on printed petition forms like the following to be sent to congressmen in Washington. Tens of thousands of them are in forty-one boxes in the files of the House of Representatives at the Library of Congress. Though women could not vote, the Constitution guaranteed their right to petition for grievances, and they argued that their opinions on moral issues were a female prerogative. Nevertheless, Congress passed a "gag law" in 1836 to prevent the petitions from being read, printed, or considered.

From Gilbert H. Barnes and Dwight L. Dimond, eds., *Letters of Theodore Dwight Weld, Angelina Grimké Weld, and Sarah Grimké, 1822–1844* (Washington, D.C.: American Historical Association, 1934), pp. 175–76.

❖

[November (?) 1834]

326

To the Hon. the Senate and House of Representatives of the U. States, in Congress Assembled

Petition of Ladies resident in _____ County, State of Ohio.

Fathers and Rulers of our Country,

Suffer us, we pray you, with the sympathies which we are constrained to feel as wives, as mothers, and as daughters, to plead with you in behalf of a long oppressed and deeply injured class of native Americans, residing in that portion of our country which is under your exclusive control. We should poorly estimate the virtues which ought ever to distinguish your honorable body could we anticipate any other than a favorable hearing when our appeal is to men, to philanthropists, to patriots, to the legislators and guardians of a Christian people. We should be less than women, if the nameless and unnumbered wrongs of which the slaves of our sex are made the defenceless victims, did not fill us with horror and constrain us, in earnestness and agony of spirit to pray for their deliverance. By day and night, their woes and wrongs rise up before us, throwing shades of mournful contrast over the joys of domestic life, and filling our hearts with sadness at the recollection of those whose hearths are desolate.

Nor do we forget, in the contemplation of their other sufferings, the intellectual and moral degradation to which they are doomed; how the soul formed for companionship with angels, is despoiled and brutified, and consigned to ignorance, pollution, and ruin.

Surely then, as the representatives of a people professedly christian, you will bear with us when we express our solemn apprehensions in the language of the patriotic Jefferson "we tremble for our country when we remember that God is just, and that his justice cannot sleep forever", and when in obedience to a divine command "we remember them who are in bonds as bound with them." Impelled by these sentiments, we solemnly purpose, the grace of God assisting, to importune high Heaven with prayer, and our national Legislature with appeals, until this christian people abjure forever a traffic in the souls of men, and the groans of the oppressed no longer ascend to God from the dust where they now welter.

We do not ask your honorable body to transcend your constitutional powers, by legislating on the subject of slavery within the boundaries of any slaveholding State; but we do conjure you to abolish slavery in the District of Columbia where you exercise exclusive jurisdiction. In the name of humanity, justice, equal rights and impartial law, our country's weal, her honor and her cherished hopes we earnestly implore for this our humble petition, your favorable regard. If both in christian and in heathen lands, Kings have revoked their edicts, at the intercession of woman, and tyrants have relented when she appeared a suppliant for mercy, surely we may hope that the Legislators of a free, enlightened and christian people will lend their ear to our appeals, when the only boon we crave is the restoration of rights unjustly wrested from the innocent and defenceless.—And as in duty bound your petitioners will ever pray.

327

[Names]	[Names]

Rosa Was to Be Free

A legal will and orders of manumission were only as good as those who could enforce them, and a slave mother had to balance the possibility of freedom against the loss of her still-enslaved children. Lydia Maria Child helped many slaves to freedom, as did many other northerners, and in 1861 Child helped Harriet Jacobs (under the pseudonym Linda Brent) publish the amazing story of her escape. But these two letters to Angelina Grimké illustrate the helplessness of even the best-intentioned abolitionists to deal with the convolutions of chattel slavery as a constitutional institution in antebellum America. Child forecasts the Civil War, twenty-three years before it occurs.

From Milton Meltzer and Patricia G. Holland, eds., *Lydia Maria Child: Selected Letters, 1817–1880* (Amherst: University of Massachusetts Press, 1982), pp. 87–89. By permission of William L. Clements Library, University of Michigan, Ann Arbor.

❖

To Angelina (Grimké) Weld

Northampton Aug. 26 1838

Dear Sister Angelina,

. . . Mrs. Martin, the wife of a clergyman in S.C. was left with two slaves, which she manumitted immediately after her husband's death. Her son held several slaves, among whom was the mother of my heroine Rosa, or Rosy. When Rosa was 3 or 4 years old, her mother died; and Mr. Martin, not knowing what to do with the child, told his mother she might have her, if she would take care of her. Old Mrs. Martin brought Rosy up as a little pet; and there was a peculiarly affectionate attachment between the child and Susan Martin, one of the old lady's grand-daughters. With this Susan Martin, Rosa says Angelina Grimké was well acquainted. When the old lady died she left a Will, that provided for Rosa. She was to serve *Susan* during her life-time, but after Susan's death, neither Rosa nor her children were to serve anyone. They were to be free. Hereupon quarrels arose between Susan Martin and her married sister, Mrs. Wagner. Mrs. Wagner had a large young family, and she thought it very hard that she could not have Rosa to wait upon her. Their daily domestic life was embittered by squabbles about their grandmother's partiality, and Rosa was made constantly uncomfortable. In the meanwhile, Susan became somewhat straitened in pecuniary circumstances, and her health failed. Physicians advised a voyage to Europe. At this juncture, Mrs. Anna Bennet, sister of Mrs. Napier, proposed to take Rosa under her protection, in order to keep her from the dreaded Mrs. Wagner, and to advance Susan Martin seven hundred dollars for Rosa and her children. Rosa was assured that neither she nor her children could be held as slaves after Susan's death. She inquired of Mr. Bentham, a lawyer, and *he* assured her she was perfectly safe. He had seen old Mrs. Martin's will, and he knew for a certainty that nobody could hold her after Susan's death. These assurances, united to a confidence in Mrs. Bennet's goodness and sincerity, induced Rosa to consent to the transfer. Susan took the $700. Before she went to Europe she made a Will, ratifying all her grandmother had promised, and giving similar directions for the comfort of Rosa and her family. This Will and old Mrs. Martin's were, very imprudently, left with Mr. Wagner. Susan returned from Europe with renovated health, contrary to her expectation. Her father died, and during his illness was very desirous to see his mother's Will; but Mr. Wagner said it was lost; and it has never been found to this day. Rosa still continues with Mrs. Bennet, who is reputed to be a kind woman, religious, and sometimes is *thought* to be a little uneasy in conscience about holding slaves. How deep, or sincere this feeling is, I know not. Rosa came to Northampton this summer with Mrs. Bennet and her daughter, Mrs. Gadsden. She is called Rosa *Gadsden*. I am afraid that among them they will play her false, and that neither she nor her 3 children will obtain the boon, which old Mrs. Martin thought she had effectually secured to her. Mr. Gadsden is an infidel and a slave-auctioneer, with every good feeling deadened by the love of gold. What can she expect from him?

She thinks it might do good if *you* would write an earnest letter to Susan Martin, impressing upon her what she owes to the memory of her grandmother. I should think she would be afraid of the old lady's ghost, unless she does something without delay to secure Rosa's freedom, and that of her children, by abundant witnesses, and with all the formalities of the law. If she is too poor to pay their expenses in leaving Carolina (as they must do, you know, if they are emancipated) has not Gerrit Smith offered to defray such expenses? I am afraid Rosa is sold outright and forever to Mrs. Bennet; but she herself feels very sure that she *could* not be thus sold. Perhaps a letter to Mrs. Bennet, *after* you have written to Susan Martin, might not be amiss. Mrs. Bennet is old, and has of *late* been scrupulous that her slaves should have their own earnings. She is reputed kind & pious. I ought to mention that Susan Martin tried to settle matters amicably with Mrs. Wagner by offering her the services of Rosa's *children* during her (Susan's) life time; but this did not suit; and Rosa had invincible repugnance to being transfered to Mrs. Wagner. . . .

Oct. 2'd 1838

. . . Rosa, I am sorry to say, had returned to So. Carolina before I received your letter of Sep. 16th; or rather she had left Northampton, to sojourn in various cities before her mistress returned to the South. The struggle in her mind between her children and freedom was evidently severe & painful. At one time, I think the balance would have turned in favor of remaining in Massachusetts, had she not received a pathetic letter from her daughter in slavery, containing these words: "Dear mother, do come back to us; for you know we have nobody but God and you to pity us. Little Johnny says, 'Tell dear mother she must come back soon'."

For my own part, I did not say a word to sway her mind, from first to last; for she was evidently a very fond mother, and I felt afraid she would be very wretched if separated from her children. I merely assured her that I would be her friend, and get a good home for her, if she chose to take her freedom.

Two slaves from Georgia were brought here by Mr. John Stoddard. (nephew of Arthur Tappan.) I understand from Rosa that the younger of the two was half a mind to take her freedom, though she left children behind her; and not being able to obtain communication with them myself, I asked Rosa to do it. The elder of the Georgians, a bold, pert, disagreeable girl, directly informed Rosa's mistress; which of course made a great deal of difficulty. After that, she was so closely watched, even after she went to bed, that she found opportunity but for one short, stolen interview with me. She was then sad enough, and her heart seemed almost torn in two by the struggle between contending feelings. I saw her no more, until I saw her follow her mistress into the stage-coach that conveyed her away from freedom. To the last, she evidently entertained hopes in connection with old Mrs. Martin's Will; though to us they seemed perfectly groundless; and we told her so. I do not know how she would answer the queries in your last letter. I confess it was rather a relief to me to hear that you had *not* written; for I felt afraid of involving the poor creature in fresh difficulties. How would it do to write to Mr. Bentham, saying merely that you have heard (without alluding to any source) that old Mrs. Martin willed Rosa to be free, after the death of her grand-daughter Susan? I do not know whether he wrote the Will, or merely witnessed it; but Rosa said he was quite familiar with its contents, and often told her to be easy, for he had seen the Will, and she might trust to him. You might mention your presumption that he wrote the Will, as a good reason for addressing him for information. Whether such a step would do good or harm, you are the best judges. Do as you think proper. Mr. Napier's family are boasting that I tried very hard to persuade Rosa to take her freedom, but that I could not coax her away from her beloved mistress. They must know this is untrue; but Christians that will steal will lie also. I do not believe the South will voluntarily relinquish her slaves, so long as the world stands. It must come through violence. I would it might be averted; but I am convinced that it cannot be.

ENSLAVEMENT AND ABOLITION

41. *Slaves Plowing Rice in Georgia*
African Americans brought the techniques of rice culture to the coastal areas of
Georgia and the Carolinas from West Africa. It was backbreaking labor in malarial
conditions for both men and women. Courtesy of Schomburg Center for Research
in Black Culture, New York Public Library, Astor, Lenox, and Tilden Foundations.

42. Slaves Picking Cotton
Women were crucial laborers in the rapidly expanding cotton economy of the
nineteenth-century South. Courtesy of Schomburg Center for Research in
Black Culture, New York Public Library, Astor, Lenox, and Tilden Foundations.

43. *Quilt*

This quilt, made in 1895 by Harriet Powers in Athens, Georgia, depicts biblical stories but utilizes techniques and symbolic forms that derive from West African tradition. It is evidence of the way women remembered and transmitted African culture both during and after the disruption and misery of slavery. Bequest of Maxim Karolik. Courtesy of Museum of Fine Arts, Boston.

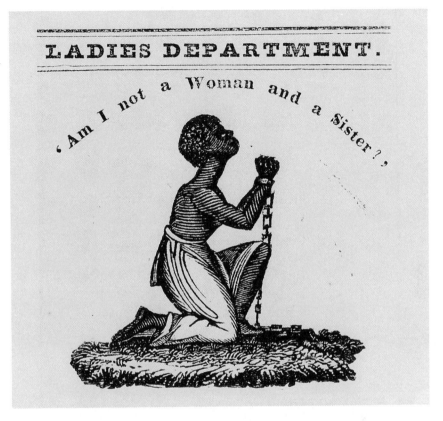

44. *"Am I Not a Woman and a Sister?"*
This drawing of a slave woman was the logo for the Ladies Department of the
Liberator, the antislavery newspaper where Maria Miller Stewart's work appeared
along with that of many other abolitionists. The quote was from one of Stewart's
speeches. By permission of the Houghton Library, Harvard University, Cambridge, Massachusetts.

45. Ad for Prudence Crandall's School

This advertisement appeared in numerous newspapers in 1833, attracting students from as far away as Philadelphia and Boston. Photo courtesy of Prudence Crandall Museum, Canterbury, Connecticut.

COLORED SCHOOLS BROKEN UP, IN THE FREE STATES.

When schools have been established for colored scholars, the law-makers and the mob have combined to destroy them ;—as at Canterbury, Ct., at Canaan, N. H. Aug. 10, 1835, at Zanesville and Brown Co., Ohio, in 1836.

46. *Cartoon against Schools for Colored Girls*

Male deference to ladies' supposedly superior moral virtue did not protect women from mistreatment if they espoused unpopular ideas. The article accompanying this cartoon mentions the attacks on Prudence Crandall's school for black girls and on similar schools in Canaan, New Hampshire, and Zanesville, Ohio. Cartoon in *Anti-Slavery Almanac*, 1839. Courtesy of Prudence Crandall Museum, Canterbury, Connecticut.

47. Sojourner Truth

Sojourner Truth was a living legend among ante-bellum abolitionists and reform-
ers. She faced both admiration and ridicule as she traveled and lectured throughout
the North, fearlessly eloquent on behalf of African Americans even into her old age.
This picture was widely circulated to publicize both abolition and women's rights.
Leslie's Magazine, December 1869. Courtesy of Schomburg Center for Research in
Black Culture, New York Public Library, Astor, Lenox, and Tilden Foundations.

An Uprooted People:
Native Americans

THE SITUATION of the native people of North America drew much less attention than that of slaves in the nineteenth century. In literature and history books, Indians began to be romanticized as "noble savages," whereas the reality of their existence was largely ignored. As Euro-American settlement expanded westward, Indian nations were again and again decimated by epidemics of smallpox and measles or were deliberately and forcefully "removed" by the U.S. government. Records show that many Native Americans sought friendship and cooperation rather than conflict, but without success. The explorers Lewis and Clark, as well as fur traders and early settlers, usually depended on Indian guides and helpers, like Sacajawea, in order to survive. But white "progress" generally brought only disaster to uprooted Indian peoples.

Isaac Knight's narrative is a rare eyewitness account of what epidemics did to Native Americans all across the country, usually well before settlers arrived. He describes the tribal devastation and his love for the Indian women who cared for him during a lethal smallpox epidemic in 1793 among the Illinois River Indians who had captured him. Settlers did not enter the area until much later. European and eastern fur traders and sailors brought smallpox and measles also to the Pacific Northwest a generation before the first settlers crossed the Rockies. The same thing had happened to Native American people in 1616, before the first Pilgrims came to Plymouth Colony in 1620. The artist George Catlin depicted the large, comfortable villages and many aspects of women's work among Plains Indian tribes—just before a deadly epidemic, caused by one sick person on a steamboat in 1836, swept the entire Missouri River valley and virtually destroyed the Plains Indian culture.

In the 1830s, Native American women and men from the long-established so-called Five Civilized Tribes of Georgia and Alabama—Cherokees, Choctaws, Chickasaws, Creeks, and Seminoles—were uprooted and forcibly marched westward, despite a ruling against such dispersal by the U.S. Supreme Court. They were called "civilized" because they had largely adopted white patterns of living, owned large farms and plantations, even owned slaves, and had developed their own alphabet. These people were deprived of their property without recompense and forced to trek the deadly "Trail of Tears," with tremendous loss of life, to the alien soil and climate of the Oklahoma Territory. Midwestern tribes were also dispossessed at various times—by broken treaties, white settlers, or disease.

The coming of white people disrupted a thriving and complex way of life. When Sarah Winnemucca hid in the sand and sagebrush east of the Sierra Nevada as the strange white people passed, she did not yet know of the destruction and death to come, and her grandfather, the chief of the Piutes, still thought he could work and negotiate with the whites on equal terms. She went on to become the Piute's designated chief and interpreter, trying again and again to stave off U.S. government representatives' exploitation of and cruelty toward her increasingly powerless people. Pretty-Shield, of the Crow tribe, remembered the joys and bounty of Plains Indian life before white settlers and soldiers killed millions of buffalo and destroyed the Indian food supply. She also described powerful women who were free to use their leadership talents in Native American society. The people of the Southwest, represented here by a Pima woman's narrative, maintained their distinctive cultural traditions until modern times, despite the unsettlement process of Anglo development after 1849.

A True and Tender Friend

The devastating effects of smallpox epidemics left Native Americans demoralized and disorganized well before white settlement or observation. Women care givers were often most affected. Isaac Knight, a twelve-year-old Kentucky boy captured in 1793 and taken to the prosperous Illinois River Indian territory just after he had been inoculated for smallpox, provides a rare glimpse of such tragedy in process. Inoculation (in contrast to modern vaccination) caused a mild but contagious form of the actual disease. Isaac infected all his captors, including the Indian woman who lovingly cleansed Isaac's sores. With fear and guilt about his own complicity, Isaac watched the Indian world crumble; food supplies were neglected, women were mourning, and death was everywhere.

From *A Narrative of the Captivity and Sufferings of Isaac Knight,* as told to Hiram A. Hunter (Evansville, Ind.: Journal Office, 1829), copy in Darlington Library, University of Pittsburgh, Pittsburgh, Pennsylvania, pp. 1–10.

❖

As they entered the town, . . . some of the warriors gave a signal, which brought out several squaws, who relieved them all of their packs. . . .

Next morning, as Isaac thought, almost all the Indians in the world collected on the opposite bank of the river, for a ball play, where they spent the greater part of the day in that exercise, both men and women sharing its pleasures. . . .

The next day . . . one of [the women] seemed to pity Isaac's situation, and in expression of her kindness, combed his hair, and, finding some sores on his head, annointed them, and was thus the means of restoring him to health sooner than he would probably have been restored . . . though he was yet quite unwell. . . .

[Later] he followed his guide . . . up the Illinois river . . . to a wigwam where lived . . . the mother of the two warriors that had taken him, and who were detained at the village by sickness, of which one of them died. . . . She immediately gave him a new blanket, and provided him something to eat. This day's travel had again freshened Isaac's sores, and so fatigued him that although he was wrapped in a new blanket, and kindly treated, he had no rest, but felt in the morning almost as bad as formerly. . . .

The squaw then, in whose care Isaac was left, with a view to cure him, made preparation for it, and with a sharp flint scarafied him, and rubbed the sores with a piece of rough bark, to make them bleed; then caused him to jump in the Illinois river. This was all done through kindness, although it was harsh treatment.

From this place Isaac, together with many Indians, started up the river, to an Indian town situated upon a small Island . . . now called Illinois lake. . . . The Indians began soon to make preparations for a crop, and Isaac was sent in company with two squaws, (who took along with them skins to smoke) to pick up and burn corn stalks; these squaws set Isaac to work in the stalks, and showed him what to do and how to do it. . . .

Soon after this time the small pox made its appearance among the Indians on this island, and the kind old squaw who had given so much attention to Isaac, and thereby endeared herself to him, was one of the first subjects and victims of that destructive disease. . . . The death of this humane and motherly old squaw gave the Author of this Narrative most unpleasant feelings, and was the cause of much distressing exercise of mind. He had found her a true and tender friend, and one who was willing to do for him all she could; but when he saw her taken from him, he found himself far from home . . . and surrounded with sickness, producing death in every direction. . . .

The death and burial of the squaw, whom Isaac recognized almost as a mother, were extremely solemn and impressive. Appearing sensible of her approaching dissolution, she gave Isaac to her daughter, who lived along with her. She was buried after their manner, with great solemnity; and many of the Indians painted themselves black and mourned for her ten days, fasting every day until evening; but all this was not expressive of Isaac's grief for the death of her who had nursed him with so much tenderness. . . . Though he afterwards witnessed the death of his own dear mother, his feelings were nothing to compare with those which harrowed up his mind at the death of her. . . .

334

A number of Indians died of the disease on the island before they left it. . . . Supposing that a change of situation would improve their health, they started, moving a short distance at a time, and spending but little time at any one place. They had moved, however, but seldom, until the squaw in whose care Isaac had been left, followed her mother, by means of the same disease. Indeed, they lost some at every place where they stopped. . . . [The epidemic and deaths continued for weeks.]

Isaac, having been committed . . . to the care of another squaw, travelled up this river in the same canoe with her, and passing the place where her husband had been buried, she steered the canoe to shore, and, taking out some venison in a bowl, had Isaac to accompany her to the grave. Here she kindled a small fire over the head of the grave, into which she threw some of the venison.—Setting down the bowl she told Isaac to eat of it, which he did, while she walked to some distance, and mourned with loud and sore lamentations for near an hour; then returned to the grave, wiped off the tears, threw some more meat in the fire and on the grave, and bade Isaac to start. Ascending the river still farther than before, they all encamped, and lived with great difficulty, in as much as the crops were very short, the corn having received no attention after it was planted, owing to the sickness that prevailed with so much fatality.

Sacajawea

The story of young Sacajawea, a Shoshoni Indian woman, has entered American history through the records of the Lewis and Clark exploration of western America from 1804 to 1806. The expedition was the first to travel over the Rocky Mountains to present-day Oregon and back, laying the foundation for all future U.S. migration and development. Sacajawea was one of two wives of a French-Canadian mountain man who guided the explorers. As such, she is an example of the importance of many Indian women in the lives and commercial transactions of early western fur traders. She had been captured in a tribal war by the Minnetares and sold by them to the Frenchman, but her skills as a guide and her courage made him, as well as the explorers, give her extra respect and even sometimes a horse to ride. (Note that Lewis mentions other Indian women as carriers, but only Sacajawea as a person.) Because of her invaluable services as a translator, which enabled Lewis and Clark to obtain the cooperation of the Shoshonis on their journey, they paid Sacajawea's *husband* very well.

From Meriwether Lewis, *The Lewis and Clark Expedition,* (Philadelphia: J. B. Lippincott, 1814), 2:333–35, 361, 368–69, 532–33, 3:780.

❖

SATURDAY, Aug. 15th [1805]

. . . On setting out at seven o'clock, captain Clarke with Chaboneau and his wife walked on shore, but they had not gone more than a mile before captain Clarke saw Sacajawea, who was with her husband one hundred yards ahead, begin to dance, and show every mark of the most extravagant joy, turning round him and pointing to several Indians, whom he now saw advancing on horseback, sucking her fingers at the same time to indicate that they were of her native tribe. As they advanced captain Clarke discovered among them Drewyer dressed like an Indian, from whom he learnt the situation of the party. While the boats were performing the circuit, he went towards the forks with the Indians, who as they went along, sang aloud with the greatest appearance of delight. We soon drew near to the camp, and just as we approached it a woman made her way through the croud [*sic*] towards Sacajawea, and recognising each other, they embraced with the most tender affection. The meeting of these two young women had in it something peculiarly touching, not only in the ardent manner in which their feelings were expressed, but from the real interest of their situation. They had been companions in childhood, in the war with the Minnetarees they had both been taken prisoners in the same battle, they had shared and softened the rigours of their captivity, till one of them had escaped from the Minnetarees, with scarce a hope of ever seeing her friend relieved from the hands of her enemies. While Sacajawea was renewing among the women the friendships of former days, captain Clarke went on, and was received by captain Lewis and the chief. . . . After this the conference was to be opened, and glad of an opportunity of being able to converse more intelligibly, Sacajawea was sent for; she came into the tent, sat down, and was beginning to interpret, when in the person of Cameahwait she recognised her brother: she instantly jumped up, and ran and embraced him, throwing over him her blanket and weeping profusely: the chief was himself moved, though not in the same degree. After some conversation between them she resumed her seat, and attempted to interpret for us, but her new situation seemed to overpower her, and she was frequently interrupted by her tears. After the council was finished, the unfortunate woman learnt that all her family were dead except two brothers, one of whom was absent, and a son of her eldest sister, a small boy, who was immediately adopted by her. . . .

Saturday 24. As the Indians . . . now said that they had no more horses for sale, and as we had now nine of our own, two hired horses, and a mule, we began loading them as heavily as was prudent, and placing the rest on the shoulders of the Indian women, left our camp at twelve o'clock. We were all on foot, except Sacajawea, for whom her husband had purchased a horse with some articles which we gave him for that purpose; an Indian however had the politeness to offer captain Lewis one of his horses to ride, which he accepted in order better to direct the march of the party. . . .

The treatment of women is often considered as the standard by which the moral qualities of savages are to be estimated. Our own observation, however, induced us to think that the importance of the female in savage life, has no necessary relation to the virtues of the men, but is regulated wholly by their capacity to be useful. The Indians whose treatment of the females is mildest, and who pay most deference to their opinions, are by no means the most distinguished for their virtues; nor is this deference attended by any increase of attachment, since they are equally willing with the most brutal husband, to prostitute their wives to strangers. On the other hand, the tribes among whom the women are very much debased, possess the loftiest sense of honour, the greatest liberality, and all the good qualities of which their situation demands the exercise. Where the women can aid in procuring subsistence for the tribe, they are treated with more equality, and their importance is proportioned to the share which they take in that labour, while in countries where subsistence is chiefly procured by the exertions of the men, the women are considered and treated as burdens. Thus, among the Clatsops and Chinnooks, who live upon fish and roots, which the women are equally expert with the men in procuring, the former have a rank and influence very rarely found among Indians. The females are permitted to speak freely before the men, to whom indeed they sometimes address themselves in a tone of authority. On many subjects their judgments and opinions are respected, and in matters of trade, their advice is generally asked and pursued. The labours of the family too, are shared almost equally. The men collect wood and make fires, assist in cleansing the fish, make the houses, canoes, and wooden utensils; and whenever strangers are to be entertained, or a great feast prepared, the meats are cooked and served up by the men. The peculiar province of the female is to collect roots, and to manufacture the various articles which are formed of rushes, flags, cedar-bark, and bear-grass; but the management of the canoes, and many of the occupations, which elsewhere devolves wholly on the female, are here common to both sexes. . . .

Saturday, 17 [1806]. The principal chiefs of the Minnetarees came down to bid us farewell, as none of them could be prevailed on to go with us. The circumstance induced our interpreter, Chaboneau, with his wife and child, to remain here, as he could be no longer useful; and notwithstanding our offers of taking him with us to the United States, he said that he had there no acquaintance, and no chance of making a livelihood, and preferred remaining among the Indians. This man has been very serviceable to us, and his wife particularly useful among the Shoshonees. Indeed, she has borne with a patience truly admirable, the fatigues of so long a route, incumbered with the charge of an infant, who is even now only nineteen months old. We therefore paid him his wages, amounting to five hundred dollars and thirty-three cents, including the price of a horse and a lodge purchased of him.

337

Petition by Cherokee Women, 1818

Cherokee women were among the most vocal opponents of the treaties designed to remove all southeastern Native Americans to beyond the Mississippi, a policy that had been adopted by the U.S. government under Thomas Jefferson and others in the new Republic. After holding a political council in 1818, Cherokee women stated their objections in a petition, with particular emphasis on the contrary influence of white men who had married Indian women and who could expand their landholdings if the tribes moved away. But by 1838 the Cherokees were forcibly removed anyway: their property in Georgia was confiscated, and their people, unprepared, were marched eight hundred miles in winter to present-day Oklahoma on the deadly Trail of Tears.

From Archives of the American Board of Commissioners for Foreign Missions, by permission of Houghton Library, Harvard University, Cambridge, Massachusetts.

❖

We have called a meeting among ourselves to consult on the different points now before the council relating to our national affairs. We have heard with painful feelings that the bounds of the land we now possess are to be drawn into very narrow limits. The land was given to us by the Great Spirit above as our common right, to raise our children upon, and to make support for our rising generations. We, therefore, humbly petition our beloved children, the head men of warriors, to hold out to the last in support of our common rights, as the Cherokee nations have been the first settlers of this land; we, therefore, claim the right of the soil.

We well remember that our country was formerly very extensive, but by repeated sales it has become circumscribed to the very narrow limits we have at present. Our Father the President advised us to become farmers—to manufacture our own clothes, and to have our children instructed. To this advice we have attended in every thing as far as we were able. Now the thought of being compelled to remove to the other side of the Mississippi is dreadful to us, because it appears to us that we, by this removal, shall be brought to a savage state again; for we have by the endeavors of our Father the President, become too much enlightened to throw aside, the privileges of a civilized life.

We therefore unanimously join in our meeting to hold our country in common as hitherto.

338

Some of our children have become Christians; we have missionary schools among us; we have heard the gospel in our nation; we have become civilized and enlightened; and are in hopes that in a few years our nations will be prepared for instruction in other branches of sciences and arts, which are both useful and necessary in civilized society.

There are some white men among us, who have been raised in our country from their youth, are connected with us by marriage and have considerable families, who are very active in encouraging the emigration of our nation. These ought to be our truest friends, but prove our worst enemies. They seem to be only concerned how to increase their riches but do not care what becomes of our Nation, nor even of their own wives and children.

Legend of the Trail of Tears

Elizabeth Sullivan, the author of the following story, is a Creek Indian descendant of one of the Trail of Tears participants. The events she describes all occurred and are documented in U.S. Army records as well as tribal legends.

From Elizabeth Sullivan, *Indian Legends of the Trail of Tears and Other Stories* (Tulsa, Okla.: Giant Services, 1974), pp. 1–29. Copyright © 1974 by Elizabeth Sullivan. Reprinted in Dexter Fisher, ed., *The Third Woman: Minority Women Writers of the United States* (Boston: Houghton Mifflin, 1980), pp. 26–30.

❖

Annakee observed the beauty around her. It was a beautiful day. The fruit tree blossoms were in bloom, corn and tobacco had been planted and the cottonwood leaves were like glass. She noticed the huge trunk of older trees whose rough scars showed where the medicine man had stripped the bark for his use for the sick Indians who were dependent on his knowledge and mercy. . . .

Little did she know that before too long, General Andrew Jackson's army would abuse them and remove all of the comforts of home life. There would be no blossoms in bloom; their crops would be destroyed and they would be driven out to go West to Indian Territory—a cruel and death journey.

When the removal began Annakee could not understand all the changes taking place. She only knew her grandmother's eyes were bloodshot, her cheeks sunken, her lips cracked. Annakee held closely to her grandmother's hand as they walked on with so many Indians. Some she did not know. Everyone appeared fearful and sad. She saw many crying. Annakee began to suffer from irritating mosquito bites. She would scatch mercilessly until she bled. Her little legs were so tired and her feet ached. . . .

Annakee remembered her home. The corn crib was full of corn. They had plenty of dried fruit and meat. Her father and mother saw to that. Her two older brothers were hunting all of the time. They even knew how to shoot with bow and arrow to kill fish when they came up for air after shoe string roots had been pounded and put into the river up stream and a dam was made.

One comfort she had and held tightly was a doll her grandmother had made from a corncob. She had long sleeves and a skirt, even had an apron on with cross stitch at the bottom just like grandmother's dress.

Along the journey they would camp for three or four days and then go on. The soldiers were mean and hateful. She began to notice, if a baby cried and cried from thirst or the fatigue in the cradle on the back of the mother, the man on the horse would say something that she could not understand and jerk the baby and take it by the legs and whip it against the trunk of the tree until it went limp and then would throw it aside.

Once she saw a mother cry and run to her dead baby. The soldier then whipped her with a long whip that would pop loud. The mother would not let go of the bleeding broken body of her child. She was whipped to death and left as they went on.

Annakee shivered and thought it was a bad dream. It appeared to her that her grandmother took command and would converse with the women at night during camp out. She told the women who had babies still suckling, "If the soldiers get your baby, let it go. Some have to look after the older children. Never look back; just march on." After that, it became a common practice.

"God lives, Creator of all things, be fearful and pray." They sang songs in whispers not audible to the soldiers who would camp nearby. The aroma of the soldiers' food reached them and hunger became almost unbearable.

Her grandmother was very stern and told her—"Learn never to cry, even if you are hurt or hungry. Never look back to see what is going on in the back." This, she learned very quickly. . . .

Some of the men folks tried to make a break. They were shot to death. Those who escaped in the forest were caught by the big dogs and in no time were destroyed by the vicious dogs. The tragedy in the wilderness was unforgettable, yet so true. Sometimes, as weeks went by these soldiers would tear the clothing off young girls twelve years of age and older or young mothers and molest them. She always turned her head the other way when these things happened.

When the journey grew into weeks and months they were allowed to camp by the body of water. They would stay at camp as long as two weeks. They were well patrolled but men were allowed to hunt nearby as food was getting low. . . .

The worst part of the trip was a time when hundreds of men, women and old women and children disappeared in a huge mean-looking river which was swift, deep and muddy—the mighty Mississippi River. Rowboats were available from the army but there were not near enough. While they camped by the river the men were allowed to make rafts six to nine feet in length. Animal skins were used for tying the rafts together. They were dangerous but a person could hold on to the log to keep from sinking. Some who were physically able swam across—other rafts capsized. Two men used feather mattresses for boats. The Big House fire was preserved and saved across the Mississippi River by three men. The three men held the container of hot coals with each hand and used only one hand to swim across this swift river. The coals were finally safely carried across to the other side. The fire was the redman's friend—significant of closeness, togetherness and cooked meals. Wild beasts feared fire so they stayed away from campfires.

To add to the misery of the trail, snow descended. It remained very cold and the trip became almost unbearable. One cold morning, they started to travel. The snow was coming down but Annakee did not cry. She noticed that grandmother was getting so thin and was getting sick. She never smiled anymore. All the army men rode horses and were in wagons. One soldier kept looking behind her. He got so close that she thought he was trying to run over her with the horse. So she looked behind her.

Her little moccasins were worn out and her little feet had been wrapped up with cloth. Suddenly each step she took left footprints of bright blood. She looked down to her feet. They did not hurt any more because her feet were numb. The soldier took her by her little thin arm and put her in the saddle in front of him. His body was warm and she snuggled next to him and was soon fast asleep.

Each day when they traveled the kind soldier wrapped her up and carried her on the horse—Annakee did not remember much when she was so sick. Food began to be short. One day she noticed two men take one bean and divide it, so that women and children could have just a little more to eat. Somehow there were less soldiers. Some began to get sick and die.

Spring came and the weather was warm. Sometimes they would come up to a camp. Those who went ahead of them had camped there. Each band of Indians was assigned to a group of soldiers. One main food was corn. The women folks had saved some corn back in case of extra need.

Months later, Annakee became stronger and was able to play with other children. This had not been allowed before. It appeared the mean soldiers became friendly and kind. The Indians were allowed to have council meeting at camp when the Medicine Man would give them a talk. He told them surely they would get to their destination and they would be left alone to start all over again. The Medicine Man noticed also that the soldiers were running out of their supplies.

The soldiers began to get sick. Some of the horses died, so some had to walk.

The Chief said, "This is our time to rebel. We need our food. We shall not give one grain of corn to them. We have suffered so much. Our loved ones they killed, they would not let us bury our dead. We will show no mercy."

They camped for a long time near a river to hunt and fish, not patrolled as before.

Regardless of what horrible scenes Annakee saw, she observed and saw the beauty in the trees and small animal life. She pretended she had to protect her doll. She talked to the doll every day. This made her almost forget the reality that was about her.

At one time all they had for food was parched corn boiled in water. One sick soldier came to the campfire and held a tin cup for broth.

The grandmother was dishing out the broth. She looked up to him in surprise. The Chief spoke up and said, "Let him starve." Annakee looked over and saw it was the soldier who had held her and let her ride the horse months and months ago. She ran up and told her grandmother to give him the broth. After that she became a symbol of mercy and took away the hate, fear and somehow helped all those who saw her. They all had to travel together in harmony. The missionaries had taught her what love was—how you felt—forgiveness. . . .

Years later after settling in Indian Territory, Annakee would gather her grandchildren around the campfire and tell them the story of her removal and she would say, "If it was not for the soldier who picked me up and cuddled me during my illness, you all would not be here."

A Sioux Cavalcade and a Mandan Village

George Catlin, an artist and careful observer of many different Native American peoples, traveled among the Sioux, Mandan, and other tribes in the early 1830s. His paintings of the Mandans and descriptions of their culture were done just four years before the tribe was decimated by a smallpox epidemic. His work thus became the only remaining evidence of a once great people uprooted by the advance of Euro-Americans. Note his comment about the frequency and necessity of marriages between white fur traders and Indian women. His description of the Sioux cavalcade neglects to mention that the entire process was the work of women, who prided themselves on the quality of their movable homes.

From George Catlin, *Letters and Notes on the North American Indians,* ed. Michael MacDonald Mooney (New York: Clarkson N. Potter, 1975), pp. 120, 142–44, 163–68.

342

❖

The manner in which Indians strike their tents and transport them is a novel and unexpected sight. I saw an encampment of Sioux, consisting of six hundred of these lodges, struck, and all things packed and on the move in a few minutes. The chief sends his runners or criers (for such work all chiefs keep criers in their employment) through the village, a few hours before they are to start, announcing his determination to move, and the hour fixed upon. At the time announced, the lodge of the chief is seen flapping in the wind, a part of the poles having been taken out from under it. This is the signal, and in one minute, six hundred tents, which have been strained tight and fixed, are seen waving and flapping in the wind. In one minute more all are flat upon the ground. Their horses and dogs, of which they have a vast number, have all been secured upon the spot, in readiness. Each one is speedily loaded with the burden allotted to it, ready to fall into the grand procession.

For this strange cavalcade, preparation is made in the following manner: The poles of a lodge are divided into two bunches, the little ends of each bunch fastened upon the shoulders or withers of a horse, leaving the butt ends to drag behind on the ground on either side. Just behind the horse, a brace or pole is tied across, which keeps the poles in their respective places. Then upon that the tent is placed, rolled up, as well as the other household and domestic furniture. On top of everything sit two, three, sometimes even four women with their children.

Each one of the horses has a conductress, with a tremendous pack upon her own back, who sometimes walks before and leads the horse, and at other times sits astride its back, with a child, perhaps at her breast and another behind her, clinging to her waist with one arm while affectionately embracing a sneaking dog-pup in the other.

In this way five or six hundred wigwams, with all their furniture, may be seen drawn out for miles, creeping over the grass-covered plains of this country. Three times that number of men, on good horses, stroll along in front or on the flank. In some tribes, at the rear of this heterogeneous caravan, at least five times that number of dogs falls into the rank, following in the train and company of the women. Every cur who is large enough, and not too cunning to be enslaved, is encumbered with a sled on which he patiently drags his load—a part of the household goods and furniture of the lodge to which he belongs. Two poles, about fifteen feet long, are placed upon the dog's shoulder, in the same manner as the lodge poles are attached to the horses, leaving the larger ends to drag upon the ground behind him. A bundle is allotted to him to carry, and with it he trots off amid the throng of dogs and squaws. . . .

On an extensive plain without tree or bush to be seen, rising from the ground and towards the heavens, are domes of dirt—and the thousand spears and scalp-poles of the semi-subterraneous village of the hospitable Mandans. . . . Their 343 lodges are closely grouped together, leaving just room enough for walking and riding between them. They appear to be built entirely of dirt, but one is surprised when entering them to see the neatness, comfort, and spacious dimensions of these earth-covered dwellings. All the lodges have a circular form, and are from forty to sixty feet in diameter. Their foundations are prepared by digging some two feet in the ground, and forming the floor of earth, by levelling the requisite size for the lodge. These floors or foundations are all perfectly circular, and vary in size in proportion to the number of inmates, or of the quality or standing of the families which are to occupy them. The superstructure is then produced by arranging, inside of this circular excavation, a barrier or wall of timbers, some eight or nine inches in diameter, of equal height (about six feet), placed on end and resting against each other, supported by a formidable embankment of earth raised against them outside.

Then, resting upon the tops of these timbers or piles, are others of equal size and numbers, of twenty or twenty-five feet in length, sending their upper or smaller ends towards the center and top of the lodge. These poles rise at an angle of forty-five degrees to the apex or sky-light, which is about three or four feet in diameter, answering as a chimney and a sky-light at the same time. The roof of the lodge thus formed is supported by beams passing around the inner part of the lodge about the middle of these poles or timbers, and themselves upheld by four or five large posts passing down to the lodge floor.

On top of the poles forming the roof is a complete mat of willow-boughs, of half a foot or more in thickness, which protects the timbers from the dampness of the earth. The lodge is covered with these from bottom to top, to the depth of two or three feet, and then with a hard or tough clay which is impervious to water, and which with long use becomes quite hard. The hardened roof becomes a lounging place for the whole family in pleasant weather. . . .

The floors of these dwellings are of earth, but so hardened by use, and swept so clean, tracked by bare and moccasined feet, that they have almost a polish, and would scarcely soil the whitest linen. In the center, immediately under the sky-light, is the fire-place—a hole of four or five feet in diameter, of a circular form, sunk a foot or more below the surface, and curbed around with stone. Over the fire-place, and suspended from the apex of diverging props or poles, is the pot or kettle, filled with buffalo meat. . . . These cabins are so spacious that they hold from twenty to forty persons—a family and all their connections.

They all sleep on bedsteads similar in form to ours, but generally not quite so high; made of round poles lashed together with thongs. A buffalo skin, fresh stripped from the animal, is stretched across the bottom poles, and about two feet from the floor. When it dries, it becomes much contracted and forms a perfect sacking-bottom. The fur side of this skin is placed uppermost, on which they lie with great comfort, with a buffalo-robe folded up for a pillow, and others drawn over them instead of blankets.

344

These beds are uniformly screened with a covering of buffalo or elk skins, oftentimes beautifully dressed and placed over the upright poles or frames, like a suit of curtains; leaving a hole in front, sufficient for the occupant to pass in and out, to and from his or her bed. Some of these coverings or curtains are exceedingly beautiful, being cut tastefully into fringe, and handsomely ornamented with porcupine's quills and picture writing or hieroglyphics. From the great number of inmates in these lodges, they are necessarily very spacious, and the number of beds considerable. It is no uncommon thing to see these lodges fifty feet in diameter inside (which is an immense room), with a row of these curtained beds extending quite around their sides, being some ten or twelve of them, placed four or five feet apart. . . .

The chiefs of the Mandans frequently have a plurality of wives. Such is the custom among all of the tribes. It is no uncommon thing to find a chief with six, eight, or ten, and some with twelve or fourteen wives in his lodge. Women are always held in a rank inferior to that of the men. They serve as menials and slaves. They are the "hewers of wood and drawers of water." It becomes a matter of necessity for a chief (who must be liberal, keep open doors, and entertain for the support of his popularity) to have in his wigwam a sufficient number of such handmaids to perform the numerous duties and drudgeries of so large and expensive an establishment.

There are two other reasons for this custom which operate with equal force. In the first place, these people have still more or less the same passion for the accumulation of wealth, for the luxuries of life, as the civilized world. A chief with a wish to furnish his lodge with something more than ordinary for the entertainment of his own people, as well as strangers who fall upon his hospitality, marries a number of wives, who are kept at hard labor during most of the year. The results of their labor enable him to procure those luxuries, and give to his lodge the appearance of respectability.

The women are kept dressing buffalo robes and other skins for the market. The brave or chief with the greatest number of wives is considered the most affluent and envied man in the tribe. His table is most bountifully supplied. His lodge is the most abundantly furnished with the luxuries of manufacture.

Manual labor among Indians is all done by the women. There are no daily laborers or persons who will "hire out" to labor for another, and it becomes necessary for him who requires more than the labor or services of one, to add to the number by legalizing and compromising by the ceremony of marriage his stock of laborers. They can thus, and thus alone, be easily enslaved, and the results of their labor turned to good account. . . . His accumulation of a household, instead of quadrupling his expenses (as would be the case in the civilized world), actually increases his wealth, as the result of his wives' labor. . . .

345

It becomes a matter of absolute necessity for the white men who are traders in these regions to connect themselves by marriage to one or more of the most influential families in the tribe. Marriage identifies their interest with that of the nation, and enables them, with the influence of their new family connections, to carry on successfully their business transactions. Young women of the best families aspire to such an elevation. Most of them are exceedingly ambitious for such a connection inasmuch as they are certain of a delightful exemption from the slavish duties that devolve upon them when married under other circumstances. They expect to lead a life of ease and idleness, covered with mantles of blue and scarlet cloth, with beads and trinkets and ribbons, in which they flounce and flirt about, the envied and tinselled belles of every tribe. . . .

Almost every trader who commences in the business of this country speedily enters into such an arrangement. It is done with as little ceremony as he would bargain for a horse, and just as unceremoniously do they annul and abolish the connection when they wish to leave the country, or change their positions from one tribe to another. . . .

The Mandan women are beautiful and modest. Among the respectable families, virtue is as highly cherished and as inviolate as in any society whatever. Yet at the same time a chief may marry a dozen wives if he pleases, and so may a white man. And if either wishes to marry the most beautiful and modest girl in the tribe, she is valued only equal, perhaps, to two horses, a gun with powder and ball for a year, five or six pounds of beads, a couple of gallons of whisky, and a handful of awls.

The girls of this tribe, like those of most of these North Western tribes, marry at the age of twelve to fourteen, and some at the age of eleven years. Their beauty soon vanishes, from the slavish life they lead. Their occupations are almost continual, and they seem to go industriously at them, either from choice or inclination, without a murmur.

The principal occupations of the women consist of procuring wood and water, of cooking, dressing robes and other skins, of drying meat and wild fruit, and of raising corn (maize).

The Mandans are agriculturists. They raise a great deal of corn and some pumpkins and squashes. This is all done by the women, who make their hoes from the shoulder-blade of the buffalo or the elk, and dig the ground over instead of ploughing it.

They raise a small sort of corn, with ears which are no longer than a man's thumb. The variety is well adapted to their climate, as it ripens sooner than other varieties, which would not mature in so cold a latitude. The green corn season is one of great festivity, and one of much importance. The greater part of their crop is eaten during these festivals, and the remainder is gathered and dried on the cob, before it has ripened, and packed away in "caches" (as the French call them), holes dug in the ground, some six or seven feet deep, the insides of which are somewhat in the form of a jug, and tightly closed at the top. The corn, and even dried meat and pemican, are placed in these *caches,* being packed tight around the sides with prairie grass, and effectually preserved through the severest winters.

Corn and dried meat are generally stored in the fall, in sufficient quantities to support them through the winter. In addition, they often store great quantities of dried squashes and dried "pommes blanches," a kind of turnip which grows in great abundance in these regions. These are dried in great quantities and pounded into a sort of meal to be cooked with the dried meat and corn. Great quantities also of wild fruit of different kinds are dried and laid away in store for the winter season, such as buffalo berries, service berries, strawberries, and wild plums.

The buffalo meat, however, is the great staple and "staff of life" in this country. There are, from a fair computation, something like two hundred and fifty thousand Indians in these western regions, who live almost exclusively on the flesh of the buffalo. During the summer and fall months they use the meat fresh, and cook it in a great variety of ways—roasting, broiling, boiling, stewing, smoking, and boiling the ribs and joints with the marrow in them to make a delicious soup.

The pot is always boiling over the fire, and anyone who is hungry (either of the household or from any other part of the village) has a right to order it taken off, and to fall to eating as he pleases. I very much doubt whether the civilized world have in their institutions any system which can properly be called more humane and charitable. Every man, woman, or child in Indian communities is allowed to enter anyone's lodge, and even that of the chief of the nation, and eat when they are hungry, provided misfortune or necessity has driven them to it.

When We Saw the White People Coming

In a book about her life and the treatment of her people, Sarah Winnemucca (1844–91) wrote this eloquent account of her first view of white people. Having learned English at the behest of her grandfather, she became the designated spokesperson and chief of the Piutes as they tried to survive among increasingly numerous white settlers and the post–Civil War army that had been sent to deal with western Indians. In the 1870s, members of her tribe were forcibly removed from their land, marched in the winter to Yakima, Washington, and repeatedly denied promised provisions and cheated by corrupt government agents. Her lecture tour in the East in 1883, sponsored by prominent women reformers, brought Indian complaints to public attention but did little to change the circumstances of Native Americans. She died of tuberculosis a few years later. The reference in this excerpt to a "band of white people" who died in the mountains probably refers to the famous Donner party tragedy of 1846.

From Sarah Winnemucca Hopkins, *Life among the Piutes: Their Wrongs and Claims* (New York: G. P. Putnam's Sons, 1883), pp. 10–13, 46–50, 52–53.

❖

That same fall, after my grandfather [Captain Truckee] came home, he told my father to take charge of his people and hold the tribe, as he was going back to California with as many of his people as he could get to go with him. So my father took his place as Chief of the Piutes, and had it as long as he lived. Then my grandfather started back to California again with about thirty families. That same fall, very late, the emigrants kept coming. It was this time that our white brothers first came amongst us. They could not get over the mountains, so they had to live with us. It was on Carson River, where the great Carson City stands now. You call my people bloodseeking. My people did not seek to kill them, nor did they steal their horses,—no, no, far from it. During the winter my people helped them. They gave them such as they had to eat. They did not hold out their hands and say:—

"You can't have anything to eat unless you pay me." No,—no such word was used by us savages at that time; and the persons I am speaking of are living yet; they could speak for us if they choose to do so.

The following spring, before my grandfather returned home, there was a great excitement among my people on account of fearful news coming from different tribes, that the people whom they called their white brothers were killing everybody that came in their way, and all the Indian tribes had gone into the mountains to save their lives. So my father told all his people to go into the mountains and hunt and lay up food for the coming winter. Then we all went into the mountains. There was a fearful story they told us children. Our mothers told us that the whites were killing everybody and eating them. So we were all afraid of them. Every dust that we could see blowing in the valley we would say it was the white people. In the late fall my father told his people to go to the rivers and fish, and we all went to Humboldt River, and the women went to work gathering wild seed, which they grind between the rocks. The stones are round, big enough to hold in the hands. The women did this when they got back, and when they had gathered all they could they put it in one place and covered it with grass, and then over the grass mud. After it is covered it looks like an Indian wigwam.

Oh, what a fright we all got one morning to hear some white people were coming. Every one ran as best they could. My poor mother was left with my little sister and me. Oh, I never can forget it. My poor mother was carrying my little sister on her back, and trying to make me run; but I was so frightened I could not move my feet, and while my poor mother was trying to get me along my aunt overtook us, and she said to my mother: "Let us bury our girls, or we shall all be killed and eaten up." So they went to work and buried us, and told us if we heard any noise not to cry out, for if we did they would surely kill us and eat us. So our mothers buried me and my cousin, planted sage bushes over our faces to keep the sun from burning them, and there we were left all day.

Oh, can any one imagine my feelings *buried alive,* thinking every minute that I was to be unburied and eaten up by the people that my grandfather loved so much? With my heart throbbing, and not daring to breathe, we lay there all day. It seemed that the night would never come. Thanks be to God! the night came at last. Oh, how I cried and said: "Oh, father, have you forgotten me? Are you never coming for me?" I cried so I thought my very heartstrings would break.

At last we heard some whispering. We did not dare to whisper to each other, so we lay still. I could hear their footsteps coming nearer and nearer. I thought my heart was coming right out of my mouth. Then I heard my mother say, " 'Tis right here!" Oh, can any one in this world ever imagine what were my feelings when I was dug up by my poor mother and father? My cousin and I were once more happy in our mothers' and fathers' care, and we were taken to where all the rest were. . . . Well, while we were in the mountains hiding, the people that my grandfather called our white brothers came along to where our winter supplies were. They set everything we had left on fire. It was a fearful sight. It was all we had for the winter, and it was all burnt during that night. My father took some of his men during the night to try and save some of it, but they could not; it had burnt down before they got there.

These were the last white men that came along that fall. My people talked

348

fearfully that winter about those they called our white brothers. My people said they had something like awful thunder and lightning, and with that they killed everything that came in their way.

This whole band of white people perished in the mountains, for it was too late to cross them. We could have saved them, only my people were afraid of them. We never knew who they were, or where they came from. So, poor things, they must have suffered fearfully, for they all starved there. The snow was too deep. . . .

Many years ago, when my people were happier than they are now, they used to celebrate the Festival of Flowers in the spring. I have been to three of them only in the course of my life.

Oh, with what eagerness we girls used to watch every spring for the time when we could meet with our hearts' delight, the young men, whom in civilized life you call beaux. We would all go in company to see if the flowers we were named for were yet in bloom, for almost all the girls are named for flowers. We talked about them in our wigwams, as if we were the flowers, saying, "Oh, I saw myself today in full bloom!" We would talk all the evening in this way in our families with such delight, and such beautiful thoughts of the happy day when we should meet with those who admired us and would help us to sing our flower-songs which we made up as we sang. . . .

All the girls who have flower-names dance along together, and those who have not go together also. Our fathers and mothers and grandfathers and grandmothers make a place for us where we can dance. Each one gathers the flower she is named for, and then all weave them into wreaths and crowns and scarfs, and dress up in them. . . .

They all go marching along, each girl in turn singing of herself; but she is not a girl any more,—she is a flower singing. She sings of herself, and her sweetheart, dancing along by her side, helps her sing the song she makes.

I will repeat what we say of ourselves. "I, Sarah Winnemucca, am a shell-flower, such as I wear on my dress. My name is Thocmetony. I am so beautiful! Who will come and dance with me while I am so beautiful? Oh, come and be happy with me! I shall be beautiful while the earth lasts. Somebody will always admire me; and who will come and be happy with me in the Spirit-land? I shall be beautiful forever there. Yes, I shall be more beautiful than my shell-flower, my Thocmetony! Then, come, oh come, and dance and be happy with me!" The young men sing with us as they dance beside us.

Our parents are waiting for us somewhere to welcome us home. And then we praise the sage-brush and the rye-grass that have no flower, and the pretty rocks that some are named for; and then we present our beautiful flowers to these companions who could carry none. And so all are happy; and that closes the beautiful day.

My people have been so unhappy for a long time they wish now to *disincrease*, instead of multiply. The mothers are afraid to have more children, for fear they shall have daughters, who are not safe even in their mother's presence.

The grandmothers have the special care of the daughters just before and after they come to womanhood. The girls are not allowed to get married until they have come to womanhood; and that period is recognized as a very sacred thing, and is the subject of a festival, and has peculiar customs. The young woman is set apart under the care of two of her friends, somewhat older, and a little wigwam, called a teepee, just big enough for the three, is made for them, to which they retire. She goes through certain labors which are thought to be strengthening, and these last twenty-five days. Every day, three times a day, she must gather, and pile up as high as she can, five stacks of wood. This makes fifteen stacks a day. At the end of every five days the attendants take her to a river to bathe. She fasts from all flesh-meat during these twenty-five days, and continues to do this for five days in every month all her life. At the end of the twenty-five days she returns to the family lodge, and gives all her clothing to her attendants in payment for their care. Sometimes the wardrobe is quite extensive.

It is thus publicly known that there is another marriageable woman, and any young man interested in her, or wishing to form an alliance, comes forward. But the courting is very different from the courting of the white people. He never speaks to her, or visits the family, but endeavors to attract her attention by showing his horsemanship, etc. As he knows that she sleeps next to her grandmother in the lodge, he enters in full dress after the family has retired for the night, and seats himself at her feet. If she is not awake, her grandmother wakes her. He does not speak to either young woman or grandmother, but when the young women wishes him to go away, she rises and goes and lies down by the side of her mother. He then leaves as silently as he came in. This goes on sometimes for a year or longer, if the young woman has not made up her mind. She is never forced by her parents to marry against her wishes. When she knows her own mind, she makes a confidant of her grandmother, and then the young man is summoned by the father of the girl, who asks him, in her presence, if he really loves his daughter, and reminds him, if he says he does, of all the duties of a husband. He then asks his daughter the same question, and sets before her minutely all her duties. And these duties are not slight. She is to dress the game, prepare the food, clean the buckskins, make his moccasins, dress his hair, bring all the wood,—in short, do all the household work. She promises to "be himself," and she fulfils her promise. Then he is invited to a feast and all his relatives with him. But after the betrothal, a teepee is erected for the presents that pour in from both sides.

At the wedding feast, all the food is prepared in baskets. The young woman sits by the young man, and hands him the basket of food prepared for him with her own hands. He does not take it with his right hand; but seizes her wrist, and takes it with the left hand. This constitutes the marriage ceremony, and the father pronounces them man and wife. They go to a wigwam of their own, where they live till the first child is born. This event also is celebrated. Both father and mother fast from all flesh, and the father goes through the labor of piling the wood for twenty-five days, and assumes all his wife's household work during that time. If he does not do his part in the care of the child, he is considered an outcast. Every five days his child's basket is changed for a new one, and the five are all carefully put away at the end of the days, the last one containing the navel-string, carefully wrapped up, and all are put up into a tree, and the child put into a new and ornamented basket. All this respect shown to the mother and child makes the parents feel their responsibility, and makes the tie between parents and children very strong. The young mothers often get together and exchange their experiences about the attentions of their husbands; and inquire of each other if the fathers did their duty to their children, and were careful of their wives' health. . . .

The chief's tent is the largest tent, and it is the council-tent, where every one goes who wants advice. In the evenings the head men go there to discuss everything, for the chiefs do not rule like tyrants; they discuss everything with their people, as a father would in his family. Often they sit up all night. They discuss the doings of all, if they need to be advised. If a boy is not doing well they talk that over, and if the women are interested they can share in the talks. If there is not room enough inside, they all go out of doors, and make a great circle. The men are in the inner circle, for there would be too much smoke for the women inside. The men never talk without smoking first. The women sit behind them in another circle, and if the children wish to hear, they can be there too. The women know as much as the men do, and their advice is often asked. We have a republic as well as you. The council-tent is our Congress, and anybody can speak who has anything to say, women and all. They are always interested in what their husbands are doing and thinking about. And they take some part even in the wars. They are always near at hand when fighting is going on, ready to snatch their husbands up and carry them off if wounded or killed. One splendid woman that my brother Lee married after his first wife died, went out into the battle-field after her uncle was killed, and went into the front ranks and cheered the men on. Her uncle's horse was dressed in a splendid robe made of eagles' feathers and she snatched it off and swung it in the face of the enemy, who always carry off everything they find, as much as to say, "You can't have that— I have it safe"; and she staid and took her uncle's place, as brave as any of the men. It means something when the women promise their fathers to make their husbands *themselves*. They faithfully keep with them in all the dangers they can share. They not only take care of their children together, but they do everything together; and when they grow blind, which I am sorry to say is very common, for the smoke they live in destroys their eyes at last, they take sweet care of one another. Marriage is a sweet thing when people love each other. If women could go into your Congress I think justice would soon be done to the Indians. . . .

Her Grinding Was Rhythmic and Easy

Anna Moore Shaw, a Pima Indian, here describes the daily work of her grand-mother and her mother in the nineteenth century in what is now southern Arizona. This area did not become part of the United States until 1854, but for two centuries Spaniards and Mexicans had settled there, and Indians had lived in the Gila River valley since at least 300 B.C. There they had established an elaborate irrigation system and had built large pueblo cities (see part 1). Their culture continued to thrive under Spanish jurisdiction but changed radically after U.S. settlers arrived.

From Anna Moore Shaw, *A Pima Past* (Tucson: University of Arizona Press, 1974), pp. 5–7, 47–52, 70–74. By permission of Adeline E. Russell.

❖

When the first Christian missionary to the Pimas and Papagos came to the Southwest, the native Pima guides told him about the Casa Grande ruins near the Gila River. In 1694 Father Eusebio Francisco Kino rode a dusty trail to visit the Big House. . . . When Padre Kino came again, he brought seeds of vegetables and fruit. These took their places among the favorite foods of the Papago, Pima, and Maricopa tribes. But the main little seed was wheat. As soon as the padre introduced it, wheat became an important part of the Indian economy. During the time of the pioneers, it saved the life of many a white tenderfoot and soldier.

Father Kino also introduced horses and cattle and helped the Indians to become better farmers. But as in the days of the Huhugam [Those Who Are Gone], the Gila River continued to play an important part in the lives of the natives, who were so dependent on water. Like the Nile, the Gila and Salt rivers used to overflow their banks, depositing rich loam. Men and women cooperated and went to the farms to plant seeds. A wooden *gihk*, or shovel, with a sharp end, was used to dig holes. When the tiny seed was thrown in the hole, bare heels were ready to shove the dirt over the seed. . . .

After Padre Kino set his feet on the Pima desert soil, a wide door was opened for the Mexicans and Europeans. "Now the peaceful Pimas will protect us from the Apaches," they thought. Some came on foot, others on horseback and in ox carts, through southern Arizona, then a part of Mexico.

This first group of settlers had little effect on the primitive Pima way of life. It is true that many Indians now had a Spanish name as well as an Indian name, but the Pimas clung to their ancient values and legends. They continued to live in their brush round houses, called *olas kih*. People helped each other and worked together in harmony. The land belonged to everyone: a man could farm as much as he could clear and work. To keep things going smoothly, each village had a chief, who allied himself under a head chief when enemies were threatening.

In 1854 the Gadsden Purchase made southern Arizona an American territory. Now a new group of strangers came to the desert country of the Pimas: white soldiers and traders and Indian agents. The rich Pima farms provided these newcomers with food, and soon the growing Pima villages formed themselves into a pattern similar to that of today. . . .

. . . The Pimas, Maricopas, and Papagos helped the white man to settle the Southwest. Besides providing the newcomers with food and water, they acted as guides, soldiers, and allies to help break the threat of Apache terrorism.

Once the Apaches were conquered, the settlers were free to arrive in great numbers. Over the prairies they came, and it was not long before the old Pima way of life was deeply affected by the white man's ideas and material culture. . . .

. . . .

Training for womanhood under the watchful tutelage of Grandmother Red Flowers had not been easy. As a mother grows old, her legs become tired, and the daughter must help with the cooking. But when one has only a grandmother, the girl must do much more, for the old one's legs are infirm and wobbly, unable to perform the many heavy chores required of a Pima woman.

Since the time of her mother's death, Dawn had arisen each day before sunrise to grind corn or wheat on the stone metate. At first, as an awkward child, it had been hard to grind the grain fine enough to be easily kneaded into the soft *chemait* (bread) Grandfather Gray Owl loved. But now that the girl was grown, her grinding was rhythmic and easy, a beautiful way to begin each day.

After the grinding and preparing the morning meal, Dawn always took a walk to a bubbling spring near the Gila River. Confidently and with grace, the maiden walked home each day with her heavy, water-filled olla balanced on a padded ring upon her head. Quail crossed her path, and rabbits played in the desert growth as the sun began to shed its warmth on the little Pima settlement.

Placing her olla in the ramada's shade, Dawn would begin the task of washing little brown tepary beans for her clay bean pot. After making a fire of just the right temperature, she would put the pot on the coals to simmer. Now the beans could take care of themselves, for when the sun was directly overhead, hungry men would return to the olas kih, anxious for pinole, cool water, and a rest before returning to the fields for the afternoon's labor.

In the evening, when the sun was setting red and gold, Dawn's simmering beans would finally be soft and delicious, ready for the major hardy meal of the old-time Pima day.

Gathering the wild desert foods was another of Dawn's chores. Sometimes this seemed hard, but more often the girl and her friends would make a holiday of it. Dawn especially loved to dig for the tiny potato-like nodules called *ihkow*. When she had collected sufficient amounts of these delicacies, she would take them home to boil in her bean pot. How her little brother Red Arrow loved the ihkow! He thought they tasted like the sugar cubes. . . .

Dawn's life did not become complete until . . . Grandmother Red Flowers decided that her young fingers had reached the stage where they could learn to weave the magnificent Pima baskets.

Dawn helped gather river willow twigs and cattail reeds with eager glee. She gladly picked the black devil's claws at the edges of the irrigated fields, for these weeds would form the striking black designs on her beautiful baskets. Red Flowers showed her granddaughter how to place the devil's claws in water for a week, to soften the tough thorns. After the two had stripped the sides of each claw with sharp awls, they threw the rest of the plant away.

Next came preparation of the cattails. Red Flowers demonstrated the trick of splitting the weeds with the teeth, then spreading them in the sun to dry. The young willow twigs were stripped free of leaves, then split in half with the teeth. These were rolled up while damp and flexible, then tied with string or strips of willow bark and hung on the rafters of the olas kih to dry until they were needed.

At first it was hard for Dawn's untrained fingers to learn the complex art. . . . It took such infinite patience! To weave intently, then unravel when it was not perfect, was the hardest thing for Dawn. But in time her fingers grew supple and skillful. When Grandmother Red Flowers finally nodded with prideful approval upon seeing a finished basket, Dawn knew she was ready to go to *Nahsa,* the famous weaver, who lived in Slippery Rock Village. . . .

Nahsa . . . lived in an olas kih of her son's household and spent all her days weaving the most beautiful of baskets. She was an exacting but patient teacher. . . .

Molly [the new bride] . . . knew that on her first night in her new home she must grind the wheat which had been left near the metate and make the breakfast tortillas to show her industry. A bride who stopped grinding before the job was done was considered lazy and worthless.

Even though she was only sixteen, Molly knew how to care for a household. As was expected of her, she took over the duties of food-gathering, cooking, and caring for Red Arrow and his family. She went about her work with industry, for she knew she must prove herself to her new family.

Red Arrow was proud of his wife and her fine cooking. He loved her succotash made with brown beans, wheat, and soup bone [and] her pinole, made from roasted ground wheat. . . . She knew how to roast beef, venison, antelope, horse meat, fish, and locusts to perfection. She expertly jerked left-over meat in the sun for future meals.

Molly's bean pot was always filled with good-smelling things, even in the summer when her days were often spent gathering wild foods in the desert. In late June and early July, she would join the other women as they took their long *kw'ipad* (saguaro rib poles) out among the giant cacti to harvest the sweet red fruit. After boiling it into a syrup, she stored it away for winter use in little ollas with round clay lids. The tiny black seeds were shaped into balls and stored; nothing was wasted. A portion of Molly's syrup always went into the large community ollas to ferment into wine for the rain-making ceremonies. During this festival, Molly would join the other women on top of the olas kih, where they made fun of the men, who grew silly and clumsy from drinking the fermented fruit.

After the saguaro gathering came foraging for the buds of the prickly pear and cholla cacti. After picking the fruit with two sticks used like scissors, she placed it in a rough willow basket made to fit her side. Then she roasted it all night on layers of sagebrush in a pit among the rocks. In the morning, she would carefully pull off the thorns, then dry and store the fruit for the winter months.

When the caterpillars were plentiful, Molly would gather them in large quantities, cut off their heads, and squeeze out their insides. Then she boiled them in salted water, and when they were cooked, she salted them again before braiding them into long strands for storage.

Next her saguaro rib poles were brought out again—this time to harvest the bean pods of the mesquite tree. Off and on during the hot month of July Molly would fill her *gioho* (burden basket) with *wihog* (mesquite pods). She would smile as she watched the village youngsters climb the trees and stamp their feet to shake down the pods for their mothers. The mesquite bean pods were an important staple in the Pima diet. Molly would dry them in the sun, then pound them to a powder in a wooden mortar with a long stone pestle. The powder was made into cakes for nourishment during the winter famine. . . .

If Red Arrow's new wife wasn't out in the desert, she might be found in the fields with her husband. In the late summer, when the Indian corn was ripe, she would gather a large pile of mesquite wood and place two or three dozen ears of corn among the twigs. When a match struck the bottom of the wood pile, the corn was roasted. The process was repeated until the desired amount was prepared. When it was cool, Molly husked the corn and spread it in the sun on top of the brush ramada to dry. The parched corn, called *ga'iwesa*, was ground on a metate with a mano, or rolling stone. Red Arrow especially liked it when it was fried and seasoned with red chile.

When the muskmelons and squash were ripe, Molly again went to the fields to help cut them into strips, then hang them to dry in the sun. She added the strips to her winter stores, to eat with or without lard when fresh vegetables were not available.

356   Because she was so industrious, Molly's huge storage baskets were filled by the time winter came. Besides wheat, saguaro syrup, cholla fruit, caterpillars, mesquite cakes, parched corn, melon strips, and squash, they contained dried salt bush leaves to flavor winter foods in the cooking pot. Next to the great storage baskets, animal skin bags held the jerky Molly had put up for winter meals. There was honey for sweetening and salt for seasoning. From the ceiling hung bunches of willow twigs, cattails, and devil's claws for weaving baskets on winter days.

When I Think of Pemmican I Grow Hungry

Frank Linderman interviewed Pretty-Shield in her old age, but she was clear of mind and glad to tell about her life and people, before and after the coming of white people. She had become a tribal "Wise-woman," and her clan included many chiefs and leaders. The Crow Indians lived in what is now southeastern Montana. Their way of life was destroyed when the United States launched a systematic campaign to kill off the buffalo and thus force the free-spirited nomadic Indians to settle down and become proper farmers—on land totally unsuited for ordinary farms.

From Frank B. Linderman, *Pretty Shield: Medicine Woman of the Crows* (New York: John Day Co., 1932), pp. 82–83, 134, 136, 145–47, 203. Copyright © 1932 by Frank B. Linderman. Copyright © renewed 1960. Reprinted by permission of HarperCollins Publishers, Inc.

❖

"How I loved to move, especially when the clans were going to meet at some selected place, always a beautiful one. . . . A crier would ride through the village telling the people to be ready to move in the morning. In every lodge the children's eyes would begin to shine. Men would sit up to listen, women would go to their doors to hear where the next village would be set up, and then there would be glad talking until it was time to go to sleep. Long before the sun came the fires would be going in every lodge, the horses, hundreds of them, would come thundering in, and then everybody was very busy. Down would come the lodges, packs would be made, travois loaded. Ho! Away we would go, following the men, to some new camping ground, with our children playing around us. It was good hard work to get things packed up, and moving; and it was hard, fast work to get them in shape again, after we camped. But in between these times we rested on our traveling horses. Yes, and we women visited while we traveled. There was plenty of room on the plains then, so that many could ride abreast if they wished to. . . .

"It was the coming of the horse that brought the best change of all to the Crows. This was long before my time, and yet I have heard my grandmother tell of the days when old women, too worn out and weak to travel afoot on the long drives when dogs dragged the travois, had to be left behind to die. She told me that when an old woman was used up, no good any more, the people set up a lodge for her, gave her meat, and wood for her fire, and then left her there to finally die. They could do nothing else. They could not pack old women on their backs, and dogs could not drag them. In those days when *men* grew too old to take care of themselves they dressed in their finest clothes and went to war against our enemies, often alone, until they found a chance to die fighting. Sometimes these old men went out with war-parties of young men just to find a chance to get killed while fighting. It was different with the old women. They sat in their lodges until their food was gone, until their fires were out; and then they died, alone.

"All this was changed by the horse. Even old people could ride. Ahh, I came onto a happy world. There was always fat meat, glad singing, and much dancing in our villages. Our people's hearts were then as light as breath-feathers." . . .

"Tell me how you made pemmican. . . ."

"Pemmican! Ahh, when I think of pemmican I grow hungry," she smiled, good-naturedly. "We cut good, lean meat into strips and dried it a little; then roasted it until it looked brown. After this was done we pounded the dry meat with stone hammers that are found nearly everywhere. They were made by The-ones-who-lived-without-fire. Next we soaked ripe chokeberries in water, and then used this water to boil crushed bones. When the kettle of boiled bones was cool we skimmed off the grease from the bone-marrow, mixed it with the pounded meat, poured this into buffalo heart-skins, and let it get solid. When it was taken out to eat—Ah, I have made myself hungry. . . .

"We Crow women had no trouble when our babies were born . . . everything was so different when I was young. I was expecting a baby, of course, but was not worrying about it. One day while playing with some girl friends I felt a little, quick pain, and sat down, laughing about it. One of my friends guessed what was about to happen, and told my mother.

"But when my mother, and a wise-one, named Left-hand, came after me I did not wish to go to the lodge with them. 'Yes,' my mother urged, 'come. We have pitched a new lodge for you, daughter.'

"Left-hand's lodge was pitched near my mother's. I noticed now that one of my father's best horses, with several fine robes on his back, was tied there. My father had already paid her for helping me, even before I needed help. Old Left-hand wore a buffalo robe with the hair-side out. Her face was painted with mud, her hair was tied in a big lump on her forehead, and in her hand she carried some of the-grass-that-buffalo-do-not-eat. Her eyes were so full of fun that I laughed at her as I might have laughed at a mud-clown. And yet she was serious, even solemn in all her actions.

"Now I must tell you about the lodge they had pitched for me. Left-hand stopped me just inside the door. A fire was burning, and my mother had made my bed, a soft buffalo robe folded with the hair side out. This bed was not to lie down on. Crow women do not lie down when their babies are born, nor even afterward, excepting to sleep when night comes, as others do. Two stakes had been driven into the ground for me to take hold of, and robes had been rolled up and piled against them, so that when I knelt on the bed-robe and took hold of the two stakes, my elbows would rest upon the pile of rolled robes.

"While I stood by the door, Left-hand took four live coals from the lodge-fire. One of these she placed on the ground at the door, then one to the left, halfway to the head [center of back], one at the head, and one in front of the bed-robe, which was on the right of the door, halfway between it and the head of the lodge. Then she dropped a little of the-grass-that-buffalo-do-not-eat upon each of these coals, telling me to walk to the left, to go around to my bed [as the sun goes], stepping over the coals. . . .

"I had stepped over the second coal when I saw that I should have to *run* if I reached my bed-robe in time. I *jumped* the third coal, and the *fourth,* knelt down on the robe, took hold of the two stakes; and my first child, Pine-fire, was there with us.

"It was always like this, in the old days. There must be some reason for the change. I have wondered about it. Perhaps it is because women have grown proud. Yes, I believe that this must be the reason." . . .

[Pretty-Shield remembered a battle when she was eight.] "Yes," she said, shortly, "a woman won that fight, and the men never tell about it. . . . Arrows were coming among the lodges, and bullets. . . .

"Several horses were wounded and were screaming with their pain. One of them fell down near my mother's lodge that was not yet half pitched. Lying there behind that pack I did not cover my eyes. I was looking all the time, and listening to everything. I saw Strikes-two, a woman sixty years old, riding around the camp on a gray horse. She carried only her root-digger, and she was singing her medicine-song, as though Lacota bullets and arrows were not flying around her. I heard her say, 'Now all of you sing, "They are whipped. They are running away," and keep singing these words until I come back.'

"When the men and even the women began to sing as Strikes-two told them, she rode out straight at the Lacota, waving her root-digger and singing that song. I *saw* her, I *heard* her, and my heart swelled, because she was a woman.

"The Lacota, afraid of her medicine, turned and ran away. The fight was won, and by a woman," she said excitedly. Then, sorrowfully, "We lost three good men in the fighting."

AN UPROOTED PEOPLE: NATIVE AMERICANS

48. Trail of Tears

Despite a Supreme Court ruling in their favor, thousands of Native Americans from the so-called Five Civilized Tribes—Cherokees, Chickasaws, Choctaws, Creeks, and Seminoles—including fifteen thousand Cherokees in 1838 alone, were forced by President Andrew Jackson's army to leave their long-established farms in Georgia and Alabama to move to a new reservation assigned to them in the Indian Territory. They had to leave in winter on short notice, with inadequate supplies, harrassed by their former neighbors and brokenhearted by their losses. This painting of their journey is somewhat idealized (there were very few wagons), but it shows the women with heavy burdens, walking west. Painting by Robert Lindneux. Courtesy of Woolaroc Museum, Bartlesville, Oklahoma.

49. *Arikara Woman*

The artist George Catlin depicted Pshan-Shaw ("Sweet-scented Grass"), an Arikara chief's daughter, during his 1832 explorations in the western territories. The twelve-year-old Pshan-Shaw wears a dress made of soft sheepskin, intricately decorated with quillwork rosettes and tiny beads; her buffalo-hide robe has a quilled sunburst design—all evidence of women's artistic achievements. George Catlin, painting. Courtesy of the National Museum of American Art, Smithsonian Institution, Washington, D.C. Gift of Mrs. Joseph Harrison, Jr.

50. Dressing Buffalo Skins
Catlin was amazed at the softness and resistance to water of Indian women's buffalo skins, and he admiringly described the quality of all their work. The women here are Comanches. George Catlin, drawing. Courtesy of the National Museum of American Art, Smithsonian Institution, Washington, D.C. Gift of Mrs. Joseph Harrison, Jr.

51. Mandan Village

The Mandan villages Catlin depicted were those of a settled agricultural people, living in homes spacious enough to hold twenty to forty people in fifty-foot-diameter shelters. In 1836, four years after his visit, a devastating smallpox epidemic ignited by one steamboat passenger on the Missouri River killed almost two-thirds of the Plains Indian people, destroying most of their culture as well. George Catlin, drawing. Courtesy of the National Museum of American Art, Smithsonian Institution, Washington, D.C. Gift of Mrs. Joseph Harrison, Jr.

52. *Pima Basket Weaver*

Indian women of many areas were noted for their beautifully designed baskets. This Pima woman in Arizona is weaving a large winter-storage basket for corn, beans, or wheat. Courtesy of Arizona Historical Society, Tucson. Photo no. 26024.

53. Grinding Grain on a Stone Metate
The process of grinding corn was so important to Native American life that women
cherished their personal grinding stones and developed many songs and rituals to
accompany their work. Courtesy of the National Anthropological Archives, Smithsonian Institution, Washington, D.C. Negative no. 2688.

Emigrants and Immigrants

NINETEENTH-CENTURY American women, white or black, free or enslaved, had to cope with the effects of massive westward migration. It was not at all unusual for a woman to move her household half a dozen times within a few years, at any stage of her life. As land in western New York State and beyond the Appalachians opened to settlement after the Revolution, heavy wagons journeyed by the hundreds through Albany or the Cumberland Gap while homemade flatboats carried entire families and their few possessions from western Pennsylvania down the Ohio River to new settlements in Kentucky, Ohio, or Illinois. Other settlers, such as Rebecca Burlend, were immigrants from Europe. Like the pilgrims and redemptioners of the seventeenth and eighteenth centuries, they endured the hard voyage to the New World and the difficult adaptation to entirely new living conditions.

Unstable frontier conditions existed from upstate New York and Michigan to Illinois, Missouri, and Texas. Women far from childhood homes and relatives could be victimized by unscrupulous "swindlers" like the one described in an ad in a Kentucky newspaper. In this case, it was bigamy; a man could desert his wife and move on to others with near impunity. Or dream-filled husbands might dash off to the western mines in search of adventure and riches, leaving women to maintain families and farms and businesses for years at a time, alone. Among New Englanders, a few women accompanied their sea-captain husbands on whaling ships, but most wives of sailors stayed behind to cope alone. Meanwhile, Mexican-American women in the West were being uprooted by the new Anglo settlers whose government replaced Mexico's in mid-century. Many Spanish-speaking Americans lost title to their lands, experienced the denigration of their long-established culture, and were reduced to penury and servitude.

Newly settled frontier women lived in crude log cabins or sod huts, reproducing the subsistence economy of earlier generations, no matter what their background or class. The log cabins that awaited Rebecca Burlend and Eliza Farnham were very different from both women's previous homes. Women coped, with humor if possible, and longed for improvements; they had good reason to concur with nineteenth-century ideologists about the importance of their "civilizing" function in society. This was one reason women like Elise Waerenskjold and Mary Austin Holley wrote letters or books about their new environments and encouraged more settlers to follow.

One of the great sagas of the nineteenth century was the overland wagon migration to Oregon Territory and California during the 1840s and 1850s. The promise of fertile land, healthful climate, and then gold was as exciting to many women as to men. At the same time, Mormons organized their two-thousand-mile handcart trek to the new Zion of Salt Lake City and built their own utopian society. Some emigrants did not survive these trips, but the many who did, like Catherine Scott Coburn and Abigail Scott Duniway or Tabitha Brown or Mary Ann Hafen, were resourceful women, proud of their accomplishment. Nineteenth-century America was a land of uprooted people, all urgently affirming and searching for economic and family stability—which existed more as an ideal than as a reality.

The *Llavera* Had Various Duties

Hispanic women had been among the settlers of present-day California and the Southwest for nearly two hundred years before the area was ceded by Mexico to the United States in the mid-nineteenth century. Eulalia Perez, who grew up in Loreta, Mexico, moved to California with her husband in 1810 and later became the *llavera*—keeper of the keys—at the San Gabriel Mission from 1821 to 1835. She was ninety-seven years old when she dictated this memoir of her experiences to Thomas Savage in Dec. 1877.

From Eulalia Perez, "Una vieja y sus recuerdos dictados," trans. Erlinda Gonzales-Berry, in Joan M. Jensen, *With These Hands* (New York: Feminist Press, 1981), pp. 47–49. The original Spanish document is in Bancroft Library, University of California, Berkeley. ❖

After consulting among themselves, the priests brought me the mission keys. This was in 1821, if I remember correctly. I do remember that my daughter Maria Rosario was seven years old. She became very ill and was looked after by Father Jose Sanchez, who gave her much skillful care; it was by this good fortune that we did not lose her. I was at that time the *llavera*.

The *llavera* had various duties. In the first place, she passed out daily rations. To do this, she had to count nuns, the single men, the day laborers, the saddle cowboys, the bareback cowboys, and also the married couples. In short, she saw to the supplies for the Indian people and for the priests' kitchen. She held the key to the clothes storeroom which contained the cotton goods for clothing for single and married women and for children. She was also charged with cutting clothes for the men.

It was my duty also to cut and sew clothing and other articles to cover the cowboys from head to foot—that is, the saddle cowboys. The bareback cowboys received no more than one cotton blanket and a breechcloth. But the saddle cowboys dressed like the Spanish-speaking inhabitants, the upper classes; they received a shirt, a vest, a jacket, trousers, a hat, boots, shoes, spurs. For their horse, a saddle, a bridle, and a lariat. Each cowboy also received a cumberbund of Chinese silk, a fine handkerchief, or whatever there might be in the storeroom.

Everything concerned with the making of clothes was done under my direction. I would cut and fit, while my five daughters sewed the pieces. When the work load was overwhelming, I would tell the priest, and he would then hire for pay some women from Los Angeles. In addition, I attended to the enormous laundry, the wine presses, and the crushing machines which rendered the oil from olives, which I worked myself. I handled the distribution of tanned hides, chamois, sheep skins, Moroccan leather, flax handkerchiefs, nails, thread, silk— all the items related to the making of saddles, as well as what was necessary in the belt and shoe-making shop.

Every eight days I delivered rations for the troops and the servants of the upper-classes—beans, maize, garbanzos, lentils, candles, soap. To help me, I had been given an Indian servant, Lucio. Whenever necessary, one of my daughters did the work I could not complete. . . .

In the San Gabriel Mission there were many neophytes [converts]. The married ones lived on their ranches while their children were young. There were two divisions for unmarried persons—one for the women, called the nunnery, and another for the men.

Little girls of seven, eight, and nine years were brought to the nunnery and reared there until they left to marry. They were cared for by an Indian nun, who was called "Mother Superior." The mayor had charge of the division for the single young men. Every evening both divisions were locked up and I was given the keys, which I in turn gave to the Fathers.

A blind Indian named Andresillo stood at the convent door and called out the name of each girl to enter. If any girl was missing, a search was initiated the following day, and the girl would be brought to the convent. Her mother, if she had one, was also brought in and punished for having kept her daughter away, and the girl was locked up for having been careless about arriving punctually.

In the morning the girls were taken out; first they went to Mass with Father Zalvidea, for he spoke Indian; afterwards to the kitchen to have breakfast, which on feast days sometimes consisted of *champurrado* (a mixture of chocolate and maize *atole,* gruel) with sugar and bread. On ordinary days, they usually had *pozole* (hominy and meat). After breaking fast, each girl went to a task which had been assigned beforehand. Her job might be at the loom, or in the sewing room, or unloading—whatever needed to be done. . . . All work ceased at eleven, and everyone came to the dining room to eat *pozole* and vegetables at twelve. At one they returned to their jobs. The work day ended at sundown when everyone returned to the dining area for a supper of *atole* and meat or plain *atole*. . . .

It was I, with my daughters, who made the chocolate, the oil, the candy, the lemonade. I made so much lemonade that some of it was even bottled and sent to Spain.

364

Is This America?

This excerpt from a narrative by Rebecca Burlend (1793–1872), who emigrated with her husband and children from Yorkshire, England, to Pike County, Illinois, in 1831, illustrates the experiences and reactions of thousands of women immigrants to the frontier. Whether they came from the eastern states or from Europe, they often left home with great reluctance. But their "submission," like Burlend's, was not entirely passive or irrational; Burlend recognized that economic difficulties required a desperate attempt to improve the family's welfare, and she even encouraged her husband to continue the trip when he would otherwise have given it up. Burlend describes a three-month, seven-thousand-mile journey, which ended at dusk at an empty riverbank landing in a seemingly uninhabited wilderness—a questionable promised land indeed!

When her husband finally located their friend's log cabin two miles away, she found it grotesque. A few months later, as their first harvest ripened, it was Burlend who had to save both the crop and her husband's life. Curing infected wounds and blood poisoning without modern antibiotics, or harvesting a wheat crop with the help of a child in order to prevent bankruptcy and starvation, certainly proved the value of a woman's labor within the home and on the farm.

From Rebecca Burlend and Edward Burlend, *A True Picture of Emigration,* ed. Milo Milton Quaife (1848; reprint, New York: Lakeside Classics, Citadel Press, 1968), pp. 7–14, 17–18, 40–44, 47–50, 89–92.

❖

Whatever may have been our success in America, I can attribute but little of it to myself; as I gave up the idea of ending my days in my own country with the utmost reluctance, and should never have become an emigrant, if obedience to my husband's wishes had left me any alternative. His motives, briefly stated, were these:—In the year 1817 we took a small farm at a village in Yorkshire on a lease for fourteen years, and as corn was at that time selling well, the rent was fixed at too high a rate for us to obtain a comfortable livelihood. We did indeed by dint of great industry and strict economy, maintain our credit to the end of the lease; but the severe struggles we had to endure to meet our payments, the gradual diminution of our little property, and the entire absence of any prospects of being able to supply the wants of a large family had tended effectually to fix my husband's purpose of trying what could be done in the western world. We accordingly disposed of our little furniture, settled our pecuniary affairs, and ultimately began our long journey the last week in August 1831.

. . . [We went] from the centre of Yorkshire to Liverpool, self, husband, and five children, the eldest a boy about nine years old, two others we were leaving behind, the one my eldest son engaged as an under teacher in a boarding school, the other my eldest daughter serving also in a respectable family. To persons such as we were, who had never been forty miles from home, a journey by waggon and railway, where every hour presents the eye with something new, does not afford the best opportunity for reflection; we in consequence reached Liverpool before we fully felt the importance of the step we were taking. . . .

. . . My dear husband, who before had displayed nothing but hardihood, on this occasion had almost played the woman. After a deep silence I not unfrequently observed his eyes suffused with tears, which though unnoticed by him, fell in quick succession down his sunbrowned cheeks. We were six days in this abode, and I may venture to assert that he did not spend six hours of the time in the forgetfulness of sleep.

At last the day dawned on which we were to embark. . . . That morning he addressed me in the following manner: "O Rebecca, I cannot do it, I cannot do it! . . . Bad as our prospects are in England we must go back! Such another night as the last has been I cannot survive! this terrible suspense and anxiety tears me in pieces."

Sentiments like these a few months ago would have been hailed with delight, and even then I must confess I felt a sort of inward satisfaction, although I knew them to be rather the effects of his feelings than his mental decisions. If we returned I knew he could not be satisfed with his condition, still less with his present conduct. . . . Never before had I felt so much to devolve on me, and perhaps never in my life did I so much feel it my duty to practise self-denial. My native land was as dear to me as ever: my two children, to whom I had bidden adieu, were strong ties. But the consciousness that it was my duty to bear up the sinking spirits of my partner, left me only one course to adopt. For a moment I raised my eyes to him "who sitteth above the water-floods," and with feelings I am not able to depict, broke silence as follows;—

"I admit, my dear husband, that our situation is a very trying one; but remember how often and how long you have resolved to go to America; hitherto we have experienced nothing that we did not anticipate; and should any calamity befall us on our journey, you have adopted emigration only from a con-viction that it would tend to the good of the family; and the Almighty is as able to preserve us and our children across the seas or in America as he is in England. Besides, if we return, we have broken up our home and sold our furniture, and should be worse situated than ever; let us even go, and look to Providence for success." The above advice on my part operated like a charm. All that has been said of the effects of martial music was here realized. His answer was rather in deed than in word. In two hours more our luggage was removed from the wag-gon, where it had just been placed with a view of returning home, to the ship in which we had taken our berths. The remainder of the day till four o'clock was spent in procuring stores, cooking utensils, &c., necessary for our voyage. . . .

[A two-month voyage took them to New Orleans, followed by a thirteen-hundred mile steamboat journey up the Mississippi.]

The time occupied in passing from New Orleans to St. Louis was about twelve days. . . .

The place at which we intended to leave the river was not more than one hundred and twenty miles from St. Louis; we therefore comforted ourselves with the idea that we should soon be there. We were finally to disembark at Phillip's Ferry, according to the directions sent by the aforementioned Mr. B. to his brother. We should then be within two miles of his residence. Mr. B., therefore, and Phillip's Ferry, occupied our thoughts almost to the exclusion of every other subject. We had already travelled nearly seven thousand miles. Our food had been principally dried provisions. For many long weeks we had been oppressed with anxious suspense; there is therefore no cause for wonder, that, jaded and worn out as we were, we felt anxious to be at our destined situation. Our enquiries of the sailors 'how much further we had to go,' almost exhausted their patience. Already we had been on the vessel twenty-four hours, when just at nightfall the packet stopped: a little boat was lowered into the water, and we were invited to collect our luggage and descend into it, as we were at Phillip's Ferry; we were utterly confounded: there was no appearance of a landing place, no luggage yard, nor even a building of any kind within sight; we, however, at-tended to our directions, and in a few minutes saw ourselves standing by the brink of the river, bordered by a dark wood, with no one near to notice us or tell us where we might procure accommodation or find harbour. This happened, as before intimated, as the evening shades were rapidly settling on the earth, and the stars through the clear blue atmosphere were beginning to twinkle. It was in the middle of November, and already very frosty. My husband and I looked at each other till we burst into tears, and our children observing our disquietude began to cry bitterly. Is this America, thought I, is this the reception I meet with after my long, painfully anxious and bereaving voyage? In vain did we look around us, hoping to see a light in some distant cabin. It was not, however, the time to weep: my husband determined to leave us with our luggage in search of a habitation, and wished us to remain where we then stood till he returned. Such a step I saw to be necessary, but how trying! Should he lose himself in the wood, thought I, what will become of me and my helpless offspring? He departed: I was left with five young children, the youngest at my breast. When I survey this portion of my history, it looks more like fiction than reality; yet it is the precise situation in which I was then placed. . . .

[Her husband found a house two miles away.]

It is however by no means to be understood that an American log house equals in comfort and convenience a snug English cottage. It is quite common to see, at least, one bed in the same room as that in which the fire is kept; a practice which invariably gives both the bed and house a filthy appearance. There was no chamber, only a sort of loft, constructed rather with a view to make the house warmer, than to afford additional room. Adjoining one side were a few boards nailed together in the form of a table, and supported principally by the timber in the wall. This was dignified with the name "sideboard." In the centre of the room, stood another small table, covered with a piece of coarse brown calico; this was the dining table. The chairs, four in number, were the most respectable furniture in the house, having bark of ichory platted for bottoms. Besides these there were two stools and a bench for common use,—a candlestick made from an ear of Indian corn, two or three trenchers and a few tin drinking vessels. One corner of the house was occupied with agricultural implements, consisting of large hoes, axes, &c., for stubbing, called in America grubbing, flails and wooden forks, all exhibiting specimens of workmanship rather homely. Various herbs were suspended from the roof with a view of being medicinally servicable, also two guns, one of them a rifle. There were also several hams and sides of bacon, smoked almost till they were black; two or three pieces of beef, &c. Under one of the beds were three or four large pots filled with honey, of which Mrs. P. was not a little lavish, as she used it to every meal along with coffee. The furniture in the other room consisted of two beds and a hand-loom, with which the family wove the greater part of their own clothes. In the cellar I observed two or three large hewn tubs, full of lard, and a lump of tobacco, the produce of their own land, in appearance sufficient to serve an ordinary smoker his life. . . .

Towards the end of June our three acres of wheat began to look ripe, and we consequently had to consider how we should reap it; we had no sickles, nor were any to be had under a dollar each; we therefore, self and husband, resolved to go to our friend Mr. B., who lent us two, for which we were thankful enough, although they were poor ones. As we were returning home, my husband had the misfortune to stumble over a log of wood, and having a sickle in his hand, he pitched upon the edge of it with his knee, and cut it severely. We were then a mile from home, and the wound bled profusely. I bound it up with a handkerchief, and after a little faintness he was able to proceed. The next day, on examining the cut, we found it to be more serious than we had imagined: the symptoms were also bad; instead of being warm and irritable, it was cold and numb. In vain did we apply lotions, it kept growing worse and worse. The following day it began to swell very much, and to be exceedingly painful at a distance from the cut.

368 The pain took away his appetite for food, and symptoms of inflammation and fever became rapidly apparent. My situation requires no comment: I could not but perceive I was likely to lose my dearest early friend, and with him all visible means of supporting myself, or maintaining my family. I was almost driven to frenzy. Despair began to lay hold of me with his iron sinews; I longed to exchange situations with my husband; there was no one near to assist or encourage me. My eldest child alone manifested any signs of sympathy: the poor boy went up to his father's bed, and with affectionate and child-like simplicity said, "don't die, father, don't die." Meanwhile the swelling increased; my husband had taken nothing but a little coffee for two days. Here was a crisis. . . . I could not give it up. I fomented the swelling with increased diligence, till at length he began to perspire, and his leg to possess its wonted sensibility. A change for the better had evidently taken place, and by degrees all the bad symptoms disappeared.

On perceiving this, I felt myself the happiest woman on earth, although my situation was still embarrassing. Our wheat was quite ripe, indeed almost ready to shake, and if not cut soon, would be lost. We had no means of hiring reapers, and my husband could not stir out. I was therefore obliged to begin myself; I took my eldest child into the field to assist me, and left the next in age to attend to their father and take care of the youngest, which was still unweaned. I worked as hard as my strength would allow; the weather was intolerably hot, so that I was almost melted. In little more than a week, however, we had it all cut down. Meanwhile my husband had continued to mend, and was now able to leave his bed and sit in a chair, or rather on a stool placed near the wall for support to his back, and made further comfortable with the help of a pillow or two. The wheat was still unhoused, and exposed to the rays of the burning sun, by which it was in danger of being dried so as to waste on the slightest movement. It was absolutely necessary that it should be gathered together forthwith. Having neither horses nor waggon, we here encountered another difficulty. The work, however, could not be postponed. With a little trouble I got two strong rods, upon which I placed a number of sheaves near one end of them; I then caused my little son to take hold of the lighter end, and in this manner we gathered together the whole of the three acres. My partner had by this time so far recovered as to be able to move about with the help of a strong staff, or crutch, and thus he came to the door to shew me how to place the sheaves in forming the stack. The reader may probably suppose I am endeavouring to magnify my own labours, when I tell him I reaped, carried home, and stacked our whole crop of wheat, consisting, as before stated, of three acres, with no other assistance than that of my little boy under ten years of age.

To Warn All Widows of the Swindler 369

Uprooted frontier women sometimes found themselves victimized by equally uprooted frontier men. Since marriage gave a husband the right to all his wife's property, and since personal histories were not easy to verify, unscrupulous men could prey on orphaned girls or needy widows and then disappear, leaving them penniless. The following newspaper ad shows one form of redress.

From *Kentucky Reporter* (Lexington), September 5, 1817, quoted in Henry B. Fearon, *Narrative of a Journey of Five Thousand Miles . . . of America . . .*, 2d ed. (London: Longman, Hurst, Rees, Orme, and Brown, 1818), p. 244.

❖

TAKE NOTICE

And beware of the swindler JESSE DOUGHERTY, who married me in November last, and some time after marriage informed me that he had another wife alive and before I recovered, the villain left me, and took one of my best horses— one of my neighbors was so good as to follow him and take the horse from him, and bring him back. The said Dougherty is about forty years of age, five feet ten inches high, round-shouldered, thick lips, complexion and hair dark, grey eyes, remarkably ugly and good-natured, and very fond of ardent spirits, and by profession a notorious liar. This is therefore to warn all widows to beware of the swindler, as all he wants is their property, and they may go to the devil for him after he gets that. Also, all persons are forewarned from trading with the said Dougherty, with the expectation of receiving pay from my property, as I consider the marriage contract *null* and *void* agreeably to law: you will therefore pay no attention to any lies he may tell you of his property in this county. The said Dougherty has a number of wives living, perhaps eight or ten, (the number not positively known,) and will no doubt, if he can get them, have eight or ten more. I believe that is the way he makes his living.

MARY DODD.

Livingston county, Ky. Sept. 5, 1817.

The Veritable House

Even in towns, frontier women could not count on the conveniences or the servants that had become common in the East. Eliza Woodson Farnham (1815–64) was one of several newly transplanted women who wrote popular books about the experience of frontier living. She had traveled to central Illinois in 1835 to visit relatives and married a young lawyer, who bought a home in recently settled Tremont. Like many other women writers of the time, she noted the contrast between the frontier towns described in lithographed advertisements and the actuality of littered and dirty streets and buildings. Widowed in 1843, Farnham later led a group of women to establish a settlement in California in the 1850s.

From Eliza Woodson Farnham, *Life in Prairie Land* (New York: Harper and Brothers, 1846), pp. 145–49.   ❖

On the morning of the third day, the house was reported to be ready. . . . We alight at the back door of a building, so small that I fancy it is one of our outbuildings, till the sight of some chairs, turned helter-skelter over each other, and a Franklin stove standing within, convinces me that this is the veritable house. It was reported to be small, and I do not find the report exaggerated. The door by which we enter is so disproportioned to the house, that one thinks it was designed to allow the house itself to walk out. It is made of heavy rough oak boards, and parts in the middle, as if it opened into a carriage-house. It is altogether one of the most extraordinary of doors; but this is explained by reference to the fact, that the building has once been used for a grocery store. The adjacent lot, on the right as we enter, is occupied by a gaping cellar, all uncovered, and affording, therefore, readier ingress than egress to sundry small pigs, chickens, et cet., who perambulate the vicinity. Its walls, however, are so weather-washed, that one of them offers a practicable way of escape when the wits of the small prisoners are sufficiently collected to try it. Beyond, on the same side, the near view is diversified by the rears of several wooden stores of different lengths, the ground about each being picturesquely ornamented with broken crockery, soiled sheets of wrapping paper, rifled boxes, and crates. On the left, is a row of three buildings, which were afterwards called "Globe Row," from the fact that the "Globe Hotel" was opened in the one farthest from us. They contain a room each and an attic. The middle one is occupied by our nearest neighbors, the family of a worthy mechanic recently from Philadelphia. The old lady's first call was made in about half an hour after our arrival, and accompanied by the tender of a barrel of rain-water, a kindness which those only can appreciate who have undertaken to clean such a house with lime-water, and that to be brought a distance of some dozen rods. Now that I am speaking of water, I may as well add, that there was no well belonging to our house, and the nearest one was at the distance just named.

Thus much for the view from the back door. I should add, that all these buildings were unenclosed, and thus presented temptations which wrought lamentable corruption in the morals of the swine. Young pigs were thus tempted, nay, heartlessly allured in all manner of offences which grow out of too close an investigation of pails, kettles, boxes, mops, brooms, and other articles that usually consort at the back doors of dwellings which have neither closet, cellar, chamber, nor entry.

But I must leave moralizing, and finish my picture. We shall have to pass through the house to get a front view, and on our way may as well take a cursory glance at its finish, proportion, and contents. The entire tenement is sixteen feet by twenty. It has a door and window in each end, and a partition of very thin boards dividing it into two rooms. One of these is nine feet deep, the other eleven. The preponderance in size has been given to the rear apartment, which is finished inside with boards of the same description as those outside, and put on in the same manner; except that, instead of lapping, they do not quite meet, and therefore hold out the most unlimited invitations to winds and vermin, to enter and examine the premises. Nearly opposite the doorway, for as yet there is no door, which leads to the other room, stands a Franklin stove, making every possible effort to look social, as if it had been an old acquaintance in some of the pleasant sitting-rooms of the east. But it appears to great disadvantage, being besmeared with a mixture of paste and tar, with which Mr. F. has been trying to fasten strong brown paper over the cracks in the ceilings. Half a dozen green wooden chairs stand about, trying to give a home look to the room. But some appear to have become disgusted with the effort, and turned themselves on their heads, in the laps of their neighbors.

We pass through into the next room. This is got up in very creditable style. The proportions, to be sure, are not just what one may call elegant, being sixteen feet one way and nine the other. But the walls are plastered, and there is a very large front door, with a very small window beside it, and a narrow side door, which affords an advantageous view of the cellar aforesaid, and the dead wall of a brown framed store, about thirty feet in length, beyond it. But the grand prospect is from the front. Here is the little niche left between the grocery next door, and Globe Row, which will be a front yard when there is a fence thrown across it. At present it is a very interesting area of black soil, on which the vegetation has been so often disturbed by ploughing matches between gentlemen who combine in themselves all the advantages of team, plough, and driver, that there is not a blade on its surface. Beyond lies the pride of the town—the Public

Square—an open space of ten acres, which has had trees enough lithographed for it to cover it three times with a dense forest, but which yet remains an obstinate and ungrateful piece of prairie turf.

. . . Our house . . . has neither cellar nor chamber. The entire establishment, including the privilege of bringing water from a distant neighbor and cultivating any degree of intimacy which fancy might dictate with the swine of the town, most of whom were distinguished for their pedestrian powers, consists of these sixteen feet by twenty, inclosed within the four walls already described. Mr. F. had, it is true, endeavored to avail himself of a trap-door in the back room by making an excavation beneath it sufficient to contain a firkin of butter or a small basket of vegetables. But this did not promise to be eminently serviceable, inasmuch as one foot of the Franklin stood upon the corner of the door, so that the latter could never be opened without first swinging the former round; a process not easy of accomplishment, and attended with imminent risk to the pipe. The floors were thoroughly wet, and exhibited every evidence of having been recently visited with other implements of cleaning than those usually employed by females. But they were still far from clean; and we addressed ourselves therefore, broom and cloth in hand, to bring affairs to a more wholesome state. If any delicate lady asks how I could have undertaken the scrubbing myself, I reply, that if I had not, no one would. No consideration could have procured the assistance of a stout Irish or colored woman, because none such were there. I might have sat myself down, folded my hands, and wept over the disorder; but that would never have brought order out of it. A much pleasanter and more efficient method was the one I adopted. It cleaned and curtained my windows, brought my stove out from the rubbish which covered it, made my chairs fit for use, and restored the floors to a comfortable degree of cleanliness before supper. Our first meal under my auspices, consisted of crackers, cheese, and cold water, served on the lid of my bureau toilet. Our first night's rest, and welcome rest it was too, was taken on a straw bed laid in the six green chairs.

The Memory of Old Norway

Women played a productive role in maintaining communication between immigrants in the New World and friends and relatives in the home country. Elise Waerenskjold (1815–95), who emigrated from Norway to Texas in 1847, was one of the most articulate of such women. In Norway, she had been a schoolteacher and an editor of *Norway and America,* a magazine promoting emigration. In America, she wrote articles and letters back to her "beloved native land," describing living conditions and persuading others to follow. Nineteen Norwegian families lived in her vicinity, all prospering and not wishing to return. Waerenskjold had divorced her first husband in Norway because of his drinking, so the local temperance society was important to her. Her work on behalf of projects like the community reading club was as significant as her help on the ranch and the care of her children. Her husband was murdered in 1867, and she managed their ranch alone for the rest of her life. She never did return to Norway.

373

From Elise Waerenskjold, *The Lady with the Pen*, ed. C. A. Clausen (Northfield, Minn.: Norwegian-American Historical Association, 1961), pp. 44–48.

❖

Four Mile Prairie

January 6, 1857

[To Mrs. Thomine Dannevig:]

It was a great as well as unexpected joy, after such a long period of time, to receive the large package of letters from you, for which I thank you sincerely.

You must not think that I have really given up hope of seeing you again, but for some years yet we cannot afford to go, and besides the children are still too small to get much benefit or pleasure out of such a trip. If all goes well for the next seven or eight years, however, it could happen that we might be able to visit our beloved native land.

No doubt you know that cattle raising is our principal means of livelihood. We do not plan to sell the cows, just the steers, until we can acquire about two hundred calves a year. This spring we can expect about seventy. Cows and calves are now $15 each, and a three-year-old unbroken ox costs about the same. When it is trained for work, it costs much more. We have four mares, a horse, and a mule. The latter is unusually gentle and sure-footed. It is the children's and my riding horse. Niels sits in my lap and Otto behind me. We do have a four-wheeled carriage but very seldom use it.

We have sixty-two sheep, and this month and next we are expecting many lambs. I help clip the sheep, but I am not very good at it. I can do only one while the others clip two, whereas Wilhelm can keep up with anyone. He is very quick at all kinds of work. I do not know how many pigs we have, not because we have so many but because pigs are so difficult to keep track of.

Because I hate liquor, it is a great joy to me that Wilhelm never tastes it. He organized a temperance society in our settlement, and since then the community has become so respectable and sober that it is a real pleasure. All of us Norwegians, about eighty persons counting young and old, can come together for a social gathering without having strong drink, but we do have coffee, ale, milk, and mead at our gatherings, and food in abundance. In the older Norwegian settlement [Brownsboro] there is a disgusting amount of drinking, among both Norwegians and Americans. A Norwegian boy shot himself as a result of his addiction to drink, and recently an American was stabbed to death by another American, likewise because of drunkenness. Drinking, quarreling, and fighting are common here. Yes, liquor destroys both body and soul.

You are really going to get a short letter in answer to your long one, but this is the twelfth letter I have written in a week, and I have three more to write by noon tomorrow—and you can well imagine how little time I have for correspondence.

374

[Four Mile Prairie, Autumn, 1857]
[To the editor of *Norway and America:*]

Even though we Norwegians find ourselves content and happy in our new home, which is thousands of miles away from our mother country, we still cherish in our hearts the memory of old Norway and our countrymen over there. Every possible link with the beloved land of our birth is important and precious to us. For that reason, the Norwegian, Swedish, and Danish immigrants of this little settlement of Four Mile Prairie have organized a reading club. As the group comprises only sixteen families, the total fund for the purchase of books is very small ($22). We are presuming, therefore, to ask our countrymen who may be interested in their distant brothers and sisters in Texas for a gift of some books, which may be delivered to the publisher, Jacob Dybwad, of Christiania. We should appreciate it if the kind donors would write their names in the book or books that they are good enough to give. We shall gratefully welcome every book, new or old. Because I am personally acquainted with several of the publishers, I am taking the liberty of appealing to them for small donations. They must have many works that will not be sold out. Many good books of the older authors have perhaps little or no value in Norway, as they have been supplanted by the more recent writers. That is not the case here, where we so rarely have the opportunity to procure Norwegian books, since very few had the forethought to bring books with them when they left Norway. The various editors would do us a great service if they would reprint these lines in their respective newspapers.

For those who may be interested, I shall add that there are three Norwegian settlements here with approximately three hundred inhabitants, including eight Danes and one Swede. The oldest settlement [Normandy], begun in 1845, is about as large as this one and the newest one combined. Most of the people were poor when they came, but all of them have prospered more or less. Families can be found who were in debt when they arrived but are now well off. Texas, on the whole, is a remarkably good place for the poor, as they can always get work with good pay and soon become independent. This is all the more true, because government land is cheap—half a dollar an acre. All white men are treated with equal courtesy. For those back home who have been accustomed to servants, life here would perhaps be less pleasant, since help is difficult to obtain and very expensive.

In 1854 a theological candidate, A. E. Fridrichsen, was called as pastor to Four Mile Prairie. That same year, a small, simple church was begun in the settlement and was dedicated immediately after the pastor's arrival the following year. Each member paid from $3 to $8 yearly toward his salary, not including the festal offerings and fees for baptisms, funerals, and the like. Some widows and spinsters subscribed $1 or $2. It would be fine if we could get a Christian-minded minister, for Pastor Fridrichsen plans to return home this winter. But he definitely must not come expecting any temporal gain, because he cannot count on more than $300 annually and a simple house, from all three settlements.

In closing, I pray that all my friends and acquaintances in Norway will accept affectionate greetings from

> Elise Waerenskjold
> (nee Tvede)

> Four Mile Prairie
> October 16, 1858

[To Mrs. Thomine Dannevig:]

You probably heard from your brother, to whom I have written a couple of times this summer, that I again expected a little boy, and now I can tell you, God be praised, that the little baby arrived happy and well on the fourth of this month. I cannot tell you how glad I was that everything went well because, after all, I am no longer young, and I was worried for fear I might have to leave my beloved children. Neither Wilhelm nor I have a single relative in this country, so it isn't easy to say what he would have done with the children if I had died. It is absolutely against the custom of this country for a white girl to keep house for a widower—and as for a stepmother, well, they are seldom good.

But, thank God, I am entirely well again and hope that the Almighty will grant me yet a few years with my sweet little boys. The little one shall be named Thorvald August after your dear Thorvald and a little German friend I had on the emigrant ship. I can truly say that the neighbors here are very kind to each other on occasions such as this, for they look after one another and provide food. That is to say, our neighbors in the country; the city women, on the other hand, follow the American customs. . . .

> Prairieville P.O.
> Kaufman County
> September 29, 1868

To Mrs. Kaja Poppe:

Health conditions have been excellent in our community this summer, but many of the old neighbors have left us and moved to Bosque, which is a more healthful district. It is also a better wheat-producing area, and there is always a good market for grain. I had sowed fifteen bushels of wheat, but the venture failed because we were struck by an Egyptian plague—grasshoppers. They came here toward the end of October and left us only when they had eaten up everything green. A most unusual spell of drought followed; we were unable to plant

376 again until just before Christmas. Then, in the spring, came a new spawn of grasshoppers that ate the sprouting wheat. When they were big enough to fly, they disappeared. The wheat had cost me $50—so it was a great loss. Moreover, I lost over half my sheep as a result of starvation, five horses, and twenty-seven milk cows, not to mention the colts. The dry grass, which the grasshoppers couldn't destroy, was burned by the prairie fires, causing us great trouble. I had never realized that grasshoppers could fly so high. The air was filled with them as far as one could see. Otherwise we have had a good harvest.

Two Texas Households

Mary Austin Holley (1784–1846), the cousin of Stephen Austin, a founder of Texas, visited Texas several times, and her descriptive books were intended to encourage both more emigration and annexation of the territory by the United States. The availability of slave labor there, and the distribution by Mexico of huge tracts of free land to American *empresarios* who would bring in other settlers during the 1820s and 1830s, led to affluence and ease for some and the opposite for others. Similar conditions could be found in many areas of the expanding South.

From Mary Austin Holley, *Letters of an Early American Traveller* (Dallas: Southwest Press, 1933), pp. 117–18; Mary Austin Holley, *The Texas Diary, 1835–38* (Austin: University of Texas, 1965), pp. 60, 66, 67–68. By permission of The Center for American History, University of Texas at Austin.

❖

Bolivar, Texas, December 1831.

Brazoria has, already, some families of education and refinement. In one of my visiting excursions, I called on Mrs. _____, who was, I found, from my native state, (Connecticut,) a circumstance sufficient to place us, at once, on the most sociable footing. The family had not been here long, and their *cabin* was not yet built. They occupied a temporary shed among the trees, or *camp,* as they call it here, not impervious to the light, though there was no window. A white curtain supplied the place of door. The single apartment contained three or four beds, as white as snow. Books, glass, china, and other furniture in polite usage, were arranged in perfect neatness about the room, as best suited the present exigence. It was Sunday evening. Mrs. _____ was seated in a white cambric wrapper and tasteful cap. The children around the door, and the servants, were at their several occupations, or sitting at leisure about the temporary fire-place without. The whole scene was an exhibition of peace and happiness. I gazed upon it with emotions of admiration and delight. . . .

In Texas, most domestic business is transacted in the open air. There has not been time to attend to the supernumerary wants of convenient kitchens. The most simple process is used for culinary purposes, and one is often reminded that hands were made before tongs, shovel and poker, as well as before knives and forks. Rumford and Franklin seemed to have laboured in vain, and the amusing melody of mother Goose is almost realised; for pots, kettles, and frying-pans, in playful confusion, greet the eyes of visiters and enjoy the benefit of fresh air, as well as of severe scrutiny.

March 22, 1837

Pleasant. Went to Quintana in the wagon—E.____ H.____, Mrs. Perry, J. Bryan & myself stopped at Mrs. McKinney's. Met there Mr. St. John & Mr. N. Williams. Ball at Velasco this evening—went over in a skiff after dark. Returned at midnight—Quite a genteel ball. The first opening of the new house which is in the form of an L—being a long room with wings—one for dancing, the other for supper—at which the ladies, 60 in number, were seated. Supper handsome—dressed cakes & sugar pyramids—other confectionary, oranges brought from N Orleans—much order & taste. The rooms new & painted white, have a neat appearance. The ball room was brilliantly lighted by rows of sperm candles over the doors, windows & all round. Mirrors were ranged at each end under which were hair sofas. Round the ceiling were flags festooned displaying the Texas Star, which also waved from the centre cake on the supper table. Had the music of 2 violins mingled with the roar of the sea, upon which you look from the gallery of the house.

March 31, 1837

We passed a month with Mrs. Sayre agreeably, but without variety enough to make a record each day. We read, played the piano, & guitar, & back gammon—& conversed a great deal. Rode & walked, & fished in the river. The fish (Buffalo & white cat) were so large as to make it difficult to get them in—Some days we had company, neighbors & from a distance.

I finished reading Zavala's Travels in the U.S. in Spanish—I like the work & mean to get it. I had then my Spanish Telemachus. I also read the astronomical sermons of Chalmers which pleased me. Had never met with it. Do not think his argument conclusive. It is a subject that puzzles me. I found there Latrobe's rambles in Mexico, a small but valuable book, giving details of that country I have not before met with.

378

April 7, 1837

Wrote to Horace—took a ride to Oyster Creek, Emily behind me, & Henrietta behind Joel. The ride is charming through the forest—the trees magnificent—meeting nearly at the top, & impervious to the sun. In some places the cane is 30 feet high—took a look at the lake—a lovely spot, nearly round, & surrounded by lofty timber. Will be a glorious residence, no doubt, a hundred years hence. The creek makes the eastern boundary of the Bolivar estate. On the opposite side lives Old Rock, as they call him, & his family. They have cut away the cane & built a house, & enclosure of it. The house is shaped like a tent, in the middle was a fire, over which on a cross piece hung an iron kettle boiling some beef bones, strips of beef undergoing the process of jerking hung on other sticks; a fine looking intelligent boy, like our James, & a laughing, curly-headed, blue-eyed girl, 2–1/2 years old—rosy & fat, were seated round it. They were left in charge of the premises while the father & mother went to Bolivar for corn. On one side, on the ground were the rags which made the bed for the whole family (5 children). This was all the furniture. A red-headed girl of 7, in rags, served as a scare crow in the corn patch—nearby—the young cane disputing ground with its rival the corn—her neck was in blisters & excited my pity, adjoining the house were some turning tools & others—for making chairs &—also covered by canes. The man is a tinker at gun-locks, chairs & springs & wheels. The high cane on every side but the creek served as a barrier to their whole clearing, where neither axe, spade nor hoe had anything to do. I never saw, nor imagined so strange a scene. I can not describe the impression it made on me. What unaccountable poverty. I longed for clothes & food to give the children—& money to place them in better situations. *Jemmy & Betty,* in particular, took strong hold of my sympathy in spite of their rags & dirt.

Returning, full of the subject, we met the old people with the corn on their backs—she, a very wild woman, to appearance slipped off into the woods, retaining, it seems, so much of her sex to be susceptible of shame. He marched on his course & we stopped to talk with him. In his attire he resembled the pictures of Robinson Crusoe.

Life and Death on the Overland Trail

Women of all sorts and ages took part in the great mid-century migration westward to Oregon, California, and Mormon Utah. Catherine Scott Coburn's young cousin, with a small baby, hoped to find health by going west; Coburn's invalid mother feared death and found it. Both were in the same wagon caravan in 1852. Abigail Scott Duniway, Coburn's sister, kept a detailed journal of the trip and wrote her grandfather about the death.

From Catherine Scott Coburn, "Narrative," in Harvey Scott, *History of the Oregon Country,* vol. 3 (Cambridge, Mass.: Riverside Press, 1924), pp. 238–41; A. J. Scott [Duniway], letter to James Scott, in Kenneth L. Holmes, ed., *Covered Wagon Women,* vol. 5 (Glendale, Calif.: Arthur H. Clark, 1986), pp. 151–53. Original in David Duniway Collection, Salem, Oregon.

❖

The second day of April, 1852, dawned on Northern Illinois through a chilly mist of scurrying snow-flakes. For days, even weeks, previous to this morning, there had been the hurry of preparation as if for a momentous event discernible about a farm house in Groveland township, Tazewell County, of that state. . . . Through all the winter preceding the April morning when the final start was made, the fingers of the women and girls were busy providing additional stores of bedding and blankets, of stockings and sunbonnets, of hickory shirts and gingham aprons, that the family might be equipped for the trip, and not left destitute in case of failure to reach the goal in season, or of opportunity to replenish the stores from the meager and high-priced stocks of a new country. Ah! the tears that fell upon these garments, fashioned with trembling fingers by the flaring light of tallow candles; the heartaches that were stitched and knitted and woven into them, through the brief winter afternoons, as relatives that were to be left behind and friends of a lifetime dropped in to lend a hand in the awesome undertaking of getting ready for a journey that promised no return.

. . . The sale of surplus belongings had been made, the wagons, five stout vehicles, had been bought, and, gorgeous in green and yellow paint, and with stout canvas covers snugly adjusted over supple hickory bows, stood just beyond the yard gate, ready for human occupancy. The stores of bacon and flour, of rice and coffee, of brown sugar and hard-tack, had been carefully disposed, a hurried breakfast was taken, and the oxen, drawn by from two to five yokes to each wagon, soon drew the five wagons into line. Into three of these were stowed the belongings of the family, an old-fashioned group, consisting of a wife and nine children. The word was given, the sluggish oxen started, and the journey of more than two thousand miles was begun. . . .

One of our five wagons was occupied by a little family of three, a man and his pale-faced wife, who held closely to her bosom, on that trying morning of last good-byes, a babe of six months. Since the advent of this child, the mother had daily drooped and faded, and this journey was resolved upon in the hope of restoring her to health. A health journey! Think of it, ye who travel in palace cars, supplied with every luxury that modern ingenuity has brought to bear upon travel to make it a delightful pastime. A heavy wagon without springs, surmounted by strong canvas stretched smoothly over bows of new hickory, drawn together in a circle at the rear by a strong cord and made fast to the front bow; a canvas door, thrown backward over the wagon sheet when opened, and fastened with large horn buttons when closed, was provided to protect the weak woman from night dews and invading storms. A rifle, dread suggestion of possible encounters with Indians, hung from a leather strap against the bows on one side, and on the other dangled a canteen, a compass and a sunbonnet. The wagon bed was packed with boxes and bundles neatly stored; a feather bed and pillows, rolled together and tied with cord during the day, were at night made up for a couch, with quilts and blankets, in a space made vacant by the removal of the boxes; a low chair, sitting sideways, with barely room in front to place the feet, a space utilized by the babe, when tired, as a place to sit, the mother providing the handbreadth of floor at the expense of her own comfort, by lifting one foot to the side of the wagon.

Thus equipped, a weak woman with her babe started on a transcontinental journey of between 2000 and 3000 miles, across mountains, streams and arid plains, in search of health, and in this wagon home she lived and journeyed patiently, even cheerfully, during the months of weakness and homesickness, jolting over the uneven roads, hungering, with an invalid's feverish longing, for proper nourishment, yearning for rest and caring daily, with such assistance as her kind husband could render after the discharge of other wearing duties that were his portion during those months of trial, for the tired, restless babe. Finally The Dalles were reached, and here the heroic health seeker found a grave. Her faithful husband prepared the worn, emaciated body for burial, and was one of three men comprising the entire funeral cortege, to bear his wife to the peaceful rest of the earth's sheltering bosom. A health journey begun in expectancy, pursued in hope, ending in disappointment. . . .

❖

Bear River Valley, Ten Miles East of Soda Springs, July 18th 1852.

My Dear Grandfather; As Father at present has no taste for writing, it becomes my duty to commence the (at this time painful task) of writing to you.

Since we last addressed you, the mysterious, relentless hand of Death has visited us and we are now mourning the decease of our beloved Mother! On the morning of the twentieth of June she was taken with a violent diarrhea which was soon followed by crampings, and in the afternoon of the same day (being Sabbath) her immortal spirit took its flight, as we have every reason to believe to fairer worlds on high; She had never been in good health since leaving home, had never performed any work, and indeed had most of the time remained in the wagon. However the day before her death she appeared much better, and walked several miles, getting much overheated. We were traveling over a range of the Black Hills, and she walked because the roads were rough. I was sick that day, and had been for some days; and during the whole of my sickness she had manifested the greatest concern for my recovery, and as I afterwards learned had frequently remarked that she did not believe I would get well. I little thought on that last Saturday of her earthly career that she so soon would be called from this unfriendly world. On Sabbath morning, (I slept that night with her) she arose early, before I was awake, and remarked to father that she was sick; he immediately went to prescribing medicine, and two physicians passed in a short time, both of whom were called to her assistance. The diarrhea was soon checked but her constitution so long impaired by disease was unable to withstand the attack and she began to sink and every effort to arouse her was vain. She remarked that her destiny was fixed, and drawing the little children to her, kissed them affectionately and speaking of Willie [three years old], who was fondly caressing her and calling her name in the kindest manner, said, "bless his little life," and when father tried to get her to talk, she said she had a great deal to say "but" said she "I shall die with weakness." These were her last words, and dear Grandfather we now feel that we are bereft indeed! She had long felt willing to go at any time, and had felt for two months that she would not get through to Oregon. . . . She rests in peace thirty miles this side of Fort Laramie on the summit of an eminence that we have named Castle Hill.

Tears Would Avail Nothing

In 1846, the sixty-six-year-old widow Tabitha Brown refused to be afraid as she guided her much older brother-in-law through the wilderness. When she got to Oregon, she seized the opportunity for useful work. She later wrote this memoir for her children.

From Tabitha Brown in Joseph Gaston, *Portland, Oregon: Its History and Builders,* vol. 1 (Chicago: S.J. Clark Publishing, 1911), 388–91.

❖

Winter had set in. We were yet a long distance from any white settlement. The word was "fly, everyone that can, from starvation; except those who are compelled to stay by the cattle to recruit them for further travel." Mr. Pringle and Pherne insisted on my going ahead with Uncle John to try and save our lives. They were obliged to stay back a few days to recruit their cattle. They divided the last bit of bacon, of which I had three slices; I had also a cup full of tea. No bread. We saddled our horses and set off, not knowing that we should ever see each other again. Captain Brown was too old and feeble to render any assistance to me. I was obliged to ride ahead as a pilot, hoping to overtake four or five wagons that left camp the day before. Near sunset we came up with the families that had left that morning. They had nothing to eat, and their cattle had given out. We all camped in an oak grove for the night, and in the morning I divided my last morsel with them and left them to take care of themselves. I hurried Capt. Brown so as to overtake the three wagons ahead. We passed beautiful mountains and valleys, saw but two Indians in the distance during the day. In the afternoon, Captain Brown complained of sickness, and could only walk his horse at a distance behind. He had a swimming in his head, and a pain in his stomach. In two or three hours he became delirious and fell from his horse. I was afraid to jump down from my horse to assist him, as it was one that a woman had never ridden before. He tried to rise up on his feet but could not. I rode close to him and set the end of his cane, which I had in my hand, hard in the ground, to help him up. I then urged him to walk a little. He tottered along a few yards and then gave out. I then saw a little sunken spot a few steps ahead and led his horse to it, and with much difficulty got him raised to the saddle. I then told him to hold fast to the horse's mane and I would lead by the bridle. Two miles ahead was another mountain to climb over. As we reached the foot of it he was able to take the bridle in his own hands and we passed over safely into a large valley, a wide, solitary place, but no wagons in sight.

The sun was now setting, the wind was blowing, and the rain was drifting upon the sides of the distant mountains. Poor me! I crossed the plains to where three mountains' spurs met. Here the shades of night were gathering fast, and I could see the wagon tracks no further. Alighting from my horse, I flung off saddle and saddle-pack and tied the horse fast to a tree with a lasso rope. The captain asked me what I was going to do. My answer was, "I am going to camp for the night." He gave a groan and fell to the ground. I gathered my wagon sheet, which I had put under my saddle, flung it over a projecting limb of a tree, and made me a fine tent. I then stripped the captain's horse, and tied him, placed saddle, blankets, and bridles under the tent, then helped up the bewildered old gentleman and introduced him to his new lodgings upon the bare ground. His senses were gone. Covering him as well as I could with blankets, I settled myself upon my feet behind him, expecting he would be a corpse before morning.

Pause for a moment and consider the situation. Worse than alone, in a savage wilderness, without food, without fire, cold and shivering, wolves fighting and howling all around me. Dark clouds hid the stars. All as solitary as death. But that same kind providence that I had always known was watching over me still. I committed all to Him and felt no fear. As soon as light dawned, I pulled down my tent, saddled my horse, found the captain able to stand on his feet. Just at this moment one of the emigrants whom I was trying to overtake came up. He was in search of venison. Half a mile ahead were the wagons I hoped to overtake, and we were soon there and ate plentifully of fresh meat. Within eight feet of where my tent had been set fresh tracks of two Indians were to be seen, but I did not know that they were there. They killed and robbed Mr. Newton, only a short distance off, but would not kill his wife because she was a woman. They killed another man on our cut-off, but the rest of the emigrants escaped with their lives. We traveled on for a few days and came to the foot of the Calipooia mountains. Here my children and my grand-children came up with us, a joyful meeting. They had been near starving. Mr. Pringle tried to shoot a wolf, but he was too weak and trembling to hold the rifle steady. They all cried because they had nothing to eat; but just at this time their own son came to them with a supply, and all cried again. Winter had now set in. We were many days crossing the Calipooia mountains, able to go ahead only a mile or two each day. The road had to be cut and opened for us, and the mountain was covered with snow. Provisions gave out and Mr. Pringle set off on horseback to the settlements for relief, not knowing how long he would be away, or whether he would ever get through. In a week or so our scanty provisions were all gone and we were again in a state of starvation. Many tears were shed through the day, by all save one. She had passed through many trials sufficient to convince her that tears would avail nothing in our extremities. Through all my sufferings in crossing the plains, I not once sought relief by the shedding of tears, nor thought we should not live to reach the settlement. The same faith that I ever had in the blessings of kind providence strengthened in proportion to the trials I had to endure. As the only alternative, or last resort, for the present time, Mr. Pringle's oldest son, Clark, shot down one of his father's best working oxen and dressed it. It had not a particle of fat on it, but we had something to eat—poor bones to pick, without bread or salt. . . .

On Christmas day, at 2 p.m., I entered the house of a Methodist minister, the first house I had set my feet in for nine months. For two or three weeks of my journey down the Willamette I had felt something in the end of my glove finger which I supposed to be a button; on examination at my new home in Salem, I found it to be a 6−1/4 cent piece. This was the whole of my cash capital to commence business with in Oregon. With it I purchased three needles. I traded off some of my old clothes to the squaws for buckskin, worked them into gloves for the Oregon ladies and gentlemen, which cleared me upwards of $30.

Later, I accepted the invitation of Mr. and Mrs. Harvey Clark, of Tualatin plains, to spend the winter with them. I said to Mr. Clark one day, "Why has Providence frowned on me and left me poor in this world? Had he blessed me with riches, as he has many others, I know right well what I would do." "What would you do?" "I would establish myself in a comfortable house and receive all the poor children, and be a mother to them." He fixed his keen eyes on me to see if I was in earnest. "Yes, I am," said I. "If so, I will try," said he, "to help you." He purposed to take an agency and get assistance to establish a school in the plains. I should go into the log meeting-house and receive all the children, rich and poor, whose parents were able to pay $1 a week, for board, tuition, washing and all. I agreed to labor for one year for nothing, while Mr. Clark and others were to assist as far as they were able in furnishing provisions. The time fixed upon to begin was March, 1848, when I found everything prepared for me to go into the old meeting-house and cluck up my chickens. The neighbors had collected what broken knives and forks, tin pans, and dishes they could part with, for the Oregon pioneer to commence housekeeping with. I had a well-educated lady from the east, a missionary's wife, for a teacher, and my family increased rapidly. In the summer they put me up a boarding-house. I now had thirty boarders of both sexes, and of all ages, from four years old to twenty-one. I managed them and did all my work except washing. That was done by the scholars. In the spring of '49 we called for trustees. Had eight appointed. They voted me the whole charge of the boarding house free of rent, and I was to provide for myself. The price of board was established at $2 per week. Whatever I made over my expenses was my own. In '51 I had forty in my family at $2.50 per week; mixed with my own hands, 3,423 pounds of flour in less than five months. Mr. Clark made over to the trustees a quarter section of land for a town plot. A large and handsome building is on the site we selected at the first starting. It has been under town incorporation for two years, and at the last session of the legislature a charter was granted for a university to be called Pacific university. . . .

You must be judges whether I have been doing good or evil. I have labored for myself and the rising generation, but I have not quit hard work, and live at my ease, independent as to worldly concerns. I own a nicely furnished white frame house on a lot in town, within a short distance of the public buildings. That I rent for $100 per year. I have eight other town lots, without buildings, worth $150 each. I have eight cows and a number of young cattle. The cows I rent out for their milk and one-half of their increase. I have rising $1,000 cash due me; $400 of it I have donated to the university; besides $100 I gave to the academy three years ago. This much I have been able to accumulate by my own industry, independent of my children, since I drew 6¼ cents from the finger of my glove.

By Handcart to Utah

In 1860 Mary Ann Hafen traveled on foot with her parents and siblings and their handcart to Salt Lake City, where the Mormon church was establishing a flourishing community. She and her family, emigrants from Switzerland, spoke no English. Mormons recruited many European converts and helped them to come to America and settle in Utah.

From Mary Ann Hafen, *Recollections of a Handcart Pioneer of 1860* (1938; reprint, Lincoln: University of Nebraska Press, 1983), pp. 20–26.

❖

The train landed us at the point of outfit. Father was a carpenter, and they asked him to stop for a while and help make handcarts, as most of the people were too poor to buy teams.

When we came to load up our belongings we found that we had more than we could take. Mother was forced to leave behind her feather bed, the bolt of linen, two large trunks full of clothes, and some other valuable things which we needed so badly later. Father could take only his most necessary tools. . . .

There were six to our cart. Father and mother pulled it; Rosie (two years old) and Christian (six months old) rode; John (nine) and I (six) walked. Sometimes, when it was down hill, they let me ride too.

Father had bought a cow to take along, so we could have milk on the way. At first he tied her to the back of the cart, but she would sometimes hang back, so he thought he would make a harness and have her pull the cart while he led her. By this time mother's feet were so swollen that she could not wear shoes, but had to wrap her feet with cloth. Father thought that by having the cow pull the cart mother might ride. This worked well for some time.

One day a group of Indians came riding up on horses. Their jingling trinkets, dragging poles and strange appearance frightened the cow and set her chasing off with the cart and children. We were afraid that the children might be killed, but the cow fell into a deep gully and the cart turned upside down. Although the children were under the trunk and bedding, they were unhurt, but after that father did not hitch the cow to the cart again. He let three Danish boys take her to hitch to their cart. Then the Danish boys, each in turn, would help father pull our cart.

After about three weeks my mother's feet became better so she could wear her shoes again. She would get so discouraged and down-hearted; but father never lost courage. He would always cheer her up by telling her that we were going to Zion, that the Lord would take care of us, and that better times were coming.

Even when it rained the company did not stop traveling. A cover on the hand-cart shielded the two younger children. The rest of us found it more comfort-able moving than standing still in the drizzle. In fording streams the men often carried the children and weaker women across on their backs. The company stopped over on Sundays for rest, and meetings were held for spiritual comfort and guidance. At night, when the handcarts were drawn up in a circle and the fires were lighted, the camp looked quite happy. Singing, music, and speeches by the leaders cheered everyone. I remember that we stopped one night at an old Indian camp ground. There were many bright-colored beads in the ant hills.

At times we met or were passed by the overland stage coach with its pas-sengers and mail bags and drawn by four fine horses. When the Pony Express dashed past it seemed almost like the wind racing over the prairie.

Our provisions began to get low. One day a herd of buffalo ran past and the men of our company shot two of them. Such a feast as we had when they were dressed. Each family was given a piece of meat to take along. My brother John, who pushed at the back of our cart, used to tell how hungry he was all the time and how tired he got from pushing. He said he felt that if he could just sit down for a few minutes he would feel so much better. But instead, father would ask if he couldn't push a little harder. Mother was nursing the baby and could not help much, especially when the food ran short and she grew weak. When rations were reduced father gave mother a part of his share of the food, so he was not so strong either.

When we got that chunk of buffalo meat father put it in the handcart. My brother John remembered that it was the fore part of the week and that father said we would save it for Sunday dinner. John said, "I was so very hungry and the meat smelled so good to me while pushing at the handcart that I could not resist. I had a little pocket knife and with it I cut off a piece or two each half day. Although I expected a severe whipping when father found it out, I cut off little pieces each day. I would chew them so long that they got white and perfectly tasteless. When father came to get the meat he asked me if I had been cutting off some of it. I said 'Yes. I was so hungry I could not let it alone.' Instead of giving me a scolding or whipping, father turned away and wiped tears from his eyes."

At last, when we reached the top of Emigration Canyon, overlooking Salt Lake, the whole company stopped to look down through the Valley. Some yelled and tossed their hats in the air. A shout of joy arose at the thought that our long trip was over, that we had at last reached Zion, the place of rest. We all gave thanks to God for helping us safely over the Plains and mountains to our destination.

EMIGRANTS AND IMMIGRANTS

54. A Sod House
This sod-roofed dugout home of an unidentified family near McCook, Nebraska,
shows how the treeless plains and prairies required innovative living among all the
new inhabitants. Courtesy of Nebraska State Historical Society, Lincoln.

55. A Log Cabin
Cabins like this one on the San Antonio River, Jemez Canyon, New Mexico, were built wherever trees were available. Its small size is typical. Ben Wittick photo, School of American Research Collections. Courtesy of Museum of New Mexico, Santa Fe. Photo no. 15621.

Civil War

THE CIVIL WAR, or War Between the States, was a tremendous cata-lyst for change, for new types of action, and for new organizational de-velopment, among women as well as men. The war was a bloody and devastating event for almost all Americans. It brought anguish and destruction and mutilation to hundreds of thousands—more casualties in proportion to the population than in any other American war. Though the war saved the Union and ended slavery, it did not resolve the multiple other problems caused by racial injustice. And it did nothing to promote equal rights for women, black or white.

During the war, women mobilized to do the work that had to be done and that no one else was doing. Nursing the Union army casualties, for which army facilities were totally unprepared, quickly became a civilian priority. More than five hundred Catholic nuns were recruited to staff military hospitals near Gettys-burg and other battlefields. Other nurses, led by Clara Barton, Dorothea Dix, and the indomitable "Mother" Mary Bickerdyke, organized rudimentary hos-pital facilities, both in huge tent camps near the battlefields and in border-city hospitals. Some women volunteers were rejected by the proper Miss Dix for being too young and attractive, but they participated with others in the Sani-tary Commission's massive organizational tasks—procuring food, bandages, clothing, and other necessities in every northern community and city. South-ern women like Mary Ann Cobb had similar responsibilities. All developed new strength from their work even as they also grieved for brothers, lovers, sons, and husbands going to war.

To African Americans, the war brought trouble as well as freedom. Most southern slaves remained at home, getting the news of emancipation only when their owners could no longer keep it secret. But Susie King Taylor was one of many who well understood the significance of events. She accompanied her hus-band to battle, participating in the shooting, as well as nursing the wounded and then teaching freed slaves. Another slave woman, Lucy Skipwith, for twenty years was her Virginia master's designated leader and teacher among the slaves on his Alabama plantation; she was promised freedom if she would let him send her to Liberia in Africa. Her "Dear Master" letters, after emancipation was proclaimed, reveal a subtle change in tone. She agreed to think over his proposal and later answered, "I have looked over my mind in regard to going to Liberia but I cannot get my consent to go there." She also told him she was leaving the abusive husband that white masters had forced her to live with, because she wished "to live a life of peace & die a death of both Joy and peace." The end of civil war and of slavery meant personal as well as public peace and freedom.

388

Mother Bickerdyke

The executive ability and determination of Mary A. Bickerdyke (1817–1901), a volunteer nurse for the Army of the West in the Civil War, became legendary in her own time. Mrs. Bickerdyke was a widow of forty-three with two young children still at home when she first volunteered to help the soldiers dying of typhoid and dysentery in filthy hospital tents in Cairo, Illinois, in 1861. One was her own son. Soon her almost superhuman feats of endurance and improvisation from 1861 to 1865, under the most primitive and unorganized circumstances of premodern warfare, endeared her to thousands of wounded veterans. As an agent of the Northwestern Sanitary Commission, which was providing food and medical supplies, she also expedited organizational efficiency and personified the active role of women in battlefield medical care. Civil War medical facilities were grossly inadequate, and "Mother" Bickerdyke was at times the only woman nurse among the hordes of wounded. Many other women, including Catholic nursing sisters and Clara Barton, the founder of the American Red Cross, organized nursing services at hospitals in Washington, D.C., and near eastern battlefields. Noncooperative doctors, however, often resented their "interference" and unwomanly lack of delicacy. Mary Livermore (1820–1905), a leader of the Chicago Sanitary Commission, who later became a founder of both the Illinois and the Massachusetts woman suffrage associations and a renowned lecturer, described the work of the commission and of many other women in a book about her wartime experiences.

From Mary A. Livermore, *My Story of the War* (Hartford, Conn.: A.D. Worthington and Co., 1896), pp. 483–90, 511–14.

❖

After the battle of Donelson, Mother Bickerdyke went from Cairo in the first hospital boat, and assisted in the removal of the wounded to Cairo, St. Louis, and Louisville, and in nursing those too badly wounded to be moved. The Sanitary Commission had established a depot of stores at Cairo, and on these she was allowed to make drafts *ad libitum:* for she was as famous for her economical use of sanitary stores as she had been before the war for her notable house-wifery. The hospital boats at that time were poorly equipped for the sad work of transporting the wounded. But this thoughtful woman, who made five of the terrible trips from the battle-field of Donelson to the hospital, put on board the boat with which she was connected, before it started from Cairo, an abundance of necessities. There was hardly a want expressed for which she could not fur-nish some sort of relief.

On the way to the battle-field, she systematized matters perfectly. The beds were ready for the occupants, tea, coffee, soup and gruel, milk punch and ice water were prepared in large quantities, under her supervision, and sometimes by her own hand. When the wounded were brought on board,—mangled almost out of human shape; the frozen ground from which they had been cut adhering to them; chilled with the intense cold in which some had lain for twenty-four hours; faint with loss of blood, physical agony, and lack of nourishment; racked with a terrible five-mile ride over frozen roads, in ambulances, or common Ten-nessee farm wagons, without springs; burning with fever; raving in delirium, or in the faintness of death,—Mother Bickerdyke's boat was in readiness for them.

"I never saw anybody like her," said a volunteer surgeon who came on the boat with her. "There was really nothing for us surgeons to do but dress wounds and administer medicines. She drew out clean shirts or drawers from some cor-ner, whenever they were needed. Nourishment was ready for every man as soon as he was brought on board. Every one was sponged from blood and the frozen mire of the battle-field, as far as his condition allowed. His blood-stiffened, and sometimes horribly filthy uniform, was exchanged for soft and clean hospital garments. Incessant cries of 'Mother! Mother! Mother!' rang through the boat, in every note of beseeching and anguish. And to every man she turned with a heavenly tenderness, as if he were indeed her son. She moved about with a deci-sive air, and gave directions in such decided, clarion tones as to ensure prompt obedience. We all had an impression that she held a commission from the Sec-retary of War, or at least from the Governor of Illinois. To every surgeon who was superior, she held herself subordinate, and was as good at obeying as at commanding." And yet, at that time, she held no position whatever, and was receiving no compensation for her services; not even the beggarly pittance of thirteen dollars per month allowed by government to army nurses.

At last it was believed that all the wounded had been removed from the field, and the relief parties discontinued their work. Looking from his tent at mid-night, an officer observed a faint light flitting hither and thither on the aban-doned battle-field, and, after puzzling over it for some time, sent his servant to ascertain the cause. It was Mother Bickerdyke, with a lantern, still groping among the dead. Stooping down, and turning their cold faces towards her, she scrutinized them searchingly, uneasy lest some might be left to die uncared for. She could not rest while she thought any were overlooked who were yet living.

Up to this time, no attempt had been made to save the clothing and bedding used by the wounded men on the transports and in the temporary hospitals. Saturated with blood, and the discharges of healing wounds, and sometimes swarming with vermin, it had been collected, and burned or buried. But this involved much waste; and as these articles were in constant need, Mother Bickerdyke conceived the idea of saving them. She sent to the Commission at Chicago for washing-machines, portable kettles, and mangles, and caused all this offensive clothing to be collected. She then obtained from the authorities a full detail of contrabands [freed slaves], and superintended the laundering of all these hideously foul garments. Packed in boxes, it all came again into use at the next battle.

This work once begun, Mother Bickerdyke never intermitted. Her washing-machines, her portable kettles, her posse of contrabands, an ambulance or two, and one or two handy detailed soldiers, were in her retinue after this, wherever she went. How much she saved to the government, and to the Sanitary Commission, may be inferred from the fact that it was no unusual thing for three or four thousand pieces to pass through her extemporized laundry in a day. Each piece was returned to the hospital from which it was taken, or, if it belonged to no place in particular, was used *in transitu*. She saw it boxed, and the boxes deposited in some safe place, where she could easily reach them in time of need. . . .

After the wounded of Donelson were cared for, Mrs. Bickerdyke left the hospitals, and went back into the army. There was great sickness among our troops at Savannah, Tenn. She had already achieved such a reputation for devotion to the men, for executive ability, and versatility of talent, that the spirits of the sick and wounded revived at the very sound of her voice and at the sight of her motherly face. While busy here, the battle of Shiloh occurred, nine miles distant by the river, but only six in a direct line. There had been little provision made for the terrible needs of the battle-field in advance of the conflict. The battle occurred unexpectedly, and was a surprise to our men,—who nearly suffered defeat,—and again there was utter destitution and incredible suffering. Three days after the battle, the boats of the Sanitary Commission arrived at the Landing, laden with every species of relief,—condensed food, stimulants, clothing, bedding, medicines, chloroform, surgical instruments, and carefully selected volunteer nurses and surgeons. They were on the ground some days in advance of the government boats.

Here Mother Bickerdyke was found, carrying system, order, and relief wherever she went. One of the surgeons went to the rear with a wounded man, and found her wrapped in the gray overcoat of a rebel officer, for she had disposed of her blanket shawl to some poor fellow who needed it. She was wearing a soft slouch hat, having lost her inevitable Shaker bonnet. Her kettles had been set up, the fire kindled underneath, and she was dispensing hot soup, tea, crackers, panado, whiskey and water, and other refreshments, to the shivering, fainting, wounded men.

"Where did you get these articles?" he inquired; "and under whose authority are you at work?"

She paid no heed to his interrogatories, and, indeed, did not hear them, so completely absorbed was she in her work of compassion. Watching her with admiration for her skills, administrative ability, and intelligence,—for she not only fed the wounded men, but temporarily dressed their wounds in some cases,—he approached her again:—

"Madam, you seem to combine in yourself a sick-diet kitchen and a medical staff. May I inquire under whose authority you are working?"

Without pausing in her work, she answered him, "I have received my authority from the Lord God Almighty; have you anything that ranks higher than that?" The truth was, she held no position whatever at that time. She was only a "volunteer nurse," having received no appointment, and being attached to no corps of relief. . . .

It was more difficult to supply the hospitals with milk and eggs than with any other necessaries. With the supplies furnished by the government, the tea, coffee, sugar, flour, meat, and other like articles, which were usually of good quality, Mother Bickerdyke could work miracles in the culinary line, even when there was a lack of sanitary stores, if she could only have an abundant supply of milk and eggs. But these were very difficult to obtain. They could not be sent from the North, and they could not be purchased in sufficiently large quantities to supply the enormous demand. In the enemy's country, where the hospitals were located, their prices were exorbitant beyond belief. Mother Bickerdyke hit upon a plan to remedy these difficulties. When the medical direction came into her hospital one morning, on a tour of inspection, she accosted him thus:—

"Dr. _____, do you know we are paying these Memphis secesh fifty cents for every quart of milk we use? And do you know it's such poor stuff,—two thirds chalk and water,—that if you should pour it into the trough of a respectable pig at home, he would turn up his nose, and run off, squealing in disgust?"

"Well, what can we do about it?" asked the doctor, between whom and herself there was now an excellent understanding.

"If you'll give me thirty days' furlough and transportation, I'll go home, and get all the milk and eggs that the Memphis hospitals can use."

"Get milk and eggs! Why, you could not bring them down here, if the North would give you all it has. A barrel of eggs would spoil, this warm weather, before it could reach us; and how on earth could you bring milk?"

"But I'll bring down the milk and egg producers. I'll get cows and hens, and we'll have milk and eggs of our own. The folks at home, doctor, will give us all the hens and cows we need for the use of these hospitals, and jump at the chance to do it. You needn't laugh, nor shake your head!" as he turned away, amused and incredulous. "I tell you, the people at the North ache to do something for the boys down here, and I can get fifty cows in Illinois alone for just the asking."

"Pshaw! pshaw!" said the doctor, "you would be laughed at from one end of the country to the other, if you should go on so wild an errand."

"Fiddlesticks! Who cares for that? Give me a furlough and transportation, and let me try it!" . . .

Before her thirty days' leave of absence was ended, Mother Bickerdyke was on the return route to her hospital, forming a part of a bizarre procession of over one hundred cows and one thousand hens, strung all along the road from Chicago to Memphis. She entered the city in triumph, amid immense lowing and crowing and cackling. She informed the astonished Memphians that, "These are *loyal* cows and hens; none of your miserable trash that give chalk and water for milk, and lay loud-smelling eggs."

General Hurlburt, who was then at the head of the department, hearing of this novel immigration within his lines, gave up to the noisy new-comers President's Island, lying in the Mississippi opposite Memphis, a stretch of land so elevated that it is above the highest stage of water. Contrabands were detailed to take charge of them; and as long as Mrs. Bickerdyke remained in Memphis there was an abundance of milk and eggs for the use of the hospitals.

Five Hundred Pounds of Biscuits

The Civil War brought grief, destruction, and hard work to almost all white Southern women. Mary Ann Cobb's husband, Howell, was a prominent Georgian and a Confederate officer. Two of their sons also went to battle while Mary Ann was left to organize the townswomen in making uniforms and gathering food provisions for the local cavalry company. Her 1861 letters suggest that these new activities were exhilarating as well as exhausting; Southern women still thought the war would soon be over. By 1863 the toll it was taking on the poor and on country people was severe, and women prayed for peace—"enough, enough." Mary Ann Cobb, born in 1818, was the mother of eight living children (four others had died); the town of Athens is in northeast Georgia.

From letters of Mary Ann Cobb to Howell Cobb in Kenneth Coleman, ed., *Athens, 1861–1865: As Seen through Letters in the University of Georgia Libraries* (Athens: University of Georgia Press, 1969), pp. 15–19, 61–62.

❖

Mary Ann Cobb to Howell Cobb, Athens, Aug. 5, 1861.

Tuesday, 5th. As I came down stairs this morning I met Mrs. Giles Mitchell's servant at the door asking for 4 pr drawers for Misses Ann & Emma Mitchell to make. At 9 o'clock I went to the Society. John A rode with me to the Church on his way to the Depot to go to Macon. Mattie Clayton went to spend the day with her Grand Mother & see her Uncle Edward Clayton. After Society I called at Jude Hillyer's & Judge Jacksons. Returned home at 1 o'clock. At dinner Mrs. Franklins servant brought two coats & a note asking me to exchange two pr pants for the coats. Mrs. W. H. Mitchell could not get them made in her Ward. I had distributed all my work, 8 coats & 5 pants for the Cavalry; but I wrote Mrs. F. if she could not dispose of the Coats I would take them. The Coats came back "with great pleasure." Since dinner I have been engaged writing a note to White & Ritch to cut a Coat & pants for Gilbert, a pr pants for Laurence, have sent a yd of shirring to Miss Sawyer to replace lost sleeve lining. Wrote a note to Mrs. Thomas sending drawers pattern for Ed Lumpkin & Joe Gerdine, and returning glass tumblers & jars in which jelly & preserves was sent for the sick soldiers. Wrote notes to Mrs. Phinizy & Mrs Smythe asking if they would take a coat apiece. Wrote a note to Mrs. Franklin asking for a name lost from a coat in its passage from Mrs. Mitchells and also for a *Model Coat* to make the others by. Sent Mrs. Phinizy & Mrs. Smythe coats a piece. Received an answer from Mrs. Smythe she was sick, but she would have it made. Dispatched Anderson back instantly to say I didn't know Mrs. S. was sick. I would send the coat to someone to whom I had sent no work. Sent home Mrs. Dents jars & bottles, Mrs. Popes jars & Bowl. A bowl & two cups going the rounds nobody claiming them. Shall send home Miss Julie mess bottle that once contained cordial. Wrote to White & Ritch for O. W. Princess Uniform. In the meantime Sarah, Lizzie and Andrew have been in for some of the Candy Pope sent. Tom Cobb, Jr., has taken his noon rations, been dandled on my knee and bo peeped with the "Constitutionalists" while I scanned the Telegraphic items. And I soon embarked Eliza & Angeline making Gilberts homespun Shirts. The above is "a glimpse" into my *every day* life. If you will not admit that I have a *few* annoyances—enough to adell a *man's* brains—then I will admit that organizing a regiment is more annoying than keeping house, raising children, and being Directress of a Volunteer Aid Society. This is the first time in my life I have been in a society. I have dodged them always, and I never will serve in another excepting under present circumstances, a state of war & blockade. I have only given you the above insight into my daily life that you may understand why I do not write. I have not the *wits* left after dribbling my brains away all through the day. Mr. Prince has written to me to have his Uniform made as he has joined Mr. Delony's Cavalry Company.

Aug. 12, 1861.

Now I will tell you of this mornings exploits. I went to the depot at 7 o'c after had called at Tailor Whites to leave some yellow cord that had been put by mistake in a suit of clothes for a servant in the Cavalry Company, which was sent to Mrs. Thomas Sr. to make up. Called at Mr. Rutherfords to leave a note offering to pay Howell's Board & Lodging bill supposing Mr. R. would want news fr John C. R. who goes in the Cavalry. Chatted with Laura—she is too busy to give *too* much—says she *often thinks* of *me*, and my *sacrifices*. Sympathy is pleasing though it may come slowly. When I returned home Mrs. Franklins carriage was at my gate. She said in her stately smiling manner, "she had come to take me from my little ones". The Cavalry Company would leave on Wednesday and the Ladies must get up provisions for them to travel upon—6 days—80 men (& horses). 300 pounds of meat was wanted (hams) and 500 lbs. *biscuit*. She wanted me to take up Milledge Avenue, and call at all the houses, for Hams & biscuit—1 ham from each householder, or 10 lbs of flour—made into biscuit. These people could afford it—ham & biscuits both. I came in, ate my breakfast hastily, nursed Tom, ordered my ham to be boiled, my 6 quarts of biscuit baked. [In] my little *Rockaway* which Lamar presented to me when he came home, and found me with *one* horse, I drove up Milledge Avenue stopping at 9 houses, going as far as Young Harris' to the left. Was successful in my applications, was returning with the intention of going up Hill Street, when Captain Delony met me and told me the Company could not get transports for Augusta, and must wait until Friday perhaps. The "Legion" is moving at one time. I came home, laid down on my bed, rested, reading—"The Still Hour"—& the "Constitutionalist," until dinner. Andrew & Sarah still my only companions. After dinner I returned to my letter which I had commenced before dinner, interrupted at intervals by messengers. At 4 o'clock a message came from Captain Delony, asking for "ham & cold biscuit to help out the soldiers' supper". I sat down immediately wrote ten *circulars* to my *neighbors,* called up Anderson & Gilbert, gave each a circular, and started them up different streets—calling upon my neighbors "to rescue the soldiers from hunger". Before 7 o'clock, I had gathered in enough biscuit & ham to last them several days. Many ladies baked biscuit after the message was sent. I made the call as a Directress, and shall report to the society tomorrow. Kept a list of names & contributions annexed. I sent a cold ham, 70 biscuit, 11 pones of *corn* bread. As no one else contributed corn bread and my name came last on the list, I wrote underneath—cornbread, "in honor of Cobb". Afterwards, Mary Athena sent in corn bread, so did Mrs. Moss & Mrs. Franklin. I packed the bread in large tin can, the hams in another. Each would have held 6 & 8 gallon. A tin bucket of fried ham, a bucket of butter, a 3 gal can of fresh milk & some candles, 2 hamper baskets of biscuit, 8 smal basket do. I received a note from Capt Delony acknowledging the receipt of all. In the meanwhile I took a list of the articles, wrote off a copy to send to Capt Delony, wrote him a note with an answer to his note, wrote a note to Mrs. Baxter, a note to Mrs. Thomas, a note to Mrs. Franklin. Sent Elija around countermanding the order for traveling biscuit. Scribbled to you as I had an opportunity. Held Tom and played with the little ones while the servants were at dinner, flew around generally, giving orders. Ate supper between 8 & 9 o'clock, finished my letter after supper, after writing a note to Mrs. [illegible] to tell her the "Georgia Troopers" will not leave on Wednesday. Now it is 5 minutes past ten o'clock, and I was up at 6 o'c this morning and must rise at 6 o'c tomorrow to go to the Depot to meet John A. and at 9 o'clock to the *Society*. I must bid you good night. God bless you.

Aug. 30, 1861.

The departure of the boys and a closing up of the work for the Mell Rifles gave me a few leisure days. The reaction from constant work and the relaxation of the tension of feeling I had assumed to bear up under the parting from my boys was too sudden and I gave up and went to bed with headache having *nothing else to do*. The Troup Artillery winter uniforms are coming in however, and I shall have to brace up and go to work again. Mrs. Franklin brought me today 3 bolts of cloth, 30 odd yd in each to distribute for *shrinking*. It is for the "Artillery" & "Guards". Then she sent me three suits of clothes—Frank Lumpkin, Joe Gerdines & Howell's—to distribute and sent me a page of "directions for making Artillery Coat" of which I have taken two copies & sent one to Mrs. J. H. Lumpkin & one to Miss Sawyer. The letter asked me to let her make Howell's. Capt Thompson of yr Regt. called to see me this morning about 8 o'clock on his way to the Depot. He said you wanted me to send you *something* but for the life of him he could not tell what it was.

July 20, 1863

Bought a white counterpane from a Mrs. Rhodes who lives 8 miles from town in the Buncombe Dist. Her son will be 18 in Dec. next, and he wants to volunteer & join Safford's (Morgan Co.) State troops to keep from being conscripted. His mother had made the counterpane for him, and for lack of other resources to buy wool to make him a uniform she brought in the counterpane to sell to buy wool. I bought it paying more than its value. The mother's appeal & tears could not be withstood. God will bless the motive that activated me. She had been in with a neighbor sometime ago whom I had enabled to buy meat for her family by buying her cloth at more than the market value. She was a soldier's wife. He went out with the first volunteers & had not been at home since, was sick in the hospital at Richmond with boils all over him produced by vaccination. Her supply of meat, a hogshead full, had been stolen. She carried her corn to mill on her back. There was energy in every movement of the woman's limbs & in the expression of her face. I thought such a woman deserved assistance. Her husband's relations the Cooks—Walton Cook is her father-in-law—had given her no assistance, and her three brothers Faulkner had fallen at Shiloh. She said "It seems to me sometimes, mine is the worst case in the settlement," and the tears stood in her eyes. Her husband did not volunteer in one of the Clark Co. cos therefore she received no assistance from the County until she was found with a bag of corn on her back by her neighbors & her case reported to the Clerk. I told her the poor soldier's wives would receive thread from the State. She smiled and said "Yes I heard that, and it lightened one little corner in my heart." I never saw a woman who moved my heart as deeply, and on inquiry if she was a member of the Church, she said she was a *Missionary* Baptist. This was a double reason for my aiding her. She was of "the household of faith" whom the Apostle recommends "especially" to our charity. She brought her neighbor Mrs. Rhodes to see me. What a difference there was in my manner to the country people to what some other ladies in town were. Mrs. Rhodes came today to sell me the counterpane. And after I bought she said, "I would not have parted with it but to buy wool for my son's clothes. But as I have to part with [it] I would rather you would have it than almost anybody else, for I have an uncommon good opinion of you." I thanked her for her good opinion. She is a worthy woman. I feel that it is the duty of all who are rich in our country to lighten the burdens of the people & especially the women as much as possible, even if we give them more than the value of the articles. The times are hard. Provisions are at extortionate prices, and as Old Mrs. Gully says, "if it was not for the rich what would become of the poor people"? What would? And being one whose granaries & coffers are filled should consider herself as a "Joseph" ordained beforehand by God "to save many souls" from starvation during this war. If this spirit prevailed throughout our land, this war would cease. But as it is, Dr. Lipscomb truly says that the speculators stand between the prayers of the women and their God, and prevents the blessing of peace descending upon our blood stained land. When will the daughters of the household cry enough, enough?

Yes, We All Shall Be Free

Born a slave on the Sea Islands of Georgia in 1848, Susie King Taylor accompanied her husband to war when he joined the South Carolina Volunteers, the first black regiment in the Union army. Both were "contrabands"—captured slaves who were glad to fight for freedom. Susie was a teacher, nurse, and laundress for the soldiers and even helped clean guns and shoot in some of the battles. Her husband died after the war, and she taught school in Savannah until she moved to Boston. In this excerpt she mentions the clandestine help of free black and some white people in providing her with an education. Note that the hymn she quotes is very similar to a verse of the twentieth-century hymn "We Shall Overcome."

From Susie King Taylor, *Reminiscences of My Life in Camp with the 33d United States Colored Troops, Late 1st S.C. Volunteers* (1902; reprint, New York: Arno Press, 1968), pp. 5–8, 11. ❖

I was born under the slave law in Georgia, in 1848, and was brought up by my grandmother in Savannah. There were three of us with her, my younger sister and brother. My brother and I being the eldest, we were sent to a friend of my grandmother, Mrs. Woodhouse, a widow, to learn to read and write. She was a free woman and lived on Bay Lane, between Habersham and Price streets, about half a mile from my house. We went every day about nine o'clock, with our books wrapped in paper to prevent the police or white persons from seeing them. We went in, one at a time, through the gate, into the yard to the L kitchen, which was the schoolroom. She had twenty-five or thirty children whom she taught, assisted by her daughter, Mary Jane. The neighbors would see us going in sometimes, but they supposed we were there learning trades, as it was the custom to give children a trade of some kind. After school we left the same way we entered, one by one, when we would go to a square, about a block from the school, and wait for each other. We would gather laurel leaves and pop them on our hands, on our way home. I remained at her school for two years or more, when I was sent to a Mrs. Mary Beasley, where I continued until May, 1860, when she told my grandmother she had taught me all she knew, and grandmother had better get some one else who could teach me more, so I stopped my studies for a while.

I had a white playmate about this time, named Katie O'Connor, who lived on the next corner of the street from my house, and who attended a convent. One day she told me, if I would promise not to tell her father, she would give me some lessons. On my promise not to do so, and getting her mother's consent, she gave me lessons about four months, every evening. At the end of this time she was put into the convent permanently, and I have never seen her since.

A month after this, James Blouis, our landlord's son, was attending the High School, and was very fond of grandmother, so she asked him to give me a few lessons, which he did until the middle of 1861, when the Savannah Volunteer Guards, to which he and his brother belonged, were ordered to the front under General Barton. In the first battle of Manassas, his brother Eugene was killed, and James deserted over to the Union side, and at the close of the war went to Washington, D. C., where he has since resided. . . .

About this time I had been reading so much about the "Yankees" I was very anxious to see them. The whites would tell their colored people not to go to the Yankees, for they would harness them to carts and make them pull the carts around, in place of horses. I asked grandmother, one day, if this was true. She replied, "Certainly not!" that the white people did not want slaves to go over to the Yankees, and told them these things to frighten them. "Don't you see those signs pasted about the streets? one reading, 'I am a rattlesnake; if you touch me I will strike!' Another reads, 'I am a wild-cat! Beware,' etc. These are warnings to the North; so don't mind what the white people say." I wanted to see these wonderful "Yankees" so much, as I heard my parents say the Yankee was going to set all the slaves free. Oh, how those people prayed for freedom! I remember, one night, my grandmother went into the suburbs of the city to a church meeting, and they were fervently singing this old hymn,—

> "Yes, we all shall be free,
> Yes, we all shall be free,
> Yes, we all shall be free,
> When the Lord shall appear,"—

when the police came in and arrested all who were there, saying they were planning freedom, and sang "the Lord," in place of "Yankee," to blind any one who might be listening. Grandmother never forgot that night. . . .

Two days after the taking of Fort Pulaski, my uncle took his family of seven and myself to St. Catherine Island. We landed under the protection of the Union fleet, and remained there two weeks, when about thirty of us were taken aboard the gunboat P_____, to be transferred to St. Simon's Island; and at last, to my unbounded joy, I saw the "Yankee."

. . . After I had been on St. Simon's about three days, Commodore Goldsborough heard of me, and came to Gaston Bluff to see me. I found him very cordial. He said Captain Whitmore had spoken to him of me, and that he was pleased to hear of my being so capable, etc., and wished me to take charge of a school for the children on the island. I told him I would gladly do so, if I could have some books. He said I should have them, and in a week or two I received two large boxes of books and testaments from the North. I had about forty children to teach, beside a number of adults who came to me nights, all of them so eager to learn to read, to read above anything else.

My Dear Master

The slave Lucy Skipwith, born in 1830, was entrusted by her master, John Hartwell Cocke, of Virginia, with the management of his household on a new plantation in Alabama during the 1840s and 1850s. Of course, there was a white overseer too, but at Cocke's request, Lucy wrote him regularly about plantation affairs, ran a school for the other slaves, and used her influence to safeguard her family and counteract unjust overseers. Cocke was preparing his slaves for migration to Liberia and freedom as part of the colonization plan by which some Southerners hoped to solve the problem of slavery. In 1863 he offered to send Lucy; she told him she would "try to deside what . . . to do." After the war ended and all slaves were emancipated, her letters no longer show the subservience of earlier years, though she remained friendly. Lucy informed Cocke, "I cannot get my consent to go there [Liberia]." She also stated that she now also felt free to leave her husband in order to live in peace and joy.

From Lucy Skipwith, *"Dear Master": Letters of a Slave Family,* ed. Randall M. Miller (Ithaca, N.Y.: Cornell University Press, 1978), pp. 253–54, 262–63. By permission of Joseph F. Johnston and John Page Elliot.

❖

Hopewell   Aug 15th 1863

Dear master

I received your last letter & have carefully considered its contents, & I hope to write more sattisfactory than I have done heretofore. the white people who have stayed on the plantation are always opposed to my writeing to you & always want to see my letters and that has been the reason why my letters has been short, but there is no white person here at present. mr Hardy is gone home to return no more. I do not know who mr Powell will get to take his place. The health of the people is not very good at preasent. we have four laid up at this time, but they are geting better. Cain has been pulling fodder for more than a week, & it will take him a week more to finish it.

The Cotton is opening very fast   it will soon be open enough to commence picking it out. The weather at preasant is quite rainy & has been for the last two or three days which maekes it bad on the fodder. There is three mulberry trees that has had fruit besides the old tree. The Scuppernong grapes have proper frames to run upon & they are full of fruit. We have two kinds of Figs the white Fig & the common Fig We have only one tree of the white Fig. there is 14/fourteen of the common Fig trees in the garden with Figs on them & 8/eight out in the fence cornors. We have 60-sixty Hogs, 32-thirty two Pigs, & 9 Sows, 53-fiftythree Sheep, 21 twentyone Lambs, 5-five Cows to the pail, 4 four young Calves, 4 four old Goats, 1 one kid. the provision lots for their support is very good.

We have our morning prayers regularly. I have not kept up the sabbath school regularly. some white people in the neighborhood has said that they would punish me if they caught me at it, and I have been afraid to carry it on unless some grown white man was liveing here, but I will commence Teaching again as soon as this talk dies out.

I Have seen mrs Dorsey. I think that she is a very nice Lady. I think that Betsey will do very well with her, but she wishes you to let Betsey stay here untell she settle herself somewhere. mrs. Witherspoon & the Children are well and talkes a great deal about you   I sent her some butter yesterday, & I sent mrs Dorsey a Loaf of light Bread. the Children all came and spent the day with me last week. I Thank you a thousand times for what you purpose doing for Maria & myself & I hope that we may both walk sattisfactory before you while you live. I cannot tell at preasent what will be best for me to do, but I will keep the subject upon my mind & try to deside what will be best to do. Maria is growing very fast and is learning to write very fast. she is a great comfort to me & to every one about her, and above all I hope that she is a true Christian.

mr Joe Borden expects to start back to the Army to day. I will now bring my leter to a close hopeing soon to hear from you again   your servant

Lucy Skipwith

Hopewell   Dec 7th 1865

my dear Master

I Received your letter a few days ago dated oct 14th it being nearly two months on the way.

I was truly glad to see that you were still alive & not yet gone the way of all the Earth & that you were able to write to me once more. I was sorry that I had to part from Armistead but I have lived a life of trouble with him, & a white man has ever had to judge between us, & now to be turned loose from under a master, I know that I could not live with him in no peace, therefore I left him for I wish to live a life of peace & die a death of both Joy and peace & if you have any hard feelings against me on the subject, I hope that you will forgive me for Jesus sake.

I Have a great desire to come to Va to see you & my relations there & I hope that I maybe able some day to do so. I have looked over my mind in regard to going to Liberia but I cannot get my consent to go there, but I thank you for your advice. none of our people are willing to go. I am still carrying on my School on the plantation & the Children are learning very fast. I had a notion of going up to Columbus another year to be with my mother & Father, but as they have moved down here to mr Keys, I have given the notion out. I do not know what Father done in Columbus but I have not seen nor heard nothing of his drinking down here. I have been thinking of puting up a large School next year as I can do more at that than I can at any thing elce, & I can get more children than I can teach, but I do not know yet whither I will be at liberty to do so or not.

I am glad that one of your Grandsons is comeing out this winter. we are looking for him every day. we have been looking for master Charles to come out, & we will be sorry not to see him.

I Have not seen mrs Dorsey for nearly three months   she is now in mobile mrs Witherspoon & her Children are well with the exception of the Whooping cough. mr Joseph Borden is not here as Mr Powell have agreed to stay with us another year. our Turnip patch failed this year. we have a small patch in the Garden. our Crop of Potatoes were very small also. Some of every bodys black people in this Neighbourhood have left their homes but us. we are all here so far but I cannot tell how it will be another year.

I will now bring my letter to a Close hopeing soon to hear from you again I am as ever your Servant

Lucy Skipwith

CIVIL WAR

Satterlee Hospital – West Phila.

56. Daughters of Charity Nurses at a Military Hospital

Catholic nuns won acceptance into American life in no small measure because of their devoted nursing during the Civil War. This photo shows the staff and Sister nurses, Daughters of Charity of St. Vincent de Paul, outside the Satterlee Military Hospital in Philadelphia, Pennsylvania, during the war. The government asked them to staff its twenty-four hundred beds plus three hundred tents; the hospital served more than eighty thousand men between 1862 and 1865. Catholic Sisters also served at twenty-one other Civil War hospitals. Courtesy of the Archives, St. Joseph's Provincial House, Emmitsburg, Maryland.